Human–Computer Interaction Series

Editors-in-Chief

Desney Tan
Microsoft Research, Redmond, WA, USA

Jean Vanderdonckt
Louvain School of Management, Université catholique de Louvain,
Louvain-La-Neuve, Belgium

The Human-Computer Interaction Series, launched in 2004, publishes books that advance the science and technology of developing systems which are effective and satisfying for people in a wide variety of contexts. Titles focus on theoretical perspectives (such as formal approaches drawn from a variety of behavioural sciences), practical approaches (such as techniques for effectively integrating user needs in system development), and social issues (such as the determinants of utility, usability and acceptability).

HCI is a multidisciplinary field and focuses on the human aspects in the development of computer technology. As technology becomes increasingly more pervasive the need to take a human-centred approach in the design and development of computer-based systems becomes ever more important.

Titles published within the Human–Computer Interaction Series are included in Thomson Reuters' Book Citation Index, The DBLP Computer Science Bibliography and The HCI Bibliography.

More information about this series at http://www.springer.com/series/6033

Rüdiger Heimgärtner

Intercultural User Interface Design

 Springer

Rüdiger Heimgärtner
Intercultural User Interface Consulting
(IUIC)
Undorf, Germany

ISSN 1571-5035   ISSN 2524-4477   (electronic)
Human–Computer Interaction Series
ISBN 978-3-030-17429-3   ISBN 978-3-030-17427-9   (eBook)
https://doi.org/10.1007/978-3-030-17427-9

This Springer imprint is published by the registered company Springer Nature Switzerland AG
The registered company address is: Gewerbestrasse 11, 6330 Cham, Switzerland

I dedicate this book to my dear parents Christa and Karl Heimgärtner.

Preface

After numerous conferences and workshops on the development of intercultural user interfaces, I summarized the relevant knowledge in this area in a book for the German-speaking market, which was published in 2017 by Springer under the title "Interkulturelles User Interface Design" to cover the most important points of this topic from an academic point of view.

Due to the rapid development of the topic and the dramatic increase in the number of publications in this field, the translation of this book into English became necessary to reach a broader audience. Some minor corrections have been made, both, in terms of content and in terms of structure.

Now, I am pleased to present the first English edition of this book covering the development of intercultural user interfaces from theory to practice.

Undorf, Germany   Dr. Rüdiger Heimgärtner
January 2019

Acknowledgements

I would particularly like to thank Kerstin Röse, who inspired me with this topic since 2003 and strongly contributed to this book as a sparring partner between 2008 and 2013.

Furthermore, I would like to thank Yvonne Schoper, Henning Brau, Helmut Windl, Lutz-Wolfgang Tiede, and Alkesh Solanki, who also contributed to this book through their joint co-authorships at conferences and in books.

In addition, my special thanks goes to Craig Mabrey for native English proof reading and valuable feedback beyond that.

I am particularly grateful to Springer especially Beverley Ford, who encouraged me to translate the German version into English as well as Helen Desmond for her input permitting me to provide different book project types to Springer. In addition, I thank James Finlay, Nancy Wade-Jones, and Divya Prabha Karthikesan for supporting me in the publication process of this book.

Thanks from the bottom of my heart go to my parents, Christa and Karl Heimgärtner, who allowed me the potential space to do such privileged things as well as to my wife Gabi Heimgärtner for her patience and for taking over many of my other tasks to have the time to finish this book.

Finally, I thank all those who have not been explicitly mentioned but have supported this book project.

Undorf, Germany   Dr. Rüdiger Heimgärtner
January 2019

Contents

About the Author

Dr. Rüdiger Heimgärtner concentrated on the continuous evaluation of the current state of research in the field of the development of intercultural user interfaces since 2003. As founder and owner of the company "Intercultural User Interface Consulting" (IUIC), he has been passing on his knowledge to industry and research in the form of training, coaching, and consulting since 2008. He develops tools and methods to support the introduction and implementation of usability engineering processes also into the context of interculturality and accessibility. He is a Founding Member and Personal Member of the "International Usability and UX Qualification Board" (UXQB) and a Member of the Standards Committee of the "Deutsches Institut für Normung" (DIN) on ambient assisted living (AAL). With this background, as a SPICE assessor, he also checks and optimizes the conformity and maturity of development processes.

Abbreviations

(C)	Chinese-speaking users
(D)	German-speaking users
(E)	English-speaking users
AAL	Ambient Assisted Living
ACM	Association for Computing Machinery
ANOVA	ANalysis Of VAriance
API	Application Programming Interface
ASPICE	Automotive Software Process Improvement and Capability dEetermination
BCD	Basic Cultural Dimension
BIG5	Common character set of the five largest Taiwanese computer manufacturers
bit	binary digit
BPMN	Business Process Model and Notation
CEO	Chief Executive Officer
cf.	compare
chapt.	Chapter
CHI	Computer–Human Interaction
CIA	Central Intelligence Agency
CII	Cultural Interaction Indicator
CJKV	Chinese Japanese Korean Vietnamese
CMMI	Capability Maturity Model Integration
CPUX	Certified Professional for Usability and User Experience
CPUX-F	Certified Professional for Usability and User Experience—Foundation Level
CTT	Concur Task Trees
DIN	Deutsche Industrie Norm (German Industry Standard)
DP	Data Processing
DP	Direct Variable
Dr.	doctor

EDP	Electronic Data Processing
etc.	and so on
etc.	et cetera
Fa.	firm
ff.	[and] the following
Fig.	picture
FMEA	Failure Mode and Effect Analysis
G11N	Globalization
GB12345	Character set for Chinese characters
ger.	german
GOMS	Goals, Operators, Methods, and Selection rules
GSR	Galvanic Skin Resistance
GUI	Graphical User Interface
HCD	Human-Centered Design (obsolete; today "user centered design", see UCD)
HCD	Human–Computer Dimension
HCI	Human–Computer Interaction
HCII	Human–Computer Interaction International
HMI	Human–Machine Interaction
HMID	HMI Dimension
HR	Heart Rate
HRV	Heart Rate Variability
i.e.	that means
I18N	Internationalization
IAD	Institut Arbeitswissenschaft Darmstadt
IBIS	Issue-Based Information System
ICCHP	International Conference on Computers Helping People with special needs
ID	Information Density
IDV	InDiVidualism Index
IF	Interaction Frequency
if applicable	as the case may be
IFIP	International Federation for Information Processing
IHCI	International Human–Computer Interaction
IIA	Intercultural Interaction Analysis
IME	Input Method Editor
IN	Information
INF	Information Frequency
INH	Information Hypothesis
INS	Information Speed
iOS	Name of Apple's mobile operating system
IP	Information parallelism
ISO	International Standard Organization
IT	Information Technologie
IU-CD	Intercultural Usage-Centered Design

IUIC	Intercultural User Interface Consulting
IUID	Intercultural User Interface Design
IV	Indirect Variable
IWIPS	International Workshop of Internationalization of Products and Systems
KSC	Korean Standard Codeset (based on ISO10646)
L10N	Localization
LTO	Long Time Orientation
M&C	Mensch & Computer
MAS	MASculinity index
MC	Mouse Clicks
MCD	Method of Culture-Oriented Design
MCI	Mensch Computer Interaction
MG	Maneuver Guidance
MICHMID	Model of InterCultural HMI design
MM	Mouse Movements
Mr.	mister
Mrs.	misses
NIT	Number of Interactions per Time unit
NLP	NeuroLinguistic Programming
NVIV	Non-Visible Intercultural Variable
OLIF	Open Lexicon Interchange Format
p.	side
PC	Personal Computer
PCII	Potential Cultural Interaction Indicator
PDCA	Plan–Do–Control–Act ("Deming Cycle")
PDI	Power Distance Index
phil.	philosophical
POI	Point Of Interest
prof.	Professor
PT	Parallel Tasks
QOC	Questions Options Criteria
ROI	Return On Investment
RTL	Right-To-Left
s.	see
sbit	semantic **bit**
SCRUM	Name of an agile process framework
SE	Software Engineering
SEM	Structural Equation Model
Shift-JIS	Japan Industrial Standard Codeset (based on JIS X 0208)
SMART	Specific Measurable Achievable Reasonable Time bound
SPICE	Software Process Improvement and Capability dEtermination (ISO/IEC 15504–5)
SUI	Speech User Interface
SW	SoftWare

Tab.   table
TBX   TermBase eXchange
TDA   Time to Deactivate Agent
TLCC   Technics Language Culture Cognition
TM   Translation Memory
TMX   Translation Memory eXchange
TPI   Time of Presentation of an Information unit
UAI   Uncertainty Avoidance Index
U-CD   Usage-Centered Design
UCD   User-Centered Design
UI   User Interface
UI4All   User Interface for All
UIT   User Interface Toolkit
UML   Unified Modeling Language
UMTM   Usability Metric Trace Model
Unicode   Universal Coded Character Set (ISO 10646)
UPA   Usability Professionals Association
URL   Unified Resource Locator
US   United States
USA   United States of America
UV   Uncertainty Avoidance
UX   User Experience
UXQB   Usability and user eXperience Qualification Board
VDMA   Verein Deutscher MaschinenAnlagenbauer
VIV   Visible Intercultural Variable
V-model   Process model
vs.   versus
VSM   Value Survey Module
XP   eXtreme Programming
z. B.   for example

Chapter 1
Introduction

1.1 Introduction

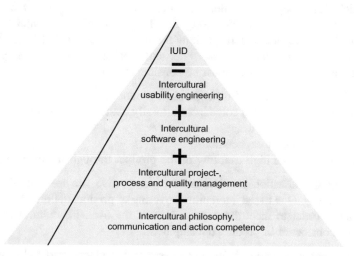

After the motivation and benefits of this book for the development of intercultural user interfaces (IUID) are presented, what is meant by IUID and its goal and procedure are further explained. In addition, the target group and structure of this book are described.

© Springer Nature Switzerland AG 2019
R. Heimgärtner, *Intercultural User Interface Design*, Human–Computer
Interaction Series, https://doi.org/10.1007/978-3-030-17427-9_1

1.2   Motivation and Benefits

"The advancing globalization, the liberalization of the world market and the increased speed of innovation for products make great demands on product and process optimization.[1] The Asian market is growing enormously (cf. Berger and Grassl 2008).[2] This requires that the product be tailored to the cultural needs of users[3] (Honold 2000). However, the development of innovative and usable products can only be realized effectively and efficiently if the underlying processes are optimized. Often, predefined goals are missed without external circumstances being able to explain this. This is simply due to a lack of usability of the products and/or processes in the required context of use. The quality of use must be increased through the usability and user experience of products through professional product development. Moreover, the processes must also be able to live in an intercultural context.

In order to be used at all, every product has a user interface, which represents the interface of the product to the user. In the case of a broom, the user interface is the broomstick, for a cup the handle, the touch screen for a mobile phone and the screen, keyboard, and mouse for a computer. The latter have electronics (hardware) with rules (software) that determine how the hardware can be used, i.e., the latter represent a system of hardware, software, and mechanics. When developing user interfaces, cultural preferences must be considered in order to

- be able to identify cultural differences in product use,
- to recognize, analyze, and solve interculturally overlapping situations of product definition and product usage,
- to meet cultural user expectations,
- to be able to create high usability of the product through familiar operability.

▸ Increasing globalization requires a new perspective on user interface design (Honold 2000). Due to the intercultural overlap of product definition and product use and in order to meet the expectations of the user, his cultural preferences must be considered in product development.

Efficient, effective, and satisfying processes and products, also and especially in an intercultural context, lead to greater sales success if you know which aspects are important for the development of intercultural user interfaces and how development guidelines can be generated from them.

---

[1]Formulation by Udo Kunder (Global Sales Manager and certified CPUX-F Usability Professional).

[2]Since 2000, sales figures for automobiles, for example, have risen steadily, especially in China, and in 2008 overtook those in the USA.

[3]With the use of words used here in this book, any other possible and desired form and address of the reader (e.g., female) is also automatically meant.

The goal is a globalized product for all (Stephanidis 2000). To this end, the product must first be internationalized, i.e., prepared for cross-cultural use, by creating a common platform that leaves room for culturally specific content. When localizing the product, the culture-specific parameters applying to the target country can then be integrated into the product (without changing the source code). The local parameters can be specified according to the target country. The internationalization process refers both to the functionality of the device and to the user interface design. Finally, the usability of interculturally designed devices increases because the operation of the device is familiar in the target country.

The development of intercultural user interfaces must take place in such a way that all relevant aspects of these areas can be used for all desired countries without time-consuming changes in the program code (= internationalization, cf. VDMA 2009). To use the product in a specific country, only the corresponding parameters should need to be changed (= localization, see VDMA 2009).

▶ Internationalization and localization can increase the modularization of software architecture.

The higher the degree of modularization in the software architecture:

- the shorter is the development time,
- the higher is the degree of system generalization,
- the lower is the programming effort,
- the better is the system robustness for future projects and platforms.

This shortens the time to market. Turnover and the market volume increase, which accelerates the return on investment (ROI). Therefore, an adaptation of the product to the desired cultures leads to advantages for

- Technicians (maintenance),
- Customers (usability),
- Product management (process control),
- Marketing (sales figures).

The product becomes comprehensible and thus easier to use, which leads to shorter training times (cf. Honold 2000; Jürgensohn et al. 2001; Röse 2002; Sun 2001). Beyond that, the probability increases that a user will buy a device from the same manufacturer again. The advantages for product developers and manufacturers are obvious:

- User-friendly product development,
- International competitiveness,
- Shorter development times,
- Cost savings,
- Increase in sales,
- Market advantage.

▸ Already the awareness that products must be adapted accordingly for the inter-national market represents the first big step in the development of international IT products. Many designers and project managers have no idea to what extent people in other countries are different and therefore need special attention, especially about the development of user interfaces. International usability has a great influence on market success. Meeting the requirements of international users is a serious design challenge that requires serious work and effort.

Studies have shown, for example, that web pages designed for a specific target country cannot be so easily used by users from other countries (cf. Marcus and Baumgartner 2004). Internationalization of IT products means more than simple translation, because the user interacts with the device and does not just read texts. Even if the translations are of excellent quality, the ideas regarding information architecture and interaction behavior can be very different due to cultural differences.[4]

▸ Not only the users differ, but also the approach of the users to solve the tasks. This results in different requirements for the design regarding usability. Therefore, intercultural usability engineering is not a "nice-to-have feature" that can be "tailored" but is a necessity.

The costs incurred for this can be kept within reasonable limits if usability tests are carried out in one's own country with test persons from the target country. The motto is: every usability test is better than none at all. Of course, the limits with regard to the number of test persons and on-site studies are open at the top. However, empirical values show that five test persons from each target group are already sufficient to identify about 80% of the largest design errors with regard to the usability of the product. Usually, at least 20 test persons are recruited for each target group in order to meet the statistical requirements. Groups from the USA, Japan, and Germany offer a first good cross-section of intercultural differences in usability. Of course, the larger the sales market, the faster the return on invest (ROI) is achieved. That is why we cannot lose sight of the emerging economic powers of the twenty-first century, such as China, India, and the Arab Emirates. The increased awareness of designers and product managers based on their experiences with these countries also means that users from other countries benefit from it.

---

[4]Information architecture includes, for example, information presentation, which is expressed, for example, by information frequency and information speed, or information structure such as information arrangement, information parallelism, and layout. Interaction behavior is described by parameters such as interaction speed and interaction frequency or by orientation during interaction ("navigation").

▸ The consideration of cultural aspects in the HMI design is just as necessary as the corresponding sensitization of the product manufacturers through training, education, and consultation with the stakeholders of the product (from the designer to the developer to the evaluator, product manager, and salesman). This book is meant to make a contribution.[5]

1.3 Definition, Goal, and Procedure

▸ The development of intercultural user interfaces encompasses all necessary process steps for the adequate design of human–machine interaction (HMI) taking cultural influences into account.

In doing so, appropriate methods for the interculturalization of user interfaces are applied. "Intercultural research in information systems is a relatively new field of research that [...] has gained in importance [...]" (Kralisch 2006, p. 17). Intercultural HMI design describes the user- and culture-oriented design of interactive systems and products, including the cultural context.

The context of the user depends on the tasks and the use of the product (Röse 2002, p. 87), i.e., the intercultural HMI design process (cf. Honold 2000, pp. 42–43). Honold presented the steps of this process of "intercultural usability engineering" (cf. Honold 2000, pp. 42-43). This approach has grown in research literature from 1990 to 2010 and stems from the processes of globalization, internationalization and localization.

▸ Intercultural user interfaces allow users of different cultural backgrounds to use products from different cultural manufacturers. Intercultural HMI design becomes beneficial and profitable when designers and developers know and apply the principles and recommendations for designing intercultural human–machine interaction in the individual product development phases (as suggested in this book).

The ultimate goal would be to create a "globalized product for all" (cf. UI4All, (Stephanidis, 2000))—especially regarding functionality and user interface. According to (Honold, 2000) the following aspects are of great importance: "1. The largest difficulties in internationalization do not lie in the field of UI design but in the field of product functionality and user requirements. While general problems and solutions are well known and limited for the UI, there are innumerable possibilities of how to do things wrong in the field of culture-specific user requirements. Therefore, procedures and methods for the elicitation and documentation of

---

[5]Further services can be obtained directly from the author and from IUIC (https://www.iuic.de, last access 29.2.2019). Illuminating examples or additional explanations are highlighted in gray.

culture-specific user requirements have to be fostered. 2. Product features are influenced by factors like infrastructure, education and training, labor organization, and also cultural values. In Germany, a high value for expertise and high technology orientation seem to influence the final design of products. Therefore, we think that for a successful internationalization, product planers should not only learn about other cultures but also become more aware of the influences their own culture has on them and their decisions." (Honold 2000): 146).

▸ The linking of theory and practice is of utmost importance, especially in an intercultural context, due to different thought patterns and approaches.

Due to the necessity of collecting current requirements and user wishes for the respective context and the respective target culture, a constant exchange between theory and practice is necessary. On the one hand, the newly collected results are to be incorporated into further theoretical research, on the other hand, new theoretical findings have an impact on the survey method(s) and the interpretation of the results. Therefore, a close integration of theory and practice is indispensable for intercultural HMI research as well as for the application of the results.

1.4   About This Book

Successful development of intercultural user interfaces (Intercultural User Interface Development—IUID)[6] includes or builds on the following areas (cf. Fig. 1.1). In this book, scientifically founded findings from intensive literature studies and research work by the author in these areas are presented and implementable knowledge is derived for practice. With this book, fundamental findings from these areas are bundled and passed on to you. The path from theory to the interculturally usable product is explained.

If any of these insights are relevant and useful to you in developing intercultural user interfaces, then this book has served its purpose.

---

[6]IUID is often simply called "Intercultural User Interface Design". "Design" is understood here in the sense of the entire development process, i.e., "design" in the sense of "development" or "process of human-centered design" as opposed to "design" as one of the more phases of the development process. The correct expression, according to that, would be "Intercultural User Interface Development". However, the term "User Interface Design" is so strongly Germanized that "Intercultural User Interface Design" was initially chosen as the title for the German-speaking market. With the second edition of the German book after its translation into English and the associated clarification of terms, an adaptation of the title of the second version of the German book may take place. For the English edition of the book the title "Intercultural User Interface Design" is just right, because in English it means the entire process of intercultural user interface development and not just the design phase.

Target audience

The know-how of developing user interfaces in an intercultural context benefits international companies and their employees as well as all those involved in the process of intercultural HMI design (such as usability professionals, user interface designers, information architects, interaction designers, software developers, project managers, product managers, sales managers). This book can also be used by students and lecturers to familiarize themselves with the topic or to prepare seminars.

Chapter overview

The subject areas of the pyramid in Fig. 1.1 are dealt with in this book. At the same time, the logical structure of the process flow for the development of intercultural user interfaces is observed and explained. In Chap. 2 the cultural basics are discussed, which mainly concern the areas of intercultural philosophy, communication, and manual competence and describe their effects on thinking (strategy) and acting (management) for intercultural product development. This primarily affects project, process, and quality management. In Chap. 3, relevant concepts of the IUID for software engineering are presented. Chapters 4–5 then focus on the human aspects of human–machine interaction: ergonomics and usability in relation to the human-centered design process and user interface design in an intercultural context. Chapter 6 allows a deeper insight into the theoretical background of IUID on the basis of scientific research. In Chap. 7, the knowledge gained on the IUID for practical implementation in industrial development projects is expanded to include technical requirements and action-relevant information.

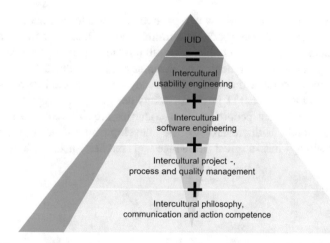

Fig. 1.1 Necessary foundation for the successful development of intercultural user interfaces (IUID). The focus of this book is marked in blue. (Source: IUIC). (The company IUIC (Intercultural User Interface Consulting) offers services in the field of IUID and has developed the pyramid in Fig. 1.1 within the framework of the development of its IUID service portfolio (more information on this can be found at https://www.iuic.de, contact details can be found in this book on p. 344).)

The development of intercultural user interfaces (IUID—Chaps. 5–7) requires interdisciplinary knowledge, which at least comes from the following areas:

- Cultural studies, communication studies, and philosophy for cultural and organizational requirements and their implementation in management (Chap. 2),
- Software ergonomics and usability engineering for human requirements and their conversion into machine requirements (Chap. 4),
- Software engineering for organizational and machine bound requirements and their implementation in products (Chap. 3).[7]

Chapter 8 concludes with a summary, a conclusion, and an outlook. Annex A (Chap. 9) lists all relevant standards and provides them with comments. By means of the summary of the checklists of this book in Appendix B (Chap. 10), the state of knowledge about the IUID topic can be reviewed and applied in practice. Appendix C (Chap. 11) contains further literature and other valuable source information as well as links to the IUID topic. The index gives you direct access to the relevant passages in the book using the most important terms. At the end of each chapter, the most important aspects of the chapter are summarized, a conclusion is drawn and, if necessary, an outlook is given. Furthermore, the standards are addressed, the literature used is listed, and a checklist for knowledge control is provided. Each chapter can be purchased separately online.

1.5 Summary, Conclusion, and Outlook

Increasing globalization requires a new perspective on user interface design. Due to the intercultural overlap between product definition and product use and in order to meet the expectations of the user, his cultural preferences must be taken into account during product development. The awareness that products for the international market must be adapted accordingly already represents the first big step in the development of international IT products. Many designers and project managers have no idea to what extent people in other countries are different and therefore need special attention with regard to the development of user interfaces. International usability has a great influence on market success. The actual

---

[7]This enumeration reflects the correct approach to the development of intercultural user interfaces, while the sequence of chapters represents the infrastructural prioritization of the areas. This means that before intercultural usability engineering (IUE) (Chap. 4) can be carried out in the development of intercultural user interfaces (IUID) (Chap. 5), software engineering (SE) must already have become intercultural software engineering (ISE) (Chap. 3) being aware of its corresponding tasks.

fulfillment of the requirements of international users is a serious design challenge that requires serious work and effort.

The development of intercultural user interfaces encompasses all necessary process steps for the adequate design of human–machine interaction (HMI), taking cultural influences into account. Intercultural human–machine design becomes beneficial and profitable when designers or developers know and apply the principles and recommendations for designing intercultural human–machine interaction in the individual product development phases (as suggested in this book). Intercultural user interfaces allow users from different cultural backgrounds to use products from different cultural manufacturers. The consideration of cultural aspects in the development of intercultural user interfaces is just as necessary as the corresponding sensitization of the product manufacturers as well as through education, training, and consultion with the stakeholders of the product (from the concept developer and designer to the developer to the evaluator, product manager and salesman).[8]

Norms	√
ISO 9241	☐
Checklist	√
Conceptual knowledge	☐
• Product	☐
• Process	☐
• User Interface (UI)	☐
• Internationalization (I18N)	☐
• Localization (L10N)	☐
• Intercultural User Interface Design (IUID)	☐
IUID includes or builds on the following areas:	☐
• Intercultural philosophy, communication and action competence	☐
• Intercultural project, process and quality management	☐
• Intercultural software engineering	☐
• Intercultural usability engineering	☐
You want to create user interfaces for products for the target markets of other cultures or to learn more about the process of intercultural HMI design? Then read this book!	☐

---

[8]This book is meant to make a contribution. You are welcome to contact the author or IUIC for questions, feedback, corrections and services (https://www.iuic.de). Further contact details can be found on page 344 in this book.

References

Berger D, Grassl W (2008) Where the auto industry is still booming. Sourcing asia, vol 4, pp 17–19

Honold P (2000) Intercultural usability engineering: a study on cultural influences on the design and use of technical products (gedr. Aufl. 647). Düsseldorf: VDI Verl

Jürgensohn T, Timpe K-P, Willumeit H-P (2001) Motor vehicle guidance: [Commemorative volume for Prof. Dr. Hans-Peter Willumeit]. Springer, Berlin

Kralisch A (2006) The impact of culture and language on the use of the internet empirical analyses of behaviour and attitudes. Dissertation, Berlin

Marcus A, Baumgartner V-J (2004) Mapping user-interface design components vs. culture dimensions in corporate websites. Visible Lang J MIT Press 38(1):1–65

Röse K (2002) Methodology for designing intercultural human-machine systems in production engineering, vol 5. University of Kaiserslautern, Kaiserslautern

Stephanidis C (2000) UI4ALL 2000: 6th ERCIM workshop on "user interfaces for all". Paper presented at the CNR-IROE–6th ERCIM WORKSHOP, Convitto della Calza, Florence

Sun H (2001) Building a culturally competent corporate web site: an exploratory study of cultural markers in multilingual web design. Paper presented at the proceedings of SIGDOC, New York

VDMA (2009) Software internationalization guide. VDMA Software Association, Frankfurt a. M

Chapter 2
Thinking and Acting

Before this chapter can deal with the influence of culture on the thinking or ideology (philosophy) and the acting (management) of people in project, process, and quality management in the development of intercultural user interfaces, an insight into the fundamentals of cultural studies is necessary.

2.1 Culture and Cultural Models

Intercultural philosophy, linguistics, cultural studies, and ergonomics deal with aspects that affect the different cultures of this earth. All disciplines that are strongly influenced by culture contribute as a multidisciplinary subject to successful cultural studies, e.g., art, literature, media, language, philosophy, religion, psychology, or sociology.

© Springer Nature Switzerland AG 2019
R. Heimgärtner, *Intercultural User Interface Design*, Human–Computer
Interaction Series, https://doi.org/10.1007/978-3-030-17427-9_2

Cultural studies explore cultures. Human behavior is examined in relation to cultural differences (cf. Straub 2007; Jäger 2004; Hansen 2003).

▸ Ethnocentrism is an important phenomenon that has effects on intercultural interaction: people tend to regard their own culture as the center of the world as well as the yardstick of all things (cf. Maletzke 1996, pp. 23–24). People from other cultures are judged according to their own customs and norms. Consequently, the customs and requirements of other cultures are often not perceived or taken into account by the developers of the HMI design (cf. Heimgärtner und Tiede 2008). Solving this problem is one of the main tasks of the intercultural HMI design process.

2.1.1   Concept of Culture

Culture is a very complex concept whose meaning differs in view of the context of use (thematic, functional, structural, historical, mental, symbolic, and normative) (cf. Kralisch 2006, p. 12, Table 2). Therefore, there are many different concepts of "culture". The word "culture" comes from the Latin word *colere,* which means "to build on something, to take care of it" and describes the way people shape their lives. This also includes thinking and shaping (cf. Maletzke 1996, pp. 22–23). "Culture is something specific human. We attribute culture only to man. Man creates culture and is shaped by it" (Maletzke 1996, p. 20). "The fact that we can laugh and weep and express feelings mimically is certainly in the nature of man. But when and how we do this depends on the culture in which we grew up" (Wahrlich 1991, p. 15). Culture arises from social, historical, political, literary, artistic, economic, legal, and spatial conditions (cf. Straub 2007; Jäger 2004; Hansen 2003). According to Kohls (2008), culture is an integrated system of learned patterns of behavior that are characteristic of all members of a society.

Culture and the associated cultural standards in the respective cultures are thus fundamental determinants of human beings, their thinking, and action. Thus, many anthropologists understand culture as a system of convictions, attitudes, and value orientations, which is expressed in human behavior and in intellectual and material products. According to the organizational psychologist (Thomas 1996), culture expresses the attributes of orientation systems. The cultural group sets standards by which an individual must orientate himself in order to feel a part of this cultural group (cf. Thomas and Eckensberger 1993, p. 112).[1] The organizational

---

[1]Thomas writes: "Culture is a universal orientation system very typical for a society, organization and group [...]. This orientation system is formed from specific symbols and passed on in the respective society, etc. It influences the perception, thinking, values and actions of all its members and thus defines their membership of society. Culture as an orientation system structures a specific field of action for the individuals who feel they belong to society and thus creates the prerequisite for the development of independent forms of environmental management" (Thomas 1996, p. 112).

anthropologist Geert Hofstede defines culture as the collective programming of the mind (cf. Hofstede et al. 2010). "It [culture] is the collective programming of the mind that distinguishes the members of one group or category of people from others." (Hofstede and Hofstede 2005, p. 4, insertion by the author). According to cultural anthropologist Edward T. Hall, culture always occurs in combination with communication. Culture is a "silent language" or "hidden dimension", which is unconscious (cf. Hall 1959). Therefore, communication problems with members of other cultures arise:

▸ If one is not aware of one's own culturally influenced motives, one cannot understand the motives and actions of others (cf. Thomas 1996). Culture thus represents a generally valid orientation system, which takes on a typical form within a certain group, organization, or society.

This system contains symbols and standards. According to (Hansen 2003), culture includes all the customs of a collective and the standardizations that include themselves in this collective, i.e., culture consists of standardization, communication, and collective and is mainly based on interactions (cf. Hansen 2003).

▸ For intercultural HMI design, the consideration of cultures on the HMI design process and the resulting user interface is of decisive importance.

2.1.2 Definition of Culture

Culture thus represents the common values of a group that enables community and communication in contrast to other groups. The common values of a group influence one's own behavior pattern, learning behavior, and cognitive processing patterns (cf. Röse 2002: 3–4). Accordingly, culture also has an influence on how technology is handled in general (cf. also Hoft 1995 and Honold 2000). This is a rather pragmatic, systematic, and structural concept of "culture", relevant for the research of intercultural HMI design. In her dissertation in 2002, Röse defined a suitable working definition for the analysis of connections between cultures and HMI design from the diversity of cultural definitions, which takes into account both the engineering–scientific, in particular, the HMI-specific applicability, and psychologically interesting aspects:

▸ "Culture (definition). An image of common values, ways of thinking and acting of a group of individuals that contributes to the formation of this community. It influences the interaction with other individuals as well as the interaction with technical devices. The common group values serve as a norm and thus for the orientation of the group members and as differentiation criteria to other groups. The common cultural identity of a group is usually reflected by a nationality." (Röse 2002, p. 7).

This definition represents a distinct demarcation with respect to the multiplicity of most different definitions in different disciplines and specifically considers the connection of culture and the relationship between culture and human technology. With this cultural definition, the following aspects can be reconciled, which play an important role in the development of intercultural user interfaces[2]:

- Description of a culture considering social factors that a group or community shares and defines as a norm,
- Identification of a culture through the behavior shown together, resulting from the common basis of thought and action patterns, common values and symbols, of the individuals belonging to it,
- The interaction between people is shaped by culture,
- The shaping of everyday behavior patterns and the everyday handling of technology and thus the human–technology interaction by culture,
- Identity of a nation based on cultural similarities.[3]

2.1.3 Cultural Differences

In order to gain an impression of how culture possibly influences the needs of users within HMI, it is useful to first look at a few examples of the differences within different cultures.

▸ Incorrect communication is a major cause of conflicts between cultures and can be avoided by respectfully considering the signs and symbols of the other culture. The form of communication can play a more important role than the content of the communication itself (cf. Maletzke 1996).

Western culture is marked by the heritage of the Greek intellect, Roman law, the Germanic idea of society and the Christian faith. This led to the modern scientific character through the epochs of the Renaissance and the Enlightenment. In comparison to Asian culture, above all the following concepts are characteristic for Western culture: Individuality, rationality, orientation toward contracts and law as well as lived ethics. Western individualism is alien to Asians from these qualities. Contrary to this, the group is clearly in the foreground in Asia (cf. Weggel 1990, p. 38). Harmony affects both thinking and individual behavior as well as the structure of society, and conflicts with Western nobility and hard work of division (cf. Nisbett 2003). The basis for interpersonal action between Asians and Western

---

[2]The cultural dimensions that describe this behavior on the basis of defined categories (e.g., power distance (cf. Hofstede 1991) or communication speed (cf. Hall 1959)) also fit in with this working definition. (see Sect. 2.1.4).

[3]The cultural similarities can vary considerably here—e.g., depending on the size of the nation and the multitude of ethnic groups in the nation.

people is the pursuit of harmony and the avoidance of open conflicts of all kinds in Asia (face-saving mentality, cf. Victor 1998). This results in different communication behavior between Europeans and Asians. Europeans express facts directly and clearly, Asians use indirect paraphrases, tips, and symbols. The more important a message is, the more cautious the design and content of the statements will be.

▸ Culture has an influence on learning behavior, expectations, and cognitive processing (cf. e.g., Brunner 2005: Sect. 2.5.1).

There are cultural differences in the perception, processing, and presentation of information as well as in problem-solving strategies, language, and behavior with regard to structure, dynamics, situation, and context:

- Information reception/perception:

  - Anticipation, selection, infiltration, forwarding

- Depth, color, time, olfactory perception
- Information processing/mental services:

  - Memory, cognitive styles, creative skills

- Problem-solving strategies:

  - Successive-sequential, monocausal, dialectical (contrasts)
  - Simultaneous-integral, multicausal, relational (relationships)

- Presentation of information:

  - Color, icons, language, formats, units

- Differences in language and behavior

  - In the age of globalization, many readers have probably already got to know or experienced such differences themselves by interacting with people from other cultures. Especially when critical interaction situations have occurred.

There are also factors which are supposed to be the same in all cultures, such as those known from Gestalt psychology, the Gestalt laws of proximity, similarity, common religion (cf. Zimbardo and Gerrig 2004), or worldwide factors in the value structure (cf. Schwartz 1992) as well as common social factors cf. (Parsons 1951). Despite all this, Schwartz and Bardi (2001) and Inglehart et al. (1998) examined these generalities across all cultures and found that even these general factors can differ or at least to some extent cause other differences. Nevertheless, there are also HMI design approaches, such as universal design or UI4All, which attempt to develop a single universal user interface that can be used by all people and contexts (cf. also the research and application of cross-cultural psychology by Berry 2007 and Altarriba 1993).

In methodological terms, it is initially easier to start from cultural differences and to take them into account in intercultural HMI design, because one progresses from the individual case to the general and not vice versa (as with the approach of cultural communities). For this reason, there is considerably more literature on cultural differences than on cultural similarities (cf. Röse 2002, pp. 17–40). D'Andrade (2001) described the development of cognitive anthropology and Tomasello (2006) explains human perception. Lee et al. (1999) show the differences in a person's personality and perceptions among cultures by examining the "Big Five" as a means of explanation (cf. Paunonen et al. 2000, 2001). Wierzbicka (1991) explains the differences in English, Japanese, and Chinese communication by considering transcultural pragmatism and the semantics of human interaction (see also Chen 1993). Matiaske (1997) investigated the structure and meaning of orientation toward the virtues of managers from China and Germany. He found out that "new" Chinese businessmen are individual materialists. Nisbett (2003) refers to cultural differences in mentality and thought. Asian people focus their perceptions more on the context than on the relevance. The Chinese very often retrieve important facts at the end of a conversation (see Fanchen and Yao 2007). There are also differences in complex decision-making processes (cf. Strohschneider 2002).

▸ Cultural aspects influence the development of intercultural user interfaces in information systems due to the intercultural HMI design process. Interaction and dialogue design, in particular, must therefore, be treated very carefully within the intercultural development process. Due to the cultural differences, this represents a corresponding challenge for all those involved, which can only be met by appropriate knowledge of the desired target cultures.

2.1.4 Cultural Models

If one follows (cf. Hofstede and Hofstede 2005), culture represents the mental programming of the mind. During the intensive learning phase in childhood, people are influenced above all by the culture with certain rules, norms, and desirable behavior patterns to which the group members adhere. Second, cultural imprinting takes place when man is also oriented toward other cultures, which coincide with the primary cultural imprinting but do not replace it. Moreover, the possibility of orientation always remains, even if culture is constantly evolving, i.e., even if the contents of cultural standards change. Therefore, there is in each case something to orientate oneself by within a group of people, a region, or a nation, which is called a cultural model. With the help of cultural models, cultural differences can be described and ordered.

One of the best-known cultural models is the iceberg model (cf. Hoft 1996). Only about 10% of the properties of a culture are visible and perceptible, the rest is invisible and subconscious, and, therefore, difficult to explore (Fig. 2.1).

Fig. 2.1 Iceberg model of cultural aspects (based on Hoft 1996)

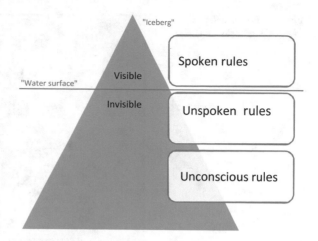

▸ Cultural models help us to look "under the surface of the cultural iceberg", i.e., to research areas of cultures that are not immediately visible at first, in order to identify and overcome methodological gaps.

Another model for the description of a cultural system was coined by the organizational psychologist Alexander Thomas.

▸ "Cultural Standards" express the normal, typical, and valid attributes for the majority of the members of a particular culture by considering modes of perception, thought, judgment, and action (cf. Thomas 1996, p. 112).

Cultural standards serve as an orientation system for the members of a group and regulate actions. The individual grows into his culture by adopting and internalizing these cultural standards. This process involves learning basic human skills in social interaction, controlling one's own behavior and feelings, satisfying basic needs, looking at the world, verbal and non-verbal communication, and the expectations of others, as well as understanding one's own role and assessment standards.

Another concept, that of the "cultural dimension", can serve as a basis for identifying cultural standards (cf. Hodicová 2007, p. 38). According to the organizational anthropologist Geert Hofstede, cultural dimensions are models for describing the behavior of people from different cultures by facilitating the quantitative analysis and comparison of characteristics of different groups (cf. Hofstede and Hofstede 2005).

▸ Cultural dimensions represent a cultural aspect that can be measured in relation to other cultures. They can be used to classify behavioral species within and between cultures.

Cultural dimensions are indicators that show trends in the interaction and communication behavior of members of cultures. Hofstede first developed four, then five, and now six cultural dimensions that describe this behavior (cf. Hofstede et al. 2010). Each dimension has a numeric index. Hofstede et al. (2010) determined

Fig. 2.2 Power distance.
(*Source* Jörg Plannerer)

the values of the indices of these cultural dimensions for 56 countries.[4] The most common are briefly addressed below.

Power Distance (PDI, Fig. 2.2): The "Power Distance Index" stands for the acceptance of social inequality and the relationship to authority, i.e., the extent to which the less powerful members of institutions or organizations in a country expect power to be unequally distributed (cf. Hofstede 1991, p. 42).

Individualism versus collectivism (IDV, Fig. 2.3): This dimension describes the attitude of an individual toward life in groups. A high individualism index points to societies in which the relationships between individuals are loose: You expect everyone to look out for themselves and their immediate family. A low individualism index points to collectivist societies in which persons are integrated into collective groups from birth, which protects them for life and demands non-binding loyalty (cf. Hofstede 1991, p. 67).

Femininity versus masculinity (MAS): This dimension stands for the social relationships of the sexes. A society indicates how clearly the roles of the sexes are separated from each other: Masculinity means being assertive, strong, and materialistic. Femininity presupposes a society in which gender roles overlap: Women and men should be down-to-earth and sensitive and attach great importance to the quality of life (cf. Hofstede 1991), S. 101). This is about the female or male role in society, i.e., what it means from a social point of view to be "typically" male or female or to act accordingly. However, the gender gaps between cultures vary.[5] In

---

[4]See the website of Geert Hofstede. https://www.hofstede-insights.com/product/compare-countries/ (last access 9th February 2019). Reimer (2005) describes and discusses Hofstede's cultural dimensions in detail.

[5]http://www.gender.sachsen-anhalt.de/, last access 9th of February 2019.

Fig. 2.3 Individualism
versus collectivism. (*Source*
Jörg Plannerer)

Fig. 2.4 Uncertainty
avoidance. (*Source* Jörg
Plannerer)

order to avoid misunderstandings, Hofstede has, therefore, renamed these cultural
dimensions into the quantity of life (e.g., competitiveness, assertiveness, ambition,
materialism, power) and quality of life (relationships, care, love).

Uncertainty avoidance (UAI, Fig. 2.4): This index represents the degree to
which members of a culture feel threatened by uncertain or unknown situations. It is
also an indicator of how the handling of uncertainty is expressed, as far as the
control of emotions and aggression is concerned (cf. Hofstede 1991, p. 133).

Long-term versus short-term orientation (LTO, Fig. 2.5): Long-term-oriented
cultures stand for lasting power, relationship resistance, and the restraint of these
relations in order to promote values toward future achievements, above all

Fig. 2.5 Long-term versus
short-term orientation.
(*Source* Jörg Plannerer)

endurance and economy (cf. Hofstede 1991: 401). Short-term-oriented societies
show a high degree of personal stability, respect for tradition and values in relation
to past and present (cf. Hofstede 1991, p. 403).

The sixth dimension was added long after the other four or five:

"Indulgence versus restraint." "Devotion" means a society that can satisfy the
basic and natural human urges relatively freely and enjoy life and spare time.
"Restraint" denotes a society that suppresses the satisfaction of needs and regulates
this through strict social norms.

Hofstede applied the cultural dimensions to nations. Their nature represents the
character of the nation. For example, China, unlike Germany, has a high power
distance. The Power Distance Index (PDI) ranges from 0 to around 100. Hofstede
found that power distance in China (PDI = 80) is high compared to Germany
(PDI = 35). This may be relevant for the development of intercultural user interfaces, e.g., accepting help or instructions (given by the system), depending on the
user's acceptance of external power.

2.1.5 Cultural Distance

▸ Cultural models describe the cultural distance between cultures, i.e., the extent of
  the differences between cultures, and allow these to be compared with each other
  (cf. Hofstede 1984).

The analysis of cultural differences reveals, for example, large cultural distances
for people from Western and Asian regions (cf. Inglehart et al. 1998, p. 16 ff.). The

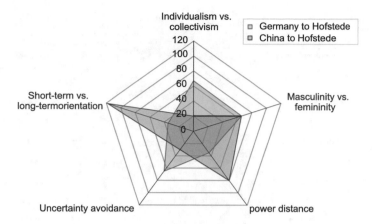

Fig. 2.6 Relatively different indices for China and Germany according to Hofstede. (*Source* Heimgärtner 2012)

distance felt between people and culture plays an important role in intercultural communication situations. It arises from the different expressions of structural characteristics of a specific culture. The probability of a misunderstanding is proportional to the size of the cultural distance (cf. Maletzke 1996, pp. 33–34). Figure 2.6 shows the characteristics of Hofstede's cultural views for China and Germany (cf. Hofstede 1991).

The greater the cultural distance, the easier it is to identify cultural differences and to transfer them to the development of intercultural user interfaces and explain them. Therefore, for didactic reasons, examples for the cultures China and Germany are mainly used in this book.

2.1.6   Tendencies of Cultural Dimensions

Hall (1959), Trompenaars and Hampden-Turner (1997), Adler (1997), Adler and Gundersen (2008), Condon (1984), Kluckhohn and Strodtbeck (1961) and Borisoff and Victor (1997) provided further cultural dimensions such as

- Universalism versus uniqueness,
- Role versus relationship orientation,
- Result versus assignment orientation,
- Neutral versus emotional behavior,
- Individualism versus community,
- Orientation according to goal achievement versus status,
- Time and space orientation.

The peculiarities of these dimensions were determined for many nations by their authors (cf. Levine and Norenzayan 1999 or Inglehart et al. 1998). Baumgartner (2003) drew up a list of 29 cultural dimensions. On this basis, literature studies can

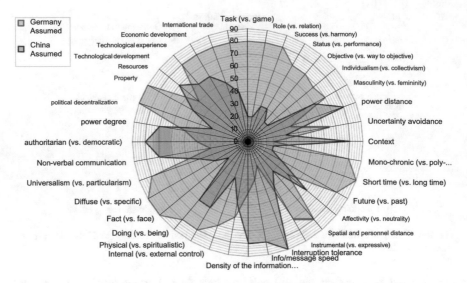

Fig. 2.7 Presumed characteristics of analyzed cultural dimensions according to the assessment of (Heimgärtner 2012) based on Hofstede indices and other literature searches

be used to assign values corresponding to the cultural dimensions for China and Germany (cf. Heimgärtner 2012). The results are shown in Fig. 2.7.

Table 2.1 lists the concrete attributes of relevant cultural dimensions for the development of intercultural user interfaces—proposed by Baumgartner (2003), Khaslavsky (1998), Marcus and Baumgartner (2004), Röse (2002), see also Heimgärtner (2012). The high cultural distance between China and Germany is obvious, as most values of cultural dimensions differ greatly.

However, cultural dimensions only describe behavioral tendencies: Generalization is not tenable, but (if one considers large groups) at least sustainable, i.e., acceptable as a first orientation value (cf. Nagy 2003). Furthermore, the knowledge about the values of cultural dimensions represents an impression of each culture to which the user could belong. Consequently, cultural dimensions are indicators of differences between cultures, which can give an impression of possible differences in intercultural user interfaces and their operation by users from different cultural backgrounds. However, all cultures are "gradable". Moreover, cultures also have many aspects in common: each culture necessarily has universal metrological relationships and basic metaphysical aspects because all cultures are made up of people, society, and knowledge of traditions. In fact, most of the essential components of a culture are shared with all other cultures (cf. Moeschler 1989). There are only minor differences.

However, if these are noticeably different, it is very important to take them into account by analyzing the interactions between the members of the cultures. Therefore, culturally conditioned aspects must be considered in the HMI design process.

The tendency character of the cultural dimensions suggests a shift in the application of cultural models. It is no longer national manifestations in the cultural dimensions that are relevant for the development of intercultural user interfaces, but

Tab. 2.1 High cultural distance between China and Germany—most cultural relations have very different values

Cultural dimension	China	Germany
Context (Hall 1959)	High	Low
Message speed (Hall 1959)	High	Low
Room (Hall 1959)	Near	Far
Time orientation (Hofstede 1984)	Long-term oriented (LTO = 118)	Short-term oriented (LTO = 31)
Time orientation (Hall 1959)	Polychronic	Monochronic
Power distance (Hofstede 1984)	High (PDI = 80)	Low (PDI = 35)
Collectivism versus Individualism (Hofstede 1984)	Collectivist (IDV = 20)	Individualistic (IDV = 67)
Uncertainty avoidance (Hofstede 1984)	Medium (UAI = 30)	High (UAI = 65)
Diffusity versus Specificity (Trompenaars and Hampden-Turner 1997)	Diffuse	Specific
Particularism versus Universalism (Trompenaars and Hampden-Turner 1997)	Universalism	Particularism
Genus (Hofstede 1984)	Feminine (MAS = 66)	Masculine (MAS = 66)
Relationship versus Tasks/role orientation (Halpin and Winer 1957)	Relation-oriented	Task-/role-oriented

their manifestations in any cultural context, i.e., between any culture (not only between nations). Interculturalization is more than globalization (internationalization and localization) of software. It also applies to personalization by storing user-specific settings and activating them by means of identifiers of the user. Interculturalization represents an "individualization" that includes intra-subjective, inter-subjective, intra-cultural, and intercultural modes of imprinting.

▸ The development of intercultural user interfaces is more than the development of international user interfaces. Due to the affinity of cultural dimensions to personality dimensions, both concepts should be applied in the design of intercultural user interfaces.

In the following section, therefore, the influence of culture on the way people think and view the world (philosophy) and act (management) in project, process, and quality management is presented, both in the development of intercultural user interfaces and in their operation.

2.2 Philosophy, Communication, and Action Competence

Culture influences human thinking, communication, and the resulting behavior, which in an intercultural context requires appropriate knowledge about culturally different ways of thinking (intercultural philosophy), relevant languages (intercultural communication), and correct behavior in unknown cultural contexts (intercultural competence).

2.2.1 Philosophy

The cradle of all cognitive styles and thought patterns are the philosophies in the different cultures of this earth. Philosophy is the love of wisdom and has been practiced since time immemorial and established over time as an academic discipline. All other disciplines have emerged from this—from the natural sciences such as mathematics and physics to the humanities such as anthropology, psychology, and sociology. But also, metaphysics, science theory, ethics—the latter strongly influences jurisprudence or genetics—are subject to strongly philosophical basic views.

▸ Humanity's patterns of thought are determined by philosophies (worldviews), which are culturally very different worldwide. In intercultural philosophy research, two main directions are distinguished: Eastern and Western philosophy.

The discipline of "intercultural philosophy" analyzes culturally conditioned ways of thinking, criticizes self-perception and external perception, promotes openness and understanding, promotes mutual enlightenment, and thus serves intercultural orientation, thereby promoting humanity and peace (cf. Wimmer 2004, p. 134).

▸ The ultimate goal of intercultural philosophy is mutual understanding.

Misunderstanding is even better than not understanding, because any misunderstanding requires a certain amount of understanding (Wimmer 2004, p. 150 ff.). However, on the way to understanding there are still a few further hurdles to overcome, which can only be solved collectively, often at the worldwide political level. These include, for example, inconsistencies in the theory and practice of regional origin or universal application, universally valid human rights ideas and general freedom of religion (cf. Wimmer 2004, p. 164). In addition, many philosophies (e.g., in India and in Islam) are religiously motivated and are, therefore, analyzed with the aid of religious philosophy, which combines metaphysics, epistemology, and ethics in order to be able to create and analyze religions (Yandell 1999, p. 17). Eastern philosophy distinguishes between Chinese, Indian, Buddhist, and Islamic traditions (cf. Deutsch et al. 1997; Komischke et al. 2003). There are concrete instructions for resolving misunderstandings, especially in dialogue-oriented contexts. Several criteria must be met in order to prevent or eliminate misunderstandings (e.g., Rationality rule (logic rule), Purpose rationality rule (functionality rule), Humanity rule (naturalness rule), Nos-quoque-rule ("We-too"-rule), Vos-quoque-rule ("You-too"-rule), Anti-cryptoracism rule, rule of personality, rule of subjectivity, rule of ontology–deontology ("actual state/should-be state" rule), rule of depolarization (rule of anti-cultural dualism), rule of inhomogeneity, rule of agnosticism, cf. Wimmer (2004, p. 147 ff.).

In order to be able to analyze cultural differences, there must be a cultural commonality. Janich (2006) explains some of these cultural universals in "Culture and Method" and details the use of these methods to attain culture in a scientific world. Such thought patterns result from the pattern of linking cognitive styles.

▸ Cognitive style patterns describe the way in which information is processed and how it is dealt with, typical of an individual.

This is a relatively stable personality trait that transcends all situations. Cognitive styles are involved in cognitive skills such as perception and thinking (Janich 2006). In differential psychology, for example, the following cognitive styles are identified:

- Field dependence (Witkin et al. 1954),
- Reflectivity versus impulsivity (Kagan 1965a),
- Analytical versus functional style (Kagan 1965b),
- Leveling versus sharpening,
- Scanning versus non-scanning,
- Tendency to interference (Hörmann 1960).

▸ In the different cultures, however, cognitive styles tend to be strongly pronounced, resulting in different patterns of thought. This, in turn, has an effect on the worldview in the respective cultures and thus on the approach to reality.[6]

The paths to wisdom (philosophies) are accordingly different. Figure 2.8 shows different types of thought patterns that entail different logical flows (thought processes).

These thought patterns have a corresponding effect on the presentation of information. For example, the structure of a lecture in Germany is very different from one in Japan. In Germany, the transition from the specific to the general is logically based on theories. In Japan, the argumentation is based on empirical values and experiments on the topic and is developed from the general to the specific.

The expectation of presentation also depends on culture (cf. Lewis 2002, p. 105 ff.). While in the USA one expects current, target-oriented, funny, and crisp presentations with effective gags, in Germany one prefers rather extensive technical background information for a solid and high-quality product without cracking jokes. In France, formality, logic, and authenticity count. Lectures are interrupted by listeners asking questions—in contrast to Finland. Here neither feedback on the lecture nor interruptions during it are usual. You want modern, well-designed, informative but concise presentations. While in Arab countries the communication

---

[6]Scientists, theologians, and philosophers think in concepts. They create concepts on the basis of theories and postulates. This way of thinking is very widespread in the West (e.g., America, Europe). Mystics and possibly inventors acquire their knowledge more intuitively, from inner experience or visions. Such intuitive thought patterns based on psychic experience are used in India, for example. Concretely relational ways of thinking, which grasp reality as active emotional relations in concrete situations, are rather practiced by artists and actors. Similar thought patterns are found in China.

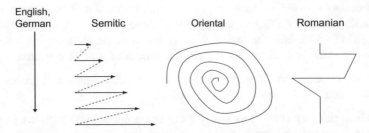

Fig. 2.8 Culturally induced different thought processes

behavior is rather personal, rhetorically brilliant, but also loud and lively, in Japan one scores with courtesy, respect, harmony, and USPs (unique selling propositions). These culturally different expectations of a presentation of information imply a correspondingly different attention span (Table 2.2, Kuhnert 2004).

Closely related to this is whether the communication partners are more task oriented as in Germany or more person oriented as in China (Reisach et al. 2007, p. 306).

Task-oriented people:

- focus on technical aspects,
- avoid personal questions and small talk,
- stay with the product—even if the seller changes,
- consider results greater than harmony and preservation of the face,
- admire specialists and experts with outstanding skills and knowledge.

▸ In contrast, person-oriented people attach great importance to relationships and the harmonious and loyal interaction with each other. Results result from loyalty, harmony, and face protection. This includes large relationship networks and frequent talking to each other.

The differences in behavior in the working environment are similarly different (cf. Reisach et al. 2007, p. 306). These differences can be explained by the different needs structure in China on the basis of Maslow's pyramid of needs (cf. Nevis 2001). In China, social needs play a more fundamental role than physical and security needs (Fig. 2.9).

According to (Schumacher 2010, p. 272 ff.) there are at least the following cognitive differences in the Western and Eastern way of thinking:

- Categorization according to role versus relationship,
- Focus versus overall view,
- Tasks versus relationship orientation.

Tab. 2.2 Culturally dependent attention duration in presentations

Country	Germany	Japan	Finland	France	USA	Arab
Attention duration	1 h	1 h	45 min	30 min	30 min	15 min

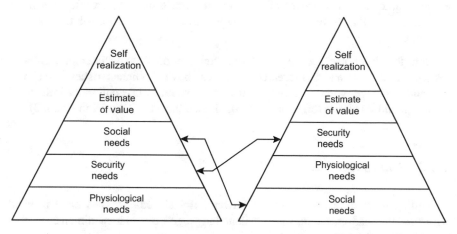

Fig. 2.9 Maslow's pyramid of needs (left) and change for China according to Nevis (right). (*Source* Nevis 2001)

- Further studies (e.g., by Nisbett 2003; Hofstede 2000; Trompenaars 1993) revealed additional differences to the following aspects (Western vs. Eastern orientation):
- Field independent versus field dependent,
- Articulated versus global,
- Individualistic versus collectivist,
- Formal versus informal,
- Impersonal versus interpersonal,
- Low versus strong social network,
- Low versus high power distance.

Thus at least Eastern and Western thought patterns can be distinguished. In addition, however, there are further and finer subdivisions. Nisbett (2003) classifies Teutonic, Anglo-Saxon, Nipponese, and Germanic thought styles. These can be further refined from an international to a regional and even individual level. This is especially true if one must understand other cultures if one wants to develop correspondingly adapted user interfaces. Thoughts, values, views, which are culturally very different, can only be experienced through the behavior of the respective person or can only be clarified and understood through conversations with the respective person.

▸ Cultural differences in thinking have an impact on the development and operation of intercultural user interfaces. These are described in detail in Chap. 5.

Regardless of the granularity of such investigations, it is clear that cultures and philosophies strongly influence each other. Thus, if one conducts comparative cultural research, one does not compare fads but fundamental and permanent aspects.

▸ The characteristics or values of a culture are not a trend but result from basic philosophies that have been handed down over a long period of time in this culture.

Here the difference between the terms "international" and "intercultural" also becomes clear: international research examines above all characteristics in technology and language, while intercultural research examines interculturally influenced cognition and its effects (cf. Honold 2000, cf. also the TLCC model in Chap. 3).

2.2.2 Communication

According to cultural anthropologist Edward T. Hall, culture goes hand in hand with communication. Culture is a "silent language" or "hidden dimension" that unconsciously controls people.

▸ Culture is mainly a communication system (see Hall 1959).

Therefore, Hall is seen as the founder of intercultural communication (cf. Moosmüller 2007, p. 16). Communication consists of verbal or nonverbal interaction and the transfer of information in human–human communication is up to 80% nonverbal (cf. Argyle and Schmidt 2002).

▸ Communication includes language (understanding, cognition, perception), material property (power and status), and behavior (emotions, conflict behavior, and coping).

Information perception depends on activity, situation, status, experience, and culture (Hall and Hall 1983, p. 21). Culture is learned and forms identity: by learning certain types of behavior, man matures according to his cultural environment. Basic behavior patterns are related to time, the density of the communication network, the communication speed, and the importance of time in chains of action. Space and time as fundamental physical factors influence human communication behavior, which has an impact on the sociological processes of a group of people and, therefore, also on their culture. Interpersonal communication has developed over thousands of years and has been shaped over time by social and cultural influences (Röse 2002, p. 42). Originally, communication rules were used to describe interpersonal communication. However, these can also be used in the HMI (see Fischer 2006). Communication is a special case of interaction, because interaction can also take place without message transmission. Communication only takes place when information is successfully exchanged; consequently, interpretation processes are involved. Communication, in contrast to pure interaction, involves the understanding of meanings through reciprocal processes and the use of language (i.e., using a common code—vocabulary and grammar)—verbal or nonverbal (cf. Dennett 1998).

Communication between humans and computers requires interaction between user and system. As soon as information is to be transmitted, interaction is simultaneously transformed into communication. HMI usually takes place to process information. For example, in road traffic, the driver uses a navigation system to obtain information (e.g., maneuvering) or to provide information (e.g., entering the destination) or to initiate a process (e.g., calculating the shortest route). For this purpose, the mental models of the communication partners should be consistent and offer the opportunity to understand dialogues. The less this is the case, the more mistakes and misunderstandings will occur in communication.

▸ Mental models, i.e., the representation of the world in the head of the user, must agree. This is particularly the case when designing human–machine dialogues in intercultural user interfaces (i.e., user interfaces that can be used by users with different cultural needs across all cultures). However, cultural aspects have not yet been considered in depth in the design of interaction processes in HMI research. Initial approaches in this regard are discussed in detail in Chap. 5.

If you are not aware of your own motives and actions that are culturally influenced, you cannot understand the motives and actions of others. Hall based his findings on cultural dimensions such as context information, news speed, monochronic or polychronic time orientation, through interviews and field studies. These process phases include the perception of time, which is highly dependent on culture (cf. Hall 1959).

This requires a certain level of confidence and trust in the communication partner (principle of forbearance, cf. Davidson 2001) and includes the knowledge of how to read between the lines of the partner's communication depending on culturally different rules. This also includes the use of linguistic rules, such as Austin's conditions of happiness or Grice's maxims. Therefore, every literal translation of a conversation is susceptible to misinterpretation, since the extension of the concept can be different in different cultures ("linguistic relativity", cf. Whorf 2008). Since the context must also be taken into consideration, it is important to consider these aspects during communication and to concentrate as much as possible on the intellectual horizon of the communication partner. This can take place primarily through personal and local communication and is particularly difficult when facial expressions and gestures are missing. In intercultural communication, even more problems arise than in intra-cultural communication due to different worldviews and different contexts in which the clarification takes place. For this reason, the empathic ability to put oneself in the situation of another is of particular importance. Finally, the application of empathy contributes to a successful communication that supports a mutual linguistic code.

▸ Successful communication depends very much on the ability of the people involved to empathize. Communication without empathy doesn't deliver the desired results.

In order not only to build understanding, but also the ability to place oneself in the position of another, it is initially necessary to be on the same wavelength in order to find a connection with the other person. This requires the adjustment of the communication coding (vocabulary and grammar) and to reach the situation in which the other person wants to communicate. In this way, a relationship is established in such a way that future communication remains possible. Once this connection is established, it is important to maintain access to the knowledge base of the other person ("faith net", cf. Quine and Ullian 1978: "Web Of Belief"), in which a common conversation theme is taken up in order to examine the knowledge base of the partner in terms of extent, nature, and quality. Only then is it possible to find the right "starting point" for future conversations and consequently to bring the other person's belief network to the most relevant point and quickly pick up the same wavelength again. The web of faith contains beliefs and desires derived from premises, assumptions, and facts, using local rules, and recursively shaped from birth by experience.

▸ By training intercultural competence, it is possible to approach the beliefs of a member of other cultures. The exchange of experiences is very effective, trust can be transferred from one person to another. The participants are introduced, and critical interaction situations can be attenuated.

This works when it is clear how the other person thinks (i.e., what worldview he or she holds, i.e., what premises and assumptions about the world that person has). This is necessary to make decisions that are relevant to the task at hand and correct for successful communication with a continuously expanding set of additional information. This is particularly the case in an intercultural context. The ability to evaluate and understand the person's thought patterns enables an adequate response for the people involved. In the same way, the leading of conversations with users, e.g., as moderators or testers, is successfully supported.

▸ Above all, intercultural user experience designers must be able to put themselves in the position of the user in order to know and understand his or her intentions or needs, experience them ideally and then take them into account in the product.

2.2.3 Decision-Making Competence

The importance of cultural differences for intercultural product development has already been demonstrated. Both the initial situation and the phases in international projects differ from national projects. All areas of project management must be

Fig. 2.10 Necessary components of intercultural action competence

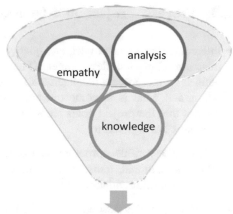

Intercultural competence to act

examined with regard to cultural influences and taken into account in the daily execution of processes within process management. Especially affected are communication and information flow, team development, conflict management, and project organization and control up to the understanding of quality within quality management.

Successful (intercultural) usability engineering requires a corresponding engineering process. If the user is to understand the developer's device and be able to use it easily and satisfactorily, it is important that the developer understands the user and knows and considers the different points of view.

▶ At least the following aspects of the user must be analyzed in detail before the product can be developed:

- User's worldview (metaphysical approach),
- General knowledge (procedural and factual knowledge) of the user,
- The context in which the product will be used by the user,
- The tasks the user tries to perform by using the product.

Only if these aspects are paired with empathy, knowledge and analysis to achieve intercultural communication as an essential condition for intercultural usability engineering and user interface design with the help of intercultural action competence (Fig. 2.10), can this lead to successful international product design. The following section deals with the project-, process-, and quality-specific effects of cultural differences on product development.

2.3 Process, Project, and Quality Management

▸ Intercultural process, project, and quality management are the basis for successful
  intercultural product development (Fig. 2.11). First of all, the processes must be
  defined by the process management in order to know what is to be done how by
  whom and what is to come out and how this is verified. Project management
  ensures that the project goals are achieved. Quality management ensures that the
  processes are adhered to.

There are various corporate structures for operating on the global market.
Global, international, transnational, and multinational forms of enterprise differ in
terms of local differentiation and global coordination within the projects (Fig. 2.12).

▸ According to the Association for Project Management, the biggest problem in
  international project work is the work culture based on cultural differences.

Communication and language, political aspects as well as infrastructure and
technologies are directly affected. It may be due to insufficient knowledge of other

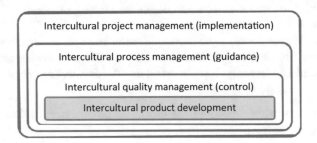

Fig. 2.11 Necessary foundations for successful intercultural product development

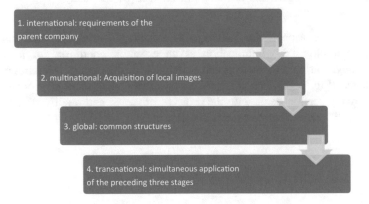

Fig. 2.12 Different forms of enterprise due to local differentiation and global coordination
(according to Hoffmann et al. 2004)

cultures as well as prejudices and stereotypes that can lead to a spiral of distrust, where international projects, in particular, can easily fail.

As already shown above using the iceberg metaphor, there is a visible and an invisible part of rules and attitudes of people. Assumptions and values are usually assumed unconsciously. Standards and behavioral patterns are usually visible but need to be interpreted. The presumed behavior of people in different countries can be inferred from cultural dimensions. However, these must first be known and their implications for intercultural product development analyzed.

▸ Misunderstandings in project work arise mainly because, without training, the complexity of the rules and norms of other cultures as well as one's own remain unconscious and thus an adequate reaction in crisis situations of interaction in project work is impossible.

This can also lead to the project failing. In addition, a fundamental prerequisite for successful training for work in intercultural projects is empathy for other cultures and avoidance of ethnocentrism. This can be achieved primarily through appropriate intercultural process, project, and quality management as the basis for all further product development activities.

2.3.1 Project Management

In order to market IT products with an intercultural user interface, they must be developed and adapted for the respective cultural context of the target market. Therefore, localization and internationalization completely permeate management.

▸ Management must be adapted to the global product development cycle (see Sect. 3.2). Therefore, localization and internationalization completely permeate management.

International projects can offer advantages and avoid disadvantages for the participating nations. For example, technology status, demographic situation, training level of employees, or skills and competencies as well as resources can be linked or balanced.

A phase model is used to structure a project. All phases of an international project are culturally influenced. In particular, the planning depth and planning commitment can be very different. Therefore, it is inevitable to reduce the complexity of the tasks of the project by a suitable phase model and an appropriate planning framework for the project work. A pragmatic working environment for phases in international projects consists of initiation, planning, implementation, conclusion, and follow-up (cf. Hoffmann et al. 2004, p. 46 ff.). Milestones are inserted between the respective project sections in order to monitor the progress of the project. Certain peculiarities from the point of view of international projects must be taken into account and pitfalls and stumbling blocks must be avoided. In each project phase, the project manager must be sensitive to changes in the project environment and take appropriate countermeasures. Project management should be internationally oriented and take into account the individual activities of national needs. For this purpose, the higher level measures and processes must be adapted to the cultural requirements of the project members. An appropriate approach must be used to achieve a common understanding of the problem (tolerance of ambiguity, adaptation of structural thinking, avoidance of uncertainty).

▸ Milestones at the end of a phase allow progress to be monitored, grievances to be identified and decisions to be made. In intercultural projects, project planning must be carried out jointly on the basis of the different cultural expectations of the project participants.

The quality of an international relationship is of crucial importance and often shaped by the first encounter. Therefore, it is extremely important to know the ways of the other cultural partner and to behave accordingly. Especially in relation-oriented countries, good relations to the upper management level as well as to the right information carriers and decision makers are indispensable. Success factors must be defined in order to meet the requirement of a consistent assessment of the success of a project. Unofficial dangers such as the takeover of the project by an informal project manager can be reduced by clearly clarifying competencies and power relations. To this end, the official project manager must be involved in the project as early as possible (i.e., as early as the initiation phase of the project) and a formal kickoff meeting must be held, since the project members get to know each other and can form initial social networks with each other. The most important task of the project manager at the start of the project is to create a project team as quickly

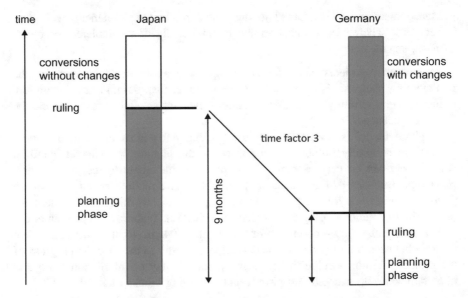

Fig. 2.13 Comparison of the time required to prepare and implement projects. (*Source* Kuhnert 2004, p. 54)

as possible that can work together on the project tasks. Depending on the culture, the intensity and design of the planning process can vary greatly.

▸ Project planning varies according to cultural background. In Japan, the project is first planned down to the last detail before being implemented without any changes. In Germany the proportions are different (cf. Fig. 2.13).
▸ There is a direct connection between the expressions of cultural dimensions and the understanding of project planning.

In the East Asian region, planning is very precise in comparison to the Southern European region. Planning must be carried out according to the cultures involved and the respective planning considerations (significance of planning, formulation, communication, acceptance, resources, risk planning). The understanding of communication in different cultures plays an outstanding role here. In order to avoid misunderstandings, the planners must adopt a common communication strategy and obtain the agreement to this communicative approach from all project members.

Due to frictional losses resulting from cultural differences and linguistic problems, a much longer time span must be planned for the solution of conflicts and crises in projects. Not only the rules governing the implementation of the project, but also all relevant tools, procedures, and methods must be made comprehensible to the project staff—if necessary, with the help of competent intercultural consultants or interpreters.

In international projects, it should be noted above all that in national projects (cf. Heimgärtner und Tiede 2008). This means that when planning events such as meetings, approximately 50% more time must be planned. In particular, depending on the language skills and cultural prior knowledge of the participants, communication problems can be expected due to insufficient clarification of misunderstandings due to stereotypes and prejudices. Decision-making processes or claims to power can distort goals and motivations through different personnel structures. Therefore, the most important points must be prepared in a politically sensitive way before discussions take place. In addition, it should be noted that the expenses for budget and resources at the start of the project can be higher than expected due to greater frictional losses (e.g., the establishment of agreed agreements and rules). One way of counteracting these problems is to use a cultural interpreter or a competent intercultural consultant to adapt the framework conditions to local conditions and to ensure that the rules are established and followed. Furthermore, it is important to establish and strengthen the relationships with the relevant parties involved in the project as early as possible. The use and elaboration of a project-specific phase model can contribute to a common understanding of the project. After all, the cultivation of a common team spirit, which results from a common understanding of the project, leads to project success.

▸ In an international project, the definition of goals has the highest priority and
  should be done together with the international team.

The latest time for this is the kickoff meeting, in which all project members
participate and if possible, should also be physically present and not only via a
virtual connection. It is particularly important to ensure that participants from
different cultures approach meetings differently. While in France, for example, a
warm-up phase is necessary, in Germany this is not necessary at all. After the
project release, the project is realized.

▸ Due to cross-cultural coordination of the processes, the effort for project management in an international context is higher than in national projects.

Project management is particularly difficult when, due to the cultural attitudes of
the project members, the current situation cannot be correctly recorded because bad
news or errors are not passed on immediately or not at all or only the successes are
passed on (face protection, control mechanism). Therefore, every effort must be
made to record the progress of the project so that problems and risks can be
countered at an early stage. This can be done, for example, by agreeing on a higher
frequency of project status meetings and informal and formal project status reports.
Moreover, a continuous reassessment of project risks should be carried out. An
additional possibility is that the project manager is in constant contact with his
project members and can recognize and solve problems early in the team spirit. The
functioning of processes and the cooperation between team members can be analyzed and improved. The project management can seek advice from cultural consultants in the event of uncertainties regarding its decisions or interventions in the
cross-cultural project.

After completion and acceptance of the project by the client, the project result is
released. A return of employees can only take place after all local completion
criteria have been met and requires a long lead time—especially for knowledge
management (transfer of knowledge to the successor team or organization). Jointly
developed project results should not be presented in a meeting with all project
members (due to their cultural differences), but a form should be chosen which is
appropriate for all cultural representatives involved. Experiences must be communicated in such a way that the project finds a worthy conclusion. For example,
individual conversations or conversations in culturally similar groups are also
meaningful with regard to the return to the home organization. In order to avoid
frustration and culture shock in the home organization, appropriate positions should
be created in good time in the home organization and the former contact persons
should be available until reintegration.

▸ The maintenance of networks and known contacts by the project manager or the
  team members plays an outstanding role.

After project completion, the follow-up phase takes place, during which final
project activities are carried out. International contacts get lost more easily due to
great spatial distance. Therefore, these valuable relationships must be put to good

use in order to remain available for future projects. This reduces the lead time for the company and the initiation phase of a follow-up project, which leads to competitive advantages. Many contacts and intercultural experience of the project manager serve his career. Furthermore, project participants are more familiar with where the knowledge is located in the company. Established knowledge management serves to ensure the flow of information between the projects and the project members among each other. In addition, the project manager should personally introduce his successor to the stakeholders.

▸ The experience gained from the international projects must be documented and passed on to the future teams (lessons learned in workshops at the end of the project and training of project members at the beginning of a new project).

2.3.2 Process Management

In addition to differences in product quality, differences in project and process quality must also be taken into account in the international context.

▸ There are different cultural views about fulfilling the requirements of the project and the processes.

Even the determination of these views takes place from an ethnocentric point of view, which puts a certain cultural stamp on it. In addition, these views are strongly influenced by the corporate culture—especially in the case of cooperation outside the parent company and subsidiaries (e.g., in the case of freelance partner companies). The resulting different understanding of product and process quality must be reduced to a minimum. Measures to this end include, for example, the joint definition of project and process quality within the project team. This makes the different views transparent and understandable and can be reduced to a common denominator.

▸ Quality understanding agreements should, therefore, be made with all stakeholders.

The agreed project and process goals should be checked regularly for compliance. German project and process understanding can be characterized as follows:

- Quality of meetings (goal orientation, adherence to the agenda, punctuality),
- Clear distribution of roles,
- Clear definition of responsibilities and responsibilities within the role,
- Applied risk management,
- Clear decision and escalation processes,
- Open, trusting project culture,
- Transparency regarding project status and deviations,
- Early presentation of problems, no covering up of problems,
- Definition and agreement of processes, deadlines, and results,

- Integration of the customers of the process results into the agreement,
- Goal orientation of the processes.

The following examples from experiences with projects in the automotive supplier industry in China and Germany are intended to illustrate which different approaches and processes are required within projects in different cultural contexts:

- Consider Guanxi,
- Gain understanding,
- Avoid prejudices.

From this, project and quality managers can derive individual, organization-specific recommendations for the respective project, process and quality management in China.[7]

2.3.2.1 Greater Project Success Through "Guanxi"

The communication between Chinese and Germans is initially difficult because the rules about how to interpret and understand the statements of the communication partner and which ones are in the faith network of the other are still unknown. For example, it is problematic to ask a Chinese for help because the structure, hierarchy, and associated rules in China are not known to the Germans. The Chinese must strictly follow the rules of the hierarchy in order to fulfill the German requirements and suffers from the dilemma of providing support without losing face within his own organization or inhibiting the good relationship with the one who demanded the help. In this sense, the Chinese cannot fulfill the request of the German participant without losing face. That is why nothing is going to happen. This example serves to give an impression of the difficulty of understanding the numerous effects of complex relations in China ("guanxi"). Figure 2.14 illustrates part of the structure of a Chinese team hierarchy and the relationships between team members.

Imagine a German team/project leader X requesting support from the Chinese project team Tc. Now the team/project manager C knows: "Our team Tc must support X." and communicates to X: "Yes, our team Tc will support you."

Nevertheless, in order to fully ensure the required support for X, C must also ask team leaders A and B of the Teams Ta and Tb, who provide subordinate project support for Team Tc. Let's say C delivers the support to X as best he and his Team Tc and Team Ta can deliver them. Nevertheless, C does not offer support from Team Tb to X. X is not satisfied with the situation and does not understand why he is not fully supported as required. What is the reason for this undesirable situation?

On the one hand, C and A have a good (personal) relationship ("guanxi"), for example, because they were at the same university. Therefore, C A asks for support

---

[7]Further recommendations for action and information on Chinese project and process understanding can be found, for example, in Lewis (2000) and are conveyed in special IUID seminars (cf. e.g., www.iuic.de).

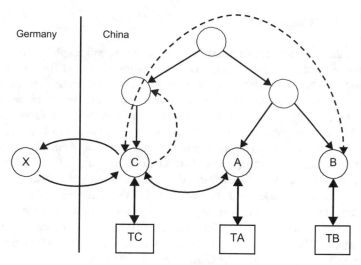

Fig. 2.14 Chinese team hierarchy

and bypasses the strict hierarchy rules. On the other hand, C is not well connected to B via "guanxi". Therefore, he must go the official way to B and follow the whole hierarchy (indicated by the dotted arrow in Fig. 2.14). The hierarchy process is defined by transfer sequences "from top to bottom." Thus, it is not C's responsibility to address requests to his boss or the boss of his boss because it is not part of his role (represented by the chain-dotted arrow in Fig. 2.14). This means that he cannot execute the request according to his job definition and the responsibility given to him. In addition, he does not want to lose face with X by explaining his inability to accomplish the task. As a result, the information that is conveyed to X is incomplete. Although X is aware of the required support/dependencies on the teams Ta and Tb, he cannot start any action, such as requesting support from senior management, because there is no feedback as to why Ta can support and Tb cannot.

2.3.2.2   Relationship Networks

Sometimes projects progress slowly while no one knows or shares each other's problems or is able to solve them. This is due to the fact that the Chinese relationship network is too difficult to understand to always find the right behavioral solution.

Nevertheless, outsiders can certainly gain an understandable overview of the situation if they have access to very high linguistic and social expertise. In order to be able to understand this network from the inner perspective, one must not only be born into this perspective, i.e., be Chinese, but one also needs the understanding of the Chinese that there are complex individual networks and how they should be used by the employees. In order to understand and include the importance of this relationship network, project team members from the target market should, therefore, be represented in the project team.

2.3.2.3 Better Understanding

Quite often the Germans complain that the Chinese speak "bad English". To understand Chinese people and vice versa, a large amount of context is needed. But Germans often don't know the Chinese context and, therefore, don't even understand questions of the Chinese counterpart. On the one hand, Chinese responses are often regarded as incorrect because the context between the explicit statements of Germans is not understood. For example, a Chinese will always answer so as not to lose face. Thus, a non-Chinese person should not be surprised by answers that cannot be understood, because they seem not to fit the question. In this case, one should sit in the position of the Chinese and ask oneself why the answer is so unusual and analyze what content must be conveyed in order to understand the question. On the other hand, direct and open answers may shock Chinese because they can easily lead to loss of face in their eyes, i.e., from the Chinese point of view. For Germans, loss of face is not as momentous as it is for Chinese people, which for Chinese people has the effect that Germans lose face without batting an eyelid. This confuses the Chinese and alienates them.

2.3.2.4 Elimination of Prejudices

The risk of prejudice is very high if one is in a foreign culture. The impressions are extremely intense but also very easily infested with prejudices which, without corresponding reflection, can quickly become generalizations. If you are in a foreign culture for a very long time, i.e., you put yourself in the position of other people for a long time, then your own impressions are weaker, but your own judgments are more rooted and finer, while the contextual background is more strongly taken into account. Regular reflection reduces stereotypes and intentional attempts to find explanations for critical interaction situations are more successful. A similar, albeit weaker, effect can be achieved if there is the possibility of forming a multicultural team. The team members can learn from each other if they are equipped with empathetic abilities and the willingness to use them.

▸ Empathic skills are required to put oneself in the position of a user as a developer and to be able to master this situation.

2.3.3 Quality Management

▸ Different cultural backgrounds require a different understanding of quality (cf. Hoffmann et al. 2004).

Intercultural differences can also be identified in the understanding of quality, which must be taken into account in international projects. While in Germany and Japan reliability and functionality are in the foreground from the customer's point of view, in China more emphasis is placed on price and in France and Italy more on design. In Great Britain and the USA in particular, brand, image, and service play the decisive role. Based on this, the quality criteria for the testing and evaluation of the products are to be applied and weighted according to the cultural target group.

▸ Quality is the measure of fulfillment of requirements that vary from product to product as well as from culture to culture.

In addition, quality is subjectively attributed to a product or service—whether by the manufacturer or the customer (or user). Good quality exists when the requirements are met. Poor quality leads to dissatisfaction with the customer or the user.

Contrary views of quality meet in an international context, but only in the course of cooperation do they finally emerge. In order to obtain a high-quality product, it is necessary that all members of the intercultural project have the same perception of process execution (for example, with regard to adherence to delivery dates, completion of tasks, problem escalation, etc., see Sect. 2.3.2). It is, therefore, necessary to identify and eliminate bottlenecks and problems within a project at an early stage through cultural sensitivity and intercultural communication skills of the project members—especially in the basic project roles such as project manager, project planner, requirements engineer, or quality engineer.

▸ The quality of the product depends on at least the following criteria, which are similar worldwide: Design, functionality/reliability, image/brand, service, applicability/up-to-date-ness and cost-effectiveness/costs. However, the priority of these criteria differs considerably in the intercultural context (Fig. 2.15).

While, for example, Italy or France tends to combine quality with design, styling, style, and aesthetics, Germany places more emphasis on reliability and functionality. In England, the aim is to restore customer confidence in quality by massively certifying products and services to ISO 9000. Therefore, good image and robustness, but also price, play an important role in England. Image in the USA is also very important, but also the pursuit of performance, which manifests itself in the desire for larger, better, faster products with more functionality and good service. Highest quality products with high reliability, topicality, and many functions from a brand manufacturer are required in Japan. While in China brand and topicality also play a role, in Japan much more importance is attached to the quality of the product than to its price.

There is an agreement in the understanding of quality for the most part between Germans and Japanese as well as English and US Americans. While Germany attaches great importance to meeting technical requirements, this aspect, in particular, is considered uneconomical in the USA, where economic efficiency and productivity have the highest priority. In order to achieve this difference in terms of capacity, persuasion, training, new methods in production and quality assurance, dissatisfaction with the customer or even losing the customer to the competitor due to nonachievement of the quality objectives as well as delays and supply bottlenecks, "it is advisable to create a common understanding of quality at an early stage" (Hoffmann et al. 2004, p. 300). This can be achieved, for example, by making opinions transparent during contract negotiations and analyzing the quality situation on site at suppliers and in the production plant.

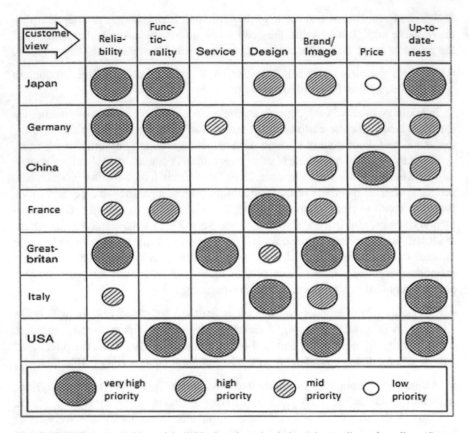

Fig. 2.15 Different priorities of individual nations in their understanding of quality. (*Source* Hoffmann et al. 2004, p. 298, Fig. 13.1)

The cultural influence on the understanding of quality can partly be explained by the cultural dimensions of uncertainty avoidance, long-term orientation, and power distance and corresponding recommendations for action can be derived from this. Approaches can be found in Triandis 2001 or Heimgärtner (2012). However, these must be further detailed and a comparison of other cultures as well as further partial declarations must be worked out.

2.4 Summary, Conclusion, and Outlook

There are many cultural terms, which make it difficult to define culture unambiguously. For the development of intercultural user interfaces, culture is understood as an image of common values, ways of thinking, and acting of a group of individuals that contribute to the formation of this community (Röse 2002).

Cultural models describe these images and allow them to be compared with each other. Cultural differences extend across all areas of human life and have an impact on the development of intercultural products ranging from project, process, and quality management to software engineering, usability engineering, and the development of intercultural user interfaces.

Culture represents an orientation system and influences the interaction with other individuals as well as the interaction with technical devices and thus has a considerable influence on human–machine interaction and thus on the operation of user interfaces. Culture influences learning behavior, expectations, and cognitive processing. Interaction and dialogue design, in particular, must therefore be treated very carefully in the intercultural development process, which represents a corresponding challenge for all participants due to cultural differences. This can only be countered by appropriate knowledge of the desired target cultures. Ethnocentrism should be avoided.

Cultural models help to look "beneath the surface of the cultural iceberg", i.e., to research the initially not directly visible areas of cultures in order to overcome methodological gaps. Cultural models describe the cultural distance, i.e., the differences between cultures and enable their comparison. Cultural standards express the normal, typical, and valid attributes for the majority of the members of a particular culture, taking into account types of perception, thought, judgment, and action. Cultural dimensions represent a cultural aspect that can be measured in relation to other cultures. They can be used to classify behaviors within and between cultures. Due to the affinity of cultural dimensions to personality dimensions, concepts should be applied in the design of intercultural user interfaces.

Patterns of thought are determined by the philosophies (worldviews) of mankind, which are very different worldwide for cultural reasons. Intercultural philosophy research distinguishes between two main directions: Eastern and Western philosophy. Cognitive styles describe the way in which information is processed and how it is dealt with, which is typical for an individual. In the different cultures, cognitive styles tend to be shaped differently, resulting in different patterns of thought. This in turn has an effect on the worldview and thus on the approaches to reality in the respective cultures. These differences in thinking also have implications for the development and operation of intercultural user interfaces. These are described in detail in Chap. 5.

Culture is mainly a communication system (cf. Hall 1959). Successful communication depends very much on the ability of the people involved to empathize. Above all, intercultural user experience designers must be able to put themselves in the position of the user in order to know and understand his or her intentions or needs, to experience them ideally and then take them into account in the product. At least the following aspects of the user must be analyzed before the product can be developed:

- User's worldview (metaphysical approach),
- General knowledge (procedural and factual knowledge) of the user,
- The context in which the product will be used by the user,

- The tasks the user wants to perform by using the product.

Overall, management must be adapted to the globalization process. Project, process, and quality management are the basis for successful intercultural product development. The biggest problem area in international project work is the work culture based on cultural differences. Misunderstandings in project work arise mainly because, without training, the complexity of the rules and norms of other cultures as well as one's own remain unconscious and thus an adequate reaction in critical interaction situations in project work is impossible. Empathic skills are, therefore, required to put oneself in the position of a user as a developer and to be able to master them. There is also a direct link between the expressions of cultural dimensions and the understanding of project planning. In an international project, the definition of goals has the highest priority and should succeed together with the international team. There are different cultural views about fulfilling the requirements of the project and the processes. Quality understanding agreements should, therefore, be made with all stakeholders. Different cultural backgrounds require a different understanding of quality. Quality represents the measure of fulfilment of requirements, which differ from product to product as well as from culture to culture. The quality of the product depends on at least the following criteria, which are similar worldwide: Design, functionality/reliability, image/brand, service, applicability/up-to-date-ness as well as economy/costs. However, the priority of these criteria varies considerably in an intercultural context.

Norms	√
ISO 3166	☐
Checklist	√
Team (at least key roles) was trained in intercultural action competence	☐
The team members are familiar with their own culture	☐
There are no fears of contact with other cultures in the team	☐
Team has been trained in intercultural communication	☐
Project managers have relevant intercultural project experience	☐
Ethno-centred thinking and procedures are avoided	☐
Cultural models are known and used to describe cultures	☐
Culturally conditioned different understanding of quality is considered	☐
Methods of intercultural project, process and quality management are known and applied	☐

References

Adler NJ (1997) International dimensions of organizational behavior, 3rd edn. South-Western College Publ, Cincinnati

Adler NJ, Gundersen A (2008) International dimensions of organizational behavior, 5 Aufl, internat. student edn. Thomson South-Western, Mason, Ohio

Altarriba J (1993) Cognition and culture: a cross-cultural approach to cognitive psychology, vol 103. North-Holland, Amsterdam

Argyle M, Schmidt C (2002) Body language & communication: the handbook for nonverversible communication, vol 5, 8th edn. Junfermann, Paderborn

Baumgartner V-J (2003) A practical set of cultural dimensions for global user-interface analy-sis and design. Fachhochschule Joanneum, Graz

Berry JW (2007) Cross-cultural psychology: research and applications, 2 Aufl, 6. print. ed. Cambridge University Press, Cambridge

Borisoff D, Victor DA (1997) Conflict management: a communication skills approach. Allyn and Bacon, Boston

Brunner G (2005) Investigation of cultural influences on human-machine interaction using driver navigation systems as an example. Regensburg

Chen MJ (1993) A comparison of Chinese and English language processing. Adv Psychol 103:97–117

Condon JC (1984) With respect to the Japanese: a guide for Americans. Intercultural Press, Yarmouth

D'Andrade RG (2001) The development of cognitive anthropology, Reprinted edn. Cambridge University Press, Cambridge

Davidson D (2001) Inquiries to truth and interpretation, 2nd edn. Clarendon Press, Oxford

Dennett DC (1998) The intentional stance, 7. printing. ed. MIT Press, Cambridge, MA

Deutsch E, Bontekoe R, Weiming T (1997) A companion to world philosophies. Blackwell, Malden

Fanchen M, Yao J (2007) Holistic thinking-harmonious action. In: Aigner-Hof T (ed) Wertorientierungen der Unternehmenspraxis, 1st edn. Hamburg, Münster

Fischer K (2006) What computer talk is and is not: human-computer conversation as intercultural communication, vol 17. AQ-Verlag, Saarbrücken

Hall ET (1959) The silent language. Doubleday, New York

Hall ET, Hall M (1983) Hidden signals. Gruner & Jahr, Hamburg

Halpin AW, Winer BJ (1957) A factorial study of the leader behavior descriptions. In: Stogdill RM, Coons AE (eds) Leader behavior: its description and measurement. Bureau of Business Research, Ohio State University, Columbus, pp 39–51

Hansen KP (2003) Kultur und Kulturwissenschaft: an introduction, 3rd, full-length ed. 1846. Francke, Tübingen

Heimgärtner, R. (2012). Cultural differences in human-computer interaction Paperback B: Einband–flex, Bd 1, (Paperback) ed. Oldenbourg Verlag

Heimgärtner R, Tiede LW (2008) Technology and culture: intercultural experience in product development for China. In: Rösch O (ed) Interkulturelle Kommunikation, Technik und Kultur, vol 6, p 149–162. Publisher News & Media, Berlin. ISBN 6

Hodicová R (2007) Mental distance and internationalization of SMEs: empirical investigation on the example of the Saxon-Czech border region. Duv, Wiesbaden

Hoffmann H-E, Schoper Y-G, Fitzsimons C-J (2004) International project management: intercultural cooperation in practice, original edn ed. vol 50883: Beck-Wirtschaftsberater; 50883. German Paperback-Verl, Munich

Hofstede G (1984) Culture's consequences: International differences in work-related values, Bd 5, Abridged ed, 1 print. ed. Beverly Hills: Sage

Hofstede GH (1991) Cultures and organizations: software of the mind. McGraw-Hill, London

Hofstede, G. J. (2000). The information age across cultures. In: Proceedings of 5th AIM Conference–Information Systems and Organizational Change [CD-Rom], pp 10

Hofstede G, Hofstede GJ (2005) Cultures and organizations: software of the mind; [intercul-tural cooperation and its importance for survival] (Rev. and expanded, 2nd edn. McGraw-Hill, New York

Hofstede GH, Hofstede GJ, Minkov M (2010) Cultures and organizations: software of the mind, 3rd edn. McGraw-Hill, Maidenhead

Hoft NL (1995) International technical communication: How to export information about high technology. Wiley, New York

Hoft NL (1996) Developing a cultural model. In: Del Galdo EM, Nielsen J (eds) International users interface. Wiley, New York, pp 41–73

Honold P (2000) Intercultural usability engineering: a study on cultural influences on the design and use of technical products Aufl 647, Als Ms. gedr. VDI Verl, Düsseldorf

Hörmann H (1960) Conflict and decision: experimental studies on the interference phenomenon. Publisher for Psychology, Hogrefe, Göttingen

Inglehart R, Moreno A, Basanez M (1998) Human values and beliefs: a cross-cultural source-book. University of Michigan Press, Ann Arbor

ISO (2000) Standard DIN EN ISO 9000 (2000): quality management systems–Fundamentals and terminology. Beuth, Berlin

Jäger, L. (ed.) (2004). Handbook of cultural studies, vol 1. Metzler, Stuttgart

Janich P (2006) Culture and method: philosophy in a scientific world, 1st edn. Suhrkamp, Frankfurt am Main

Kagan J (1965a) Reflection-impulsivity and reading ability in primary grade children. Child Dev 36:609

Kagan J (1965b) Impulsive and reflective children: significance of conceptual tempo. In: Krumboltz J (Hrsg) Learning and educational process (S 133–161). Rand Mcnally, Chicago

Khaslavsky J (1998) Integrating culture into interface design. In Paper presented at the CHI 98 conference summary on Human factors in computing systems, Los Angeles

Kluckhohn F, Strodtbeck FL (1961) Variations in value orientations. Greenwood Press, Westport

Komischke T, McGee A, Wang N, Wissmann K (2003) Mobile phone usability and cultural dimensions: China, Germany & USA. In: Mühlbach L (Hrsg) Human factors in telecommunica-tion. Proceedings of the 19th international symposium on human factors in telecommunication (HFT 03). Berlin

Kralisch A (2006) The impact of culture and language on the use of the internet empirical analyses of behaviour and attitudes. Dissertation, Berlin

Kuhnert I (2004) Business with the Japanese. Gabal, Offenbach

Lee YT, McCauley CR, Draguns JG (1999) Personality and person perception across cultures. Erlbaum, Mahwah

Levine RV, Norenzayan A (1999) The pace of life in 31 countries. J Cross Cult Psychol 30 (2):178–205

Lewis J (2002) Cultural studies–the basics. Sage, London

Lewis RD (2000) Handbook international competence: more success through the right dealings with business partners worldwide. Campus-Verl, Frankfurt am Main

Maletzke G (1996) Intercultural communication: interaction between people from different cultures. Westdt. Verl, Opladen

Marcus A, Baumgartner V-J (2004) A practical set of culture dimensions for global user-interface development. In: Masood M, Jones S, Rogers B (Hrsg) Computer human interacti-on, 6th Asia Pacific conference, APCHI 2004, Rotorua, June 29–July 2, 2004, proceedings, S 252–261

Matiaske W (1997) Structure and significance of value orientations for managers from the People's Republic of China and the Federal Republic of Germany

Moeschler J (1989) Dialogue modeling: representation of the argumentative inference. Hermès, Paris

Moosmüller A (2007) Intercultural communication: contours of a scientific discipline, vol 20. Waxmann, Münster

Nagy C (2003) The hidden dimension. Cultural dimensions as orientation in intercultural cooperation. Intercult Online 5:1–4

Nevis EC (2001) Organizational consulting: a Gestalt approach. GestaltPress, Cambridge, MA

Nisbett RE (2003) The geography of thought: How Asians and Westerners think differently ... why. Free Press, New York

Parsons T (1951) The social system. Free Press of Glencoe, New York

Paunonen SV, Zeidner M, Engvik HA, Oosterveld P, Maliphant R (2000) The nonverbal assessment of personality in five cultures. J Cross Cult Psychol 31(2):220

Paunonen SV, Ashton MC, Jackson DN (2001) Nonverbal assessment of the Big Five personality factors. Eur J Pers 15(1):3–18

Quine WVO, Ullian JS (1978) The web of belief. McGraw-Hill, New York. Reimer, A. (2005). *The significance of Geert Hofstede's cultural theory for the international Management.* Wismar: University, Department of Economics

Reimer A (2005) The significance of Geert Hofstede's cultural theory for the international Management. University, Department of Economics, Wismar

Reisach U, Tauber T, Yuan XU (2007) China-Economic partner between desire and reality: a handbook for practitioners. Redline Economy, Heidelberg. https books google de books id LtRaSp-c O. Y. C

Röse K (2002) Methodology for the design of intercultural man-machine systems in production engineering, vol 5. Univ, Kaiserslautern

Schumacher RM (2010) The handbook of global user research. Morgan Kaufmann, Burlington

Schwartz SH (1992) Universals in the content and structure of values: theoretical advances and empirical tests in 20 countries. Adv Exp Soc Psychol 25:1–65

Schwartz SH, Bardi A (2001) Value hierarchies across cultures: Taking a similarities perspec- tive. J Cross Cult Psychol 32(3):268

Straub J (2007) Intercultural communication and competence handbook: basic terms-theories-fields of application. Metzler, Stuttgart

Strohschneider, S. (2002). Cultural factors in complex decision making. In: Lonner WJ, Dinnel DL, Hayes SA, Sattler DN (Hrsg) Online readings in psychology and culture, Bd 4/1. Center for Cross-Cultural Research, Western Washington University, Bellingham/Washington, DC

Thomas A (1996) Psychology of intercultural action. Hogrefe, Seattle

Thomas A, Eckensberger LH (1993) Comparative cultural psychology: an introduction. Hogrefe, Göttingen

Tomasello, M. (2006). The cultural development of human thought: the evolution of cognition, 1st edn, vol 1827. Suhrkamp, Frankfurt am Main

Trompenaars F (1993) Global management handbook: How to understand cultural differences in business life. ECON-Verl, Düsseldorf

Trompenaars F, Hampden-Turner C (1997) Riding the waves of culture: understanding cultu-ral diversity in business. Nicholas Brealey, London

Victor DA (1998) International business communication, 7th edn. Harper Collins, New York

Wahrlich H (1991) Wortlose Sprache-Verständnis und Mißverständnis im Kulturkontakt. In: Thomas A (ed) Kulturstandards in der internationalen Begegnung, Saarbrücken, Fort Lauderdale, Breitenbach 1991. Saarbrücken: Verlag für Entwicklungspolitik Saarbrücken GmbH

Weggel O (1990) The Asians (2nd, straight through). Beck, Munich

Whorf BL (2008) Language-thinking-reality contributions to metalinguistics and philosophy of language. Rowohlt, Reinbek near Hamburg

Wierzbicka A (1991) Cross cultural pragmatics: the semantics of human interaction, vol 53. Mouton de Gruyter, Berlin

Wimmer FM (2004) Intercultural philosophy: an introduction, vol 2470. WUV: Vienna

Witkin HA et al (1954) Personality through perception. Harper, New York

Yandell KE (1999) Philosophy of religion: a contemporary introduction. Routledge, New York

Zimbardo PG, Gerrig RJ (2004) Psychologie, Aufl 16, aktualisierte, S 17–25. Pearson studies, München

Chapter 3
Software Engineering

Before a short overview of the individual elements of a software to be localized is given, a delimitation of important terms takes place. The relevant concepts which must be known for the process of intercultural software engineering are explained.[1] Subsequently, the context of the localization is presented using the iceberg model (cf. Fig. 2.1 in Chap. 2) and its effects on the phases of software development processes are discussed. Finally, the core components for software localization are presented.

---

[1]The entire book serves to explain the influence of culture over the phases of a project to develop intercultural user interfaces. Chapter 7 also presents knowledge relevant to these phases for IUID practice in industrial development.

© Springer Nature Switzerland AG 2019
R. Heimgärtner, *Intercultural User Interface Design*, Human–Computer Interaction Series, https://doi.org/10.1007/978-3-030-17427-9_3

3.1 Intercultural Software Engineering

Most projects for the development of intercultural user interfaces are carried out in the context of a product development cycle.

The influence of culture is present and noticeable in all phases of a research and development project:

- Initiating analysis of the market and the context of use of a system,
- Implementation of the system using localization and internationalization methods,
- Evaluation and validation of the system or product or service test.

The results from software ergonomics research (cf. Chap. 4) support intercultural software engineering by taking into account the transfer of working conditions and their optimal adaptation to the user and the use of software in an intercultural context in the global engineering and product development process (see Sect. 3.2).

▸ Intercultural software engineering considers cultural influences during software development based on the results of software ergonomics research and usability engineering. The ultimate goal of incorporating software ergonomics into software engineering is to create software that is easy to understand and use, with which the user is satisfied (= software with user interfaces with optimal usability).

3.1.1 "Ethnocomputing"

▸ Due to the importance of multimedia cross-device computer applications in today's global information society, there is an increasing demand for software solutions that are not only adapted to the language, but also to other cultural needs of the users.

The translation of the texts contained in the product is generally not sufficient here. However, software designers are often unaware of their own cultural imprint, which "tempts" them to develop a certain design—so after their development, each software product automatically meets the requirements of the culture from which its developer originates (cf. Taylor 1992, p. 5). Just as translation scholars emphasize the importance of functional translation, localized software should also function in the target culture and give the user the impression of an original product developed for his culture.

▶ Ethnocomputing refers to everything that is computer science in relation to culture. This can mean not only ethnic groups but also nations or individual regions down to the smallest user groups with their very own cultural context.[2]

In connection with the culture-specific design of human–machine systems, the terms "internationalization" (L18N) and "localization" (L10N) of software as well as the terms "globalization" (G11N) and "glocalization" are mentioned in the field of the development of intercultural user interfaces. It should be mentioned here that all these terms in this context have a strong connotation based on information—and thus on software development—and therefore have a very narrow extension ("ethnocomputing"). The terms internationalization, localization, and globalization are often abbreviated as I18N, L10N, and G11N in specialist literature. These abbreviations are derived from the number of letters between the first and last letter in the English terms "Internationalization", "Localization", and "Globalization".

Globalization (G11N) comprises all activities relating to the marketing of a (software) product outside a national market. The aim is to achieve successful branding in one or more regional markets by taking into account the technical, economic, and legal conditions in the respective market (Schmitz and Wahle 2000). In addition, Marcus calls for cross-cultural HMI design to take into account the relationship between cultural dimensions and user interface characteristics (cf. Marcus 2001); Shen et al. (2006) introduce a culture-centric HMI design process based on the results of research on cross-cultural user interface design by Marcus (2006). Röse and Zühlke (2001) conducted iterative analyses to consider target users and their cultural requirements. Yeo (2001) presents a two-part internationalization and localization process for developing software for the global market that is relevant to a large part of intercultural user research.[3]

---

[2]Vgl. Matti Tedre "Ethnocomputing—A Multicultural View on Computer Science" (Master-Thesis): "[..] Ethnocomputing refers to local points of entry to: Organized structures and models used to represent information (data structures); Ways of manipulating organized information(algorithms); Mechanical and linguistic realizations of the above (tools and theory); and Applications of all of the above (uses). [..] Ethnocomputing does not take computing out of the center of CS. Instead, it rests on the principles of computing, and aims to widen the current perspective by adding some complementary points of view to technology, science, and society. These different dimensions are not necessarily at odds with one an- other but can support each other. The challenge is: How to create a smoothly working combination of disciplines that would benefit people in the form of intuitive technologies and ICT education with mini- mal cognitive overhead. It should benefit societies by allowing technological development without un- dermining local cultures or traditions and by supporting local identity rather than undermining it. The ICT industry should benefit from better user satisfaction and larger markets. Finally, this new per- spective should benefit CS in the form of different points of view on old concepts or even offering novel concepts."

"Researchers and users from developing countries would be able to bring in new resources, fresh view- points, and novel innovations." (vgl. Matti et al. 2006, S. 130).

[3]The topic of intercultural HMI analysis is particularly interesting from the point of view of information science, because this discipline is concerned with generating new knowledge, new requirements, and new goals for the design of information-processing systems, including software engineering, software ergonomics, and usability engineering.

3.1.2 Localization (L10N)

▸ Localization means the adaptation of a system to certain cultural requirements of a local market, e.g., the adaptation of the look and feel of the user interface or the internal data structures to the cultural requirements of the user (see VDMA 2009).

The localization of a product is aimed at specific countries and culture-specific requirements. The localization process therefore adapts the product to a country and its culture-specific needs.

▸ Software localization is the translation and adaptation of a software product to the language and culture of a foreign market (according to Carter 1992, p. 1).

Software localization describes the adaptation and translation of a software application to make it linguistically and culturally appropriate for a selected local market using internationalized software (Schmitz and Wahle 2000, pp. 3–4). Localizing a software product involves adapting the software to the specific cultural context in which it will be used. It means "to adapt an existing product to the local conditions of a region, taking into account its cultural, religious, historical and sociological conditions. So, it is not enough to transfer names, texts and logos literally into the foreign language and script. The product can only be successful in the local market if it awakens familiar associations with the customer and has a positive connotation. On the other hand, disregarding local conditions can lead to a complete rejection of the product" (Heimgärtner 2006).

The localization process includes at least the adaptation of the following aspects to the desired culture:

• Letter set and character sets,
• Formats (e.g., date, address, currency),
• Signs, icons, and metaphors,
• Documentation, online help,
• Colors.

▸ Software localization applies to the entire software package, i.e., both the program and the complete documentation are translated into another language and culture.

This includes the adaptation of the user interface with the components dialogue boxes, menus, and messages of all kinds as well as technical documentation, online help, and user manuals (see Esselink 1998).

Many differences are obvious (language, writing, formats, sorting, etc.), but many things remain hidden and only come to light during real use (to the manufacturer's disadvantage), such as

• Everyday rules and work organization,
• Regulations and laws,
• Environment, climate, working context,
• Understanding symbols and communication modes,
• Education and learning habits.

Hoft (1995) distinguishes between different degrees of localization and differentiates between general localization (surface localization) and radical localization (depth localization). The latter concerns those cultural specifics which affect, inter alia, the user's values.

▶ Hoft (1995) illustrates visible (language, colors, icons, symbols) and verbal localization elements (context, behavioral norms, thinking, communication, behavior, time aspect) using the iceberg model (cf. Fig. 2.1 in Chap. 2, cf. also the iceberg model in the intercultural context in Hoft 1995, p. 59).

Iceberg model of localization:

- Surface: The culture specifics "above the water surface" are immediately visible to the observer and thus self-evident, but account for only about ten percent of the specific characteristics of the culture under consideration. In addition to the language, these include national variables such as currency, time, and date, but also colors, icons, and symbols (so-called "explicit", i.e., immediately perceptible or visible cultural differences). This layer falls into the range of general localization.
- Unwritten (or unspoken) rules: The cultural characteristics on this level are "beneath the water surface"—they are initially hidden from the observer and only become visible and comprehensible after the context of the situation in which they occur has been identified. As an example, socially recognized norms of conduct can be cited here.
- Unconscious rules: The lowest layer of the iceberg contains the rules that control the thinking and behavior of the members of a specific culture without their being aware of it. These include, for example, nonverbal communication, the perception of time, or learning and problem-solving styles.

At the center of radical localization is the consideration of unwritten and unconscious rules. Hoft recommends that this model be used for target group analysis, as it is on this basis that the strategy for software development and marketing is determined. It can be used to determine the degree of localization required for a particular software product.

▶ In order to achieve complete culture-specific usability of a software product, the localization of program elements in which the cultural differences are explicit is not sufficient.

The usability of the design goes beyond accommodating the requirements of localization and translation. Although this is a complicated task, producing a product that is localizable and translatable may only be scratching the surface (Del Galdo und Nielsen 1996, S. 82).

▸ It is also necessary to adapt those program modules which are assigned to the
  levels of unwritten and unconscious rules, i.e., which are not explicit, such as the
  navigation concept, the structuring of information, or the formulation of system
  messages.

Localization can also be understood as a follow-up concept to "customization", the
aim of which is to provide an additional program version for a foreign market, but
which also requires the development of new individual software components.
A disadvantage of this strategy—apart from additional development costs—is a
considerably delayed market launch of the adapted software, which leads to sales
losses in the target markets (see Tuthill and Smallberg 1997, p. 4). The strategy of
"internationalization" was therefore developed.

3.1.3   Internationalization (I18N)

In the course of increasing global economic relations and the expansion of the sales
markets for software companies, the need for the development of the concept of
"internationalization" was recognized at the beginning of the 90s of the last century,
which allows a more efficient and faster adaptation to local user needs (cf. Esselink
1998, p. 1). "Internationalization is a way of designing and producing software that
can be easily adapted to local markets. Unlike customized software, which must be
largely revised or rewritten before it can be used with different languages and
customs, internationalized software does not require revision. It is able to support
any number of language markets without change" (Tuthill and Smallberg 1997,
p. 5).

▸ Internationalization of a product means that the product is equipped with a basic
  structure on the basis of which a cultural adaptation for use in the desired target
  countries can later be carried out (cf. International 2003).

According to Esselink (1998), internationalization means designing software in a
way that allows it to be translated into other languages without the need for a new
design or redesign of the software. But internationalization is much more than that.
Internationalization describes the process of preparing software so that it can be
used in any country of the world (see VDMA 2009). Internationalization means the
development of (software) products with a view to easy adaptation to other markets,
i.e., to other (technical) principles, cultural idiosyncrasies, and languages (Schmitz
and Wahle 2000, p. 3). It means that the product is prepared for its use in the
desired (at best all) countries (see International 2003). Internationalization of a
software product thus provides a basic structure in which a later cultural customization or localization can be carried out.

The software is divided into a culture-independent and a culture-dependent
component. The culture-independent component as a generic core contains most of
the software and is free of culture-sensitive elements. This provides many

advantages—especially if you also separate dialogue-relevant core components from the actual processing parts of the dialogues:

- Processing, application, and dialogue parts can be developed independently of each other in terms of time and personnel.
- This is a prerequisite for the introduction of iterative prototyping.
- Surface development can be carried out by specially trained dialogue authors who do not necessarily have to be IT specialists (cf. Usability Professionals, Sect. 4.4.3).
- Different surfaces can be developed for the same application (user class-specific variants).
- External consistency (consistency across different applications) is achieved to a large degree if representation- and manipulation-relevant parts are realized with a single tool. If it turns out that requirements on the surface become necessary during use of the application, these can be met without changing the application part.
- If the tool is available on different hardware platforms, the porting of applications is greatly facilitated.
- Once good solutions have been found, they can be made available as building blocks for reuse (design samples).

In the phase of internationalization, a software package is first created which, due to its universal design and the interchangeability of individual program components, can easily be converted into local program versions. The subsequent localization phase for the various target markets is possible with minimal effort by setting the respective culture-dependent program elements such as sign systems, symbols, or national formats as default values for the respective target countries or cultures. Accordingly, the development of an internationalized software system is a prerequisite for the implementation of localization.

▸ The advantages of the internationalization approach are obvious: not only can it save costs for new developments, but it also makes it possible to quickly offer a local version on the respective target markets.

Characteristics of an internationalized software that the internationalization process must take into account are (cf. Esselink 1998, p. 2; Nielsen 2000, p. 315 ff.):

- Support of Unicode strings;
- Support for all languages (e.g., provision for writing control, typography and input options, e.g., through an input method editor (IME), cf. Lunde 1999);
- Increased use of universal icons and symbols that have been defined as standards to simplify international communication processes;
- Generalization of online help, documentation, project management, and localization tools;
- Generalization of HMI forms and HMI logic (cf. Stephanidis 2001, 2007);
- Separate storage of the text parts visible to the user and the actual program code (separation of strings from source code);

- Menus and dialogue boxes whose design is not affected by translation-related changes in string lengths;
- Removal of inscriptions from illustrations, as otherwise the graphics must be edited;
- Provision and support of various national number, currency, or data formats.

Common errors in software internationalization are as follows (VDMA 2009, p. 6):

- "In software internationalization, the user interface is externalized so that the software can be translated."
- "Translators select the best wording in the target language."
- "The software is programmed in Java and therefore already internationalized."
- "My product is internationalized because it supports Unicode."
- "My product is based on Open Source. That's why software internationalization doesn't concern us."
- "All our employees speak English. That's why we only need English for our internal tool."
- "User interfaces for administrators do not require internationalization."
- "We will never localize this product/module/component. That's why we don't need software internationalization."
- "We realized the software internationalization in the last version. So, we're done."
- "If something's wrong, our client will tell us."
- "My product is internationalized because it supports Japanese."
- "Software internationalization is implemented after the basic software has been completed by another group of developers."
- "Software internationalization is only needed in a software development department."

▶ If software is not internationalized, there will be unnecessary localization and product realization efforts.

If terminology is not uniformly used by the software developers or technical writers (e.g., use of synonyms for the same process or term), this leads to inconsistencies as well as to incomprehensible documentation and lack of self-descriptiveness of the system.

The same names are used for different processes or terms in the same context (for example, using the same name for different commands of the user interface), which leads to ambiguities.

Texts for an international audience—as is the case with the development of intercultural software applications—contain local-specific references, so that a software redesign is necessary for each target country or cultural context. Therefore, no local-specific references (such as colors, hairstyles, facial features, cultural markers, flags, culture-specific symbols, etc., cf. Barber and Badre 2004) should be used (Figs. 7.18 and 7.19). Text in graphics should also be avoided (Fig. 7.20).

▸ Moreover, such challenges and efforts can be considerably reduced through the use of "locales" (cf. Sect. 7.3.2) within an internationalized software architecture.

3.1.4 TLCC Model of Internationalization

The software internationalization takes place in several stages—historically grown and almost identical in coverage according to the effort (Sturm 2002).

▸ Sturm (2002) analyzed the internationalization processes of software since the invention of the computer and thus the historical development of the consideration of cultural aspects in HMI design. The resulting TLCC model shows the historical growth of the steps of internationalization and localization in the HMI design. It comprises four levels which categorize the activities of I18N and L10N into the classes of technology, language, culture, and cognition (Fig. 3.1).

At the technical level, the infrastructure is first adapted (e.g., electricity connection). The language is then adapted by using appropriate character sets and a possible conversion of the entire software architecture to Unicode. The adaptation of software to Unicode is an example of the prerequisite for processing Asian languages and language levels. Adaptation at the cultural level concerns country-specific aspects such as format, currency, colors, modalities, menu structure, menu content, help, number of messages, text length, number of notifications, level of entertainment, or the relationship between information and entertainment. At the highest level, for example, cognitive styles can be considered that describe the types of

Fig. 3.1 TLCC model of Sturm (2002)

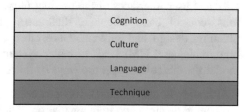

Cognition

Culture

Language

Technique

human thought (cf. Chap. 2, Nardi 1996; Norman and Draper 1986). These processes not only strongly influence the functionality and the user interface of the product (i.e., monitor, keyboard, hard and soft keys, control buttons, voice dialogues, etc.) but also the interactive behavior.

▸ Cultural and cognitive aspects must be considered in addition to technical and linguistic aspects.

3.1.5 "Interculturality"—Opportunities and Limits of L10N and I18N

On the one hand, the internationalization process does not start with the product development, but already with the product idea and influences product planning, product development, production, and product tests. In this way, internationalization concerns complete product management. On the other hand, the concepts of localization must also be integrated into the development process from the outset in order to achieve an optimal internationalization effect.

▸ Internationalization and localization are interwoven processes. In their application, it is essential to take into account the different cultural backgrounds of the users in order to generate adequate user models and thus be able to adapt the system and its parameters to the cultural needs of the user.

It must also be possible to adapt the parameters so that the product can easily be used in the target country or for the respective cultural target context in accordance with the required culture. To this end, the results of cultural and cognitive anthropology and psychology must be integrated into the concept of internationalization in order to create the necessary preconditions for a successful localization at a later date. Therefore, software internationalization research and software development must also consider the basic principles of software ergonomics as well as intercultural differences for dialogue design. Furthermore, the localization parameters must be selected in such a way that the product can be used appropriately in the future target country or cultural target context. These processes primarily concern the functionality and user interfaces of the product (e.g., graphic user interface, keyboard, buttons, control bars, language, dialogues, etc.). This causes increased analysis, planning, design, and implementation efforts. However, an improvement in software ergonomics and HMI leads to better system acceptance by the user if the system model fits the culture-specific ways of thinking of the user (cf. Chap. 2).

▸ Although these I18N and L10N processes require additional effort in the analysis, planning, design, and implementation of software, the long-term benefits result in higher product acceptance by the user as the HMI is optimized very carefully by applying software ergonomics and deep (intercultural) usability methods.

The aim of globalization is to successfully market in one or more local markets, taking into account local technical, economic, and legal conditions (Schmitz and Wahle 2000, p. 2).

▸ Globalization comprises all activities with regard to the international up to the worldwide marketing of a (software) product (e.g., using the methods of I18N and L10N).

The neologistic term "glocalization" results as a portmanteau word formation from the opinion that user interfaces should be globally applicable but must be localized for this purpose. In addition, other terms such as "universal design" and "culture-oriented context" are already linked to "goldilocksical" (You et al. 2016), which expresses that information design should in each case use the best aspects of universal design and culture-related design. But let us now move on to the development cycle of global products.

3.2 Global Product Development Cycle

▸ A product can only be successful in the international market if it awakens familiar associations (within its cultural character) in the customer and is positively connotated. Failure to comply with this point of view may lead to a complete rejection of the product.

Therefore, in global product development, the need for software solutions that not only address the language, but also the cultural needs of the user, is very high. Localization and internationalization methods are used for this purpose. A mere translation of the texts contained in the product is not sufficient.

▸ Intercultural product development spans the entire product development cycle and consists of software internationalization and software localization (Fig. 3.2).

3.2.1 Activities Within the Global Product Development Cycle

If one considers internationalization and localization in connection with the process of developing products for the world market (cf. Fig. 3.2), one realizes how comprehensive the spectrum of activities required for localization and internationalization is.

▸ Localization and internationalization are not just additional steps that need to be considered when developing a software product. They are a fundamental part of the entire software development process, from the analysis of product requirements (local/global), through modeling, development, implementation, and

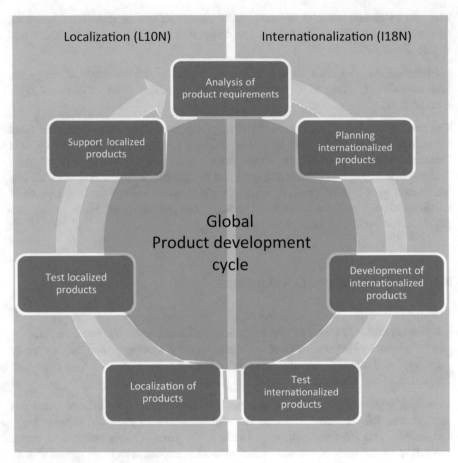

Fig. 3.2 Global product development cycle based on eCoLoTrain (2009). (*Source* VDMA 2009, p. 53)

testing to product maintenance and quality assurance (cf. Fissgus und Seewald-Heeg 2005, pp. 190–191).

For the global market, products are developed in such a way that they can easily be adapted to local requirements. This affects the entire software package as well as the hardware of a machine under certain circumstances (e.g., memory expansion due to new character sets). This includes aspects that directly affect the HMI, such as the user interface with its components (e.g., dialogue boxes, menus, or messages of all kinds) as well as indirect factors such as documentation (e.g., technical descriptions, online help, user manuals, etc.).

In order to achieve a complete culture-specific user-friendliness of a software product, it is also necessary to adapt the program modules, which can be assigned to the levels of unwritten and unconscious rules. This includes, for example, the navigation concept, the structuring of information, or the formulating of system messages.

▸ At the beginning of the internationalization process, it must be decided which
  components are to be localized. On the basis of this definition, appropriate
  measures can then be taken to internationalize the software.

It must also be decided whether a simultaneous display of several languages on the
user interface is required. A user interface that completely focuses on text also has
special requirements (e.g., regarding colors and icons).

▸ In localization projects, the project objectives (e.g., scope and type of software
  localization, definition of exchange formats, and review of the localization
  database) must first be defined. This is followed by the preparation of a project
  schedule and a cost calculation, followed by the implementation of the plan in
  accordance with the specifications defined in the planning process.

This includes, for example, the preparation of the material to be translated (e.g.,
source strings of the user interface elements) with information on the target text
recipients as well as explanations on the use of terminology, style and language
level, the translation itself, revisions, proofreading, or review and testing. Aligning
previous materials, preparing terminology, and translation memory terminology can
be done by using button labels, menus, functions, and concepts. Preparing files and
texts for translation includes, for example, specifying whether the original files are
source or binary files, identifying the translatable strings of the files, locking strings
or codes that may not be deleted or modified during translation, and so on.

▸ A localization kit or package is then prepared and delivered with all the resources
  required by the translators for translation. After translation, at least one linguistic
  test must be carried out to ensure the quality of the translated product.

This quality assurance phase, which runs with the help of special tools, includes

- Revision (comparison of source and target texts to ensure that the translation is
  consistent with the agreed objectives),
- Proofreading (checking that the target text corresponds to its destination and its
  recipients),
- Review (final review).

▸ After translation/localization, some software components (such as user interfaces
  and help files) may require recompilation.

A new technical test (e.g., integration test) is usually performed by software
developers to ensure that all localized components of the software application
function correctly. The translated/localized elements are assembled to form the
target product. Before translating the documents, the user interface should be
carefully checked in order to avoid correction tasks for a translation that has not yet
been completed (Müller 2005; Johnson 2002), even if the localization of the documents and that of the user interface must be carried out simultaneously and usually
within a very tight timeframe (cf. Heimgärtner et al. 2011).

You can then make screen copies of the user interface and insert them into the help files and documentation. After all quality checks have been carried out, the localized applications, components, and documentation are delivered.

▶ In intercultural projects, the monitoring and control of projects, i.e., the checking and recording of project progress and costs as well as the correction of deviations from the project management plan, are of central importance (see Chap. 2).

This includes, for example, checking partial deliveries and problem reports from translators to ensure consistent use of terminology and spelling, or change management and replanning. If unexpected changes occur in the terminology or functions of the application at certain points in the project, these should be integrated into the localized versions as quickly as possible. Delayed feed-in of changes leads to increased costs and possible delays in delivery. Finally, project completion includes delivery of the localized product to the client, revision, and evaluation of project activities, and updating of data and materials (such as localization kits, terminology databases, translation memories, glossaries, etc.).

▶ One of the best strategies for using language and designing a localized product is to know the purpose of the translation and localize it directly in the target country with local translators and specialists.

Projects for the localization of user interfaces include the translation and adaptation of all text-containing user interface elements as well as the use of software localization tools (cf. Chap. 7), which enable the extraction and editing of text to be translated from the user interface. Usually, project managers or software developers are responsible for the preparation of source files containing software elements to be translated.[4] The preparation of these files varies depending on the text translation and editing method used, tools, client requirements, etc. The translators then translate the texts into the target language. Often the adaptation of graphics, images, symbols, user manuals, etc. is done by a software developer or UI designer. Sometimes, translators can also work with software developers to test the software. Both translators and software developers can be responsible for reformatting menus, dialogues, etc. to adapt the target texts to the available space.

▶ It is advisable to bring localization experts on board.

3.2.2 Project and Process Planning

The first step in the process is aimed at identifying the necessary attractiveness and market penetration of a new product. This step places the user in the focus of the

---

[4]See also the role descriptions in the GUPA Quality Standard for Usability Engineering, Version 1.0, April 2012, URL http://docplayer.org/8048330-German-upa-qualitaetsstandard-fu-er-usability-engineering.html, last access 29.02.2019.

new design to be developed, regardless of whether it is a technical device, an electronic product, or new software.

▸ The study of the human-centered design process in the current ISO 9241-210 with regard to aspects of intercultural management, in particular intercultural project management, clearly shows that precisely these aspects are still missing in this process, especially in the important early project phase.

The resulting weaknesses in the current human-centered design process of ISO 9241-210 can be summarized as follows:

- There must be a strong interest in a well-managed project start by an experienced project manager.
- The product development team for a globally successful future product should consist of representatives from the most important target markets.
- The first task of a UI Design (UID) team should be to acquire a solid understanding of the underlying complexity of the design task and its requirements.

The user interface is often only given attention when the later phases of the software lifecycle begin. The correct development process, however, requires attention to the human user from the beginning of the development process. The numerous design operations must be performed in parallel and determine how each process is affected by other processes. A large design team may need to provide specialists for the tasks of analysis, specification, and evaluation of user interface aspects. The design of user interfaces consists of a complex set of activities, all of which should focus on the human side of the system. Software engineers tend to model the user interface according to the structure of the implementation mechanism instead of the structure of the task domain.

Intercultural project management measures are the first step in an intercultural user-centric design process:

- Recruit a diverse team with representatives from all relevant user groups (e.g., from Japan, China, India, South America, North America, Arab Emirates, Sub-Saharan Africa, and Europe). Such a cross-cultural team has the potential to be far more effective and innovative than a mono-cultural one if the team is well managed.
- For your high-performance team, appoint an experienced leader who knows the different development process phases well and is able to lead his team in a moderated manner.
- Examine the current market situation with regard to existing products, main competitors, and environmental factors such as politics, new

legislation, economic trends, worldwide sociological, and technological developments.

- Perform an analysis of political, economic, social, and technological aspects that provides a framework for strategic management factors of the macro-environment and describes existing and new user groups worldwide.

▸ The challenges facing global software development all have something to do with distance: time, geography, and sociocultural distance.

In a similar way, the challenges of software development can be classified into the following three categories:

- Communication and collaboration between team members. Individual team members have to exchange information and work together.
- Coordination of tasks: The work that is carried out at different locations must be coordinated.
- Work control: Management must remain in control of the work carried out in different locations.

Table 3.1 summarizes the main challenges in the development of global systems.

3.2.3 Requirements Analysis in an Intercultural Context

▸ The communication between designer and user plays a decisive role in the requirements analysis. Successful intercultural communication depends on the personal ability to understand each other's network of faith by using empathic abilities (cf. Heimgärtner et al. 2011).

Even a simple survey, an interview or a guided discussion between an HMI designer and users to record their needs may lead to user interfaces with excellent

Table 3.1 Challenges in the development of global systems

	Distance in time	Geographical distance	Sociocultural distance
Communication	Effective communication	Effective information exchange and team building	Cultural understanding
Coordination	Coordination costs	A feel for the prioritization of tasks	Ability to work effectively together
Check	Minimization of delays	Status quality and process uniformity	Quality tolerance

usability and, in addition, an excellent user experience (UX). Accordingly, empathy is a key factor for the successful design of an intercultural user interface.

When it comes to designing functionality and interaction for global devices, the cultural background must be taken into account: intercultural HMI design is much more than just the implementation of a set of requirements for the user interface, such as the consideration of different languages, colors, or symbols.

Successful intercultural HMI design looks much further behind the regular design process by considering different mentalities, thought patterns, and problem-solving strategies anchored in the target culture, e.g., linear vs. nonlinear differences. For example, utility models that do not appear in everyday life in the source country may appear in the target country due to different power structures (flat vs. hierarchical). In addition, the designer must know exactly what the user needs or wants (i.e., why, in which context, etc.).

▸ Knowledge about users and their needs can be obtained most precisely by using methods based on communication, such as user surveys or interviews.

Relying only on quantitative observation techniques or on expert opinions results in less reliable information, although these results are also very useful. Nevertheless, problems in intercultural communication—especially those in requirements analysis —inhibit the possibilities of obtaining good usability and (the associated) UX (user experience).

▸ Understanding difficulties within the requirements analysis must be identified and solved to improve the cooperation between designers, managers, users, and customers. Intercultural communication can contribute here to solving problems arising from cultural differences, since these are strongly influenced by the philosophy of the cultures concerned (cf. Chap. 2).

3.2.4 Concept Creation in the Design Phase

▸ In the design process step, the culturally diverse UI design team must generate new innovative solutions.

Research results show that the more diverse the team members are in terms of age, gender, cultural background, and education, the greater the chance of capturing new innovative ideas (cf. Kochan et al. 2003; Sethi et al. 2001). The processes in intercultural product design teams are much more complex management tasks than in comparable monocultural teams. Problems will arise daily in time and budget planning, project management, task extensions, conflict management, risk management, and different quality expectations in the design phase (cf. Hoffmann et al. 2004; Binder 2007). Because of the different cultural imprints and hidden underlying assumptions of the team members, processes such as team building will take longer than in monocultural teams. Communication remains a challenge in diversified teams: misunderstandings arising from the use of a common but non-native language will often emerge and lead to anger and frustration.

▸ Interculturally induced problems require an interculturally experienced, professional project manager who will resolve them in a professional manner and avoid potential obstacles.

3.2.5 Implementation of Requirements in Products

Cultural influences must also be taken into account during the implementation of the requirements in the intercultural product, especially through software. Many aspects are covered by using the approach of internationalization and localization including the corresponding tool support (see Sect. 7.3.2 on the localization kit and Sect. 7.4.4 on localization tools).[5]

3.2.6 System Evaluation for Requirements Validation

The system evaluation serves to check the fulfillment of derived requirements from the usability and corporate goals for the intercultural context. The better and more precisely the product goals are defined at the beginning of a development project, the easier it is to compare the goals with the current status of design. Such comparisons of performance objectives must be made on an ongoing basis to ensure that the design solutions generated are in line with the defined objectives.

▸ In the international context, it is important to evaluate the design status from the perspective of different user groups defined to ensure that the design meets the different and often conflicting requirements of all stakeholders.

The ongoing control strategy provides the basis for meeting the diverse requirements and objectives of all cultural target groups of the new product, whereby (i) the current design has been reviewed by all relevant main cultural target group leaders, who in turn know the environmental factors as well as local user requirements and conditions in detail, and (ii) the design is adapted on the basis of this feedback.

In the event of a conflict of interest that cannot be resolved with a single product solution, but which nevertheless has the highest priority for success on the market (e.g., incompatible legal requirements for the display size of a navigation system) and which cannot be reconciled with these requirements, another option needs to be

---

[5]Furthermore, Chap. 7 (IUID in practice) deals in more detail with design elements in an intercultural context and their implementation possibilities.

found. In the worst case, these requirements cannot be met with a single user interface design and management must decide how to proceed.

3.3   Summary, Conclusion, and Outlook

The challenges facing global software development all have something to do with distance: time, geography, and sociocultural distance. Intercultural software engineering considers cultural influences during software development based on the results of software ergonomics research and usability engineering. The ultimate goal of incorporating software ergonomics into software engineering is to produce software that is easy to understand and use, with which the user is satisfied (= software with high usability and UX). Ethnocomputing refers to everything that is comprehensive in relation to computer science and culture. Not only ethnic groups are meant, but also nations or even individual regions down to the smallest user groups with their very own cultural context.

A product can only be successful in the international market if it arouses familiar associations and positive connotations in the customer. The disregard of this aspect can lead to a complete rejection of the product.

Intercultural product development spans the entire product development cycle and consists of software internationalization and software localization. Internationalization and localization are interwoven processes. In their application, it is essential to take into account the different cultural backgrounds of the users in order to generate user models and thus adapt the system and its parameters to the cultural needs of the user.

Internationalization of a product means that the product is equipped with a basic structure on the basis of which a cultural adaptation for use in the desired target countries can later be carried out (cf. International 2003), which saves costs. The TLCC model (cf. Sturm 2002) shows the historical growth of the steps of internationalization and localization in HMI design and comprises four levels which categorize the activities into the following classes: technology, language, culture, and cognition. At the beginning of the internationalization process, a decision must be made as to which components should be localized. On the basis of this definition, appropriate measures can then be taken to internationalize the software. When internationalizing and localizing software, all parties involved should always be aware of the core elements of localization and take them into account accordingly; otherwise, they could be potential sources of problems that can cause user effort and inacceptance in the development process.

Localization means the adaptation of a system to certain cultural requirements of a local market, e.g., the adaptation of the look and feel of the user interface or the internal data structures to the cultural requirements of the user (see VDMA 2009). Hoft (1995) illustrates visible (language, colors, icons, symbols) and hidden localization elements (context, behavioral norms, thinking, communication, behavior, time aspect) using the iceberg model. In localization projects, the project objectives (e.g., scope and type of software localization such as definition of exchange formats and checking the localization database) must first be defined. This is followed by the preparation of a time schedule for the project and a cost calculation, followed by the implementation of the plan in accordance with the specifications defined in the planning process. After that, the preparation and delivery of a localization kit or localization package with all the resources required by the translators for the translation must be prepared and delivered. After translation, at least one linguistic test must be carried out to ensure the quality of the translated product. After translation/localization, some software components (such as user interfaces and help files) may require recompilation. One of the best strategies for using language and designing a localized product is to know the purpose of the translation and to localize it directly in the target country with local translators and specialists. It is advisable to bring localization experts on board.

The investigation of the human-centered design process in the current ISO 9241-210 with regard to aspects of intercultural management, in particular, intercultural project management, shows that precisely these aspects are not taken into account in this process and especially in the important early project phase. Interculturally induced problems require an interculturally experienced, professional project manager who will resolve them in a professional manner and avoid potential obstacles. In intercultural projects, the monitoring and control of projects, i.e., the checking and recording of project progress and costs as well as the correction of deviations from the project management plan, is of central importance. The communication between designer and user plays a decisive role in the requirements analysis. Successful intercultural communication depends on the personal ability to understand each other's network of faith by using empathic abilities (cf. Heimgärtner et al. 2011). Knowledge about users and their needs can be obtained most precisely by using methods based on communication, such as user surveys or interviews. Difficulties in understanding the requirements analysis must be identified and solved in order to improve the cooperation of designers, managers, users, and customers. Intercultural communication can contribute to the solution of problems arising from cultural differences, as these are strongly influenced by the philosophy of the cultures concerned. In the design process step, the culturally diverse UI design team must generate new innovative solutions. In the international context, it is important to evaluate the design status from the perspective of different user groups defined to ensure that the design meets the different and often contradictory requirements of all stakeholders. The introduction of agile methods can accelerate the process of disentangling diverse and changing stakeholder interests from different cultures.

Normally, software products contain two main components: software and documentation. Localization projects usually begin with software translation, which includes the translation of the components of the graphical user interface of an application such as menus, dialogue boxes, and strings (error messages, questions, etc.) and any sample files that may be provided with the software for demonstration purposes. In times of globalization, it is very important for companies, institutions, or products to be present on the Internet. This presence in the form of a website should also be tailored to the local target markets. Since the content of websites changes very often, it is recommended to develop and systematize a localization workflow. A "Locale" is the culture-dependent component of the software and is rich in units that are specific to a particular target culture. A localization kit (LocKit) should contain all the information the translator needs for localization. Zerfaß (2005a) provides step-by-step tips for creating a LocKit. One way to avoid communication problems within a localization team is to give everyone involved in the project an overview of all project phases using an L10N plan.

Norms	√
ISO 9241-210	☐
Checklist	√
Cooperation with other cultures is the mindset of the team	☐
Team is trained in intercultural communication and action competence	☐
SW development team is trained in intercultural software engineering	☐
Team (at least owners of process roles with pronounced intercultural contact) are trained in intercultural project management (e.g. PM, QM, TM, RM)	☐
HMI developers are trained in intercultural usability engineering and UI design	☐
Planning system adapted to target culture	☐
Requirements analysis is culturally appropriate (not ethnocentric, empathic), systematic, culture-oriented	☐
The context of use (user, tasks, system and environment) was defined with adequate Identification and description of resources for the (inter-)cultural context	☐
Requirements were met with adequate funding for the (inter-)cultural Context derived and specified	☐
Methods of internationalization and localization are familiar to the team	☐
Team knows the possible cultural influence on the context of use and on the Product design (information architecture and interaction design) and acts accordingly	☐
Team knows potential recommendations for the development of intercultural user interfaces (e.g. intercultural design guidelines)	☐
Team knows the TLCC model and is guided by it	☐
Team knows the core elements of localization	☐
Localization KIT available	☐
Localization tools are known and used	☐
Intercultural differences in quality are known and corresponding understanding of quality is given is available	☐
Relevant norms and standards are used and applied in an intercultural context (e.g. assessed and used on the basis of cultural dimensions)	☐
Problems with the evaluation of intercultural user interfaces are known and recommendations are taken into account	☐

References

Binder J (2007) Global project management: communication, collaboration and management across borders. Gower, Aldershot

Carter D (1992) Writing localizable software for the Macintosh. Addison-Wesley, Reading

Del Galdo EM, Nielsen J (1996) International user interfaces. Wiley, New York

Esselink B (1998) A practical guide to software localization: for translators, engineers and project managers, vol 3. Benjamins, Amsterdam

Esselink B (2000) A practical guide to localization, 2 Aufl, Bd 4. Benjamins Publishers, Amsterdam/Philadelphia

Fernandes T (1995) Global interface design: [A guide to designing international user interfaces]. AP Professional, Chestnut Hill/Boston

Fissgus U, Seewald-Heeg U (2005) Software localization. IT-MUNCHEN 47(4):220–225

Heimgärtner R (2006) On the necessity of intercultural usability engineering in the design of driver information systems. i-com 5(2):66–67. https://doi.org/10.1524/icom.2006.5.2.66

Heimgärtner R, Windl H, Solanki A (2011) The necessity of personal freedom to increase HCI design quality. In: Marcus A (Hrsg) Design, user experience, and usability, HCII 2011. LNCS 6769, S 62–68. Springer, Heidelberg

Hoffmann H-E, Schoper Y-G, Fitzsimons C-J (2004) International project management: intercultural cooperation in practice (Orig-Ausg Aufl Bd 50883: Beck-Wirtschaftsberater; 50883). German Paperback-Verl, Munich

Hoft NL (1995) International technical communication: how to export information about high technology. Wiley, New York

International, Dr (2003) Developing international software, 2nd edn. Microsoft Press, Redmond

Johnson D (2002) How to begin a localization project. In: The guide to translation and localization. Lingo Systems: American Translators Association (ATA), Portland, S 8–11

Kochan T, Bezrukova K, Ely R, Jackson S, Joshi A, Jehn K, Thomas D et al (2003) The effects of diversity on business performance: report of the diversity research network. Hum Resour Manag 42(1):3–21. https://doi.org/10.1002/hrm.10061

Lunde K (1999) CJKV information processing: [Chinese, Japanese, Korean & Vietnamese computing], 1 Aufl. O'Reilly, Beijing

Marcus A (2001) Cross-cultural user-interface design. In: Smith MJSG (ed) Proceedings conference on human-computer interface internat (HCII), New Orleans, vol 2. Lawrence Erlbaum Associates, Mahwah, pp 502–505

Marcus A (2006) Cross-cultural user-experience. Design diagrammatic representation and inference. Springer, Heidelberg, pp 16–24

Matti T, Erkki S, Esko K, Piet K (2006) Ethnocomputing: ICT in cultural and social context. Commun ACM 49(1): 126–130. https://doi.org/10.1145/1107458.1107466. ISSN: 0001–0782

Müller E (2005) „Step-by-step localization". Localization. The guide from multi lingual computing & technology. Beiheft 75:16–18

Nardi BA (1996) Context and consciousness: activity theory and human-computer interaction. MIT Press, Cambridge, MA

Nielsen J (2000) Usability engineering ([Nachdr] Aufl). Merchant, San Diego

Norman DA, Draper S (eds) (1986) User centered system design: new perspectives on human-computer interaction. Lawrence Erlbaum Associates, Hillsdale

Röse K, Zühlke D (2001, September 18–20) Culture-oriented design: developers' knowledge gaps in this area. In: Paper presented at the 8th IFAC/IFIPS/IFORS/IEA symposium on analysis, design, and evaluation of human-machine systems, Kassel

Schmitz K-D, Wahle K (2000) Software localization. Stauffenburg-Verl, Tübingen

Sethi R, Smith DC, Park CW (2001) Cross-functional product development teams, creativity, and the innovativeness of new consumer products. J Mark Res 38(1):73–85. https://doi.org/10.1509/jmkr.38.1.73.18833

Shen S-T, Woolley M, Prior S (2006) Towards culture-centred design. Interact Comput 18(4):820–852. https://doi.org/10.1016/j.intcom.2005.11.014

Stephanidis C (2001) User interfaces for all: concepts, methods, and tools. Lawrence Erlbaum Associates, Mahwah

Stephanidis C (Hrsg) (2007) Universal access in human-computer interaction. In: Ambient interaction. 4th international conference on universal access in human-computer interaction, UAHCI 2007 held as part of HCI international 2007, Beijing, July 22–27, 2007 proceedings, Part II, Bd 4555. Springer, Heidelberg

Sturm C (2002) TLCC-towards a framework for systematic and successful product internationalization. In: Paper presented at the international workshop on internationalisation of products and systems, Austin

Taylor D (1992) Global software: developing applications for the international market. Springer, New York/ Berlin/Heidelberg/London/Paris/Tokyo/Hong Kong/Barcelona/Budapest

Tuthill B, Smallberg D (1997) Creating worldwide software: Solaris international developer's guide. Prentice Hall, Upper Saddle River

VDMA (2009) Software internationalization guide. VDMA Software Association, Frankfurt a. M.

Yeo A (2001) Global software development lifecycle: an exploratory study. In: Jacko J, Sears A, Beaudouin-Lafon M, Jacob R (Hrsg) CHI 2001: conference on human factors in computing systems. ACM Press, S 104–111

You S, Kim Ms, Lim YK (2016) Univ Access Inf Soc 15:369. https://doi.org/10.1007/s10209-014-0393-9

Zerfaß A (2005a) Assembling a localization kit. The guide from multilingual computing & technology. Supplement 75:8–11

Zerfaß A (2005b) Localization of internet presences. In: Reineke D, Schmitz K-D (eds) Introduction to software localization. Gunter Narr Publishers, Tübingen, pp 127–143

Chapter 4
Usability Engineering

In order to achieve usability and positive user experience also in an intercultural context, cultural influences on usability and UX as well as cultural influences on usability engineering have to be investigated. In this chapter, the theoretical background regarding interculturally adapted human–machine interaction (HMI) is examined and cultural aspects are linked with models, roles, and principles of the human-centered design process (planning and design activities) and then transferred to intercultural usability engineering. Subsequently, the steps of the process of the intercultural usability engine are presented.

© Springer Nature Switzerland AG 2019
R. Heimgärtner, *Intercultural User Interface Design*, Human–Computer
Interaction Series, https://doi.org/10.1007/978-3-030-17427-9_4

4.1   Human–Machine Interaction (HMI)

▸ The interaction in which information is exchanged between user and system via
the user interface (UI) is referred to as "human–machine interaction" (HMI) or
"human–computer interaction" (MCI) (cf. Jacko and Sears 2003).

The interaction of a human being with a machine is often also referred to as
"human–machine communication", since the human being applies similar rules to
his interaction with the computer or the machine as to interpersonal communication
(Reeves and Nass 1998; Fischer 2006). Both situations are processes that involve
the exchange of information, i.e., communication processes. Here cultural influences become effective, as they are partly known from the studies on intercultural
communication in humans. Although experience and research results can be used,
they cannot be directly transferred to the field of technically oriented communication between human and machine. An intermediate stage of interpretation and
analogous reasoning is necessary for intercultural HMI design.

In human–machine systems, human and machine both pursue the same goal (cf.
Charwat 1992). According to (Timpe and Baggen 2000), the user works with the
man–machine system together with the goal of solving a task selected by the user.
The user initiates tasks and the system answers with solutions, also vice versa.

▸ HMI takes place on a man–machine system consisting of three parts embedded in
a work environment or context of use: Task, user, system (cf. Wandmacher 1993,
p. 1).

Wandmacher (1993) describes the man–machine system with his ABC model as a
triad of: Task, user and computer (tool or machine) embedded in the working
environment (Fig. 4.1). This unit is also called the context of use (cf. DIN 1999).

In addition, cultural dependence increases from phase to phase. In Japan, for
example, a very short system response time is very important. On the other hand,
Japanese users are obviously more patient than users from European countries when
it comes to long-term tasks (cf. e.g., Rößger and Rosendahl 2002).

4.1.1   User Interface

Human-Machine Interaction (HMI) describes the exchange of information between
humans and machines.

▸ The interface between the user and the technical system is formed by the
operating system, the so-called "user interface" according to ISO standard 9241
(often simply but not standardized referred to as user interface or user interface).

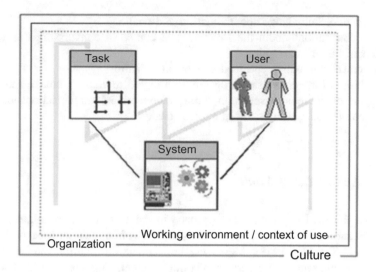

Fig. 4.1 Scheme of a human–machine system according to (Wandmacher 1993; Röse 2002), extended to the cultural environment by the author

The user interface contains those components of a human–machine system that are necessary for interaction with the user (cf. Timpe and Baggen 2000). The use of the user interface depends on the context of use, which includes the system (tool, computer, and machine), the tasks, the environment, and the user himself.

The design of human-machine systems always depends on the respective context, i.e., also on the respective cultural context:

- Consideration of the context of use (e.g., work environment),
- Integration/reflection of work organisation (e.g., access rights),
- Consideration of the user qualification,
- Adaptation to existing user knowledge,
- Consideration of user constitution (e.g. attention control),
- Consideration of technological conditions and possibilities,
- Consideration of the intercultural context.

The tasks are gradually divided into hierarchically structured steps (cf. Herczeg 1994, pp. 10–11). The environment and the tasks are recorded, whereby human abilities should be at the center of design considerations (cf. Röse 2002, p. 10).

The rules of human–machine interaction are derived from the information-theoretical consideration of interpersonal communication. Interpersonal communication is characterized by (cf. Kraiss 1993):

- Shared prior knowledge about situation and context,
- Fixed conventions about the structure and course of conversations as well as mechanisms of interruption,
- Conversation initiative and feedback or confirmation,
- Flexibility of the conversation design with regard to content, course and speed,
- Support of content presentation through nonverbalCommunicationsnonverbal communication (gestures, facial expressions).

4.1.2 Action Level Model

Normally, the HMI is a reciprocal approach to the person you are talking to. The communication model of Shannon and Weaver is often used as a basis for HMI models (cf. Shannon 1948). Messages, i.e., coded information, are exchanged between the communication partners via one channel. This task can be disturbed, and the messages deformed accordingly. The communication partners need codes to encode and decode the information. However, interpersonal communication cannot be transferred 1:1 to human–machine interaction, since the tasks of the human–machine system must be adapted according to the capabilities of man and machine. Among the main tasks of man are Planning, communication, management, and navigation (Timpe and Kolrep 2000). These tasks must be supported by a meaningful and ergonomic design of the user interface. Components of interaction (conceptual, communicative, and situational) and thus depictable model levels (task level, etc.) serve as descriptive characteristics. Performance characteristics of humans can be derived from the model level, which can be described by corresponding objectives. The corresponding strategic action steps then describe the implementation or action-relevant characteristics.

▸ The action level model according to (Herczeg 2005) describes the steps of human–machine communication.

The user wants to solve a certain task with the help of the system. Therefore, the user must interact with the system to obtain information or relevant knowledge. This interaction takes place on several levels in parallel (Fig. 4.2).

The processing of a task by means of a computer system can be tracked from the user's point of view on logical levels using models. The processes initiated by the user activities in the computer system can be modeled on the computer at the same logical levels as from the user's point of view. There is an input page (processing user input) and an output page (generating computer output). The user processes a task by successively breaking it down hierarchically into activities of different abstraction. While at the beginning, the task is divided into a sequence of intended, roughly structured activities; at the end there are individual motor activities.

To solve a task, a user develops intentions on the intentional level. They are the starting point for planning several activities. Once the activities have been carried

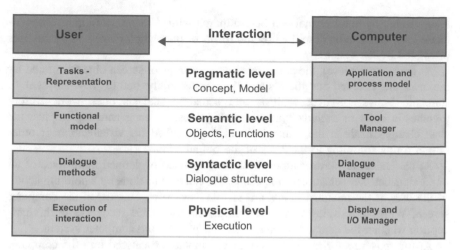

Fig. 4.2 The semiotic mode 1 of interaction between humans and computers according to Herczeg. (*Source* Herczeg 2005)

out, the results are compared with the original intentions and evaluated. Activities will be considered successful if positively evaluated. In the case of negative evaluations, the intentions or activities are modified in such a way that they are likely to lead to success in a new dialogue step. The user may also recognize that the system used is not appropriate for the task and stop using it. The computer system has a model of the application world for processing user orders. Based on the evaluations of the user orders, appropriate strategies are selected. The computer system can become independently active, i.e., take the initiative, in defined situations without user intervention by interpreting the system state. The interaction cycle then starts at the computer system.

At the pragmatic level, the intentions are translated into more concrete objectives (expected work results). Concrete procedures (procedures) are applied to the activities. The extent to which the objectives are later classified as achieved depends on the interpretations of the work results. If the objectives appear to have been achieved, the planned follow-up activities are carried out. If the interpretations are negative, the objectives or procedures are modified, and other activities are carried out.

At the semantic level, the procedures are translated into the operations possible with the computer system. The user plans to create or delete objects or change their states. The extent to which these objects are subsequently classified as successfully processed by the user depends on the detected states that the computer system reflects in its output. If the objects appear to be in the desired state, subsequent operations are performed. If this is not the case, changed operations are executed. The computer output shows whether the input was successful on a syntactic level and whether the computer system accepted the input form and evaluated the contents. The output generated by the computer system can form structures recognizable by the user that can be compared with the syntactic input. The syntactic level can also be described by the forms of interaction perceived by the user or offered by the system.

At the syntactic level, the characters and selections of screen objects entered by the user are checked for their syntactic permissibility before they are sent to semantic analysis. Syntax analysis and semantic analysis often work closely together in order to exclude syntactic ambiguities. When generating outputs, the state changes made at the semantic level are prepared for visualization or other output forms according to the rules of the output syntax.

At the lexical level, user input must be composed of defined input lines of an input alphabet. The selection of the characters can also be done by a pointing action of the user, if the intended inputs are visible as existing outputs on the computer screen. With the resulting computer output, the user must recognize by his perception whether the characters have been accepted by the computer system.

At the sensorimotor level, the articulated inputs are entered into the computer system via the user's motor system. Such inputs or signals are mostly transmitted by keys of a keyboard or by movement and keys of a pointing instrument (e.g., mouse). The entries can also be made using spoken commands or gestures.

When we talk about actions in the following, we mean individual user activities (work steps) on all levels of the action level model of human–computer communication mentioned above. For example, an action at the semantic level is an operation, that is, the application of an operator to a usage object (the top-level information unit with which the user interacts, such as a document). On the sensorimotor level, an action is, for example, the pressing of a key or a completed pointing action with the pointing instrument.

Important for information-intensive applications is the organization, placement, and manipulation of complex data. Using mental models and metaphors, users can draw on their existing knowledge, e.g., about visual formalisms based on simple objects such as tables, graphs, diagrams, etc.

4.1.3   Mental Models

People gain mental models of their environment from experience with their environment in order to find their way around it more quickly. Semantic or episodic mental models in the brain represent human knowledge about the world, i.e., about oneself, the environment, computers, tasks, and organizational structures, as well as about the relationships existing between them, which form the basis for their action planning and execution. Models are not "formulated" at the beginning, they are only gradually supplemented. Often the "mere view/seeing/observing" is sufficient to find the right models or to recognize them.

▸ Mental models are means of depicting the shared knowledge of communication partners (cf. Johnson-Laird 1983). In HMI research, mental models serve as the basis for user models to explain the user's expectations of the system in order to pursue their intentions or fulfill their tasks (cf. Herczeg 1994, p. 9; Schlungbaum 1996, 1997; Blank 1996).

These are simplified models of complex events which a user creates using the operational and functional possibilities of a system in order to work with them (cf. Herczeg 1994, p. 17). The best HMI takes place when user and system models match. Then the system meets the expectations of the user. If the models match, the system is self-explanatory and accordingly easy to learn. Cultural aspects must be taken into account if one or more cultures are involved during the HMI or if a user interface of a culture is to be used in another culture or in another cultural context. This is the case if the user of the system is not at the same time the developer of the system or if the cultures of user and developer differ (cf. Honold 2000; Röse 2002). Therefore, the conceptual models of the developers for intercultural HMI research must also be taken into account because systems reflect the cultural influence of their developers. Human–machine communication turns into intercultural communication if the user belongs to a different culture than the system developer (and accordingly the system itself) (cf. Honold 2000). Consequently, the successful use of a computer system depends on the compatibility of the mental models of the user and the system designers (see Herczeg 1994, pp. 18–20; Honold 2000, p. 45).

▸ The product developer is not forced to prognosticate the mental models of the users, but they can empirically collect them systematically with the help of the methods of intercultural usability engineering. Intercultural usability engineering is indispensable for intercultural product development.[1]

The creation of an HMI system involves different groups of people and stakeholders such as product managers, designers, developers, customers, users, etc. All the ideas of these parties are taken into account in the product creation process. Therefore, there are different perspectives which are relevant for human–machine interaction and which have to be clearly differentiated in order to avoid misunderstandings, especially in the requirements analysis of an HMI system. The human-centered design process according to ISO 9241-210 focuses on the user and his mental model for using the system.

These ideas can be represented by mental models (A = area of application, S = system, U = user, D = designer):

- U(S(A)): mental model of the user of the implementation of the system,
- D(U(A)): System designer's model of user's mental model equals the prescriptive model ("what should the user know about the scope?"),

---

[1]For example, iconized graphics serve to activate mental models, thereby reducing the complexity of the screen display and avoiding a quantitative cognitive overload ("massive mental overload", "high mental work load") (Andersen 1997).

- P(U(A)): Model of work psychologists of the mental model of the user equals descriptive model ("what does the user know about the scope of application?"),
- S(U(A)): Model of the system from the mental model of the user,
- S(S(A)): Model of the system of the implementation of the system (quasi of itself).

▸ The main problem is the incompatibility of the user's mental model (U(S(A))) with the implementation of the system (S(A)): The reason for this lies in the inadequacy of the system designer's model of the user's mental model (D(U(A)). This problem arises in particular if the user is not involved in the development process of the product in good time (e.g., through the application of the human-centered design process, cf. ISO 9241-210, as explained in detail in Sect. 4.4).

Cultural schemata influence these mental models, which are each limited to the area of application. Rößger (2003, p. 130) describes culture as a phenomenon that presents itself through continuous phases of interaction with its surroundings. In addition, cultural differences influence expectations when dealing with technical systems. The link between culture and mental models lies in the permanent behavioral patterns that form the mental models. Consequently, it is important to capture and describe these behavior patterns in relation to the interaction of users with the system in a cultural context in order to derive design recommendations. It is therefore worthwhile to invest the effort for the consistent implementation of mental models in practice while incorporating software ergonomic findings.

Software ergonomic findings serve to optimize work design and thus, for example, to relieve the burden on the user through a division of labor between man and computer. Working together can be supported by cooperative systems, for example, which can minimize physical and/or mental stress. Nevertheless, in order not to undermine the motivation of the user, a certain amount of strain must remain. Systems can be complex, but they must not be complicated. In particular, the handling of the system must be considered according to the restrictions in the application filters (hierarchies, patterns, query languages, etc.), contexts/modes (window/"insert—overwrite mode") and default settings (defaults, user profiles). In this context, the efficiency of communication plays a crucial role (cf. Herczeg 2005 action level model). The prerequisite for this is the compatibility of U(S(A)) and S(A). This is the only way to reduce user input as much as possible, simply and consistently. Also, input help or the use of system output visible on the screen ("interreferential input–output") and direct manipulation can support this. In the case of system expenditure, the aim is to achieve the best possible perceptibility, meaningful connection between the signs and comprehensibility.

4.1.4 Metaphors

▸ Metaphors represent a known real situation or object, facilitate learning for the user and give his expectations a certain direction.

Metaphors are often used, especially by users with little experience, to form their own impressions of the new systems (cf. z. B. "Office" applications, with "new documents", "recycle bin", "filing cabinet", etc.). In reality, metaphors that no longer exist are also used (e.g., a scroll bar for scrolling a document apart). (Nevertheless, this metaphor is recognized relatively easily and quickly).

Design features of metaphors have an influence on:

- Learning ability (measure: time for learning),
- Manageability (measure: time to complete the task),
- Scope of duties (measure: number of tasks).

Further reasons for the necessity of metaphors are described by Hülzer-Vogt (1995):

- Partial analogy to things of physical world (induction by analogical conclusion),
- Learning strategy,
- "Decorative effect",
- Constitutive and unavoidable components of communication,
- Means to systematically process and determine the entire everyday experience with the physical and cultural environment,
- Distinguish preparatory thought work ("conceptual metaphor") as an inner action from linguistic implementation ("metaphorical linguistic expression"), which is theoretically important for multimedia considerations,
- Reconstruction of human experiences and their systematic classification into a structural structure,
- Not always necessary: e.g., if the effect of an analogous conclusion can also be achieved.

In addition to mental models and metaphors, cultural influences affect above all interaction and dialogue design (cf. Röse 2002). Therefore, in the following, the most important information science terms concerning intercultural HMI design "interaction", "information", and "dialogue" are presented.

4.1.5 Information and Interaction

Reischer (2006, pp. 8–11) very impressively describes the status of research with regard to the concept of "information". There are many attempts at approximation but no uniform terminology. The meaning of the term "information" is rather fixed in relation to the context of the discipline that uses it. For example (Kuhlen 1991), defines the concept of information in the field of information science as "knowledge in action and context" (cf. Kuhlen 1991, p. 100; Hammwöhner und Kuhlen 2004; Reischer 2006, S. 112). Reischer (2006) uses a semiotic concept of information by integrating syntactic, semantic and pragmatic aspects, to which he was motivated by the everyday handling of the information concept in life. In contrast, (Fox and Hofkirchner 2002) argue that the information concept can be very clearly specified and does not have to be derived from everyday life (cf. Fox and Hofkirchner 2002). Another definition of "information" by Shannon uses a syntactical-quantitative concept of information that represents the amount of information measured by the reciprocal value of the delay in [bit] (cf. Shannon 1948). Floridi's semantic-quantitative information concept measures the amount of semantic information in [sbit] (cf. Floridi 2004). There are many definitions of the information concept (cf. Reischer 2006) but no uniform one. Therefore, the information concept must be defined in the context of use.

▸ Since the focus of this work is on intercultural HMI, the more pragmatic than syntactic information concept of Kuhlen (1991) "Information as Knowledge in Action" is used as a working definition primarily from the perspective of information reception and information processing. In contrast to purely syntactic information concepts such as Shannon's, Kuhlen's concept is also easier to reconcile with the cultural concept presented in Chap. 2.

All typologies of human–machine interaction (cf. Schomaker et al. 1995) can be based on a reasonable working definition of the interaction between humans and technical systems by (Stary 1994): "interaction" in the HMI between user and system means the process of using means of interaction and application functions (cf. Stary 1994, p. 35).

▸ Interaction is a specification of communication and implies that a person acts in accordance with the interpretation of received signs (Hohmann 2003, p. 29).

Interaction with explicit information ("interactive information", i.e., explicitly expressed messages) occurs primarily in spoken dialogues. Nevertheless, less than 20% of communication is based on speaking (cf. Argyle and Schmidt 2002). According to the study, more than 80% of the transmission of information takes place in interpersonal communication without verbal language. In this case, there is an interaction with implicit information ("informative interaction"). "Informative interaction" is involved in "indirect interaction" and "interactive information" in "direct interaction". "Direct interaction involves a dialogue with feedback and control during task execution. Indirect interaction can also involve background or batch processing." (Dix et al. 2001, p. 3).

▸ Both verbal and nonverbal communication between humans and computers must be investigated.

In order to analyze informative interaction, the interactive behavior of the communication partners must be analyzed: there must be communication between humans and computers in order to achieve reasonable results and effects in feed-back for the communication partners. This is informative interaction (i.e., interaction with sense and meaning) because communication between humans and computers takes place predominantly nonverbally (e.g., pointing the mouse cursor at something).

By analyzing the interaction between user and system, relevant information can be obtained that describes or at least suggests the characterization of the user in interaction and communication ("interaction/communication type").

Interaction depends on time and happens only through time. It is therefore necessary to analyze the interaction process over a certain period of time (inter-action process analysis) (cf. Bales 1950; Frey and Bente 1989). There are many aspects that need to be considered and that can be observed by the user during interaction with the system. Long pauses in interaction may imply "problems" in the interaction ("communication") between user and system or otherwise—by recording the interaction history and analyzing it, solutions can be inferred and suggested to the user. Not only the use of interaction offers of a system such as softkeys (e.g., buttons or links) can be recorded and analyzed but also interaction times, interaction paths, and interaction frequency. In addition, the analysis of interaction pauses can also reveal important information about the user. Why are there these interaction pauses by the user? Is he active or passive? Does he consume information, e.g., by reading or listening? Is he trying to enter something (e.g., via mouse or keyboard)? Which input device is used and how often? The interface can be set manually by the user (personalization) or automatically by the system (adaptivity). This allows many rather heterogeneous parameters to be analyzed during interaction: User, session time, mouse coordinates, mouse clicks, menu items/entries, and key status, context (mouse, menu, etc.), explicit, implicit and step-by-step prompts, messages, speech speed, pauses, etc. The graphic design also influences the interaction behavior (e.g., colors, characters, language, line spacing, etc.). In addition, the interactive behavior can be changed by the functional depth of the system and the application types. For example, when driving a car, the number of functionalities should be kept very low (each licensed user should be able to drive a car), whereas applications in research and development in industry and science can have a very high number of functions (only experts can handle these user interfaces). This is only an incomplete list of aspects that can be considered.

4.1.6   Dialogue—Combination of Information and Interaction

Dialogue is a reasonable means of exchanging information with the communication partner through interaction. According to Wittig (1979), a user's interaction with the system continues dialogues. It specifies five criteria for identifying a dialogue between human and machine (Wittig 1979, p. 86):

(i)   A "dialogue" is a conversation during which one of the two partners can be a machine.
(ii)   Certain remarks to the partner are evaluated and answered thematically (intentionality is therefore omitted).
(iii) Knowledge expansion occurs for at least one of the partners.
(iv)   The dialogue does not have to be communicative but can also be an instrumental action with a rational purpose.
(v)   The roles of the two partners in points (i)–(iv) are interchangeable.

▸ A dialogue is the interaction between a user and an interactive system in the form of a sequence of actions by the user (input) and responses by the interactive system (output) to achieve a goal.

"Interaction" with computer systems means to conduct "dialogues" according to the above meaning, because the direction of interaction is also reversible, and the types of speech action can be the same as a result of which knowledge expansion occurs. There are several types of dialogues at the HMI (called "dialogue windows"). Dialogues combine interaction and information because they present information and need interaction. Consequently, the principles for interaction design and information processing determine the principles for dialogue design (cf. Dybkjær et al. 2004). Principles of dialogue (e.g., change of speaker, initiation of dialogue, multimodal principles, etc., cf. McTear 2002 or Searle and Kiefer 1980) should be considered similar to those in interpersonal communication, because human understanding is involved (cf. Reeves and Nass 1998; Fischer 2006). The system should at best function as if it were a human being in the same situation. Furthermore, HMI depends on many parameters related to situation, context, user preferences, and world knowledge as well as aspects of space and time (see Del Galdo and Nielsen 1996). All these aspects are culturally influenced. Therefore, it is important to consider fundamental intercultural differences when dealing with the interaction of users of different cultures with computers or machines. In addition, knowledge of the cultural characteristics of the communication partners as well as their culturally accepted communication behavior in intercultural communication situations is necessary.

4.1.7   Dialogue Principles

▸ Dialogue principles are general objectives for the design of dialogues. Dialogue principles are abstract guidelines for top-level dialogue design derived from experience (UXQB 2015).

The details of a dialogue that meets the needs of a user within the identified context of use are defined as dialogue requirements. Due to their universality, it can be difficult to implement them in a concrete context. The DIN EN ISO 9241 standard defines requirements for the ergonomics of human–system interaction. The aim of this series of standards is "the ergonomic design of computer workstations taking into account the individual needs of users" (ISO 9241-110, p. 9). Part 110 specifies seven principles of dialogue design, which are to be applied as guidelines in the design and evaluation of dialogue systems.

Part 110 of DIN EN ISO 9241 lists the following seven dialogue principles (see ISO 9241-110):

- Suitability for the task,
- Self-descriptiveness,
- Conformity with user expectations
- Suitability for learning,
- Controllability,
- Error tolerance,
- Suitability for individualization.

The following detailed descriptions of these dialogue principles are based on the UXQB's publicly accessible and generally available curriculum and glossary for the certification exam to obtain the degree of Certified Professional for User Experience and Usability-Foundation Level (CPUX-F)[2] based on the ISO 9241-110 standard.

▸ A dialogue is task appropriate if it supports the user in completing his task.

Functionality and dialogue are based on the characteristic properties of the task rather than on the technology used to complete it. Recommendations for following the dialogue principle: The dialogue should show the user information related to the successful completion of the task. The dialogue should not display information to the user that is not required for the successful completion of relevant tasks. The form of input and output should be adapted to the task. If certain input values are typical for a task, these values should automatically be available to the user as default values. The dialogue steps required by the interactive system should fit the workflow, i.e., necessary dialogue steps should be included, and unnecessary dialogue steps should be avoided. Adequacy of tasks is understood to mean the ideal work design of internal and external tasks, the division of tasks and the orientation of the I/O of information to the task at hand ("interreferential I/O"). This includes, for example, the creation of macros and adequate default settings to facilitate the performance of routine tasks, i.e., also the adaptation of the system to the needs of the tasks.

---

[2]See https://uxqb.org/en/documents/, last access 9th February 2019.

▸ A dialogue is self-descriptive to the extent that it is at any time obvious to the user which dialogue he is in, where he is and which actions can be carried out and how.

Self-describability of the system exists when an adequate mental model of the user of the system $(B(S(A)))$ is created with regard to the momentary functional possibilities. This includes, for example, that help is adapted to the user's knowledge, context-dependent help/explanations/relevant information is provided, passive help (comprehensibility of the system, help called up) and active help (automatic notification, automatic correction after errors).

▸ A dialogue conforms to expectations, i.e., in accordance with user expectations, if it meets the user requirements foreseeable from the context of use as well as generally accepted conventions.

The dialogue design criterion of expectation conformity must be met in order not to disappoint the expectations regarding the operation of the interactive system from the user's previous experience. The dialogue should meet the user's expectations. Consistency is an aspect of expectation conformity that is achieved by adhering to the following rules:

• Uniformity and consistency of dialogue behavior,
• Internal consistency (within an application system),
• External consistency (of dialogues between application systems),
• Metaphorical consistency (of dialogues with the real working world).

▸ A dialogue is conducive to learning if it supports and guides the user in learning to use the interactive system.

Recommendations on compliance with the dialogue principle: The dialogue should provide sufficient feedback on intermediate and final results of actions so that users learn from successfully performed actions. If it fits the tasks and learning objectives, the interactive system should allow the user to try out dialogue steps without adverse effects. Example: When users reserve a room using a hotel room reservation system, users receive step-by-step feedback to refine their request and more and more details about the progress of successful room reservation.

▸ A dialogue is controllable if the user is able to start the dialogue flow and influence its direction and speed until the goal is reached.

There are system controlled, user-controlled and hybrid dialogues. Usually, there is a hybrid dialogue—only the dominance of the control system varies. The speed of the system shall be adaptable to the working speed of the user (no "working cycle" shall be specified by the system). The working route and means must be freely selectable. Interruptible and restartable partial dialogues (control information) must be possible, as must the cancelation of actions ("undoability").

▸ A dialogue is error-tolerant if the intended work result can be achieved despite recognizably incorrect entries either with no or with minimal correction effort on the part of the user.

Examples: When an error occurs, the interactive system should provide a constructive, accurate, and understandable explanation. If a user action can have serious consequences, the interactive system should offer an explanation and give a confirmation before carrying out the action. Errors must be made understandable to the user (for rectification). In the case of automatically corrected errors, a message must be sent without interfering with the dialogue flow. Error messages should attract attention (e.g., by color, flashing). It is also helpful to be able to select the level of detail of error messages.

▸ A dialogue is customizable when users can customize human–system interaction and presentation of information to their individual abilities and needs.

Beu et al. (1999) point out in their guidance on the application of ISO standard 9241 that the principles of dialogue should not always be regarded as equivalent in their relevance to the design of dialogue systems. Their relative relevance is determined by the characteristics of the work task and the characteristics of the potential users. The use of an adaptive learning program by learners from different cultures, for example, represents a scenario in which the guidelines of expectation conformity and the individualization of the system are of primary importance.

> A dialogue is expectation-conform to the degree, as it corresponds to the knowledge from past operational sequences, the training and the experience of the user, as well as generally recognized conventions. (Beu et al. 1999, p. 18, translated by the author).

4.2   Ergonomics

▸ Ergonomics deals with the relationship between human characteristics and artifacts.

Ergonomics develops methods and techniques to allow adaptations between humans and artifacts—often in the form of tools, complex systems, organizations or procedures. In classical ergonomics, the main focus is on anthropometry, which deals with peculiarities such as human muscle power and human perception.

The user interface can be seen from two different points of view:

- Design aspect: Design everything that is relevant to the user.
- Human aspect: What does the user need to understand and what ability does he need?

These aspects must be considered together, otherwise, the user may not understand the system properties. According to Susanne Maaß, software ergonomics is about optimizing the interplay of all components that make up the work situation of computer users: Human, task, technology and organizational framework. Software ergonomics is expressly not limited—as often wrongly assumed—to the treatment of presentation aspects of interactive software (cf. Maaß 1993, pp. 191–205). Winograd and Flores (1991) justify the necessity of considering the results of software ergonomics research by the fact that better understanding and more user context-oriented theories for the development of HMI systems and their user interfaces result from it.

▸ Software ergonomic criteria or guidelines are used to design, evaluate and compare user interfaces and their dialogues.

"The main task of software ergonomics is to provide recommendations and guidelines for modeling dialogues and to develop criteria for their evaluation. Since important basic conditions for the employment of a computer system are very numerous and variable, generally only minimum requirements and unclear recommendations can be given (Herczeg 1994, p. 103). Among the framework conditions relevant here is Herczeg's assessment of the users' mental abilities to absorb and process information, but also the task that the system is intended to accomplish (e.g., learning specific content) (cf. the action model in Sect. 4.1.2).

Software ergonomics research fulfills the following tasks:

• Exploration of the characteristics of user- and task-oriented software,
• Development of procedures for the design of user interfaces,
• Software support of the procedures,
• Optimization of the work situation of computer users.

Software ergonomics deals with people and technology in relation to the tasks to be performed in the work situation. The results are highly sought-after in practice because, due to their normative character, they represent guidelines and checklists which can be applied immediately—adapted to the respective situation. Standards (national and international standards), recommendations (nonbinding), design rules and tools (development tools, building blocks) cover the areas of technology (optimization and new development of hardware for human–computer interaction), human beings (adaptation to human perceptions, thought processes, learning processes and problem-solving) and work (adaptation to tasks and work organization). By considering these results unnecessary physical or mental strain, high training effort, unnatural working methods, shifts in the relevance of work processes, senseless division of activities and waste of human thinking ability by routine work are to be avoided. Software should be written in a way that no help function must be used, or no manual is necessary because it is self-explanatory and all other design principles according to ISO 9241 are fulfilled.

▸ The main principle of software ergonomics is that the software must be adapted to the people and not vice versa.

4.2.1 Design Rules

General dialogue design objectives described in official standards, although explained by a large number of explanatory examples, are not suitable as instructions for the person who has to develop a user interface. Although they give hints as to what can be done wrong in the design of a surface, due to the necessity to remain sufficiently general as a standard and not to use technical or paradigm-specific features, they do not offer the developer a design orientation and enable him to use the appropriate design means in a concrete design situation.

▸ Generic recommendations (such as guidelines, norms, standards, dialogue principles, etc.) must be broken down by experts (such as usability professionals, cf. Sect. 4.4.4) to the specific design situation and filled with the appropriate knowledge.

For example, a correct but generic recommendation such as "Surface design is all the more profitable the less time and memory must be spent on the interaction itself and the more exclusively the user's attention can be devoted to the planning and execution of his work task" could be expressed in a concrete design situation as follows[3]: A user wants to rent a car from 21 October 2016. On an American car rental website, the user enters 21-10-2016 as the start date for the rental. The error message is "invalid date". The problem is that the site requests the date in US format month-day-year. The best concrete solution from the point of view of usability could be to prevent this interaction between the user and the website by addressing the problem and providing a graphical calendar from which the user can select the date.

Similarly, in the case of dialogue principles, as described in Sect. 4.1.7, which are also quite general and can only serve as a guide in the user analysis to be carried out in a specific application case, expert advice must be called into generate the right solutions for specific design cases.

"In order to use these principles in practice, they need to be interpreted in relation to the context of use. Simply applying guidelines will not lead to good design" (Preece et al. 1994, p. 488). The design guidelines drawn up by (Shneiderman 1998) have been largely incorporated into the content of ISO Standard 9241, Part 110. They are less abstract and therefore easier to follow. On the other hand, such a specification also creates the danger of misinterpretation in more complex situations (cf. Herczeg 1994, p. 114).

In the following, for example, the dialogue principles of ISO 9241-110 are supplemented by further specifications proposed by Preece et al. (1994):

---

[3]The example corresponds to the content of the public CPUX-F exam question #30, version 3.15 EN, 23 March 2018, publisher: UXQB e. V., contact: info@uxqb.org, https://uxqb.org/wp-content/uploads/documents/CPUX-F_EN_Public-Test-Questions.pdf, last access 9th February 2019.

1. "Try to maintain consistency": This rule requires that users be confronted with similar action sequences in similar situations. In menus, prompts or help information, compliance with identical terms should be ensured. The same applies to colors, layout, fonts, etc. In this context (Preece et al. 1994) calls for the use of understandable metaphors that help the user to create a mentalModelmental model of the system structure that can serve as an additional orientation aid in addition to consistency.

2. "Provide abbreviations": As the frequency of use increases, the need for an abbreviation of action sequences that lead to the desired interaction result grows. A system should therefore take into account the different levels of experience of the different user groups and provide experienced users with abbreviations such as function keys ("shortcuts") or macros.

3. "Provide informative feedback": Each user action should be followed by a visible response from the system. The visualization of usage objects whose state can be changed by the user by means of direct manipulation is particularly suitable for displaying informative system feedbackSystemfeedback.

4. "Make sure dialogues are complete": Action sequences should be arranged in such a way that the beginning, the middle and the end are recognizable. An IT feedback at the end of a sequence of actions, for example, signals the successful conclusion of a dialogue, which at the same time has a motivating effect on the user.

5. "Do error-avoiding designDesignerror-avoiding, offer simple error handling": In principle, users should not be able to make serious mistakes. All user errors should be detected as such by the system and corrected accordingly, e.g., by notices and instructions or by preventing a change in the system state. The system should, however, allow less serious user errors to go through, as these also promote the learning of the functionality, among other things.

6. "Allow simple reset of actions": It should be possible in principle to undo actions. The certainty that wrong interaction steps can be reversed at any time enables users to work with the system without fear and promotes explorative user behavior.

7. "Support user-controlled dialoguesDialogueuser-controlled": Experienced users attach great importance to controlling the dialogue system, i.e., initiating actions or retrieving the desired information at any time as required. Unexpected system reactions or lengthy data entry procedures, on the other hand, lead to dissatisfaction and demotivation.

8. "Reduce the information burden of short-term memory": The limitation of human short-term memory (the rule is that users cannot memorize more than 7 ± 2 items of information) requires that the user is able at any time to understand content presentation and which interaction steps lie behind him and which he can carry out next (cf. Beu et al. 1999, S. 17). Basically, if required, simple online access to all relevant information such as syntax forms for commands or abbreviations should be possible.

4.3 Usability

When assessing the usability of a software system, it is analyzed how accurately and completely the user's work goals are achieved (effectiveness), how the user's effort is related to the work equipment used (efficiency and how satisfied the user is with the application (satisfaction). It is emphasized that user-friendliness is primarily dependent on the context of software use (cf. Beu et al. 1999, p. 25), i.e., the system can be used appropriately, as (Bevan 1995) writes: "Usability means that the product can be used for its intended purpose in the real world" (Bevan 1995, p. 2).

Usability is a product quality of interactive systems. It is defined in ISO 9241-11:1998 (formerly ISO 13407):

- ▸ Usability is the extent to which a product can be used by specific users in a specific context to achieve specific goals effectively, efficiently and satisfactorily. (DIN 1999, p. 94).

Satisfaction is defined as freedom from interference and a generally positive attitude towards system use.

A definition by Nielsen (1997), for example, summarizes the topic of usability even more broadly and generally (in the direction of "user-friendliness"): "Usability is the measure of the quality of the user experience when interacting with something —whether a Web site, a traditional software application, or any other device the user can operate in some way or another." (Nielsen 1997).[4]

The essential core statement in which all definitions agree is that the user is to be considered in interaction with the used (mostly software). The user, what is being used and the environment form a unit and, together with the tasks to be performed, are referred to as the context of use (cf. Sect. 4.3.2).

With the human-centered design process (user-centered design), the focus during development is on the requirements of the user and not on technical specifications. The user is involved in the design process as early as possible. Technology is seen as a tool to support the tasks of the user (social and organizational context is included—people and technology form socio-technical systems). Usability is the yardstick by which technology must be measured. The usability engineering process has an iterative course with strong user participation (see Sect. 4.4).

4.3.1 Properties of Systems with a High Degree of Usability

By default, usability comprises three criteria. Effectiveness refers to the accuracy and completeness of the results. Efficient refers to the necessary resources (e.g., time expenditure, concentration expenditure, etc.) which had to be spent in order to

---

[4]Accordingly, this could include a paper questionnaire or a dustpan. In the context of ISO 9241, however, usability primarily concerns software ergonomic systems, i.e., human–machine systems.

achieve a goal (i.e., the relation between expenditure and result). Satisfaction—difficult to describe and difficult to measure—but a very important criterion of good usability, refers to freedom of obstacles. Although this aspect is so significant, it is often overlooked, underestimated or misjudged by developers—especially in the cultural context.

▸ Users evaluate the quality of a software system based on the degree to which it helps them perform their tasks and the pleasure they experience when using it.

This assessment is largely determined by the quality of the user interface. Good user interfaces contribute to the quality of a system in the following way:

- Increased efficiency: If the system fits the way its users work and if it has a good ergonomic design, users can perform their tasks efficiently. You don't lose any time fighting with the functionality and its appearance on the screen.
- Improved productivity: A good interface does not distract the user, but rather allows him to concentrate on the task at hand.
- Fewer errors: Many so-called "human errors" can be attributed to poor user interface quality. Avoidance of inconsistencies, ambiguities and so on reduces usage problems.
- Less training: A bad user interface makes learning more difficult. A well-designed user interface encourages its users to create appropriate models and supports the learning process, thus shortening the exercise time.
- Improved acceptance: Users prefer systems with well-designed user interfaces. Such systems make it easy to find information and make it available in a way that is easy to use.

A system in which interaction takes place on a level that is understandable to the user is accepted more quickly than a system in which this is not the case.

4.3.2   Context of Use

The context of use includes the user himself, his work tasks, the resources (tools) available to him as well as the physical and social environment (Fig. 4.3). The acquisition of user properties also plays an important role in the usability and acceptance of a software system. According to Herczeg (1994, p. 37), the main user associations to be examined in the context of this are:

- The user's area of responsibility,
- The knowledge background of the users,
- The computer knowledge and experience of the users in the use of a particular application system,
- The users' tasks, expectations, preferences with regard to the functionality and characteristics of the system.

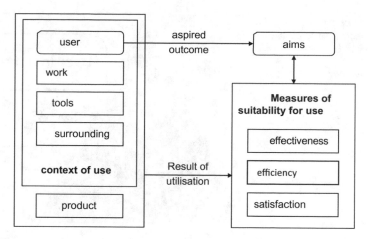

Fig. 4.3   Application frame for usability (according to DIN 1999)

▸ A usability problem occurs when aspects of a system make it unpleasant, inefficient, cumbersome, or impossible for users with sufficient prior knowledge to achieve the goals for which the system was designed in a typical context of use (Sarodnick and Brau 2011).

In the specialist literature on intercultural research, empirical studies confirm the effects of culturally influencing factors on HMI (e.g., Honold 2000; Röse 2002; Heimgärtner 2007a). The perception of the usability of a system also changes according to the cultural background of the recipient (cf. Badre and Barber 1998; Vöhringer-Kuhnt 2002; Clemmensen 2010a, b). Badre and Barber (1998) empirically demonstrated the direct influence of cultural markers on the performance of user interaction with the system and thus on the connection between culture and usability. Vöhringer-Kuhnt (2002) stated, for example, that Hofstede's individualism index is related to user satisfaction and usability of the product and has a significant influence on usability in an intercultural context.

4.3.3   User Experience

However, it is too superficial to understand usability as the sole quality requirement for interactive systems in the sense of the standard. The existence of objective quality features does not ensure the actual positive experience of these features by the user, because users also have "user experiences" (UX) with interactive systems, which are meaningfully embedded in an overall context and do not all refer to whether and how a usage goal has been achieved. Hassenzahl et al. (2003) show

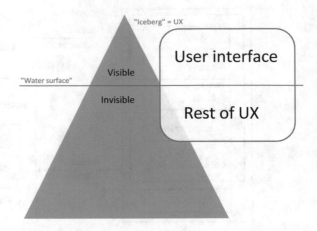

Fig. 4.4 User experience involves more than just experiencing the user interface

that people rather strive to improve their own knowledge and abilities (stimulation) and to express their selfhood (identity). Therefore, a distinction can be made between "pragmatic" qualities (utility, usability) and "hedonic" qualities (stimulation and identity) of systems. Technical products should therefore be both novel, interesting and stimulating, as well as communicate (help) the identity of the user in order to create a positive usage attitude. The user experience therefore includes more than just experiencing the user interface (Fig. 4.4).

There is now a broad consensus on the importance of these nonfunctional hedonic aspects (Hassenzahl et al. 2003; Preim and Dachselt 2010). Various authors argue for making experience the object of design rather than the thing itself (e.g., Norman 2002; Buxton 2010).

▸ According to DIN EN ISO 9241-210 (DIN 2010), the user experience includes all effects that an interactive product has on the user both before (anticipated use) and during or after use (identification with the product or dissociation) (Fig. 4.5).

Good usability as product quality is therefore an important factor, but only one of the factors that determine or influence the user experience.

4.4   Usability Engineering Process

▸ Usability engineering is the methodical way to generate the property of usability. It is a subprocess of the development and design of technical systems and supplements classical engineering—for example software engineering—with ergonomic perspectives.

It provides approaches, methods, techniques, and activities for a user-oriented development process. Part 210 of DIN EN ISO 9241 (DIN 2010) contains a set of

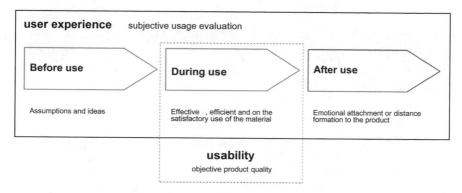

Fig. 4.5 View of DIN EN ISO 9241-210 on Usability and User Experience

requirements and recommendations for a human-centered design process (HCD often referred to as "user-centered design" (UCD)) of computer-based systems. In this process, both hardware and software components of the system are taken into account.

Figure 4.6 shows the essential process steps of a human-centered design that are necessary to consistently ensure the usability of interactive systems during their development.

In culture-related contexts, many questions regarding levels of interaction, mentality and thinking as well as action in the application of "usability engineering" methods—and especially in the use of the "usability engineering" process—remain only partially answered at best.

How do different cultures influence or hinder navigation within applications? Are there significant improvements compared to applications in which intercultural differences were not taken into account adaptively? Can users from other cultures have different experiences with applications from their own or foreign cultures? Such questions must be answered if one wants to provide useful hints to developers and designers of intercultural user interfaces.

Some of these questions have already been answered (see, e.g., Heimgärtner 2012) but many are still open, especially regarding the tolerability of the human-centered process in different cultural contexts.

Explanation models for the culturally influenced difference of experience in a usage situation as well as the methods and processes of an intercultural usability engine are so far hardly found in enough detail in the literature. The often-decisive cultural influences on the usability of technical systems exist, particularly in the industrial context, but both remain too unknown and insufficiently explained. The analysis of cultural dimensions or cultural standards and the resulting derivation of implications for usability engineering is a methodical approach for incorporating findings based on cultural theory into the practice of intercultural usability engineering processes. Knowing the cultural differences of HMI also helps to improve the intercultural usability of technical systems. Companies that develop such

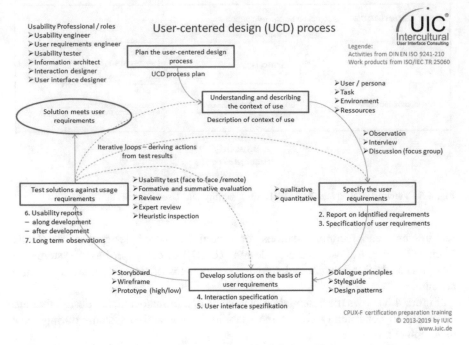

Fig. 4.6 Human-centered design process according to ISO 9241-210. (*Source* IUIC)

systems should therefore be sensitized to the fact that it is almost impossible to dispense with cultural differences for successful global product marketing. Results of the author are presented in Chap. 6 (IUID in theory: Research in science).

4.4.1   Principles of the Human-Centered Design Process

▸ The human-centered design process follows six principles, which must also be taken into account in the intercultural context.

(i)   The design is based on an explicit understanding of the user, the task and the environment: The explicit understanding of the user, the task and the environment remains one of the greatest challenges—especially in intercultural contexts—because of the different explicit, implicit or even concealed knowledge of facts or processes resulting from different worldviews, assumptions, methods and processes (Heimgärtner et al. 2011).

(ii)   The user is involved throughout the entire design and development process. Nevertheless, cultural behavior exists that contradicts the expected and required user behavior throughout the entire design and development process

(Hofstede et al. 2010). Users of different cultures understand things differently and behave accordingly in certain design and development situations (Honold 1999b), which in turn affects the next principle of human-centered design.

(iii)   The design is driven and refined by user-centric evaluation: in this case, there are cultural differences in the way one responds to questions or surveillance (Clemmensen and Goyal 2005). The phenomenon of "saving face" (Victor 1998) must also be taken into account so that the evaluation methods can be adapted or changed accordingly in good time.

(iv)   The process is iterative: this principle seems superficially not to be particularly problematic for application in different cultures, because the need for iterative learning concerns users around the world. Nevertheless, it must be considered, whether problems arise here when this phenomenon is examined more closely. For example, different learning styles that affect iteration cycles (e.g., iteration duration or iteration frequency) may come into play.

(v)   The design faces the complete user experience: this principle seems to be universally valid for all users of all cultures. The perception and reactions with regard to the expected use of a product, a system or a service can, however, be different depending on the requirements of use in the corresponding cultural context. This increases the effort required to implement this principle.

(vi)   The design group comprises interdisciplinary skills and perspectives: Empathy and sincere openness are necessary in order to be able to understand objects from other disciplines, which is all the more difficult and important in intercultural contexts due to the complexity of cultures (Thomas et al. 2010). In addition, some cultures are more closed than open (Hofstede et al. 2010; Trompenaars and Hampden-Turner 2012; Hall and Hall 2009).

The human-centered design process comprises the following main tasks:

- Understanding and describing the context of use,
- Specifying user requirements,
- Developing solutions based on user requirements,
- Testing solutions against user requirements.

In the following, the planning of this process and its main tasks will be analyzed with regard to their usability in intercultural contexts and some ideas on cultural effects on this "usability engineering process" (human-centered design process) will be presented. The weaknesses of the process resulting from intercultural use are identified in order to identify suggestions for improvement. After a brief description of the respective process step, an assessment of the possible cultural effects on it and possibly applicable implications for the process, its actual products as well as the overall product achieved follows.

4.4.2 Planning the Human-Centered Design Process

   (i) General: The phases of the product life cycle seem to be independent of culture because they reflect generic human behavior:

- Capturing an idea (conception),
- Gathering the means necessary for the realization of the idea (analysis),
- Planning the physical realization of the idea (design),
- Implementation of the idea itself (implementation),
- Verification of the implementation on the basis of the intended idea (evaluation),
- Supporting the idea until it is no longer in demand (maintenance).

       Each person follows these steps independently of the respective culture. And there are still cultural differences to consider here. For example, unlike Germans, Japanese people plan very long before they implement something (Kuhnert 2004).

   (ii) Responsibility: Responsibility is very strongly influenced by cultur e. Cultures with high power distance and high uncertainty avoidance show a different attitude towards assuming responsibility than cultures with low power distance and low uncertainty avoidance (Hofstede et al. 2010).

  (iii) Content of the plan and integration of the project plan: In accordance with the respective world view, different methods must be applied in order to achieve reasonable results (Heimgärtner et al. 2011). For example, a plan can be very detailed or very agile. Its acceptance depends on the respective culture. Negotiations and the conclusion of treaties constitute a further area which, in addition to the agreement on time restrictions for iterative process cycles in different cultures, can pose problems depending on monocausal or multicausal thinking style (Röse 2005).

  (iv) Timing and resources: The cultural influence is described here using cultural models of time recording (mono-chronic vs. poly-chronic, cf. Hall and Hall 2009) and resource consumption (cf. Chap. 2).

▸ In order to establish a stable intercultural engineering process, cultural aspects have to be considered in the phases of the software engineering process as well as in the usability engineering process (human-centered design process) (see also Chaps. 3 and 7).

4.4.3 Human-Centered Design Activities

(i) Understanding the context of use: The aim of this process step is to collect all the requirements, interests, expectations and behavior patterns of the most diverse user groups.

In an international context, it is important to note that not only one homogeneous user group exists. In order to specify the cultural context of use in the corresponding usage situations, it is important to develop a thorough understanding of the individual culture-dependent needs of the users. The current process does not fully cover this aspect of the cross-cultural context because it does not yet place sufficient emphasis on a deeper analysis of the cultural aspects and their influence through the use of HMI dimensions, user interface characteristics, cross-cultural variables, and cultural definitions. HMI dimensions describe the style of human–machine interaction as it can be captured with information frequency, information density and arrangement, and with interaction frequency and interaction speed. User interface characteristics capture relevant attributes of user interfaces: Metaphor, presentation, navigation, interaction, and mental model (Marcus and Baumgartner 2004). Intercultural variables capture the levels of localization: Function, interaction and presentation (Röse and Zühlke 2001). Direct cross-cultural variables directly affect the HMI in terms of color, icon, language, image layout, and interaction speed and frequency. Indirect cross-cultural variations cover HMI-related topics such as operating instructions or packaging. Trompenaars and Hampden-Turner (2012), which refer to human interaction such as universality, neutrality, specificity, continuity, and control. They can be associated with HMI dimensions in order to establish a connection between the cultural imprint of a user and his HMI style (Heimgärtner 2013) and to describe from the cross-cultural context the analytical basis of the specification of the context of use and thus support the next activity:

(ii) Specification of user requirements: The challenge in this human-centered activity is to gain a deep understanding of the complexity of the task at hand and its requirements (see Schoper and Heimgärtner 2013) through a market analysis of the current situation with regard to existing products, main competitors, environmental factors such as politics, legislation, economic trends, and finally sociological and technological developments on the target market.

Recommendations from ISO 9241-210 can be extended to tasks and roles in cross-cultural contexts. Elements of the "usage-centered design" process such as culture-specific user tasks and user roles as well as an additional culture model can be used to systematize the intercultural "usability engineering" process (cf. Windl and Heimgärtner 2013).

(iii) Creating design solutions: In this process step, a culturally diverse design team has to generate new, innovative design solutions for user interfaces.

The better and more precise the product objectives are defined at the beginning of the development project, the easier it becomes to compare them with the actual state of the design. Communication represents a challenge within the various teams: Misunderstandings arising from the use of a common nonnative language (at least for the majority of employees) will be common and lead to anger and frustration. The distribution of subtasks and feedback loops is also negatively affected by this which then leads to development activity ad absurdum because it is misdirected by wrong or missing feedback (or its interpretation).

(iv) Design evaluation: In a cross-cultural context, it is crucial to evaluate the design status from the perspectives of different cultural user groups, which are defined in such a way that the design fits the different and sometimes contradictory requirements of all stakeholders.

4.4.4   Roles in the Human-Centered Design Process

However, stubborn adherence to standards does not guarantee good usability or a good user experience. This requires experienced people who master the craft of usability engineering and are able to implement product-relevant processes, norms, standards and design guidelines in practice.

▸ The Usability Professional is a person who is qualified to methodically derive, implement or verify the usability of interactive systems (hardware and software).[5]

> According to the human-centered design process, a usability professional is typically specialized in one or more of the following areas of work:
>
> - Analysis—Survey of context of use, derivation of user requirements,
> - Design—Conception of the interaction between humans and interactive systems, structuring and presentation of action-guiding information,
> - Evaluation—Performing inspection-based evaluations (without users) and usability tests (with users),
> - Process design and application of methods—definition, introduction and operation of a human-centered design process.

---

[5]Usability Professionals are organized in professional associations (e.g., German UPA, https://www.germanupa.de/, last access 9th of February 2019). The UXQB (International Usability and UX Qualification Board) has created the personal certification program "Certified Professional for Usability and User Experience" (CPUX) for this purpose (see www.uxqb.org, last access 9th of February 2019). Recognized training providers (e.g., IUIC, see https://www.iuic.de, last access 9th of February 2019) offer appropriate preparatory seminars for the certification examinations.

The activities of a usability professional are based on the international standards for the usability of interactive systems and their design process (ISO 9241) as well as up-to-date, published specialist knowledge.

Usability Professionals work in projects for the production of interactive systems and associated services and processes for use in numerous project contexts (e.g., interactive systems for commercial use, household appliances, interactive games, mobile devices). A usability professional can fill one or more roles. Some of the most important roles are addressed below.

The Usability Engineer is responsible for the human-centered design process in a cross-sectional function. He is competent and experienced in the process steps and available methods of human-centered design and knows design rules for user experience so that he can plan the development projects under the aspect of human-centered design and ensure the quality of the execution of human-centered design related activities. This includes the integration of human-centered design into the company's product development process, the definition of success criteria for such projects and the training of project teams involved. He is in a position to identify the relevant work results for the respective project, suitable procedures as well as working aids and definitions (e.g., principles of dialogue and design rules) for the human-centered design process and to define them for a project.

The Usability Tester evaluates user interfaces at various stages of implementation. In consultation with the process participants, he defines the structure of the evaluations and is responsible for the valid execution of the evaluations. The usability tester creates usability reports after executing "formative usability evaluations" during the development having the aim of product improvement as well as a usability report on the final "summative usability evaluation". He communicates these results to the stakeholders (project participants) or is responsible for their communication.

This can take place, for example, within the framework of an acceptance test in cooperation with the User Requirements Engineer, who is responsible for the collection of the context of use and the specification of user requirements.

Further essential roles are user interface designer, information architect and interaction designer. For further information see UPA Usability Professionals' Association (2009).

4.4.5 Usability Heuristics

Software ergonomic guidelines not only serve as a working aid for modeling dialogues (cf. Herczeg 1994) but can also be used to evaluate and compare existing dialogue systems (Nielsen 1994). In this context, heuristic evaluation is also frequently spoken of. The term heuristics derives from the Greek term for "discovery" and, in the context of usability engineering, refers to "procedures or principles that help users to systematically work on a discovery, a decision or a solution" (Geest and Spyridakis 2000, p. 1).

▸ Usability heuristics are derived from experience and represent generally accepted rules of thumb, which serve the implementation of dialogue principles but are more concrete and easier to apply.

The ten usability heuristics according to Nielsen (1994), which are listed below, overlap with the rules established by Shneiderman (1998) but offer additional specifications in some points.

1. Visibility of the system status: A system should keep the user "up-to-date" on current events by providing appropriate feedback within a reasonable time.
2. Consistency between the system and the real world: A system should "speak the user's language", i.e., the dialogue with the user should be simple, clear and understandable, both at the linguistic and conceptual level. Every piece of information should be presented in a logical sequence, system messages and designations should be formulated simply, and technical terminology should be avoided as far as possible. The consideration of culture-specific notions of the real world or a logical representation is of high relevance for the development of systems for an international audience.
3. User control over the system and user freedom: Since users often mistakenly select wrong system functions and can thus unintentionally reach the wrong program positions, a system should offer a clearly marked "emergency exit" so that they can leave the unwanted state at any time. An example is the button to cancel a dialogue.
4. Consistency and Standards: The user should not be surprised about different word choices, fonts, graphics or system actions, which however should mean the same.
5. Error prevention: Better than providing suitable error messages is a carefully conceived design that does not allow the user to perform any erroneous actions in the first place.
6. Recognition instead of Reminder: All objects, actions, and options available should always be visible to the user, so he doesn't have to remember the information that was relevant in another area of the dialogue. Also, all instructions for the use of the system should be clear, uncomplicated, and always visible or easy to find.
7. Flexibility and efficiency of use: For advanced users, the system should offer shortcuts that are not visible to the beginner but allow the experienced user to perform frequent actions faster. In this way, both user groups can be satisfied.
8. Aesthetic and minimalist design: Dialogues should only contain the information that is relevant and necessary, as any extra information distracts the user's attention from the important one and reduces its relative visibility.
9. Supporting the user in the detection and correction of errors: A system should provide precise and constructive error messages that provide comprehensible, formmulated hints for solving the problem.
10. System help and documentation: Although it speaks for a system if its functionality and structure are self-explanatory and it can be used without

documentation or the help function, these tools should always be made available to the user. It is important that a documentation or help function is user-oriented, e.g., with proposed solutions in the form of predefined step sequences.

4.5 Dialogue Principles and Their Use

▸ ISO 9241-110 " […] deals with the ergonomic design of interactive systems and describes principles of dialogue design which are fundamentally independent of a particular dialogue technique and which should be applied in the analysis, design and evaluation of interactive systems". (German version of DIN EN ISO 9241-110/2008-09, p. 4, DIN 2006, p. 4).

It is questionable whether Part 110 of ISO 9241 covers all contexts of use. It is conceivable, for example, that safety-critical applications or special cases of collective cooperation could be envisaged, as well as new forms and areas of application of HMI (such as gesture control and ambient assisted living), in which the seven dialogue principles described therein would not be effective or additional ones would become necessary. Culture also influences the entire context of use. If the dialogue principles of ISO 9241-110 are to be applied, then the intercultural context must always be taken into account. To date, however, questions relating to the level of interaction, user mentality, cognitive capacity and behavior of users when using dialogue principles in cultural contexts have often not been answered, or only partially. How, for example, can or must the "controllability" dialogue principle be correctly implemented in an intercultural context in order to evaluate how different cultures interfere with each other and impair navigation within applications? How are other principles of dialogue such as "appropriateness in individualization" involved or how can they be applied in an intercultural context? Are there any significant improvements when comparing an application that does not take international differences into account with an adapted version? Can users from different cultures have different experiences when interacting with applications of their own or foreign culture? These questions concern the entire user experience and affect all dialogue principles. Such questions regarding the framework conditions for the use of dialogue principles, dialogue requirements and dialogue techniques must be answered before these dialogue principles can be correctly used in intercultural contexts. Many such questions require an answer regarding the compatibility of dialogue principles in intercultural contexts. In the following are some initial thoughts that lead to a basic answer to the question of the possible impact of cultural influences on the principles of dialogue in ISO 9241-110 and their use in intercultural contexts.

▸ Dialogue principles are a collection of general objectives (intended outcomes) for designing dialogues.

ISO 9241-110 describes the relationships between the dialogue principles:

The principles of dialogue design are not strictly independent of each other and can overlap in terms of content. It may be necessary to balance principles in order to optimize usability. The applicability and significance of each individual principle depend on the respective context of use, the user groups, and the selected dialogue technique. This means that the following points of view must be taken into account: Objectives of the organization; user interests of the intended user group; tasks to be supported; available techniques and resources. The applicability and significance of each principle are determined by the specific context of use. Each of the principles must be taken into account in the analysis, design, and evaluation, but may vary in importance depending on the context of use and other design requirements. In practice, in design situations, concessions will be made for an interactive system. (DIN EN ISO 9241-110/2008-09, p. 8).

▸ Dialogue principles can often not be strictly separated in their application. In addition to this context-related variability in the use of dialogue principles, culturally sensitive aspects must be taken into account and analyzed in the definition of user dialogues so that the dialogue principles can be used correctly according to the intercultural context.

In the following, the accomplishment of this task is demonstrated using the example of the first dialogue principle of ISO 9241-110 ("suitability for the tasks") to confirm the hypothesis that dialogue principles are "culturally sensitive", i.e., that their expressions change in intercultural contexts because they contain terms whose meanings or reference variables also change in intercultural contexts. A special method using cultural models is used to analyze the use of dialogue principles in intercultural contexts. Culture-sensitive terms in the definitions of the dialogue principles are set in bold and italics in the following. They are exemplary for culturally strongly influenced concepts.

4.5.1 Example: Suitability for the Tasks

An interactive *system* is appropriate to the task if it supports the *user* in *completing* his *task*, i.e., if *functionality* and *dialogue are* based on the characteristic properties of the task (instead of the technology). (DIN EN ISO 9241-110/2008-09, p. 8)

▸ A dialogue should show the user the information related to the successful completion of the task. But both the presentation of the information, the requirement to fulfill the task and the task itself can be culture-specific (see Windl and Heimgärtner 2013). If the requirements of the task are culture-specific, the required quality, quantity, and type of information to be presented are also culture-specific.

In addition, according to the ISO standard, any presentation of information is to be avoided which is not required for the completion of the relevant task. However, this facet of the principle of dialogue must be weakened somewhat in view of some cultural dimensions such as the avoidance of uncertainty (Hofstede et al. 2010), network density (Hall und Hall 2009) or relationship orientation (Halpin and Winer 1957). Nevertheless, the note and the first part of the example from the standard also apply to intercultural contexts:

> NOTE: Displaying inappropriate information can lead to reduced performance and unnecessary mental stress. EXAMPLE: In a context of use where travelers want to book a hotel room for a specific date, the slide log system only displays hotels with free rooms for that specific date. Information about fully booked hotels in this region or additional travel information, e.g. special sights, will only be displayed on request. (German version of DIN EN ISO 9241-110/2008-09, p. 9).

The number of displayed information units as well as their frequency and arrangement can also vary in different cultures (see Heimgärtner 2012). The dialogue principle "expectation conformity" also plays a role here. A user of a particular culture may expect information at a point where a user of another culture expects information only upon request.

The general objective for dialogue design that input and output formats should be appropriate can easily be achieved if localization tools (see Symmonds 2002; Fissgus and Seewald-Heeg 2005) and internationalization guidelines (see VDMA 2009; W3C 2010) are taken into account when designing for intercultural contexts.

> EXAMPLE 1: An application for converting currencies for travelers displays the amounts with an accuracy that matches the destination currency (e.g., two decimal places for most European currencies). EXAMPLE 2: A dialogue intended exclusively for the domestic market clearly indicates this to the user. (DIN EN ISO 9241-110/2008-09, p. 9).

At first glance, the automatic assignment of typical input values seems to be culture-independent depending on the task. However, it may be necessary for the system to identify the user so that reasonable specifications can be offered for selection. However, such identity allocation can lead to problems in cultures with a high "uncertainty avoidance" or "power distance" (see Hofstede et al. 2010), which then have an impact on a user's need for information mentioned above and his willingness to provide the system with personal data (e.g., e-mail address or password).

A further subgoal of the dialogue design on task adequacy is: "The dialogue steps required by the interactive system should fit the workflow, i.e., necessary dialogue steps should be included, and unnecessary dialogue steps should be avoided." (DIN EN ISO 9241-110/2008-09, p. 9). The steps necessary to fulfill the task, however, depend on the culturally conditioned concepts of "task" and "necessary steps". Depending on the monocausal or multicausal way of thinking, a user expects more or less steps to fulfill his task (see Röse et al. 2001). Again, the dialogue principle of "expectation conformity" is strongly involved. Here, input and output channels can vary greatly and be burdened differently according to the cultural imprint of the user. For example, there are users with holistic or analytical perceptions (see Nisbett and Miyamoto 2005). In an evaluation of a chat program with regard to the task adequacy of systems and functions, German and Indian engineers showed a significantly different evaluation of the task adequacy of the system as a communication tool in the work context (Brau 2009). While the Indian engineers used the system to create social proximity with their team via the short messages and to save distances with smaller voting volumes, their German colleagues found the relatively frequently arriving text messages to be a source of disturbance and too short to transport relevant information (cf. Hall 1959, high vs. low context orientation). In addition to the low information density, the messages cannot be standardized. The separation between professional and private communication is less pronounced in Indian culture, which is why flexible communication was rated as far more appropriate to the tasks. There are indications that this is more an influence of labor than of national culture: This reverses the willingness to use among users who have been abroad for a long time: Indian returnees from Germany rate chat systems in the work context less positively than Germans who have lived in India for several years (cf. Kosma 2011).

4.5.2 Discussion and Conclusion

If ISO 9241-110 is to be regarded as an international standard, it must be possible to apply the contents of ISO 9241-110 in a meaningful way worldwide, regardless of cultural contexts.

In contrast, however, the analysis of the application of the dialogue principle of "suitability of the tasks" in the intercultural context on the basis of cultural dimensions at the national level shows the following:

▸ The existing dialogue principles defined in ISO 9241-110 must be applied with care in order to be successful in intercultural contexts as well.

If only one of the dialogue principles of ISO 9241-110 cannot be applied internationally because of an intercultural conflict at the national level, optimizations or modifications of all other dialogue principles must also take place (as they are not independently applicable) to ensure that they function at least in international contexts at the national level.

▸ The seven principles of dialogue design DIN EN ISO 9241-10 (DIN 1996) (task adequacy, error tolerance, self-explanatory ability, learning ability, expectation conformity, controllability, and individualizability) are not laws but lead to interculturally variable interpretations. Therefore, they need to be thoroughly analyzed in order to derive recommendations on how to correctly apply these principles of dialogue in international contexts.

Even if these remarks on task adequacy in the cultural context are preliminary and need to be further examined and described in detail in order to be universally valid, they can still serve as a reasonable basis for future research. In addition, the examples presented, which bridge the gap between the principle of dialogue and culture, should be sufficient to give an impression of how principles of dialogue can be affected in intercultural contexts.

▸ It remains to be seen whether the postulated hypothesis that dialogue principles are "culturally sensitive" can be empirically proven, namely that their core characteristics change in intercultural contexts because they contain concepts whose meaning, or reference variables change in intercultural contexts. Until then, a more profound discussion on the relationship between dialogue principles and culture has yet to take place.

4.6 Intercultural Usability Engineering

The process of intercultural usability engineering comprises the collection of usability requirements, the design of global and culture-specific user interfaces as well as the international evaluation of the products. This results in important requirements for the individual employee such as intercultural action competence, internationalization competence, experience in the field of HMI design as a software architect or software developer, empathy for other cultures, good knowledge of the target languages and intercultural communication as well as decision-making power. In addition, the same conditions (functional, conceptual and operational equivalence) must be established for the investigation of different user groups by using a mix of methods, building a local team and interpreting, discussing and evaluating the results in bi- or multinational teams, e.g., together with the developers. In order to make the right decisions within this process at an early stage and to learn from mistakes, an evaluation of the process results is necessary right from the start.

For the developer of an intercultural user interface there is therefore a considerable need for intercultural knowledge in order to (better) understand the user of another culture. He also needs intercultural communication skills in order to initiate and maintain an exchange of information with the user, which should lead to the developer ultimately knowing exactly which product the user needs (Honold 1999c; Röse 2002). But also the knowledge and use of relevant methods in this area is unavoidable and must be conveyed accordingly. The evaluation of a survey conducted in July 2007 with 30 software developers revealed that the concept of "Internationalization" is more well known than the concepts "Intercultural User Interface Design", "Software Ergonomics" or "Usability Engineering", but all these aspects are considered to be very important (Heimgärtner 2007b). The significance of each of these four areas was not particularly high in the training of the test persons. Furthermore, the use of appropriate methods within the software engineering process was very moderate. However, the interviewees would like to be more involved with these areas and would like them to be more firmly anchored in the university curriculum.

▸ Intercultural usability engineering requires knowledge of intercultural differences in human–machine interaction as well as the corresponding methodological competence and its consideration in the design and implementation of the product.

In addition to the usual misunderstandings between developers and users, there are misunderstandings due to cultural conditions. There is not only a different understanding regarding the requirements of the product but also different cultural views and perspectives on it. In addition, it must be ensured that the human–machine interface (colors, dialogue elements, frequency or arrangement of information, etc.) keeps the mental strain on the user as optimal as possible with regard to interaction with the system (Heimgärtner 2005a; Piechulla et al. 2003; Röse und Heimgärtner 2008). The adequate application of usability engineering methods can contribute to achieving this goal.

▸ Through the use of specific intercultural usability engineering, differences in approaches and preferences of different cultures can be addressed more intensively in order to be globally successful (Holzinger 2005; Honold 2000).
▸ "Intercultural" Usability Engineering is a method for designing good usability products for users from different cultures (Honold 2000).

"Intercultural" in this context refers to the special methods necessary to perform usability engineering for different cultures (cf. Honold 1999a). Honold (2000) coined the term "intercultural usability engineering ring", presented cultural differences in the product development process and suggested solutions.

▸ The prerequisite for applying the usability engineering method is knowledge of cultural differences in the HMI.

Critical interaction situations that arise due to problematic user interfaces or are based on the given system functionality are analyzed. One of the most promising methods to preserve cultural differences in HMI is to observe and analyze user interaction with the system.

▸ Differences between cultures can be found by analyzing critical interaction situations (Thomas 1996).

Honold (2000) made the method of analyzing critical interaction situations for cultural differences in HMI available. In the collection of culture-specific user requirements and in the culture-specific evaluation of the concepts used, it must be examined how suitable the improved methods for intercultural usability engineering are. The existing cultural model should be considered in the process of product design in the context of intercultural usability

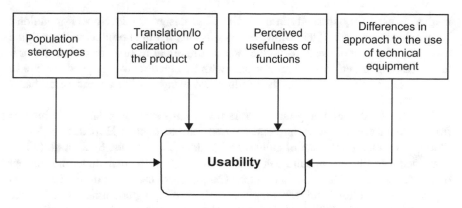

Fig. 4.7 Factors leading to differences in usability between cultural user groups (according to Honold 2000)

engineering. First of all, product developers must be sensitized to the difficulties of cultural influences on product development and product use. Then the developers must be provided with cultural facts that influence the HMI and integrated into the product. The procedures that serve to realize the created knowledge in a concrete product design must be institutionalized. A distinction must be made between the functionality desired by the user regarding the system and the functionality of the system that is actually implemented. Analysis and implementation of the functionality desired by the user in relation to an optimally usable system with joy and simplicity are decisive for software with ergonomic and intercultural characteristics. This requires knowledge about software ergonomics and intercultural user interface design as well as about the application of usability evaluation methods. In contrast, if the currently implemented functionality of a system of a certain culture is used as a basis for the analysis of user interface characteristics, it can lead to erroneous or simply wrong design guidelines if the requirements do not correspond to the actual needs of the users. Therefore, the user requirements of the users or the desired user groups (e.g., Chinese and German) must be determined and taken into account (Fig. 4.7).

The prerequisites for successful intercultural usability engineering are knowledge of the cultural differences of HMI and their consideration in product design and implementation (Honold 2000; Röse 2002; Heimgärtner 2005b) (Fig. 4.7).

The usability of a system depends heavily on how well the developer knows how well the user is getting along with the system. This knowledge can be obtained by observing and questioning the user during his interaction with the system. In this case, the user articulates his or her wishes, which can be used to derive his or her needs with regard to the usability of the system. Unfortunately, even today this method is used very sparingly in industrial HMI design, so developers often don't know what users need. If this knowledge is missing, the final product will not fit the user: The user cannot use it due to the lack of important features or properties, or it takes too long to perform a particular task with this incorrectly designed system. In the worst case, this can lead to the product not being used at all and being badly talked about.

Honold (2000) therefore presented a framework for extracting cultural influences from product use, taking culture and context into account in HMI design. Simon (2000) examined the impact of culture and gender on websites. Shah et al. (2012) examined the influence of culture in global software development under the concept of cultural models. Dasgupta and Gupta (2010) conducted an empirical study on organizational, cultural and technological use in developing countries. Based on the research of Honold (2000) several researchers have invested a lot of effort in identifying the best methods and attitudes for testing usability and user experience in cultural contexts.

One of the most active researchers in this field is Torkil Clemmensen and colleagues. Clemmensen and Goyal (2004) examined cross-cultural "think aloud" narrative techniques in usability tests in order to then develop proposals for an experimental paradigm. Clemmensen et al. (2007) examined usability engineering in a cross-cultural study of the user experience when using information systems. Clemmensen (2010a, b) discovered the components of usability testing in three countries. Clemmensen also worked with Apala Chavan, Anirudha Joshi, Dinesh Katre, Devashish Pandya, Sammeer Chabukswar and Pradeep Yammiyavar to describe interaction design and usability from an Indian perspective (Clemmensen 2008). Yammiyavar et al. (2008) investigated the cultural influence on nonverbal communication in the usability testing situation. Paterson et al. (2011) interpreted cross-cultural usability evaluations based on a case study of a hypermedia system for the management of rare animal species in Namibia. Bidwell et al. (2011) investigated settlement media in Africa in the transfer of rural knowledge to support indigenous rural populations. Röbig et al. (2010) published the results of a workshop on the international understanding of usability and the application of usability methods.

Finally, there is a tendency to consider cross-cultural differences in the development of design methods in general (see Dinet et al. 2011).

▸ Bad or missing intercultural usability engineering within the development process of the product increases the development and maintenance costs considerably due to frequent change requests.

A detailed analysis of product requirements can save up to 80% of the maintenance and implementation costs of such change requirements (cf. Mutschler and Reichert 2004).

▸ The development of intercultural HMI begins long before the context of use and requirements analysis and therefore long before the actual design of the HMI is started.

In addition, the preferences of many people all over the world can be taken into account using intercultural usability engineering methods, which are essential for expansion into larger markets (Holzinger 2005) as well as the extension of universal access (Heimgärtner et al. 2008).

The results of the intercultural HMI design and the software architecture from cultural studies in the HMI are an important prerequisite for the usability and sale of software for global markets. An international software product, which can be used effectively and efficiently by users from different cultures to their satisfaction, increases customer satisfaction as well as functional safety. A satisfied user will not change the product brand because he appreciates the manufacturer's efforts to develop applicable products with optimized HMI.

▶ In an intercultural context, knowledge about the target culture and about which methods can be used for intercultural usability engineering and how is necessary to allow the development of adequate intercultural user interfaces. This is discussed in detail in Chap. 5.

4.7   Summary, Conclusion, and Outlook

Ergonomics deals with the relationship between human characteristics and artifacts. Software ergonomic criteria or guidelines are used to design, evaluate and compare user interfaces and their dialogues. The supreme principle of software ergonomics is that the software must be adapted to people and not the other way around.

The interaction in which information is exchanged between user and system via User Interface (UI) is referred to as "human–machine interaction" (HMI) or "human–computer interaction" (MCI) (cf. Jacko and Sears 2003). The interface between the user and the technical system forms the "user interface" according to ISO standard 9241. The action level model according to Herczeg (2005) describes the steps of man–machine communication. Metaphors represent a known real situation or object, facilitate learning for the user and give a certain direction to his expectations.

Mental models are means of depicting the shared knowledge of communication partners (cf. Johnson-Laird 1983). The product developer is not forced to prognosticate the mental models of the users, but they can empirically collect them systematically with the help of the methods of intercultural usability engineering. Therefore, intercultural usability engineering is indispensable for intercultural product development.

Interactive systems shall be designed to meet all user requirements. The more different the cultural imprint between designer and user is, the higher the transformation effort of the user is to bridge the distances and differences in the interaction on all levels of the action level model. Generic recommendations (such as guidelines, norms, standards, dialogue principles, etc.) must be broken down by experts (such as usability professionals) to the specific design situation and filled with the appropriate knowledge. A usability professional (see Sect. 4.4.4) is a person who is qualified to methodically derive, implement or verify the usability of interactive systems (hardware and software).

A dialogue is the interaction between a user and an interactive system in the form of a sequence of actions by the user (inputs) and responses by the interactive system (outputs) to achieve a goal. Principles of dialogue are general objectives for the design of dialogues. Dialogue principles are derived from experience and are abstract guidelines for dialogue design at the highest level. Dialogue principles often cannot be used strictly separately. The seven principles of the dialogue design DIN EN ISO 9241-10 (DIN 1996) (task adequacy, error tolerance, self-explanatory ability, learning facilitation, expectation conformity, controllability, and individualization) are not laws but lead to interculturally variable interpretations. They therefore need to be thoroughly analyzed in order to make recommendations on how to correctly apply these principles of dialogue in international contexts. For example, a dialogue on the dialogue principle of task proportionality should provide the user with information related to the successful completion of the task. But both the presentation of the information, the requirement to fulfill the task and the task itself can be culture-specific (see Windl and Heimgärtner 2013). If the requirements of the task are culture-specific, the required quality, quantity, and nature of the information to be presented are also culture-specific.

The "adequacy of tasks" in an intercultural context with cultural dimensions at the national level shows that the existing dialogue principles defined in the ISO 9241-110 must be applied with caution in order to be successful in intercultural contexts.

Usability is the extent to which a product can be used by certain users in a certain context of use to achieve certain goals effectively, efficiently and satisfactorily (DIN EN ISO 9241-11 1999, p. 94). Users evaluate the quality of a software system based on the degree to which it helps them perform their tasks and the pleasure they experience in using it. The context of use includes the user himself, his work tasks, the tools at his disposal, and the physical and social environment (Fig. 4.3). A usability problem occurs when aspects of a system make it unpleasant, inconvenient, or impossible for users with sufficient prior knowledge to achieve the goals for which the system was designed in a typical context of use (Sarodnick and Brau 2011).

User Experience (UX) comprises all effects that an interactive product has on the user both before (anticipated use) and during or after use (identification with the product or dissociation) (Fig. 4.5).

Usability engineering is the methodical way to generate the properties of usability and UX. It is a sub-process of the development and design of technical systems and supplements classical engineering—for example, software engineering —with ergonomic perspectives. The human-centered design process (usability engineering process) follows six principles, which must also be taken into account in the intercultural context. In order to establish a stable intercultural engineering process, cultural aspects have to be considered in the phases of the software engineering process as well as the usability engineering process (human-centered design process) (see also Chaps. 3, 4, and 7). Empathy is an essential prerequisite for successful intercultural communication, which promotes successful intercultural HMI design and intercultural usability engineering and, as a consequence, a good user experience. It should therefore be ensured and disseminated that usability professionals receive, know and apply empathy.

The analysis of the human-centered design process (cf. ISO 9241-210) with regard to intercultural management showed that aspects in this process are missing with regard to the cultural context of use (cf. Heimgärtner 2014). In drafting this standard, no particular emphasis has yet been placed on an in-depth analysis of the cultural aspects and their impact within the process, because the necessary concepts such as HMI dimensions, UI characteristics, intercultural variables, and cultural dimensions have not yet been sufficiently received. The examples presented on the principle of dialogue of task adequacy, which bridge the gap between the principle of dialogue and culture, should be sufficient to give an impression of how principles of dialogue should be used in intercultural contexts.

"Intercultural Usability Engineering is a method for designing good usability products for users from different cultures (Honold 2000). Through the use of specific intercultural usability engineering, differences in the approaches and preferences of different cultures can be addressed in order to be globally successful (Holzinger 2005; Honold 2000). The application of this engineering method requires knowledge of cultural differences in HMI as well as the corresponding methodological competence and its consideration in the design and implementation of the product. In an intercultural context, knowledge about the target culture is necessary and about which methods can be used for intercultural usability engineering and how thus permitting the development of adequate intercultural user interfaces. This is discussed in detail in Chap. 5.

The development of intercultural HMI begins even before the context of use and requirements analysis and therefore long before the actual design of the HMI is started. Differences between cultures can be found by analyzing critical interaction situations (Thomas 1996). Due to the intercultural overlapping situation of product definition and product use and in order to meet the expectations of the user, his cultural preferences must be taken into account in product development. To achieve this, the product must be internationalized and localized. This process refers both to the functionality of the device and to the user interface design. The use of methods of intercultural usability engineering ensures the usability of the products. Therefore, intercultural user interface design should be included in the curriculum of HMI design.

Culture influences all phases and all participants in the development of intercultural user interfaces. The knowledge about these influences and the use of the measures does not represent insurmountable problems for a project in theory or in the practical application of methods but motivates to include cultural aspects in research and development. Ultimately, users of any cultural imprint and in any cultural context should be able to use the product—through Intercultural Usability Engineering. Bad or missing intercultural usability engineering within the development process of the product significantly increases the development and maintenance costs due to frequent change requests. Comparative cultural studies by HMI are a necessary prerequisite for improving the intercultural usability of software, which in turn is a necessary prerequisite for global sales opportunities. It is necessary to examine the cultural context of use and the user culture on site. An international software product, which can be used effectively and efficiently by users of different cultures due to the use of intercultural usability engineering, increases both customer satisfaction with the product and its functional security. A satisfied user will not change the manufacturer of the product in the future, because he appreciates his efforts for usable products and optimized user interfaces. Intercultural usability engineering is therefore a must for every product development in the global market.

Even if these initial ideas are a basis for further research, they are of a provisional nature and must therefore be examined in more detail in order to be considered as general statements. For example, it remains to be seen whether the postulated hypothesis that dialogue principles are "culturally sensitive" can be empirically proven, namely that their core characteristics change in intercultural contexts because they contain concepts whose meaning, or reference variables also change in intercultural contexts. Until then, a more profound discussion on the relationship between dialogue principles and culture has yet to take place. In this sense, a thorough discussion is still pending. Nevertheless, some of the ideas suggest that the HMI development process currently defined in ISO 9241-210 could be extended with roles and activities in order to be used successfully worldwide in all cultural contexts and thus meet its international requirements.

In addition, the methods for developing user interfaces should be systematically complemented by cultural aspects to ensure that new systems can be designed for one or more cultures from the outset and that developers can adapt to the various global user requirements and thus react faster to changes using agile methods and modules of usage-centered design.

In any case, it is reasonable for experts in international HMI standardization committees to have intercultural experience and knowledge in the development of intercultural user interfaces and intercultural usability engineering.

Norms	√
ISO 3166	☐
DIN 66234	☐
ISO 9241-8	☐
ISO 9241-10	☐
ISO 9241-11	☐
DIN EN ISO 9241-110	☐
ISO 9241-210	☐

Checklist	√
The principle of human-machine interaction is well known	☐
Concepts and meaning of ergonomics, usability and user experience are well known and introduced	☐
Users, tasks, context and technology are taken into account (PACT)	☐
Dialogue principles and usability heuristics are used and applied	☐
Usability and user experience of the system are given	☐
Influence of culture on usability is known	☐
Influence of culture on usability engineering is well known	☐
· Process	☐
· Methods	☐
· Application	☐
· Interpretation	☐
· Documentation	☐
The influence of culture on the principles of dialogue and their application is well known.	☐
Basic methods and approaches of intercultural usability engineering are known and organizationally installed	☐

References

Andersen PB (1997) A theory of computer semiotics: semiotic approaches to construction and assessment of computer systems. Cambridge University Press, Cambridge/New York

Argyle M, Schmidt C (2002) Body language & communication: the handbook for non-verbal communication, 8th ed, vol 5. Junfermann, Paderborn

Badre A, Barber W (1998) Culturabilty: the merging of culture and usability. In: Proceedings of the 4th conference on human factors and the web. Basking Ridge: AT and T Labs

Bales RF (1950) Interaction process analysis: a method for the study of small groups. Addison-Wesley, Cambridge, MA

Beu A, Görner C, Koller F (1999) The VDU workstation: software development with DIN EN ISO 9241, vol 1. Beuth-Verlag, Berlin/Vienna/Zurich

Bevan N (1995) Usability is quality of use. Paper presented at the proceedings of the 6th international conference of human computer interaction, Amsterdam

Bidwell NJ, Winschiers-Theophilus H, Koch Kapuire G, Rehm M (2011) Pushing per- sonhood into place: situating media in the transfer of rural knowledge in Africa. Int J Hum-Comput Stud. Special Issue on Locative Media. Hrsg Cheverst K, Willis K 69(10):618–631

Blank K (1996) User modeling for adaptive interactive systems: architecture, methods, tools and applications, vol 131. Dissertations on Artificial Intelligence, Sankt Augustin: Infix

Brau H (2009) Daimler AG. Unpublished internal project report

Buxton B (2010) Sketching user experiences: getting the design right and the right design. Morgan Kaufmann, San Francisco. ©2007

Charwat HJ (1992) Lexikon der Mensch-Maschine-Kommunikation. Oldenbourg, Munchen/Wien

Clemmensen T (2008) Interaction design & usability from an Indian perspective—Talks with: Apala Chavan, Anirudha Joshi, Dinesh Katre, Devashish Pandya, Sammeer Chabukswar, Pradeep Yammiyavar C. B. S. Institut for Informatik I. N. F. Department of Informatics I. N. F. Copenhagen Business School (Hrsg). http://blog.cbs.dk/culturalusability_cbsdk/wp-content/uploads/2014/07/interaction-design-and-usability-from-an-indian-perspective.pdf, accessed 29 Feb 2019

Clemmensen T (2010) A comparison of what is part of usability testing in three countries. In: Katre D, Orngreen R, Yammiyavar P, Clemmensen T (Hrsg) Human work interaction design: Usability in social, cultural and organizational contexts, Bd 316. Springer, Heidelberg, S 31–45

Clemmensen T (2010) A comparison of what is part of usability testing in three countries. In: Clemmensen T (Hrsg) Human work interaction design. Springer, Heidelberg, S 31–45

Clemmensen T, Goyal S (2004) Studying cross cultural think-aloud usability testing. In: Proceedings of fourth danish human-computer interaction research symposium, 16th November 2004. Aalborg University, Denmark, S 4

Clemmensen T, Goyal S (2005) Cross cultural usability testing: the relationship between evaluator and test user. Copenhagen Business School, C. B. S. Institut for Informatik I. N. F. Department of Informatics I. N. F.

Clemmensen T, Hertzum M, Hornbæk K, Kumar J, Shi Q, Yammiyavar P (2007). Usability constructs: a cross-cultural study of how users and developers experience their use of information systems

Dasgupta S, Gupta B (2010) Organizational culture and technology use in a developing country: an empirical study. Paper presented at the proceedings of SIG GlobDev third annual workshop, Saint Louis, USA, 12 Dec 2010

Del Galdo EM, Nielsen J (1996) International user interfaces. Wiley, New York

DIN (1996) DIN EN ISO 9241-10 (1996): ergonomics requirements for office work with display screen equipment—Part 10: principles of dialogue design. Beuth-Verlag, Berlin/Vienna/Zurich

DIN (1999) DIN EN ISO 9241-11 Ergonomic requirements for office work with display screen equipment Part 11, requirements for suitability for use: Principles = Guidance on usability = Guidelines for usability, vol DIN, Teil 11. Beuth-Verlag, Berlin

DIN (2006) DIN EN ISO 9241-110 ergonomics of humans-system interaction Part 110: dialogue principles. Beuth-Verlag, Berlin

DIN (2010) DIN EN ISO 9241-210 ergonomic requirements for human-system interaction—Part 210: process for designing usable systems. Beuth-Verlag, Berlin

Dinet J, Vivian R, Brangier E (2011) Towards future methods to take into account cross-cultural differences in design: An example with the „Expert Community Staff" (ECS). In: 1st international conference on design, user experience and usability: theory, methods, tools and practice, DUXU 2011, held as part of 14th international conference on human-computer interaction, HCI international 2011. (July 25, 2011). Lecture notes in computer science (including subseries Lecture Notes in Artificial Intelligence and Lecture Notes in Bioinformatics), 6769 LNCS (Part 1), S 53–61

Dix A, Finaly J, Abowd G, Beale R (2001) Human-computer interaction, 2 Aufl, 11 Pr ed. Prentice Hall Europe, London

Dybkjær L, Bernsen N, Minker W (2004) Evaluation and usability of multimodal spoken language dialogue systems. Speech Commun 43(1–2):33–54. https://doi.org/10.1016/j.specom.2004.02.001

Fischer K (2006) What computer talk is and is not: human-computer conversation as intercultural communication, vol 17. AQ-Verlag, Saarbrücken

Fissgus U, Seewald-Heeg U (2005) Software localization. IT-MUNCHEN 47(4):220–225

Floridi L (2004) The Blackwell guide to the philosophy of computing and information. Blackwell, Malden

Fox C, Hofkirchner W (2002) A uniform concept of information for a uniform information science. In: Floyd C, Fuchs C, Hofkirchner W (ed) Steps to the information society. Studies commemorating the 65th birthday of Klaus Fuchs-Kittowski, vol 65. Lang, Frankfurt am Main, pp 241–281

Frey S, Bente G (1989) Microanalysis of media-mediated information processes for the application of time-series-based notation principles to the investigation of television news. Cologne J Sociol Soc Psychol. Special edition 30(1989):515–533

Hall ET (1959) The silent language. Doubleday, New York

Hall ET, Hall MR (2009) Understanding cultural differences: Germans, French and Americans. Intercultural Press, Boston [u. a.]

Halpin AW, Winer BJ (1957) A factorial study of the leader behavior descriptions. In: Stogdill RM, Coons AE (eds) Leader behavior: its description and measurement. Bureau of Business Research, Ohio State University, Columbus, pp 39–51

Hammwöhner R, Kuhlen R (2004) Wissen in Aktion: Der Primat der Pragmatik als Motto der Konstanzer Informationswissenschaft; Festschrift für Rainer Kuhlen, vol 41. Constance: UVK Verl.-Ges.

Hassenzahl M, Burmester M, Koller F (2003) AttrakDiff: a questionnaire to measure perceived hedonic and pragmatic quality. In: Ziegler J, Szwillus G (eds) Man computer 2003: interaction in motion. B.G. Teubner, Stuttgart/Leipzig, pp 187–196

Heimgärtner R (2005a) Measuring cultural differences in human-computer interaction. In: Auinger A (ed) Workshop-proceedings mensch und computer 2005. OCG Vienna, Vienna, pp 89–92

Heimgärtner R (2005b) Research in progress: towards cross-cultural adaptive human-machine-interaction in automotive navigation systems. In: Day D, del Galdo EM (Hrsg) Proceedings of the seventh international workshop on internationalisation of products and systems (IWIPS 2005). Grafisch Centrum Amsterdam, Amsterdam, S 97–111

Heimgärtner R (2007a) Cultural differences in human computer interaction: results from two online surveys. Paper presented at the Open innovation, Konstanz

Heimgärtner R (2007b) Intercultural user interface design. In: Paul-Stueve T (ed) Mensch & computer 2007, vol. Mensch & Computer 2007 workshop volume. Publishing House of the Bauhaus University, pp 11–14

Heimgärtner R (2012) Cultural differences in human-computer interaction: towards culturally adaptive human-machine interaction. Oldenbourg, Munich

Heimgärtner R (2013) Reflections on a model of culturally influenced human computer interaction to cover cultural contexts in HCI design. Int J Hum Comput Interact 29:205

Heimgärtner R (2014) ISO 9241-210 and culture?—the impact of culture on the standard usability engineering process. In: Marcus A (Hrsg) Design, user experience, and usability. User experience design practice: third international conference, DUXU 2014, held as part of HCI international 2014, Heraklion, Crete, June 22–27, 2014, proceedings, Part IV. Springer International Publishing, Cham, S 39–48

Heimgärtner R, Tiede LW (2008) Technology and culture: intercultural experience in product development for China. In: Rösch O (ed) Interkulturelle Kommunikation (Technik und Kultur, vol 6, pp 149–162). Publisher News & Media, Berlin

Heimgärtner R, Holzinger A, Adams R (2008) From cultural to individual adaptive end-user interfaces: helping people with special needs. In: Miesenberger K, Klaus J, Zagler WL, Karshmer AI (Hrsg) Computers helping people with special needs, 11th international conference, ICCHP 2008, Linz, July 9–11, 2008. Proceedings, Bd 5105. Springer, Heidelberg, S 82–89

Heimgärtner R, Tiede L-W, Windl H (2011) Empathy as key factor for successful intercultural HCI design. Paper presented at the proceedings of 14th international conference on human-computer interaction, Orlando

Herczeg M (1994) Software ergonomics: basics of human-computer communication, 1st AuflBonn. Addison-Wesley

Herczeg M (2005) Software ergonomics: basics of human-computer communication, 2nd, fully revised. Aufl. Oldenbourg, Munich

Hofstede GH, Hofstede GJ, Minkov M (2010) Cultures and organizations: software of the mind, 3rd edn. McGraw-Hill, Maidenhead

Hohmann S (2003) Man - Machine - Interface: studies on a theory of human interaction. PhD, Duisburg-Essen. http://duepublico.uni-duisburg-essen.de/servlets/DocumentServlet?id = 5483, accessed 29 Feb 2019

Holzinger A (2005) Usability engineering methods for software developers. Commun ACM 48 (1):71–74. http://doi.acm.org/10.1145/1039539.1039541, accessed 29 Feb 2019

Honold P (1999a) „Cross-cultural" or „intercultural"—some findings on international usability testing. In: Prabhu GV, Del Galdo EM (eds) Designing for global markets 1, first international workshop on internationalisation of products and systems, IWIPS 1999. Backhouse Press, Rochester/New York, pp 107–122

Honold P (1999b) Cross-cultural usability engineering: development and state of the art. Paper presented at the proceedings of HCI international (the 8th international conference on human-computer interaction) on human-computer interaction: ergonomics and user interfaces-volume   I.   http://dl.acm.org/citation.cfm?id=647943.742510&coll=DL&dl= GUIDE&C-FID=145069547&CFTOKEN=47400189, accessed 29 Feb 2019

Honold P (1999c) Learning how to use a cellular phone: comparison between German and Chinese users. J STC 46(2):196–205

Honold P (2000) Intercultural usability engineering: a study on cultural influences on the design and use of technical products (Als Ms gedr ed Bd 647). VDI Verl, Düsseldorf

Hülzer-Vogt H (1995). Metaphor basics of linguistic communication. Man - World - Action - Language - Computer. Wilhelm Fink Publishers, Munich, pp 176–197

Jacko JA, Sears A (2003) The human-computer interaction handbook: Fundamentals, evolving technologies and emerging applications. Erlbaum, Mahwah

Johnson-Laird PN (1983) Mental models: towards a cognitive science of language, inference and consciousness, vol 6. Harvard University Press, Cambridge, MA

Kosma F (2011) Construction and evaluation of a culture assimilator for the German-Indian project work at an automobile manufacturer. Unpublished [He1] diploma thesis. University of Potsdam

Kraiss K-F (1993) Man-machine dialogue. In: Schmidtke H (ed) Ergonomics. Carl Hanser Publishers, Munich, pp 446–458

Kuhlen R (1991) Information and pragmatic value-adding: language games and information science. Lang Resour Eval 25(2):93–101. https://doi.org/10.1007/BF00124146

Kuhnert I (2004) Business with the Japanese. Gabal, Offenbach

Maaß S (1993) Software ergonomics, user- and task-oriented system design. Inf Spectr 16:191–205

Marcus A, Baumgartner V-J (2004) Mapping user-interface design components versus culture dimensions in corporate websites. Visible Lang J 38(1):1–65

McTear M (2002) Spoken dialogue technology: enabling the conversational user interface. ACM Comput Surv 34(1):90–169. https://doi.org/10.1145/505282.505285

Mutschler B, Reichert M (2004) Usability metrics as proof of the cost-effectiveness of improvements to the human-machine interface. Paper presented at the proceedings of the IWSM/MetriKon workshop on software metrics (IWSM/MetriKon 2004), Königs Wusterhausen, Germany

Nielsen J (1994) Usability inspection methods. Wiley, New York

Nielsen J (1997) Usability engineering, 4 [print] ed. AP Professional, Boston

Nisbett RE, Miyamoto Y (2005) The influence of culture: holistic versus analytic perception. Trends Cogn Sci 9(10):467–473

Norman DA (2002) The design of everyday things. Basic Books, London

Paterson B, Winschiers-Theophilus H, Dunne TT, Schinzel B, Underhill LG (2011) Interpretation of a cross-cultural usability evaluation: a case study based on a hypermedia system for rare species management in Namibia. Interact Comput 23(3):239–246. https://doi.org/10.1016/j.intcom.2011.03.002

Piechulla W, König W, Gehrke H, Mayser C (2003) Reducing drivers' mental workload by means of an adaptive man-machine interface. http://www.sciencedirect.com/science/jour-nal/13698478, Zugegriffen am 29 Feb 2019

Preece J, Rogers Y, Sharp H, Benyon D, Holland S, Carey T (1994) Human-computer interaction. Addison-Wesley, Wokingham

Preim B, Dachselt R (2010) Interactive systems-volume I: basics, graphical user interfaces, information visualization. Springer Verlag, Heidelberg

Reeves B, Nass C (1998) The media equation, 1st paperback ed. CSLI Publications, Stanford

Reischer J (2006) Signs, information, communication. Analysis and synthesis of the sign and Information concept. https://epub.uni-regensburg.de/10483/, accessed 29 Feb 2019

Röbig S, Didier M, Brother R (2010) International understanding of usability as well as metrology application in the field of usability. Paper presented at the Grundlagen - Methoden - Technologien, 5th VDI symposium USEWARE 2010, Baden-Baden. http://tubiblio.ulb.tu-darmstadt.en/46312/, accessed 29 Feb 2019

Röse K (2002) Methode für das Design interkultureller HMI Systeme in der Produktion, vol 5. University of Kaiserslautern, Kaiserslautern

Röse K (2005) The development of culture-oriented human machine systems: specification, analysis and integration of relevant intercultural variables. In: Kaplan M (ed) Cultural ergonomics, advances in human performance and cognitive engineering research, 4th edn. Elsevier, Amsterdam

Röse K, Heimgärtner R (2008) Kulturell adaptive Informationsvermittlung im Kraftfahrzeug: 12 Uhr in München–Stadtverkehr, 18 Uhr in Shanghai–Stadtverkehr. i-com 7(3 Usability and aesthetics):9–13

Röse K, Zühlke D (2001, September 18–20) Culture-oriented design: developers' knowledge gaps in this area. Paper presented at the 8th IFAC/IFIPS/IFORS/IEA symposium on analysis, design, and evaluation of human-machine systems. Vor Druck, Kassel

Röse K, Zühlke D, Liu L (2001) Similarities and dissimilarities of German and Chinese users. In: Johannsen G (ed) Preprints of 8th IFAC/IFIP/IFORS/IEA symposium on analysis, design, and evaluation of human-machine systems. Vor Druck, Kassel, pp 24–29

Rößger P (2003) An international comparison of the usability of driver-information-systems. In: Röse V, Honold K, Coronado P, Day J, Evers D (Hrsg) Proceedings of the fifth international workshop on internationalisation of products and systems, IWIPS 2003, Germany, Berlin, 17–19 July 2003. University of Kaiserslautern, Kaiserslautern, S 129–134

Rößger P, Rosendahl I (2002) Intercultural differences in the interaction between drivers and driver-information-systems. Paper presented at the SAE world congress

Sarodnick FF, Brau H (2011) Methods of usability evaluation. Scientific basics and practical application, 2nd, revised & updated edition. Huber, Bern

Schlungbaum E (1996) Model based user interface software tools: current state of declarative models. Graphics, Visualization & Usability Center, Georgia Institute of Technology, Atlanta

Schlungbaum E (1997) Individual user interfaces and model-based user interface software tools. Paper presented at the proceedings of the 2nd international conference on intelligent user interfaces, Orlando

Schomaker L, Nijtmans J, Camurri A, Lavagetto F, Morasso P, Benoît C, Adjoudani A (1995) A taxonomy of multimodal interaction in the human information processing system: report of the esprit   project   8579   MIAMI.   http://www.ai.rug.nl/~lambert/papers/ TaxonomyMultimodalInteraction-RepEsprit-Project8579-MIAMI.pdf, accessed 29 Feb 2019

Schoper Y, Heimgärtner R (2013) Lessons from intercultural project management for the intercultural HCI design process. In: Marcus A (Hrsg) Design, user experience, and usability. Health, learning, playing, cultural, and cross-cultural user experience, Bd 8013. Springer, Heidelberg, S 95–104

Searle JR, Kiefer F (1980) Speech act theory and pragmatics, vol 10. Reidel, Dordrecht, Holland

Shah H, Nersessian NJ, Harrold MJ, Newstetter W (2012) Studying the influence of culture in global software engineering: thinking in terms of cultural models. Paper presented at the proceedings of the 4th international conference on intercultural collaboration, Bengaluru

Shannon CE (1948) A mathematical theory of communication. Bell Labs Tech J 27(379–423):623–656

Shneiderman B (1998) Designing the user interface. Addison-Wesley, Reading

Simon SJ (2000) The impact of culture and gender on web sites: an empirical study. SIGMIS Database 32(1):18–37. https://doi.org/10.1145/506740.506744

Stary C (1994) Interactive systems, 1st edn. Vieweg, Wiesbaden

Symmonds N (2002) Internationalization and localization using Microsoft.NET. Apress, Berkeley

Thomas A (1996) Psychology of intercultural action. Hogrefe, Seattle

Thomas A, Kinast E-U, Schroll-Machl S (2010) Handbook of intercultural communication and cooperation. Basics and areas of application. Vandenhoeck & Ruprecht, Göttingen

Timpe K-P, Baggen R (2000) Human-machine system technology, 1st edn, as of October 2000 ed. Symposion Publishing

Timpe K-P, Kolrep H (2000) The human-machine system as an interdisciplinary object. In: Timpe K-P, Jürgensohn T, Kolrep H (eds) Mensch-Maschine-Systemtechnik. Concepts, modelling, design, evaluation. Symposium Publishing, Düsseldorf, pp 9–40

Trompenaars F, Hampden-Turner C (2012) Riding the waves of culture: understanding diversity in business (Rev and updated, 3 Aufl). Nicholas Brealey Publishing, London [u. a.]

van der Geest T, Spyridakis JH (2000) Developing heuristics for web communication: an introduction to this special issue. Tech Commun 47(3):301–310

UXQB e.V. (ed) (2015). CPUX-F curriculum and glossary Version 2.11 EN, 22 Mar 2016

Usability Professionals' Association, UPA (2009) http://uxpa.org/, accessed 29 Sep 2016

VDMA (2009) Software internationalization guide. VDMA professional Association Software, Frankfurt am Main

Victor DA (1998) International business communication, 7. Aufl. Harper Collins, New York

Vöhringer-Kuhnt T (2002) The influence of culture on usability. MA master thesis, Freie University Berlin

W3C (2010) W3C internationalization activity. http://www.w3.org/International/questions/qa-mono-multilingual, accessed 29 Feb 2019

Wandmacher J (1993) Software ergonomics, vol 2. de Gruyter, Berlin

Windl H, Heimgärtner R (2013) Intercultural design for use—Extending usage-centered design by cultural aspects. Paper presented at the HCII 2013, Las Vegas

Winograd T, Flores F (1991) Understanding computers and cognition: a new foundation for design, 6th printing ed. Addison-Wesley, Reading

Wittig T (1979) The dialogue between man and machine. In: Heindrichs W, Rump GC (ed) Dialogues: contributions to interaction and discourse analysis, Gerstenberg, Hildesheim, pp 86–98

Yammiyavar P, Clemmensen T, Kumar J (2008) Influence of cultural background on non- verbal communication in a usability testing situation. Int J Des [Online] 2(2)

Chapter 5
User Interface Design

This chapter provides the framework for understanding the influence of culture on the development of user interfaces. After the presentation of the influence of culture on the HMI, HMI-relevant cultural dimensions for the development of intercultural user interfaces are presented. Finally, the most important approaches, concepts and methods for intercultural user interface design (IUID) are presented.

© Springer Nature Switzerland AG 2019
R. Heimgärtner, *Intercultural User Interface Design*, Human–Computer
Interaction Series, https://doi.org/10.1007/978-3-030-17427-9_5

5.1   Human–Machine Interaction (HMI) in a Cultural Context

There are numerous books on intercultural communication that give advice on how to behave in Japan, China or India. In addition to the exchange of information between humans, there is also the exchange of information between humans and computers/machines. The interaction of a human being with a machine is often referred to as human–machine communication. This term makes clear the parallels between "human–human" communication and "human–machine" communication. Studies have shown that humans apply the same rules to their interaction with computers or machines as they do to interpersonal communication (see Reeves und Nass 1998 and Fischer 2006). Both situations are processes that involve the exchange of information, i.e., communication processes (see also Chap. 2).

▸ At HMI, cultural influences become effective, as they are partly known from studies on intercultural communication between people. The experience and research results gained in this area can be used, but not transferred 1:1 to the field of technically oriented communication between man and machine. Instead, it requires appropriate know-how and appropriate procedures in order to be able to carry out an appropriate transformation.

Culture can influence HMI in many ways. The cultural distance between Western and Asian regions suggests that cultural differences in HMI are to be expected from users of different regions in terms of interaction style, way of thinking and action models. Therefore, design, application and use of interactive systems should not only consider the general usage criteria, but also include cultural cases that address relevant issues such as planning, presence, data protection, entitlement, control, awareness, security, error, trust, convenience, coordination, conflict, communication and collaboration (see Liang 2003).

▸ Intercultural overlapping situations (cf. Honold 2000, p. 42 ff.) arise when a product is defined and shaped within a culture and this product is then transferred to another culture and used there.

Further forms of intercultural overlapping situations are random interpersonal intercultural situations as well as comparative cultural studies, arranged by means of technical systems with direct cultural factors influencing the HMI (cf. Honold 2000, pp. 42–43). Information presented in the same way can have different meanings in different cultures due to experiences of values, symbols and behavioral patterns, each with its own meanings and interpretations. These aspects influence the coding or decoding of messages during communication (cf. Röse 2002, p. 21).

The effects of cultural differences in product use can be identified and compared across cultures by comparing behavior in the same action contexts of those cases where a person X' in culture X uses a system and a person Y' in culture Y uses the same system. Action contexts are shaped, e.g., by communication, understanding, conversation code, world view, methods, processes, web of belief and empathy.

In the comparative cultural view, there is no cultural exchange. Only characteristics of an interaction with a technical system and the expression of these characteristics in the respective culture are compared.

▸ A developer from Kultur X must make the operation of the product understandable for a user from Kultur Y (see Röse 2002, p. 68 ff.) (see also Fig. 5.1).

Example (cf. Fig. 5.1): A test person X' from culture X (e.g., China) and a test person Y' from culture Y (e.g., USA) solve the same problem and their solutions and actions are compared with regard to previously defined characteristics (2) and

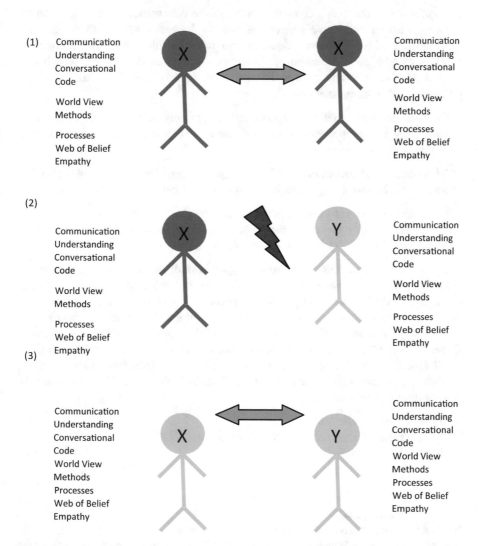

Fig. 5.1 Adaptation of the developer (left figure) to the user (right figure)

adapted accordingly (3) in order to achieve a common understanding of product development and product operation. Within the same culture, this adaptation is less necessary for (1).

In the following, the influence of culture on user interaction will be discussed in more detail.[1]

5.1.1 User Interaction

The influence of the user's cultural imprint on the effectiveness and perception of working with an interactive system can already be easily seen from the diverse requirements of the different languages and fonts of this world. Research from psychology and the comparison of similar products from different cultural backgrounds also showed that cultural differences also affect mental models, cognitive processes and working methods.

▸ The consideration of cultural aspects should not only refer to visual design and elementary UI components, but also to basic design concepts, metaphors, and workflows.

   This concerns above all information perception, mental models, cognitive styles, creativity, problem-solving strategies, language, and behavioral differences.

▸ The perception of information is influenced by the cultural context of the perceiver. The filtering process in the acquisition of information described therein is determined by the acquired regulations of the culture.

   Color perception is culture-specific. People from different cultures see different colors because they have different definitions of the colors they perceive. These conceptual worlds have mostly grown traditionally and show clear regional differences. "Each culture determines more or less arbitrarily, where one draws borders in the continuum of the color spectrum and distinguishes thus different colors. The reasons for these culture-specific idiosyncrasies are sometimes obvious in their significance, but often they are not recognizable either." (Maletzke 1996, p. 50).

   Time perception can be described according to Thomas (1993) using the following time dimensions:

- Time course (cyclic vs. linear),
- Abstractness of time (concrete vs. abstract),
- Social pace (slow vs. fast).

---

[1]I would like to take this opportunity to thank Dr. Kerstin Röse very much for the content and, in part, the preparation and formulation of parts of Sects. 5.1.1–5.1.3. She deserves most of the credit for these sections.

In general, the assignment of cultures to the spectrum of time dimensions is always context-specific. Thus, the cultures also have different characteristics for different areas of life (e.g., business vs. private).

▸ The cultural conditions under which a person grows up agree with what is imprinted and stored in his memory. This also has an influence on structuring and memory. The resulting actions—as a result of the information processing process—are also dependent on it.

Shorter access times and less required storage capacity due to culturally different language structures and characteristics can be seen as the cause for better memory performance, e.g., in Chinese: "Chinese-language stimuli obviously represent particularly favorable conditions for chunking processes, and they make little use of short-term memory capacity when phonologically encoded" (Lass 1997, p. 265).[2] Jensen and Whang (1994) come to the conclusion when investigating the access time to the long-term memory that simple memorization in the Chinese tradition is practised with children at an early age and that they are therefore very quick in simple retrieval tasks.

▸ There are cultural performance differences in the area of short- and long-term memory. Culture thus also shapes people's learning and performance. User expectation is also the result of the cognitive processing and learning processes of the user and is thus culturally shaped in the same way as user life.

Creative skills are also culturally shaped. Kuo et al. (1979) defined the descriptive dimensions for creative thinking (agility, flexibility, originality, and complementarity) and thus determined an investigation metric for creativity. American students showed better values for "originality" and "complementarity", but lower values for agility. More specifically, individuality—as a cultural marker for more freedom for creative achievements—was markedly higher, even though Chinese students had a higher number of ideas. In addition to the aspects of information reception and cognitive interpretation, problem-solving strategies are also interesting in connection with information processing.

▸ Problem-solving is a mental process of developing and integrating new action strategies at the knowledge-based human action level (cf. Action Level Model of Herczeg 2005 in Sect. 4.1.2).

New incoming information is compared with existing patterns of action. Assuming that there is no adequate pattern of action for the problem to be processed, existing patterns of action must either be newly combined or supplemented. If this does not lead to success, then completely new patterns of action must be developed. Top-down or bottom-up strategies are used for this purpose. Under the assumption of a hierarchical structure of conditions and the logic based on it to represent the

---

[2]Chunking means the organization of information into meaningful units. Humans can keep about 7 ± 2 chunks in their short-term memory at the same time (Miller 1956).

abstract–formal relationships are thus given two essential solution paths: inductive and deductive reasoning.

Inductive reasoning is a form of generalizing thought. The conclusion is drawn from the special to the general ("bottom-up" strategy). Deductive reasoning is a derivation of new statements from already existing statements. The conclusion is drawn from the general to the particular ("top-down" strategy). These approaches and theories are very common and "state of the art" in Western cultures. The presented forms of problem-solving are so-called *successive* forms of problem-solving. There is a hierarchical structure of conditions with abstract relationships that are linked monocausally.

Another form of problem-solving is *simultaneous* problem-solving. This is determined by a relational structure of conditions with situational relationships and multicausal connections. This form of simultaneous problem-solving is widespread in Asian-Confucian cultures and is mostly known through the symbolism of the "Yin–Yang". The differences between "successive versus simultaneous", "monocausal versus multicausal", and "opposite versus relation" are illustrated in Fig. 5.2.

Strohschneider has carried out research into this in a cultural context (Strohschneider 2006). Table 5.1 illustrates the results on the culturally different problem-solving behavior of Indian and German test persons within a usability engineering life cycle.

Indians have a greater need for background and context information than essential decision prerequisites. Germans want more information regarding system parameters in order to be able to perform an adequate action quickly. Overall, a

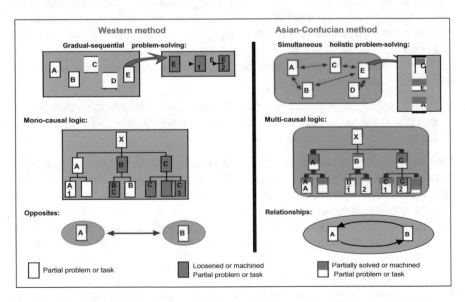

Fig. 5.2 Culturally different problem-solving strategies *Source* Röse 2002, p. 37, Fig. 2.20

Table 5.1 Results of comparative cultural studies between Indians and Germans on problem-solving behavior (Strohschneider 2001)

Range	Indian volunteers	German volunteers
Coping strategy	Express less stress behavior, cannot be disturbed, patient approach to problem-solving various solutions with problem space extension	Clear stress behavior, sometimes slight aggression, impatient pressure Search for relevant system parameters, limited to correlations in the problem area
Problem-solving strategy	Manifold inhomogeneous solution approaches Problems with independent decisions inflexible strategies; once selected, strategy was retained	More homogeneous approaches no problems with decisions more flexibility of strategies
Tactics and Decision	More background questions to understand the overall context (e.g., "indeterminacy reduction" because problem-solving action must be integrated into the context). Concentration on a few key sub-aspects	More concrete questions about the current state and thus more active use of interaction options (change parameters) Consideration of several aspects of the task

higher decision-making intensity was observed in the German subjects of the studies.

▶ Language is an obvious feature for differentiating cultures. Asian cultures have a "top/bottom" typeface and Western cultures have a "Left/Right" typeface. The same arrangement principle also applies to the horizontal or vertical menu arrangement (see Röse 2002 and Heimgärtner 2012).

Cultural differences in behavior are also decisive for the design of human–machine systems. Cole (1997) describes the cultural influences on behavior as the result of a model learning process. The child imitates behavioral patterns of the parents. The parents give the child appropriate positive or negative feedback on the behavior depending on the values and behavior patterns communicated by the grandparents. They compare the values and behavioral patterns communicated to them with their own and with those shown by the child. Thus, a behavior-based feedback process takes place in child development as an "enculturation cycle" between three generations. Enculturation means the integration of an individual into the culture by adopting values and norms (cf. Hansen 2003). The imprints acquired in this way are very stable, as they were reinforced by a mostly intensive positive feedback process. Such acquired behavioral patterns are also regarded as stable cultural influence factors on the interaction behavior towards humans and technology.

5.1.2   User(Groups)

▸ According to Röse (2002), a cultural user group is a group of persons who consciously (assigning their own values) or unconsciously (assigning them by feature/context/role from outside) share values, rules and behavioral patterns and thus represent a culture. The assignment to a cultural user group is made by the affiliation to a culture and the characteristics implicitly assumed. The cultural focus is not on single individuals, but on user groups. This means that the user is considered an individual or representative of a group/role.

In many cases, several groups of users must be differentiated according to their tasks. For example, the case of an ATM. A type of user, the bank customer, inserts his card into the machine to perform a financial transaction. Other users are specially trained people who ensure the correct functioning of the machine and supply it with money. Their role is to maintain the machine and replenish the cash. Lawyers could constitute a third class of users. You have to consider whether a certain transaction was actually fraudulent. You would need to have access to a memory or some kind of transaction track that is maintained by the system. Each of these users has a different perspective on the proper functioning of ATMs. Each of these roles will require a slightly different user interface or variant of the user interface.

▸ Multiple user groups require different user interface styles for the same application, and sometimes a single user will require different user interface styles to run the same application.

This would be the case, for example, if the same user accesses the application via several different devices: Mobile phone, PDA, laptop or desktop PC (see Responsive Design). Each of these devices has different characteristics, such as the size and resolution of the screen, the number and types of buttons on each display, and the different environments in which each of these devices could be used. For example, the user may be in a hurry and exposed to distracting sources of noise while working with the mobile phone and repeatedly viewing or using the desktop at the same time. Technically, the multi-device user thus poses some new challenges, which come into play in an intercultural context due to the different user expectations.

5.1.3   Context of Use

Software systems are used by humans. Cognitive aspects play a prominent role in the effectiveness of the users' work with the system. Why is one system more understandable or user-friendly than another? The development of user interfaces requires more than just the size and placement of buttons and menus. Rather, aspects of human factors that are relevant for the development of interactive systems must be considered.[3]

Culture influences the interaction of the user with the computer due to the movement of the user in a cultural environment (Röse 2002). Based on the socio-technical background of man–machine systems, corresponding triangular relationships result (task, human being, environment). Cultural imprinting, analysis, and design go hand in hand with norms, user interfaces and tasks. In order to master these requirements, "intercultural UI designers" with intercultural competence and sound knowledge of internationalization and localization are in demand. These competencies require knowledge of the respective cognitive structures and philosophies in the target cultures, as already described in detail in Chap. 2.

Thoughts, values, views, which are culturally very different, can only be experienced through the behavior of the respective person or can only be clarified and understood through conversations with the respective person. Eliza del Galdo illustrated this with the iceberg metaphor (see Chap. 2 "Culture and cultural models"). The cultural imprinting of the user therefore takes place in a variety of ways depending on the role of the user in life and his or her location in the world (local, regional, national or international) as well as his or her relationships to his or her communication partners (intrasubjective, intersubjective, intracultural, and intercultural) (Fig. 5.3).

Among the cultural user specifics are cognitive peculiarities or different, culturally influenced preferences, differences in the technical approach and culturally varying user expectations.

▸ Cultural differences in the context of use (different users, tasks, environment, and resources) must be taken into account in the design of user interfaces and meaningfully integrated into product development.

5.2   Cultural Models for the HMI Design

Culturally dependent dimensions (cultural dimensions) are part of cultural models that enable the comparison of human behavior between different cultures.

▸ The multidimensional cultural imprinting of users can be described using cultural models.

Baumgartner (2003) interviewed thirty international experts from 21 different countries about their opinions on the influence of cultural dimensions on user interface design and asked them to assess the dimensions in relation to their importance for HMI design. According to the experts surveyed, their results contain

---

[3]Cf. https://www.se.uni-hannover.de/, last access 9th February 2019.

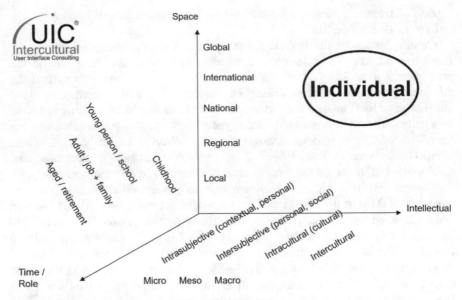

Fig. 5.3 Multidimensional cultural imprinting of a user *Source* IUIC

a summary of the following relevant cultural dimensions for the HMI design, arranged according to importance (Baumgartner 2003, p. 46):

- Context,
- Technological development (combination of environment/technology and technological development),
- Uncertainty avoidance,
- Perception of time,
- Authority view.

The dimension "context" is related to the amount of information needed in a culture in a certain situation (cf. Hall 1976). "Technological development" covers both technological progress and experience in dealing with technology found in a culture. "Avoiding uncertainties" describes the circumstances in which the members of a culture feel threatened by unknown situations (cf. Hofstede 1991). "Time perception" refers to mono-chronic time orientation, i.e., doing things more planned and sequentially, and poly-chronic time orientation, doing things more arbitrarily and in parallel (cf. Hall 1976, p. 17 ff.). The "view of authority" includes the attitude to power distance, organizational power, and leadership, because people are aware of the members of an organization (cf. Hofstede 1991). These results are based on estimates by usability experts and still require empirical validation.

Since there are a multitude of cultural dimensions (see Chap. 2), considerations are now being made as to which cultural dimensions are the most relevant for the development of intercultural user interfaces and why.

5.2.1   Reduction of the Conceptual Complexity of Cultural Models

According to Reimer (2005, p. 39), many of the cultural dimensions of different authors have similar qualities, which makes it possible to compare them with each other (even if they may vary in their use). For example, the cultural dimension "individualism versus collectivism" can be used dichotomously or holistically. In addition, there is a close semantic relationship between some cultural dimensions (cf. Hodicová 2007, p. 38). For example, the cultural dimension "role versus relationship orientation" strongly corresponds to Hofstede's concept of "individualism versus collectivism", which describes societies with loyal members. It also corresponds to Trompenaar's cultural dimension "specificity versus diffusion", which means the division of work and private areas (cf. Hodicová 2007, p. 38).[4]

Some cultural dimensions obviously cannot be separated because they are inherently connected. According to Kralisch (2006), individualism and power distance influence private behavior in contrast to previous studies. Empirical results provided evidence that the combination of both cultural views actually has the strongest influence: "In contrast to previous studies, we argued that both Individualism and Power Distance affect privacy attitudes and cannot be considered independently from each other. Empirical results provided evidence that the combination of both cultural dimensions has in fact the strongest impact." (Kralisch 2006, p. 223).

In addition, the Ohio State Leadship Study (cf. Halpin and Winer 1957) revealed a similar cultural dimension: task versus person orientation (cf. Schriesheim et al. 1995). In task-oriented cultures, people with a focus on workplace the completion of the job as the highest priority over any consideration of people, which contrasts with person-oriented cultures and resembles the effects of the dimension "individualism versus collectivism".

This and the reduction to some main cultural dimensions is also supported by the evaluation of Cox (1993), which also sees the dimension individualism versus collectivism immediately connected with task/role versus relationship orientation. Many authors of cultural dimensions indirectly describe the effects of the individualism versus collectivism dichotomy (cf. Cramer 2008, p. 37). This conclusion can also be applied to the work of Vöhringer-Kuhnt (2002), which stat es that only one of Hofstede's five dimensions, namely "individualism versus collectivism", is in a reciprocal relationship to the user-friendliness of a system (Vöhringer-Kuhnt 2002, p. 17), suggesting that this dimension has the greatest significance for intercultural HMI design. In addition (Podsiadlowski 2002, p. 43), the one-dimensional construct "individualism versus collectivism" was used as the basis for its extension to a multidimensional construct in order to derive cultural and

---

[4]In order to explain intercultural communication and cooperation, several cultural dialogues must be used simultaneously (cf. e.g., also Rösch 2005).

individual subdimensions. Podsiadlowski (2002, p. 45) also emphasizes time and space as well as the communicative aspects.

▸ Cultural dimensions can be reduced to a basic cultural dimension (BCD), in which the very similar dimensions of "individualism versus collectivism", "tasks versus personal orientation" and "roles versus relationship orientation" are "combined".

It is assumed that the differences in behavior in relation-oriented cultures *compared* to task-oriented cultures are greater than the differences in behavior *within* relation-oriented or task-oriented cultures. For example, Chinese and French people exhibit similar behavior in relation-oriented aspects, since both cultures are strongly relation-oriented. German and US Americans also base their relationship-oriented behavior on similar behavior, because both cultures are task-oriented. It can therefore be assumed that the differences in interaction behavior between Germans and Americans or between Chinese and French are smaller than between Germans/ Americans and Chinese/ French.

The cultural dimensions "activity orientation" (do—will—be), "human nature" (good, bad/changeable, not changeable), "instrumental versus explicit" (depending on human nature), "universalism versus particularism" and all cultural dimensions affecting the development of a country are difficult to subsume beyond the basic cultural dimensions. These dimensions contain more common, personally motivated objectives than group-motivated ones. Accordingly, they cannot so easily be classified into role/task/individualism or relation/person/collectivism-oriented categories on the socially oriented level.

5.2.2   Relevant Cultural Models for HMI Design

▸ For the design of intercultural HMI, those cultural models most interesting are those that are directly linked to communication, information, interaction, and dialogue design, e.g., those cultural dimensions that directly address the culturally different concepts of space, time and communication (Heimgärtner 2005, 2007, 2012).

Space and time are physical variables that influence people's communicative behavior, which shapes the social processes of a group of people and their culture: by learning certain behaviors, people mature with regard to their cultural environment. Therefore, the influence of the cultural imprint of the user on his behavior in interaction with other communication partners is immense.

Vöhringer-Kuhnt (2002) investigated the influence of culture on usability. Hofstede's individualism index is significantly linked to the behavior towards the satisfaction of the user and the behavior towards product usability. In his conclusion, Vöhringer-Kuhnt writes, "Individualism/ collectivism is connected with and has effects on usability". (Vöhringer-Kuhnt 2002, p. 17).

In addition, communication in the HMI is defined by the user and the system. Consequently, cultural differences in interpersonal communication can and must be transferred to interaction with technical devices (Röse 2002, p. 74 ff.).

Cultural dependencies in user–system interactions primarily affect interaction and dialogue design (cf. Röse 2002). According to Röse, this effect can also be observed if the user's communication partner is a computer system: culture influences the user's interaction with a computer system or a machine due to the user's movement in a cultural environment (cf. Röse 2002, p. 18). Thus, cultural imprinting has a direct influence on the user's interaction with the system.

Cultural dimensions and specific values are indirectly relevant to intercultural UI design and those cultural dimensions that are directly linked to the complicated basic cultural dimension (BCD) are most directly relevant to the development of intercultural user interfaces because they reveal different patterns of behavior of users depending on their role or relationship orientation.

▸ Of the 29 cultural dimensions (cf. Fig. 2.7 in Chap. 2), the author found four supercategories that are directly relevant to intercultural user interface design (Heimgärtner 2012), primarily on the basis of analytical evidence:

• Individualism (task) versus collectivism (relationship) (containing related cultural dimensions such as face-saving or power distance),
• nonverbal communication,
• Perception of space (e.g., distance between user and system, network density, context),
• Time perception (containing all related cultural dimensions such as uncertainty avoidance or communication speed).

These supercategories overlap predominantly with the results of (Baumgartner 2003). In addition (Khaslavsky 1998) supports the relevance of the four supercategories by providing "a package of nine descriptive variables useful for the assessment of culture and design" (Khaslavsky 1998, p. 365 seq.). This package contains well-known cultural dimensions of Hall (speed of communication, density of information networks, personal space, and time orientation), Hofstede (power distance, collectivism vs. individualism and avoidance of uncertainties) and Trompenaars (diffuse vs. specific and particularism vs. universalism). Relevant variables for intercultural HMI design can be derived from this package of cultural dimensions, such as speed at which people can decode and respond to messages (message speed) and the amount of information in which it occurs, depending on the context.

Table 5.2 Most relevant cultural dimensions for intercultural interaction analysis (IIA) in intercultural HMI design and its characteristics for China and Germany. (Source: own representation)

Authors of cultural dimensions	Cultural dimension relevant to HMI design	China	Germany (German)
Hofstede	Individualism versus collectivism	Collectivism	Individualism
Trompenaars	Role versus relationship orientation	Relation	Role
Halpin and Winer	Tasks versus personal orientation	Person	Assignment
Hall	Context	High	Low
Hall	Communication speed	High	Low
Hall	Time orientation	Poly-chronic	Mono-chronic
Hall	Type of action chains	Parallel	Sequential
Hall	Density of the information network	High	Low
Hall	Personal distance	Low	High
Hall	Nonverbal communication	More pronounced	Weaker

> Table 5.2 presents a summary of the most important cultural dimensions that can be considered relevant for intercultural interaction analysis (IIA) within intercultural HMI design. It is clear that the reduction of the number of cultural models leads to a loss of information. However, reduction is justified and sensible for the argument of proving concepts and preserving initial tendencies in cultural differences in the HMI. The same reasoning also applies to HMI dimensions.

The basic relationship between cultural dimensions and variables for the HMI design lies in the basic dimensions of time and space (see Hall 1959) and is fundamental to the derivation of all other variables for the HMI design.

▸ All cultural dimensions analyzed provide space and time-specific aspects. It therefore makes sense to assume that cultural dimensions based on time deal with interaction and information processing in HMI (e.g., use of dialogue). Cultural dimensions, which instead refer to space, concern the presentation of information as well as the structure and layout of user interfaces.

The most prominent cultural dimensions related to these aspects were identified by Hall and Hall (1983), who assumed that seven cultural dimensions were relevant for intercultural interaction analysis because they served three of the four supercategories relevant for user interface design. In addition, the work of Hall and Hall (1983) is the basis for the most important intercultural variables for HMI design, since its cultural dimensions directly address five of the eight information science categories and the other three indirectly.

Accordingly, the cultural model of Hall and Hall (1983) is the cultural and information science basis because it implicitly integrates cultural and information science aspects. Space, time and communication are central concepts in Hall's cultural model. According to Hall and Hall (1983, p. 23) time is fundamental for communication systems. The bridge of understanding to culture is communication, which is based on the basic categories of space and time that Kant presupposed in 1789 (cf. Kant 2006).

5.2.3   Implications of Cultural Models for Intercultural HMI Design

Messages and individual information must therefore be designed in such a way that the user from culture Y can understand them without problems. Masao Ito and Kumiyo Nakakoji already demonstrated the influence of culture on user interface design in 1996 for the modes "hear" and "speak" between user and system (see Masao and Kumiyo 1996). In "listening mode", the presentation of information from the system to the user takes place in the recording, context and conclusion. Cultural dependency grows from the first to the last phase: colors and forms in the reception phase are less dependent on culture than standards in language and metaphors within the cohesion phase. Finally, in the final phase, which is based on logical and social norms, the inference mechanism depends heavily on culture. In the "speaking mode" the instructions for the system are divided into four phases by the user. At first, the user recognizes the possibilities of the system use. For example, he understands the meaning of the layout, chooses alternatives or initiates functions. Then he tests their applicability by examining the semantic consequence using trial and error. In the third phase, he determines the expectation of the system in view of his actions and recognizes the system instructions in the last phase. These processing phases involve time perception, which depends very much on the culture (cf. Hall 1959). In addition, cultural dependence grows from phase to phase. In Japan, for example, a very short system response time is very important. On the other hand, Japanese users are obviously more patient with lengthy tasks than users from European countries.

▸ Culture influences HMI at all levels of the interaction model (see acting level model according to Herczeg 2005; Heinecke 2004; Norman and Draper 1986).

Miscommunication has a negative impact on the usability of the product. Numerous scientists have pointed out that a change in the cultural environment takes place when a technology or product is transferred from the country of origin to another country and must be taken into account in the development of intercultural human–

machine interaction (cf. Heimgärtner 2012; Clemmensen and Clemmensen 2012; Hoft 1995; Honold 2000; Hermeking 2001, p. 55); Röse 2002).

▸ It is important that there is an agreement between the developer and the users in different cultures about the meaning and interpretation of information—otherwise there will be misunderstandings or no understanding at all (see Chap. 2).

5.3   Intercultural User Interface Design (IUID)

IUID has grown steadily in recent years. "Intercultural research in information systems is a relatively new field of research that has gained in importance in recent years [...]" (Kralisch 2006, p. 17). The influence of culture was recognized and addressed (cf. Snitker 2004).

Nevertheless, there is still no final, generally valid theory on the influence of culture on HMI—even though research in this area has gained considerable momentum in recent years and a possible approach to a culture-dependent HMI model is presented in Chap. 6.

This is largely due to the fact that the context that has to be considered is very complex (cf. the results of the Dagstuhl workshop in 2014 at Schloss Dagstuhl).[5] Context includes circumstances, environment and background knowledge (history) that determines the meaning of an event within an interactive system.

Field studies are suitable, for example, to determine the context of use. Honold (2000) has investigated Indian households to find out why certain washing machines were not accepted in India. Observations and interviews with Indian families showed, for example, that the washing cycle of the washing machine, which was too long, did not fit into the daily routine of the Indians because the power supply or servants were not available at the time of washing.

▸ In order to be competitive as a product manufacturer on the world market, it is important that users accept the product. Therefore, cultural influences must be taken into account during the development of products for other markets.

In order for the user to understand the developer's device and thus be able to operate it easily and satisfactorily, it is important that the developer understands the user. But they have different cultural backgrounds. Therefore, at least the following aspects must be analyzed in detail before the product can be developed (see also Chap. 2):

• User's worldview (metaphysical approach),
• General knowledge (procedural and factual knowledge) of the user,

---

[5]URL = https://www.dagstuhl.de/de/programm/kalender/semhp/?semnr=14131, last access 9th of February 2019.

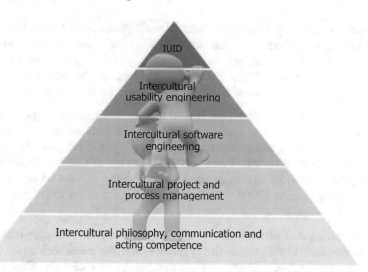

Fig. 5.4 Steps on the way to the successful development of intercultural user interfaces Source: IUIC

- The context in which the product is used by the user,
- The tasks the user wishes to perform by using the product.

Only if these aspects are taken into account and further prerequisites are met such as intercultural communication as an essential condition for intercultural usability engineering, user interface design and user experience, will the development of intercultural user interfaces be crowned with success and ultimately lead to a successful international product. To achieve this, intercultural know-how from several levels is required (Fig. 5.4).

▸ The communication level forms the basic level, followed by the levels of project management, software and usability engineering on the way to the successful development of intercultural user interfaces (Fig. 5.4).

Accordingly, intercultural communication skills at the basic level at all levels (strongly influenced by the philosophy of the cultures concerned) can contribute to solving problems arising from cultural differences at the upper levels. IUID is built on levels 1–4 (Fig. 5.4).

5.3.1   Intercultural HMI Design

According to (Röse and Zühlke 2001), culture-oriented HMI design describes the culture-oriented design of interactive systems and products that takes into account the cultural context of the user with regard to the corresponding tasks and product use (Röse 2002, p. 87). Honold presented the steps of this process which she called "intercultural usability engineering" (cf. Honold 2000, pp. 42–43). This approach has grown in the research literature from 1990 to 2000 and has emerged from the processes of globalization, internationalization and localization of products (cf. Chap. 3). Intercultural usability engineering includes insights from human–machine interaction, software ergonomics and comparative cultural knowledge (cf. Chap. 6).

▶ Intercultural HMI design describes the user and culture-oriented design of interactive systems and products, including the cultural context of the user depending on tasks and product use (Röse 2002, p. 87; Honold 2000, p. 42–43), and thus representing the "Process of HMI Design in Cultural Context".
▶ The process of HMI design generally refers to the process of human-centered design according to ISO 9241210 and in particular to the development of user interfaces.

Cultural studies deal with all cultural aspects. All disciplines strongly influenced by culture contribute to cultural studies as multidisciplinary cases such as art, literature, media, linguistics, philosophy, religion, psychology or sociology. Cultural studies are concerned with the exploration of culture as human behavior forming in connection with social, historical, political, literary, artistic, economic, legal, and spatial conditions by investigating cultural differences with regard to, e.g., gender, age, education, nationality, etc. (cf. Straub 2007; Jäger 2004 and Hansen 2003). Ethnocentrism is an important phenomenon that has effects on intercultural interaction situations: people tend to see their own culture as the center of the world as well as the yardstick for all things (Maletzke 1996, pp. 23–24, see also Chap. 2). In addition, other people are considered from their own point of view, customs and standards, which are used as a standard for each assessment (cf. Heimgärtner and Tiede 2008).

▶ The perception and consideration of the customs and requirements of other cultures by the developers of intercultural user interfaces is one of the main tasks within intercultural HMI design.

5.3.2   Approaches of Intercultural User Interface Design

At least the following concepts or approaches of the IUID can be named, which consider cultural aspects in the HMI design:

- Intercultural HCI design (Honold 2000; Röse and Zühlke 2001 (IUID in China), Heimgärtner 2012, 2017),
- Cross-cultural HCI design (Marcus 2001, b; Rau et al. 2012),
- Culture-oriented HCI design (Röse and Zühlke 2001),
- Culture-centered HCI design (Shen et al. 2006).
- Semiotic-oriented approach for HCI design (Pereira et al. 2015),

However, rather than their content, the connotations of the names of the approaches are different (Heimgärtner 2013a). These mainly determine how different the approaches are used in different contexts. In the following, all these approaches are summarized under the term "Intercultural User Interface Design".

▸ Intercultural User Interface Design (IUID) refers to the process of adequately designing human–machine interaction (HMI) taking into account the cultural requirements of the context of use.

For the development of successful intercultural user interfaces, a suitable approach is necessary to ensure user interfaces with good usability and a positive user experience in the desired cultural context.

▸ The development of Intercultural User Interface Development (see Chap. 1) focuses on a particular product or service and its use in a particular cultural context. It is checked whether the user interface is suitable for its use in the respective cultural context or whether it can be adapted accordingly by the user.

Galdo et al. (1996) speak of "international user interface design" in 1996. Here the difference between "international" and "intercultural" becomes clear: international research examines above all characteristics in technology and language, while intercultural research examines interculturally influenced cognition and its effects (cf. Honold 2000).

▸ Intercultural user interface design is a necessary prerequisite for improving the intercultural usability of software, which in turn is a necessary prerequisite for global sales opportunities.
▸ Using methods of intercultural usability engineering, further design guidelines can be iteratively derived from the results of the tests and the feedback of potential users from all over the world for intercultural user interface design.

A software product that can be used effectively and efficiently by users of different cultures due to the use of such methods increases both customer satisfaction with the product and its functional safety. The demand in the industry for the methods of intercultural user interface design in the course of globalization will be in line with the export market (first and foremost for Asians) and must therefore also be increasingly offered in teaching in science and industry.

▸ In order to be able to design user interfaces for the global market that meet the cultural needs of users (or even adapt automatically, cf. "Culturally-Aware HCI Systems", Heimgärtner 2018, the first step is to find out the differences in the cultural needs of users and thus the cultural differences in HMI at all levels of HMI localization (surface, functionality, and interaction) (Röse and Zühlke

2001). Areas such as information presentation and language or dialogue design as well as interaction design are affected (Lewandowitz et al. 2006) (cf. Chap. 7).

▸ Cultural dimensions are too rough for intercultural user interface design. For this reason, additional cultural variables are necessary which—related to user interface design—break down the cultural aspects into smaller units (cf. Röse 2002). These cultural aspects can be empirically determined using qualitative and quantitative methods.

Qualitative methods such as interviews, focus groups or participatory observation generally require a higher level of interpretation with lower reliability than quantitative methods whose data can be objectively verified. These include, for example, log file or questionnaire capture and analysis. Usability tests, for example, can be counted among the hybrid processes. Unfortunately, all procedures require interpretation with regard to hypothesis formation, overall evaluation, and implication formation and are therefore always associated with a certain subjectivity and thus with uncertainty as to their objective validity.

▸ Although cultures are constantly changing, trends can be identified for a product life cycle of a few years at least, and for special applications even sharply defined parameters can be identified that serve intercultural user interface design.

One promising method to accomplish this task is to observe the interaction of users from different cultures with the system using an appropriate automated analysis tool and to define different patterns of interaction with regard to the cultural background of the users (cf. Chap. 6). With this tool you can reach thousands of test persons and simulate any use cases. A study using this tool covered different interaction patterns regarding the cultural background of the users in terms of, e.g., design (extensive to simple), information density (high to low), menu structure (high width to high depth), personalization (high to low), language (symbols versus signs) and interaction devices (Heimgärtner 2007).

▸ There are correlations between the interaction behavior of the user and his culture or between the cultural dimensions and information science variables such as information density or interaction frequency at the interaction level (cf. middle level of the "iceberg" in Fig. 6.3 in Chap. 6).

The cultural differences in the HMI were determined quantitatively (Heimgärtner et al. 2007). Therefore, intercultural usability metrics can be used for the design of intercultural (even adaptive) user interfaces (Heimgärtner 2013b).

5.3.3   Levels of Intercultural User Interface Design

▸ Intercultural UserInterfaceDesign is divided into three levels according to Thissen (2008).

▸ The first stage (characters) is the cultural coding of characters, i.e., way of presenting information (= semiotic systems of a culture—(Cassirer 1994))—signs as expressions of cultural values ("cultural markers").

"Cultural symbols, signs or markers" are not perceived as culture-specific within culture and have two kinds of meanings, which should not be confused in design, but should be given equal consideration. On an emotional level, the sense of belonging to and identity with the culture are addressed, and on a semantic level, the meaning of signs. The aim of the first stage is to facilitate the understanding of information and to generate trust through the conscious use of culture-specific signs. Culture-specific characters include:

- Language,
- Body language,
- Way of dressing,
- Design of living, working and public spaces,
- Hero worship,
- Spelling,
- Typography,
- Pictures,
- Symbols,
- Colors.

> Cultural markers in HMI design are the elements of interface design adopted in a culture (Badre and Barber 1998) such as icons and metaphors, colors, images, national symbols, grouping of elements, languages, geographical elements, general direction, sound, typographic elements, geometric elements, showing buildings. They strongly influence the usability of software interfaces and information products: "Ultimately, we argue, cultural markers can directly impact user performance, hence the merging of culture and usability." (Badre and Barber 1998). The research of Sheppard and Scholtz (1999 and Sun 2001) confirmed the theory of cultural markers. They are significant, recognizable, usability-enhancing, cultural differences and will therefore be used even more in the future.

▸ The second stage (social behavior) deals with forms of cultural perception described on the basis of cultural models.

Cultural patterns are defined, which describe phenomena of reality as models. All societies and cultures have the same basic social problems (cf. Mead 2005) and basic anthropological problems (cf. Inkeles and Levinson 1996). These include, for example:

- The relationship of the individual to authority,

- The relationship of the individual to the group,
- The perception of masculinity and femininity,
- The way in which conflicts and aggression are dealt with,
- The expression of feelings.

The characteristics of these basic problems can be described, for example, by means of cultural dimensions or cultural standards (see Chap. 2).

▸ On the third level of intercultural user interface design, culture is captured and understood in its entirety and complexity (understanding the differentness/alienity).

Problems arise when followers of different cultures meet and do not master the following activities:

- Consideration of the strangeness of other cultures,
- Understanding the otherness,
- Understanding as a prerequisite and basis of all communication,
- Empathy and ethnorelativism:

  - to see the world through the eyes of others
  - Getting involved with the others

- More than just perceiving the signs (1st stage) or social value systems (2nd stage) of a free culture,
- Foreign culture becomes partly a part of one's own,
- Real dialogue becomes possible.

The encounter models developed by Sundermeier (1996) describe these complete behavior patterns in dealing with other cultures in more detail (cf. Sundermeier 1996).

5.4 IUID Concepts and Methods

In the following, the most important concepts and methods for acquiring relevant knowledge at the IUID will be discussed (culturally dependent variables, dimensions, system characteristics, procedures, models and theories as well as processes, standards and tools).

5.4.1 Intercultural and Cultural Variables

▸ Intercultural variables describe the differences in HMI design in terms of user preferences from different cultures (Table 5.3).

Table 5.3 Intercultural variables after (Röse 2002, p. 97 ff.) (estimated values regarding the difficulty of identifying variables were added by the author)

Intercultural variable	Localization level	Relationship to HMI design	Perceptibility of the variables	Estimated detection difficulty [0 (easy)–10 (difficult)]
Dialogue design	Interaction	Straight	Hidden/Over long time and Extensive analysis	10
Interaction design	Interaction	Straight	Hidden/Over long time and Extensive analysis	9
System functionality	Function	Obliquely	Visible/ immediately recogni zable	8
Service (Maintenance)	Function	Obliquely	Visible/ immediately recognizable	7
Technical documentation	Function	Obliquely	Visible/ immediately recognizable	6
Information presentation	Surface	Straight	Visible/ immediately recognizable	4
Language	Surface	Straight	Visible/ immediately recognizable	2
General system design	Surface	Obliquely	Visible/ immediately recognizable	0

"Intercultural" variables represent the relevant knowledge for the internationalization of software and system platforms that can be gained by observing at least two cultures and their differences, i.e., conducting intercultural research (cf. Honold 1999). These can also be simply called "cultural" variables because the values of these variables represent the knowledge of a specific culture (relevant for system and software localization). Therefore, in the following the term "intercultural variable" will be used in cases where the intercultural research character is meant to obtain values of variables and the term "cultural variable" in cases where the use of value variables is the main focus concerning a specific culture.

There are "direct" (DV) and "indirect" (IV) variables (Fig. 5.5) which influence the HMI parameters either directly (e.g., interaction, presentation of information or language) or indirectly (e.g., through maintenance, documentation or technical environment).

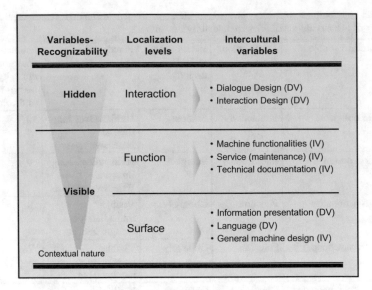

Fig. 5.5 Properties of intercultural variables *Source* Fig. 4.28 from Röse 2002

▶ Direct intercultural variables have a direct and significant influence on HMI design. According to Röse (2002), direct variables can be divided into visible variables (surface levels) and hidden variables (influence on interaction levels) (Fig. 5.5), which together reflect the concept of the "iceberg metaphor" (cf. Fig. 4.4 in Chap. 4).

Both types of variables have a strong influence on the design and determination of usability as well as on the acceptance of the system. Visible intercultural variables (VIV) concern the presentation level (e.g., colors, time and date format, icons, font size, window size, position of the navigation bar) and language level (e.g., font, writing direction, designations) of a product which appear above the "water surface You can be very easily identified because they are less defined by cultural context. Invisible or "hidden" intercultural variables (NVIV) ("under the water surface" of the "cultural iceberg") influence the dialogue design (e.g., menu design and complexity, changes to the dialogue form, layout, widget positions, information presentation speed, frequency of dialogue changes) and the interaction design (e.g., navigation concept, system structure, interaction path, interaction speed, use of the navigation bar, etc.), which are closely related to the cultural context. These variables concern the interaction and dialogue levels of a product and require a high research priority (e.g., by using special tools as proposed by Heimgärtner 2008). In addition, the temporal aspect extends the definition of visible and hidden intercultural variables and complicates their collection.

▶ "Visible" intercultural variables (VIVs) are immediately perceptible at a specific time (font, color, window size, navigation bar, etc.).

It is very easy to understand that intercultural relationships of static aspects are easy for HMI design to recognize because they represent contrasts in direct comparison, i.e., if they do not normally change, they can be studied more easily than those aspects that can only be defined by observing them over a period of time. It is therefore relatively easy to find access to them, and they are also very easy to analyze.

▶ "Invisible" (or "hidden") intercultural variables (NVIVs) are only recognizable over a certain period of time (speed of interaction, duration of information display, frequency of dialogue display, use of navigation bar, etc.). It is therefore relatively difficult to analyze and access these variables (Table 5.3).

First, dynamic aspects require recognition by monitoring elements of the aspects over a period of time and, moreover, a comparison of the patterns that have emerged from the individual components. Consequently, the attention here must be directed to time-dependent components.

▶ The localization of hidden intercultural variables is very difficult to realize because the contextual relation to the cultural background as well as to the product is very strong for interaction and dialogue design. However, it is precisely this culturally distinct context and consequently the cultural dependency that makes these patterns and invisible intercultural variables so important for information architecture and interaction design and for the resulting dialogues (Röse 2002, p. 98).

It follows that the crucial reason for exploring direct hidden intercultural variables is their high contextual dependence on cultural background (higher than the directly visible intercultural variables). They have a "congenital culture" which is very helpful in determining the main "cultural effects" in the variable content. Table 5.4 shows some examples of visible and non-visible direct intercultural variables and their assumed values, which have been partially confirmed by the literature (see footnotes in Table 5.4).

5.4.2   Method of Culture-Oriented Design

According to Röse (2002, p. 93–96), intercultural variables describe the differences in HMI design with regard to the preferences of users from different cultures. "Intercultural" variables represent knowledge that can only be acquired by observing at least two cultures and their differences, i.e., by intercultural research (cf. Honold 1999) with the aim of recording relevant knowledge for the international adaptation of software and operating systems. Röse (2002) proposed the "Method for Culture-Oriented Design", which integrates the factors of new concepts of culture-oriented HMI design and the knowledge of cultural differences into existing concepts of HMI design.

Table 5.4 Examples of visible and non-visible direct intercultural variables with their manifestations for China and Germany (partly from Röse (2002, p. 125 ff.), supplemented with presumed characteristics/values by the author)[a]

	Characteristics/Value	
Variable/Parameters	Germany (German)	China
Visible intercultural variable (VIV)		
Color of warnings[b]	Red	Red/orange
Color of the normal operating condition[c]	Green	Yellow
Extent of color use[d]	Low	High
Tilt "Touch" devices to use[e]	Low	High
Non-Visible Intercultural Variable (NVIV)		
Number of information units	Low	High
Number of system messages	Low	High
Number of mouse movements	Low	High
Number of words in messages	Low	High
Number of explanation dialogues	Extremely important	Less important
Argument structure[f]	X, because Y	Because Y, X

[a]The estimation of the values for the number of information units, system messages, mouse movements, words in messages and explanatory dialogues was based on the author's reflections (Hall 1976)
[b]Röse (2002, p. 125 ff.) and Vanka (1999)
[c]Röse (2002, p. 31) and Courtney (1986, p. 90)
[d]Röse (2002, p. 32) as well as the results of the qualitative study by (Heimgärtner 2012)
[e]Rößger (2003)
[f]Scollon and Scollon (1995)

▸ Röse (2002, p. 108) uses intercultural variables within her "Method of Culture-Oriented Design" (MCD), which she has defined for the development of intercultural human–computer systems (Fig. 5.6).

MCD integrates factors from established, culture-oriented design into existing concepts of HMI design. Figure 5.6 shows the procedure of the MCD. Knowledge about cultural differences is integrated into existing methods. Relevant cultural variables for intercultural HMI design must be identified analytically on the basis of literature searches and requirement studies can be determined.

Their values represent culture-dependent variations that occur at all levels of HMI localization (surface functionality and interaction) (Röse 2002) and can be used for intercultural user interface design (IUID) (Heimgärtner 2007).[6]

However, the most culturally influenced aspects (such as cognition or ethics) are not directly visible on the surface. Rather, these aspects are reflected in the behavior of the user. Therefore, the analysis of user behavior in particular provides

---

[6]More detailed information on the MCD can be found in (Röse 2002). Training on IUID topics (including the IUID methods addressed in this chapter) is offered by the author, e.g., via IUIC (see https://www.iuic.de).

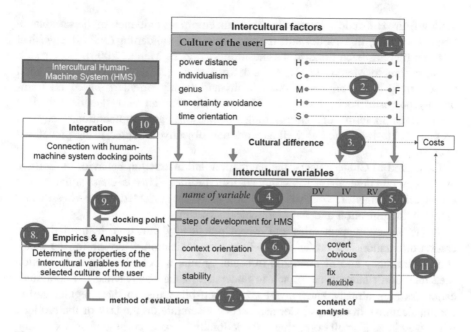

Fig. 5.6 Method of culture-oriented design (MCD) according to (Röse 2002) *Source* Fig. 5.5 from Röse 2002, p. 108

information on the cultural imprinting of the user (Röse 2002). One of the most promising methods to preserve cultural differences in HMI is therefore the observation and analysis of user interaction with the system (see Heimgärtner 2008). Empirical qualitative and quantitative studies must show whether culturally influenced user behavior correlates with cultural models. Finally, the values of the cultural variables can be used for guidelines of intercultural HMI design and for intercultural usability engineering (see Heimgärtner 2013b).

5.4.3 User Interface Characteristics

In order to make cultural dimensions tangible for user interface design, Marcus developed (Marcus 2001, b) characteristic factors for user interfaces and gives examples that can have an influence on the development of user interfaces.

▸ The user interface characteristics "Metaphor", "Mental Model", "Navigation", "Interaction", and "Presentation" are linked to five of Hofstede's cultural dimensions (see Chap. 2).

Marcus used a purely deductive approach to obtain these connections. Many possible recommendations for web design were made by Marcus and Gould (2000) mainly from Hofstede's knowledge without empirical evidence of these connections. Therefore, this model still requires empirical validation (even if empirical work on this has been done in the meantime, cf. z. B. Marcus 2006).

According to Marcus (2001, b) and Röse et al. (2001) Chinese people (and consequently users) are more relationship and family oriented, based on traditionally powerful social hierarchies. In contrast, German users are described as event-driven in terms of actions, tools, work, jobs, and competition. They are product and task-oriented as well as work and objective oriented using predefined structures.

Compared to Chinese users, the navigation and interaction behavior of German users does not depend on roles but on user profiles. This is characterized by a user-specific behavior, which is game and individual oriented and addresses distanced communication and flat hierarchical structures.

Chinese users respect roles and accept practicality, function, team, and cooperation orientation and prefer face-to-face communication. They prefer the mediation of intimacy and membership in social groups with high context connection (i.e., they don't have to say much to understand each other, since the communication partners already know a lot about each other due to their regular earlier communication). In contrast, German users concentrate on the task or the product, while they have a small contextual connection and mostly communicate explicitly.

Röse compared the user interface characteristics for China and Germany in detail (Table 6.3 in Röse 2002, p. 138). The summary of the attributes of the user interface characteristics was rearranged by Röse (2002) by classifying the user interface characteristics into additional subcategories in order to present the cultural aspects relevant for the HMI design more clearly (Table 5.5).

▸ User interface features can be used in conjunction with empirical studies of their characteristics for the respective cultural target context to derive recommendations for the development of intercultural user interfaces.

5.4.4 HMI Dimensions

Many things in our world are subject to space and time and can therefore be assigned to the dimensions "space" and "time"—including cultural dimensions. Both physical and material things can be perceived in space under the influence of time. Imagined and nonphysical or immaterial things are part of the mental world and only involve time— therefore do not need space. All categories derived from the dimensions space and time such as density, speed or frequency as well as the space dimension itself are based on the time dimension (cf. Kant 2006). Space and time as physical basic quantities also have an influence on the communication behavior of humans, which in turn affects the social processes of a group of humans and thus their culture: by learning certain behavior patterns, humans develop according to their cultural environment. For Hall (1959), the handling of time, the

Table 5.5 Differences in User Interface Characteristics for China and Germany with additional subcategories of User Interface Characteristics corresponding to Table 6.3 in Röse (2002, p. 138)

User interface characteristics	Subcategory of user interface characteristics	China	Germany
Metaphor	Orientation	Hierarchical	Event, work, competition
		Relation	Target
		Role	Assignment
	Thinking	Concrete	Abstract
	Texture	Solid	Modifiable
		Hierarchical	Flat
Mental Model	Reference to prioritized data	Yes	No
	Orientation	Role	Assignment
	Texture	Socially	Work/business
	Mental model	Simple	Complex
	Articulation	Clear	Ambiguous
	Choices	Limited	Multifarious
	Type of logic	Binary	Blurred (fuzzy)
User interface characteristics	Subcategory of user interface characteristics	China	Germany
Navigation	Choices	Limited	Multifarious
		Prespecified	Arbitrary
	Paths	Limited	Open
		Prespecified	Individual
	Navigation	Role-dependent	Role-independent
		Nonuniform/inconsistent	Uniform/consistent
	Paths	Long	Brief
		Ambiguous	Clear (referenced, taxonomic)
Interaction	Type of error messages	Straight/direct	Supporting
	Help	Wizards	Cards
	Search	Limited	search word
	Profiles are based on	Role	user/individual
	Orientation	Game	function
		Team	individual
	Preferred Interaction	Face-to-face	gap
	Notifications	Personalized	anonymous
Presentation	Language	Formal	Informal
	Context	High	Low
	Colors	Feminine	Masculine
	Orientation	Relation	Assignment

density of the information network, the speed of communication and the temporal behavior of action chains are basic patterns of such behavior.

▸ Information science quantities such as information speed (speed of dissemination and frequency of occurrence of information), information density (number and distance of information units) or information order (order of occurrence and arrangement of information) correlate with culturally different basic patterns of behavior.[7]

Dialogues, interaction, information presentation and thus the HMI are subject to time (interaction, communication) and space (layout, structure) as well as mental aspects (relationships, thoughts). Because the view of space, time, and mental aspects is strongly dependent on culture, the HMI is subject to culture (Heimgärtner 2007).

Physical subdimensions that are important for HMI design can be derived from the basic physical dimensions (space and time) and can be described by classifying the attributes of "culture" using culture models, such as cultural denominations (Heimgärtner 2007). Table 5.6 shows the derived physical subdimensions from the basic physical dimensions as well as from which cultural model and which cultural dimension they originate.

Frequency and speed are derived from time and depend on time orientation and communication speed. Action chains can explain ordering and sequential interactions. The density of communication networks and context orientation determine the context of use (cf. Chap. 4) of the HMI.

Because dialogues predominantly contain information and interaction, the physical subdimensions are summarized on the basis of information-related and interaction-related categories.

At least the following information-related subdimensions form the type/style/ type "Culture" of the user's information processing:

• Frequency (sequential density),
• Density (static: spatial distance, dynamic: temporal distance),
• Sequence/Sequentiality,
• Structure/Arrangement.

At least the following interaction-related aspects form the type/style/"culture"/ characteristics of the user's interaction:

• Frequency,
• Speed,

---

[7]The correct number and arrangement of information units is very important, for example, in applications in which the display surfaces are very small and at the same time the mental strain must be kept at an optimum level, such as driver navigation systems (cf. Heimgärtner and Holzinger 2005)—and in an intercultural context it is of course also dependent on the cultural requirements of the HMI system (cf. Heimgärtner et al. 2007).

Table 5.6 Physical subdimensions—derived from basic physical dimensions and culture models

Derived physical subdimensions (fundamental physical dimensions)	Cultural model(s)/ concept(s)	Cultural dimension (s)
Frequency (Time)	Hall: Dealing with time	Mono/poly-chronic time orientation Information network density
Speed (Time)	Hall: Communication speed	Density of the information network
Sequentiality/Priority/Sequence (Space and Time)	Hall: Action chains	Mono/poly-chronic time orientation
Context (Space and Time)	Hall: context density	Information network density low versus high context orientation
Density/Quantity (Space and Time)	Hall: context density	Information network density low versus high context orientation
Structure (Space and Time)	All cultural models	All cultural dimensions
Complexity (All categories)	All cultural models	All cultural dimensions
Quality (All categories and User characteristics)	All cultural models	All cultural dimensions

- Sequence/Sequentiality,
- Type of interaction tool.

▸ HMID dimensions (HMID) describe the behavior of a user (HMIStil) with an interactive information processing system (Heimgärtner 2007).

HMI dimensions can be derived from the basic physical dimensions of space and time. All HMI variables (expressions) of the HMI dimensions can also be derived from the physical subdimensions such as speed, frequency or density (Heimgärtner 2007). The "style of information processing" and "interactional characteristics" of the user are represented by information-related and interaction-related HMI dimensions (Table 5.7).

▸ HMI dimensions represent classes of HMI variables useful for HMI design (manifestations of HMI dimensions) that are operationalized by (interaction) indicators in HMI metrics (Table 5.8).

The indicator "Number of information units per room unit" belongs to the HMI dimension "Information density" and can be expressed by the number of words on the display. The HMI dimension "Interaction frequency" contains the variable "Number of interactions per time unit" represented by the number of mouse clicks per second.

▸ At least one potential indicator must exist as a measurement variable in order to represent the expression of an HMI dimension. For real use, however, several empirically proven indicators should be used.

Table 5.7 HMI dimensions

Derived physical sub-dimension (Physical basic dimension)	Information-related HMI dimension	Interaction-related HMI dimension
Frequency (Time)	Information frequency	Interaction frequency
Speed (Time)	Information speed	Interaction speed
Sequence/Priority/Order (Time and Space)	Information sequence/ information parallelism	Interaction sequence/ Interaction parallelism
Density/Quantity (Time and Space)/ Context (Time and Space)	Information density	

Table 5.8 HMI dimensions represented by certain characteristics and indicators

HMI dimension	HMI variable(s) (characteristic(s) of the HMI dimension)	HMI metric(s) (indicator(s) of the expression(s) of the HMI dimension)
Interaction frequency	Number of interactions per time unit	Mouse clicks and mouse movements per second or session
Information density	Number of information units per room unit	Number of words per message or on the display
Information/ interaction parallelism/ sequence	Sequence of publication of information units	Number and sequence of dialogue steps (e.g., number of message windows for a system error)

The quality of information and interaction processing is mainly defined by its efficiency and effectiveness. To measure these parameters, the specific values of the HMI dimensions (HMIDs) must be very precise and concrete.

▶ If HMI dimensions are consistently represented on the basis of cultural variables, one can speak of "(inter)cultural HMI dimensions", which express a culturally influenced HMI style.

Chapter 6 presents thoughts on a model of culture-dependent HMI that models the relationship between cultural dimensions and HMI dimensions using cultural interaction indicators (CIIs) and thus describes "intercultural HMI dimensions".

5.4.5   Models and Theories

Hoft (1996) developed a cultural model (iceberg metaphor) relevant to international user interface design (see Fig. 2.1 in Chap. 2). (Marcus 2000) referred user interface features to Hofstede's cultural dimensions (as described above). Shi and Clemmensen (2007) constructed a relationship model for testing cultural applicability. Kappos and Rivard (2008) postulated a cultural model with three perspectives: Information system, its development, and application. Other authors used cultural models to investigate the relationship between culture and HMI. Shah et al (2012) adhered to the concepts of cultural models in researching the influence of culture on global software development.

Based on previous findings in the field of IUID research (Heimgärtner 2012), Heimgärtner 2013b considered a preliminary model of culturally influenced HMI in order to integrate the cultural contexts in HMI design that encompass the relationship between cultural dimensions and HMI dimensions.

In line with the results of an empirical study (see Heimgärtner 2007), some of the correlations between cultural dimensions and the HMI ratios could be determined and numerically evaluated (see Heimgärtner 2010), which led to the concept of HMI style coefficients (see Heimgärtner 2014).

▸ The HMIStile coefficient describes the cultural HMIStyle of a user by representing the average amount of information density, information frequency, interaction frequency and interaction speed expected by members of the intended cultural group.

The HMI style coefficients can be calculated on the basis of Hofstede's indices (cf. Sect. 2.1.4) for the intended population group. The lower the normalized HMI style coefficient is in the range from 0 to 100, the lower the quantity of information to be expected and the lower the frequency of interaction. The resulting style coefficients allow the determination of countries with similar coefficients.

According to these country groups identified on the normalized HMI style coefficient continuum (group average) one can expect that the countries of these country groups show a similar HMI style due to their cultural determination by means of the values of the cultural dimensions of Hofstede PDI, IDV, MAS UAI and LTO (Table 5.9).

These taxonomic results partly resemble the findings in Galtung (1981) related to "saxonic", "teutonic", "Gallic" and "Nipponic" behavioral styles. But in order to arrive at a generalization of the postulated correlation, it may be necessary to examine further cultural groups. To achieve this, both the values of the cultural dimensions by means of empirical surveys, e.g., using the value survey model (VSM, cf. Hofstede 1994), and the values of the HMI dimensions (e.g., number of information units presented per minute, cf. (Heimgärtner 2012)) for each desired population. This can also be done for indigenous groups if the same user cases and test environments are used in arbitrary cultural interest groups. A test tool developed by the author can be used to support this survey (see Heimgärtner 2008). As long as there are no empirically collected values for cultural dimensions at the national level than those of Hofstede, these must be used to test the model. In order to confirm empirical results and to statistically calculate the corresponding HMI style weights resulting from the grouping of Hofsted indices according to HMI style values, a factorial analysis can be carried out. On the basis of the empirical results, the currently valid rules describing the relationship between cultural imprinting and the HMI group style (at least 20 members) should then be refined. The explanatory

Table 5.9 HMI Styles

HMI style	Cultural characterization	HMI style coefficient
Asian	PDI high, IDV low, MAS medium, UAI low, LTO high	90
Indian	PDI high, IDV medium, MAS medium, UAI medium, LTO medium	70
African	PDI high, IDV low, MAS medium, UAI medium, LTO low	60
Scandinavian	PDI Low, IDV High, MAS Low, UAI Medium, LTO Low	40
Slavonic	PDI high, IDV medium, MAS medium, UAI high, LTO low	30
Anglo-Saxon	PDI Low, IDV High, MAS Medium, UAI Low, LTO Low	20
German	PDI low, IDV medium, MAS high, UAI medium, LTO low	10

potential of this currently still purely descriptive model still has to be worked out. In addition to this descriptive model, there are several other approaches to a theory of culturally influenced HMI.

Martinsons and Westwood (1997) have developed an explanation theory for the use of management information systems within Chinese business culture. The use of activity theory plays a very prominent role in the treatment of cultural contexts (see Nardi 1996, p. 1279; Kaptelinin and Nardi 2006, p. 956; Constantine 2009, p. 2242). Maier (2005) applied activity theory as a framework in which cultural factors can be located in HMI studies. Constantine (2009) integrated activity theory into a user-centric design approach to cover environmental contexts. Faiola (2006) aimed at an HMI theory on cultural cognition. Heimgärtner et al. (2011) worked on extending the user-centered design approach to cover cultural contexts by including a cultural model as a new component. Vatrapu (2010) outlined a theory about socio-technological interaction to explain culture. Wyer et al. (2009) integrated theory, research and application to understand the corresponding culture. Clemmensen and Clemmensen (2009) compared common theories to derive a theory of "cultural usability".

► However, there is still no definitive theory that explains all the relevant factors that would be necessary to derive general design recommendations for culture-centric HMI design. This remains a challenge for the future.

5.4.6   Processes, Standards, and Tools

Even if companies invest a lot in the development and acquisition of software, the use of the software does not always run smoothly. In order to ensure the necessary usability of software, a number of standards have therefore been developed.

Bevan (2001) describes the international standards for HMI design and usability engineering.

▸ The human-centered HMI design process is defined in ISO 9241210 and the emerging extension ISO 9241220.

In addition, for example, ISO 9241-171 can also be used to consider cultural aspects necessary to develop user interfaces for users with special skills in intercultural contexts. In addition, the Working Group "Quality Standards" of the German UPA (German Usability and User Experience Professionals Association) has developed a standard for usability engineering which could be provided with the necessary tools, roles, tasks, methods and documents and extended in a way to take cultural aspects into account and in an intercultural context.

Gould and Marcus (2011) proposed cultural audits to improve collaboration, communication, and cooperation between development teams. Heimgärtner (2008) developed an intercultural interaction analysis tool (IIA tool) to measure differences in HMI in a cultural context.

▸ Relevant parts of the ISO 9241 series for usability professionals and user interface designers are practically summarized in a two-volume edition of the DIN VDE paperback 354.

The DIN VDE paperback 354/1 contains standards with basic recommendations for product and process design, while the DIN paperback 354/2 provides standards with concise recommendations for interaction and information design. The four to ten standards printed in this DIN VDE pocketbook 354 are of a general nature and contain principles of dialogue design, processes and evaluation standards within the framework of the development of usable software. This also includes the usability of medical devices. The following standards are printed in DIN VDE Paperback 354/1:

- DIN EN 29241-2 Ergonomics requirements for office work with display screen equipment—Part 2: Requirements for work tasks; Guidelines (ISO 9241-2: 1992); German version EN 29241-2: 1993,
- DIN EN 62366 Medical devices—Application of usability to medical devices (IEC 62366: 2007); German version EN 62366: 2008,
- DIN EN ISO 9241-1 Ergonomics requirements for office work with display screen equipment—Part 1: General introduction (ISO 9241-1: 1997) (includes amendment AMD 1: 2001); German version EN ISO 9241-1: 1997 + A1: 2001,
- DIN EN ISO 9241-11 Ergonomics requirements for office work with display screen equipment—Part 11: Fitness for use requirements; Guidelines (ISO 9241-11: 1998); German version EN ISO 9241-11: 1998,

- DIN EN ISO 9241-20 Ergonomics of human-system interaction—Part 20: Guidelines for accessibility of equipment and services in information and communication technology (ISO 9241-20: 2008); German version EN ISO 9241-20: 2009,
- DIN EN ISO 9241-110 Ergonomics of human-system interaction—Part 110: Principles of dialogue design (ISO 9241-110: 2006); German version EN ISO 9241-110: 2006,
- DIN EN ISO 9241-171 Ergonomics of human-system interaction—Part 171: Guidelines for accessibility of software (ISO 9241-171: 2008); German version EN ISO 9241-171: 2008,
- DIN EN ISO 9241-210 Ergonomics of human-system interaction—Part 210: Process for designing usable interactive systems (ISO 9241-210: 2010); German version EN ISO 9241-210: 2010,
- DIN EN ISO 14915-1 Software ergonomics for multimedia user interfaces— Part 1: Design principles and framework conditions (ISO 14915-1: 2002); German version EN ISO 14915-1: 2002,
- Technical regulation DIN SPEC 33441–100 Ergonomics of human-system interaction—Part 100: Overview of standards for software ergonomics (ISO/TR 9241-100: 2010),
- ISO/TR 16982 Ergonomics of human-system interaction—Methods to ensure suitability for use supporting user-oriented design,
- Pre-standard ISO/TS 18152 Ergonomics of human-system interaction— Specification for the process evaluation of human-system related facts,
- ISO/IEC TR 25060 Quality criteria and evaluation of software products (SQuaRE)—Common industrial format (CIF) for usability—General framework for usability information,
- ISO/IEC 25062 Software Engineering—Quality Criteria and Evaluation of Software Products (SQuaRE)—Common Industrial Format (CIF) for usability test reports.

In addition, DIN Paperback 354/2 contains standards with recommendations for interaction and information design to ensure the necessary usability of the software. They reflect the current development in the standardization of the ergonomics of user interfaces. The standards DIN EN ISO 9241-12 to DIN EN ISO 9241-16 were developed before the restructuring of the DIN EN ISO 9241 series of standards. They also contain valid design notes for information presentation, user guidance, menus, command languages, and manipulation. The newly developed standards deal with individualization, screen forms, user interfaces in the World Wide Web and speech dialogue systems.

5.5 Summary, Conclusion, Outlook

Culture-related user differences must be taken into account when designing user interfaces and integrated sensibly into product development. The design of intercultural HMI has a lot to do with intercultural communication and requires appropriate know-how and appropriate procedures. Intercultural overlapping situations (cf. Honold 2000, p. 42 ff.) arise when a product is defined and formed within a culture and this product is then transferred to another culture and then also used there. A developer from culture X must make the operation of the product understandable for a user from culture Y (see Röse 2002, p. 68 ff.). A cultural user group is a group of people who consciously (their own assignment) or unconsciously (by characteristic/context/role assigned from outside) share values, rules, and behavioral patterns and thus represent a culture. The assignment to a cultural user group takes place through belonging to a culture and the characteristics implicitly assumed with it. Single individuals are not always at the center of cultural considerations, but user groups. This means that the user is regarded as an individual or representative of a group/role. Several user groups require different versions of the user interface for the same application. Conversely, an individual user can also require different versions of the user interface to execute the same application.

The cultural conditions under which a person grows up determine what is memorized and stored in his memory. This also has an influence on structuring and memory. The resulting actions—as a result of the information processing process—are also directly dependent on it. There are cultural differences in performance in the area of short-term and long-term memory. Culture thus also shapes people's ability to learn and perform. Language is an obvious characteristic for the differentiation of cultures. Asian cultures have an "up/down" typeface and Western cultures have a "Left/Right" typeface. The same arrangement principle also applies to the horizontal or vertical menu arrangement (see Röse 2002 and Heimgärtner 2012). The consideration of cultural aspects should not only refer to visual design and elementary UI components, but also to basic design concepts, metaphors, and workflows. There is still a significant need for mediation between science and industry with regard to cultural and cognitive aspects in the development of intercultural user interfaces (IUID).[8]

The multidimensional cultural imprinting of users can be described on the basis of cultural motives. The most interesting cultural models for the design of intercultural HMI are those that are directly linked to communication, information, interaction, and dialogue design, i.e., those cultural dimensions that directly affect the culturally different concepts of space, time, and communication (Heimgärtner 2005, 2007, 2012):

---

[8]This book is intended to contribute to this. As the author of this book, I am happy to answer your questions and provide feedback on the book and IUID. Further information can be found at URL = https://www.iuic.de.

- Individualism (task) versus collectivism (relationship) (containing related cultural dimensions such as face-saving or power distance),
- Nonverbal communication,
- Perception of space (e.g., distance between user and system, network density, context),
- Time perception (containing all time-related cultural dimensions such as uncertainty avoidance or communication speed).

All analyzed cultural dimensions provide space- and time-specific aspects. It therefore makes sense to assume that cultural dimensions based on time deal with interaction and information processing in HMI (e.g., use of dialogue). Cultural dimensions, which instead refer to space, concern the presentation of information as well as the structure and layout of user interfaces. Culture influences the HMI at all levels of the interactive model (cf. action level model after Herczeg 2005 and Heinecke 2004, as well as Norman and Draper 1986). Cultural dimensions can be reduced to a basic cultural dimension (BCD) in which the very similar dimensions "individualism versus collectivism", "task versus personal orientation" and "role versus relationship orientation" are combined. It is important that there is an agreement between the developer and the users in different cultures about the meaning and interpretation of information; otherwise misunderstandings or no understanding at all arise (see Chap. 2). In order to be competitive as a product manufacturer on the world market, it is important that users accept the product. Therefore, cultural influences during the development of products for other markets must be taken into account. The communication level forms the basic level, followed by project management, software, and usability engineering on the way to the successful development of intercultural user interfaces (Fig. 5.4). In order to be able to design user interfaces for the global market that meet the cultural needs of the users, the first step is to identify the differences in the cultural needs of the users and thus the cultural differences in the HMI at all levels of the HMI localization (user interface functionality and interaction) (Röse and Zühlke 2001). Areas such as information presentation and language or dialogue design as well as interaction design are affected (Lewandowitz et al. 2006) (cf. Chap. 7). Bevan (2001) describes the international standards for HMI design and usability engineering.

Intercultural HMI design describes the user- and culture-oriented design of interactive systems and products, taking into account the cultural context of the users in relation to tasks and product use (Röse 2002, 87; Honold 2000, pp. 42–43) and thus the "process of HMI design in a cultural context". The term "process of HMI design" generally refers to the process of human-centered design according to ISO 9241-210 and in particular the development of user interfaces. The perception and consideration of the customs and requirements of other cultures by the developers of intercultural user interfaces are one of the main tasks of intercultural HMI design. Intercultural User Interface Design (IUID) refers to the process of adequately designing the HMI taking into account the cultural requirements of the context of use. The development of intercultural user interfaces concentrates on a specific product or service and on its use in a specific cultural context. It is checked whether the user interface is suitable for its use in the respective cultural context or whether it can be adapted accordingly by the user. Intercultural user interface design is a necessary prerequisite for improving the intercultural usability of software, which in turn is a necessary prerequisite for global sales opportunities. Using methods of intercultural usability engineering, further design guidelines can be iteratively derived from the results of the tests and the feedback of potential users from all over the world for intercultural user interface design. Intercultural interface design is divided into three levels according to (Thissen 2008). The first stage (signs) involves the cultural coding of signs, i.e., the implementation of the way in which information is presented (= semiotic systems of a culture—(Cassirer 1994))– signs as expressions of cultural values ("cultural markers"). The second stage (social behavior) deals with forms of cultural perception described on the basis of cultural models. At the third level of intercultural user interface design, culture is captured and understood in its entirety and complexity (understanding of its identity/alienity).

Cultural dimensions are too rough for intercultural user interface design. For this reason, additional cultural variables are necessary which—in relation to the user interface sign—divide the cultural aspects into smaller units (cf. Röse 2002). These cultural aspects and their manifestations can be empirically determined using qualitative and quantitative methods. Although cultures are constantly changing, for a product life cycle of a few years at least trends can be determined, and for special cases of application, even selective parameters can be determined which serve the intercultural user interface design. there are correlations between the user's interaction behavior and his culture or between the cultural dimensions and information science variables such as information density or interaction frequency at the interaction level (cf. middle level of the "iceberg" in Fig. 6.3 in Chap. 6).

Intercultural variables describe the differences in HMI design with respect to the preferences of users from different cultures (Table 5.3). Direct intercultural variables are most important because they have a direct and essential influence on the HMI design. "Visible" intercultural variables (VIVs) are immediately perceptible at a certain time (font, color, window size, navigation, etc.). In contrast, "invisible" (or "hidden") intercultural variables (NVIVs) are only recognizable over a certain period of time (interaction speed, information display duration, dialogue display frequency, use of the navigation bar, etc.). The localization of hidden intercultural variables is very difficult to realize because the contextual relation to the cultural background as well as to the product is very strong for interaction and dialogue design. However, it is precisely this culturally distinct context and consequently, the cultural dependency of the reason why these patterns and non-visible intercultural variables are so important for information architecture and interaction design and for the resulting dialogues (and dialogues) is that they are not visible (Röse 2002, p. 98). Röse (2002, p. 108) uses intercultural variables within her "Method of Culture-Oriented Design" (MCD), which she has defined for the development of intercultural human–computer systems (Fig. 5.6).

The user interface characteristics "Metaphor", "Mental Model", "Navigation", "Interaction" and "Presentation" are linked to five of Hofstede's cultural dimensions (see Chap. 2). User interface characteristics can be used in conjunction with empirical surveys on their characteristics for the corresponding cultural target context to derive recommendations for the development of intercultural user interfaces.

Information science quantities such as information speed (speed of dissemination and frequency of occurrence of information), information density (number and distance of information units) or information order (sequence of occurrence and arrangement of information) correlate with culturally different basic patterns of behavior. HMI dimensions (HMID) describe the behavior of a user (HMI style) with an interactive information processing system (Heimgärtner 2007). HMI dimensions represent classes of HMI variables (expressions of HMI dimensions) useful for the HMI design, which are operationalized by means of (interaction) indicators in HMI metrics (Table 5.8). There must be at least one potential indicator as a measurement variable in order to be able to represent the character of an HMI dimension. For real use, however, several empirically proven indicators should be used. If HMI dimensions are consistently represented on the basis of cultural variables, one can use "(Inter-) Cultural HMI Dimensions", which express a culturally influenced HMI style. The HMI style coefficient describes the culturally influenced HMI style of a user by representing the average amount of information density, information frequency, interaction frequency and interaction speed expected by members of the previous cultural group. In addition to descriptive models, there are several other approaches to a culturally influenced HMI theory. However, there is still no definitive theory that explains all the relevant factors that would be necessary to derive general design recommendations for culture-centric HMI design. First considerations for an approach are presented in Chap. 6.

The human-centered HMI design process is defined in ISO 9241-210 and the detailed extension in ISO 9241-220. Relevant parts of the ISO 9241 series for usability professionals and user interface designers are practically summarized in a two-volume edition of DIN VDE paperback 354 by Beuth-Verlag.

Norms

√ ☐ ☐

DIN EN 29241-2
DIN EN 62366   ☐ ☐ ☐
DIN EN ISO 9241-1   ☐ ☐
DIN EN ISO 9241-11   ☐ ☐
DIN EN ISO 9241-20   ☐ ☐
DIN EN ISO 9241-110   ☐ ☐
DIN EN ISO 9241-171   ☐ ☐
DIN EN ISO 9241-210   ☐ ☐
DIN EN ISO 9241-220   ☐ ☐
DIN EN ISO 14915-1   ☐ ☐
DINSPEC 33441-100
ISO/TR 16982   ☐ ☐
ISO/TS 181S2
ISO/IEC TR 25060   ☐
ISO/IEC 25062

                                                         ☐

Checklist

Basics of the intercultural user interface design are known (Cultural influences on context of use   ☐
(PACT), Essential new findings from research are available)

                                                                                                         ☐

Stage 1 of intercultural user interface design achieved (cultural differences in languages and
symbols taken into account)   ☐

Level 2 of intercultural user interface design achieved (cultural behavior considered)

Stage 3 of intercultural user interface design achieved (cultural values considered)   ☐

Level 1of TLCC model s is implemented (technique) Level 2 of TLCC model s is implemented   ☐
(language) Level 3 of TLCC model s is implemented (culture) Level 4 of TLCC model s is   ☐
implemented (cognition)   ☐

Relevant cultural dimensions for MMI development are well known User interface characteristics   ☐
are well known and are applied MMI definitions are well known and are applied   ☐

The relationship between cultural dImensIons and MMI dImensIons is reflected and included in the   ☐
design process   ☐

Intercultural variables are known and used Method of culture-oriented design is systematically   ☐
applied

Challenges in the application of the methods and approaches of intercultural usability engineering
and corresponding solutions are known (data level, hypothesis level and hybrid approaches).

Procedure for the creation of explanatory models for the relationship between culture and human-
machine interaction is known

Empathy as a key factor in the development of intercultural user interfaces is known and is
applied

The possibility of using agile methods in the development of intercultural user interfaces is well
known
                                                                                                         ☐

References

Badre A, Barber W (1998) Culturabilty: the merging of culture and usabilty proceedings of the 4th conference on human factors and the web. AT and T Labs, Basking Ridge

Baumgartner V-J (2003) A practical set of cultural dimensions for global user-interface analysis and design. Fachhochschule Joanneum, Graz, Austria

Bevan N (2001) International standards for HCI and usability. Int J Hum Comput Stud 55(4):533–552

Cassirer E (1994) Nature and effect of the concept of symbol. Scientific Book Society, Darmstadt

Clemmensen T, Clemmensen T (2009) Towards a theory of cultural usability. A comparison of ADA and CM-U theory, vol 5619, pp 416–425

Clemmensen T, Clemmensen T (2012) Usability problem identification in culturally diverse settings. Inf Syst J 22(2):151–175. https://doi.org/10.1111/j.1365-2575.2011.00381.x

Cole M (1997) Cultural psychology: a once and future discipline (2. print. Aufl.). Belknap Press of Harvard University Press, Cambridge

Constantine L (2009) Human activity modeling: toward a pragmatic integration of activity theory and usage-centered design human-centered software engineering. In: Seffah A, Vanderdonckt J, Desmarais M (eds). Springer, London, p. 27–51

Courtney AJ (1986) Chinese population stereotypes: color associations. Hum Factors 28(1):97–99

Cox T (1993) Cultural diversity in organizations: theory, research, and practice. Berrett-Koehler Publishers, San Francisco

Cramer PDT (2008) Intercultural cooperation in multinational teams. GRIN Publishing OHG, Munich

Del Galdo EM, Nielsen J (1996) International user interfaces. Wiley, New York

Faiola A (2006) Toward an HCI theory of cultural cognition. In: Ghaoui C (Hrsg) Encyclopedia of human computer interaction. IGI Global, Hershey, PA, USA, S 609–614

Fischer K (2006) What computer talk is and is not: human-computer conversation as intercultural communication, vol 17. AQ-Verlag, Saarbrücken

Galtung J (1981) Structure, culture, and intellectual style: an essay comparing saxonic, teutonic, gallic and nipponic approaches. Soc Sci Inf 20(6):817

Gould E, Marcus A (2011) Company culture audit to improve development team's collaboration, communication, and cooperation design, user experience, and usability. In: Marcus A (Hrsg.) Theory, methods, tools and practice, Bd. 6769. Springer, Berlin, S. 415–424

Hall ET (1959). The silent language. Doubleday, New York

Hall ET (1976) Beyond culture. Anchor Books, New York

Hall ET, Hall M (1983) Hidden signals. Gruner & Jahr, Hamburg

Halpin AW, Winer BJ (1957) A factorial study of the leader behavior descriptions. In: Stogdill RM, Coons AE (Hrsg) Leader behavior: its description and measurement. Bureau of Business Research, Ohio State University, Columbus, S 39–51

Hansen KP (2003) Culture and cultural studies: an introduction (3rd, full-length, vol 1846). Francke, Tübingen

Heimgärtner, R. (2005). Measuring cultural differences in human-computer interaction. In: Auinger A (ed) Workshop-proceedings mensch und computer 2005. OCG Vienna, Vienna, p 89–92

Heimgärtner R (2007) Cultural differences in human computer interaction: results from two online surveys. In: Oßwald A (Hrsg) Open innovation, Bd 46. UVK, Konstanz, S 145–158

Heimgärtner R (2008) A tool for getting cultural differences in HCI. In: Asai K (Hrsg), Human computer interaction: new developments. InTech, Rijeka, S 343–368

Heimgärtner R (2010) Cultural differences in human-computer interaction–Towards culturally adaptive human-machine interaction. PhD Dissertation, Universitätsbibliothek der Universität Regensburg

Heimgärtner R (2012) Cultural differences in human-computer interaction: towards culturally adaptive human-machine interaction. Oldenbourg, Munich

Heimgärtner R (2013a). Intercultural user interface design–culture-centered HCI design–cross-cultural user interface design: different terminology or different approaches? In: Marcus A (Hrsg) Design, user experience, and usability. Health, learning, playing, cultural, and cross-cultural user experience, Bd 8013. Springer, Berlin, S 62–71

Heimgärtner R (2013b) Reflections on a Model of Culturally Influenced Human-Computer Interaction to Cover Cultural Contexts in HCI Design. Int J Hum Comput Interact 29(4):205–219. https://doi.org/10.1080/10447318.2013.765761

Heimgärtner R (2014) Intercultural user interface design. In: Blashki K, Isaias P (Hrsg) Emerging research and trends in interactivity and the human-computer interface. Information Science Reference (an imprint of IGI Global), Hershey, S 1–33

Heimgärtner R (2017) Using Converging Strategies to Reduce Divergence inIntercultural User Interface Design (Vol. 05)

Heimgärtner R, Holzinger A (2005) Towards cross-cultural adaptive driver navigation systems. In: Holzinger A, Weidmann K-H (Hrsg) Empowering software quality: How can usability engineering reach these goals? 1st Usability symposium, HCI&UE workgroup, Vienna, 8 Nov 2005, Bd. 198. Austrian Computer Society, Vienna, S 53–68

Heimgärtner R, Tiede LW (2008) Technology and culture: intercultural experience in product development for China. In: Rösch O (ed.) Interkulturelle Kommunikation (Technik und Kultur), vol 6. Publisher News & Media, Berlin, p 149–162

Heimgärtner R, Tiede L-W, Leimbach J, Zehner S, Nguyen-Thien N, Helmut W (2007) Towards cultural adaptability to broaden universal access in future interfaces of driver information systems. In: Stephanidis C (Hrsg) Universal access in human-computer interaction. Ambient interaction, 4th international conference on Universal Access in Human-Computer Interaction, UAHCI 2007 Held as Part of HCI International 2007 Beijing, 22–27 July 2007 Proceedings, Part II, Bd 4555. Springer, Heidelberg, S 383–392

Heimgärtner R, Tiede L-W, Windl H (2011) Empathy as key factor for successful intercultural HCI design. Paper presented at the proceedings of 14th international conference on human-computer interaction, Orlando

Heinecke AM (2004) Human-computer interaction. Reference book edition Leipzig in the Carl Hanser Verl, Munich

Herczeg M (2005) Software ergonomics: basics of human-computer communication, 2nd, fully revised. Aufl. Oldenbourg, Munich

Hermeking M (2001) Cultures and technology. Waxman, Munich

Hodicová R (2007) Psychological distance and internationalization of SMEs: empirical investigation on the example of the Saxon-Czech border region. Duv

Hofstede GH (1991) Cultures and organizations: software of the mind. McGraw-Hill, London

Hofstede G (1994) VSM94: values survey module 1994 manual. IRIC, Tilberg

Hoft NL (1995) International technical communication: How to export information about high technology. Wiley, New York

Hoft NL (1996) Developing a cultural model. In: Del Galdo EM, Nielsen J (Hrsg) International users interface. Wiley, S 41–73

Honold P (1999) "Cross-cultural" or "intercultural"–some findings on international usability testing. In: Prabhu, GV, Del Galdo EM (Hrsg) Designing for global markets 1, first international workshop on internationalisation of products and systems, IWIPS 1999. Backhouse Press, Rochester/New York, S 107–122

Honold P (2000) Intercultural usability engineering: a study on cultural influences on the design and use of technical products. VDI Verl, Düsseldorf. (Als Ms. gedr. Aufl. 647)

Inkeles A, Levinson DJ (1996) National character: a psycho-social perspective. Transaction Publishers, New Brunswick

Jäger L (ed) (2004) Handbook of cultural studies, vol 1. Metzler, Stuttgart

Jensen AR, Whang PA (1994) Speed of accessing arithmetic facts in long-term memory: a comparison of Chinese-American and Anglo-American children contemporary educational psychology, Bd 19. Academic-Press, New York, S 1–12

Kant I (2006) Critique of pure reason ([Nachdr.] ed. 6461). Reclam, Stuttgart

Kappos A, Rivard S (2008) A three-perspective model of culture, information systems, and their development and use. MIS Q 32(3):601–634

Kaptelinin V, Nardi B (2006) Acting with technologie: activity theory and interaction design. MIT Press, Cambridge

Khaslavsky J (1998) Integrating culture into interface design. Paper presented at the CHI 98 conference summary on human factors in computing systems, Los Angeles

Kralisch A (2006) The impact of culture and language on the use of the internet empirical analyses of behaviour and attitudes. Dissertation, Berlin

Kuo, You-Yuh J, Paschal B, Schurr KT (1979) Creative thinking in Indiana and Taiwan college students. Coll Stud J 13(4):319–327

Lass U (1997) Influence of language on processing processes in short-term memory-an experimental study with German and Chinese rehearsals. In: Lüers G, Let U (eds) Remember and retain: paths to the exploration of human memory. Vanderhoeck & Ruprecht, Göttingen, pp 244–268

Liang SFM (2003) Cross-cultural issues in interactive systems. Paper presented at the proceedings of the international ergonomics. Ergonomics in the digital age

Lewandowitz L, Rößger P, Vöhringer-Kuhnt T (2006) Asian vs. European HMI solutions of driver information systems Useware 2006, vol 1946. VDI, Düsseldorf, S 279–287

Maier E (2005) Activity theory as a framework for accommodating cultural factors in HCI studies. In: Auinger A (Ed) Workshops-proceedings of the 5th interdisciplinary conference man and computer 2005. Internationalization of information systems: cultural aspects of human-machine interaction. Vienna, pp 69–79

Maletzke G (1996) Intercultural communication: interaction between people from different cultures. Westdt. Verl, Opladen

Marcus A (2001a). Cross-cultural user-interface design. In: Smith MJSG (Hrsg), Proceedings conferences, human-computer interface internat (HCII), New Orleans, Bd 2. Lawrence Erlbaum Associates, Mahwah, S 502–505

Marcus A (2001b) International and intercultural user interfaces. In: Stephanidis C (Hrsg) User interfaces for all: concepts, methods, and tools. Lawrence Erlbaum, Mahwah, S 47–63

Marcus A (2006) Cross-cultural user-experience design. In: Barker-Plummer D, Cox R, Swoboda N (Hrsg) Diagrammatic representation and inference, vol. 4045. Springer, Berlin, S 16–24

Marcus A, Gould EW (2000) Crosscurrents: cultural dimensions and global web user-interface design. Interactions 7(4):32–46

Martinsons MG, Westwood RI (1997) Management information systems in the Chinese business culture: an explanatory theory. Inf Manag 32(5): 215–228. https://doi.org/10.1016/s0378-7206 (96)00009-2

Masao I, Kumiyo N (1996) Impact of culture on user interface design international users interface. Wiley, New York, pp 105–126

Mead R (2005) International management: cross-cultural dimensions, 3rd edn. Blackwell, Malden

Nardi BA (1996) Context and consciousness: activity theory and human-computer interaction. MIT Press, Cambridge, MA

Nisbett RE (2003) The geography of thought: How Asians and Westerners think differently … why. Free Press, New York

Norman DA, Draper SW (1986) User centered system design; new perspectives on human-computer interaction. L. Erlbaum Associates Inc, Hillsdale, NJ, USA

Pereira (2015) A value-oriented and culturally informed approach to the design of interactive systems. International Journal of Human-Computer Studies vol 80, Aug 2015, pp. 66–82

Podsiadlowski A (2002) Multicultural working groups in companies, vol 12. Waxmann, Münster

Rau P-LP, Plocher TA et al (2012) Cross-cultural design for IT products and services. Taylor & Francis, Boca Raton

Reeves B, Nass C (1998) The media equation (1. paperback Aufl.). CSLI, Stanford

Reimer A (2005) The importance of Geert Hofstede's cultural theory for international management. Department of Economics, Hochsch

Rösch O (2005) Common goals–different ways? On the simultaneity of the non-simultaneous in German-Russian cooperation TRANS. Internet J Cult Sci 14. http://www.inst.at/trans/14Nr/roeschfv14.htm. Accessed 29 Feb 2019

Röse K (2002) Methodology for the design of intercultural man-machine systems in production engineering, vol 5. Univ, Kaiserslautern

Röse K, Zühlke D (2001). Culture-oriented design: developers' knowledge gaps in this area. Paper presented at the 8th IFAC/IFIPS/IFORS/IEA symposium on analysis, design, and evaluation of human-machine systems, Kassel (18–20 Sept)

Röse K, Zühlke D, Liu L (2001) Similarities and dissimilarities of German and Chinese users. In: Johannsen G (Hrsg) Preprints of 8th IFAC/IFIP/IFORS/IEA symposium on analysis, design, and evaluation of human-machine systems. Kassel, S 24–29

Rößger P (2003) An international comparison of the usability of driver-information-systems. In: Röse U, Honold K, Coronado P, Day J, Evers D (Hrsg) Proceedings of the fifth international workshop on internationalisation of products and systems, IWIPS 2003, Germany, Berlin, 17–19 July 2003. University of Kaiserslautern, Kaiserslautern, S 129–134

Schriesheim CA, Cogliser CC, Neider LL (1995) Is it "trustworthy"? A multiple-levels-of-analysis reexamination of an Ohio State leadership study, with implications for future research. Leadersh Q 6(2):111–145

Schumacher RM (2010) The handbook of global user research. Morgan Kaufmann, Burlington

Scollon R, Scollon SW (1995) Intercultural communication: a discourse approach, vol 21. Blackwell, Oxford. (Reprinted)

Shah H, Nersessian NJ, Harrold MJ, Newstetter W (2012) Studying the influence of culture in global software engineering: thinking in terms of cultural models. Paper presented at the proceedings of the 4th international conference on intercultural collaboration, Bengaluru

Shen S-T, Woolley M, Prior S (2006) Towards culture-centred design. Interact Comput 18(4):820–852. https://doi.org/10.1016/j.intcom.2005.11.014

Sheppard C, Scholtz J (1999) The effects of cultural markers on web site use. Paper presented at the proceedings of the 5th conference on human factors and the web, Gaithersburg

Shi Q, Clemmensen T (2007) Relationship model in cultural usability testing usability and internationalization. In: Aykin N (Hrsg) HCI and culture, Bd 4559. Springer, Berlin, S 422–431

Snitker TV (2004) Breaking through to the other side. Nyt Teknisk Forlag

Straub J (2007) Intercultural communication and competence handbook: basic terms–theories–fields of application. Metzler, Stuttgart

Strawcutter S (2001) Culture–thinking–strategy: an Indian suite. Bern [et al.]: Huber

Strawcutter S (2006) Cultural differences in problem solving. In: Funke J (ed) Encyclopedia of psychology, subject area C, series II, volume 8: thinking and problem solving. Hogrefe, Göttingen, S 549–618

Sun H (2001) Building a culturally-competent corporate web site: an exploratory study of cultural markers in multilingual web design. In: Proceedings of the 19th annual international conference on computer documentation. ACM, Sante Fe, S 95–102

Sundermeier T (1996) Understand the stranger: a practical hermeneutics. Vandenhoeck & Ruprecht, Göttingen

Thissen F (2008) Intercultural information design. In: Weber W (ed) Compendium Informationsdesign. Springer, Heidelberg/Berlin, pp 387–424

Thomas A (1993) Perceptual psychological aspects in cultural comparison. In: Thomas A (ed) Comparative cultural psychology. Hofgrefe-Verlag, Göttingen/Bern/Toronto/Seattle, pp 147–171

Vanka S (1999) Color tool: the cross cultural meanings of color. In Prabhu GV, del Galdo EM (Hrsg) Designing for global markets. 1st international workshop on internationalization of products and systems. Rochester, N.Y. USA, 20–22 May 1999, pp 33–43

Vatrapu R (2010) Explaining culture: an outline of a theory of socio-technical interactions. In: Hinds P, Søderberg A-M, Vatrapu R (Hrsg) Proceedings of the 3rd international conference on Intercultural collaboration 2010, Copenhagen, Denmark 19–20 Aug 2010. Association for Computing Machinery, New York, S 111–120. https://dl.acm.org/citation.cfm?id=1841853.1841871. Accessed 29 Feb 2019. https://doi.org/10.1145/1841853.1841871

Vöhringer-Kuhnt T (2002) The influence of culture on usability. M.A. master thesis, Freie University of Berlin

Wyer RS, Chiu Chi-yue, Hong Ying-yi (2009) Understanding culture: theory, research, and application. Psychology Press, New York

Chapter 6
IUID in Theory—Scientific Research

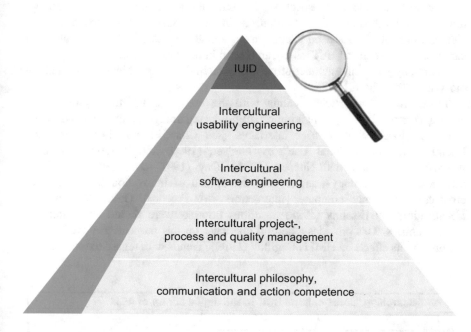

In this chapter, the state of research in the field of the development of intercultural user interfaces and the connection between culture and HMI is presented and some main research questions regarding the culture-centered HMI designs are categorized. A look at the connection between theory and practice, then, opens the way to an explanatory model for culture-dependent human–machine interaction relevant to IUID. Both theoretical knowledge and the results of empirical studies are used. Finally, the first possible model is presented from which recommendations for the development of intercultural user interfaces can be derived.

© Springer Nature Switzerland AG 2019
R. Heimgärtner, *Intercultural User Interface Design*, Human–Computer Interaction Series, https://doi.org/10.1007/978-3-030-17427-9_6

6.1   Status of IUID Research

▸ In order to capture the paradigms and latest aspects of methodology, technology transfer, and innovation diffusion and to get an impression of what the most important tasks in IUID research can, should or must be, it is useful to know and analyze the relevant literature.

6.1.1   Historical Development

In order to obtain the latest aspects of the IUID, e.g., on methodology, technology transfer, and diffusion of innovation, a literature search was carried out by Heimgärtner (2012) based on Clemmensen and Roese (2010). For example, you can enter "cross-cultural HCI" as a search term in the digital library of the ACM, an exponentially increasing number of publications in this area is obtained from about the year 2000 (Fig. 6.1).

There are several articles dealing with the use of information systems in a cultural context. Two of the first important books regarding internationalization and especially localization of user interfaces (see Chap. 3) are "Designing User Interfaces for International Use" by Nielsen (1990) and "International User Interfaces" by Galdo and Nielsen (1996). Day (1991) compiled the research methods, the technology transfer, and the spread of innovation in the field of cross-cultural human–computer interaction. "A Practical Guide to Software Localization" by Esselink (1998) describes how software should be written for other countries. This provides a helpful checklist for this purpose. An overview of culture and its effects on HMI is Cagiltay (1999). Trends with regard to intercultural

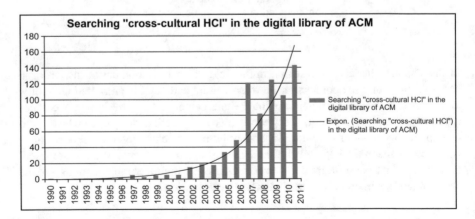

Fig. 6.1 Approximately exponential increase of publications in the IUID area

HMI are also investigated (cf. Jetter 2004). Leidner and Kayworth (2006) conducted a literature search on the connection between culture and information systems and postulated a theory of conflict between culture and information technology. Vatrapu and Suthers (2007) examined the connection between culture and computers through an analysis of the concept of "culture" and the implications for intercultural collaborative online learning. Clemmensen and Roese (2010) offer an overview of a decade of journal publications on culture and HMI.

▸ From the analysis of publications in the field of intercultural HMI, some IUID "hypes" can be identified. The first hype occurred in the early 1990 s. The next one was around 2000 and since about 2010 research in the field of intercultural HMI and IUID has increased by leaps and bounds.

Within these "hypes", the number of publications is high, indicating a strong interest in research and correspondingly high research efforts:

Before 1990: almost no publications available that would link the concepts "culture" and "HMI",

1990–1999: (Pioneers): (Galdo and Nielsen 1996; Aykin 2004; Hoft 1996; Badre and Barber 1998),

2000–2004: (First systematic works): (Honold 2000a; Röse and Zühlke 2001; Hermeking 2001; Rößger and Hofmeister 2003; Marcus 2001; Sun 2001; Vöhringer-Kuhnt 2003; Röse and Zühlke 2001, 2002),

2005–2010: (Exploring the field for extended systematic work): (Clemmensen and Goyal 2004; Reinecke et al. 2007; Heimgärtner 2007; Shen et al. 2006; Clemmensen and Goyal 2004; Thissen 2008),

Since 2010: (Strongly developing research in this field): (Abdelnour-Nocera et al. 2011; Rau et al. 2012; Heimgärtner 2012; Sun 2012; Lee et al. 2008).

6.1.2 Research Questions and Disciplines Involved

The following selection of disciplines and related fields of activity/activities can be identified in relation to some key issues of research in intercultural HMI design:

(i) What are the different cultural user preferences?

    a. Cultural Studies [cultural dimensions (Hall 1959; Hofstede 1991)], cultural standards (Thomas 1996),

    b. Culture, perception, and decision-making regarding cognitive styles, metaphors, problem-solving, knowledge representation, information recognition, and processing (cf. Heimgärtner 2008; Kaplan 1966; Oldenburg 1992: 31; Dörner 2001; Dong and Lee 2008),

    c. Communication science (intercultural communication) (cf. Gudykunst and Mody 2002), speech analysis, dialogue analysis, speech analysis ("conversations are dialogues") (cf. Heindrichs 1979), speech representation theory (Kamp and Reyle 1993), communication analysis and speech act theory (Austin and Savigny 1962; Searle et al. 1980; Grewendorf 1979; Wunderlich 1978), communication modes, communication modes, inter-active dialogues (Moeschler 1989), and language games (Wittgenstein and Schulte 2000),

d. Linguistics (monitoring and analyzing natural language (Reischer 2002), principle of cooperation (Grice 1993), dialogueical speech behavior, illo-cution, intentionality (Searle et al. 1980), conventionality, text analysis ("dialogues are texts"), semantics (Brekle 1972), cognitive linguistics (Saffer 2008), translating (Wilss 1988), and linguistic pragmatics (Wunderlich 1975),

e. Philosophy [Theory of Action (Davidson 1993; Dennett 1998)], Universal Pragmatics (Apel 2002; Habermas 2006), Hermeneutics (Gadamer 1975), Meeting Models (Sundermeier 1996), Intercultural Philosophy (Wimmer 2004),

f. Others: Cognitive technology (Beynon et al. 2001), cognitive language processing (Rickheit and Strohner 1993), regional studies, applied geogra-phy, and dialectology, etc., (e.g., sinology, which is also part of linguistics), cultural engineering.

(ii) Which aspects of HMI depend on culture (i.e., which aspects need to be adapted to the cultural needs of the user)?

Aspects of HMI can be drawn primarily from the fields of information science and applied computer science (intercultural HMI design, software ergonomics):

- Information Science (Information Theory Shannon 1948), Information Concept (e.g., Lyre 2002 or Reischer 2006),
- HMI design [sequence pattern, interaction design (cf. Preece and Rogers 1994, Meta-communication as design principle for dialogue design in HMI Galdo and Nielsen 1996; Shneiderman 1998)],
- Intercultural HMI design: Variables of intercultural HMI design (e.g., Khaslavsky 1998; Badre and Barber 1998; Marcus 2001; Röse 2002; Fitzgerald 2004; Callahan 2005b).

(iii) Do usability and user experience (e.g., simplicity and joy of use) improve through cultural adaptation?

▸ To date, there are only a few qualitative studies or tests on intercultural user experience that would provide reasonable answers to these questions (cf. Jameson 2007). Even though there is now relevant literature on usability engineering (e.g., Nielsen 1993; Holzinger 2005, etc.), reliable and above all generalizing literature on intercultural usability engineering [e.g., on evaluation in an intercultural context (cf. Clemmensen and Clemmensen 2012)] and above all on intercultural usability engineering is increasing only very moderately (cf. Heimgärtner 2014).

6.1.3   Studies and Contents

▸ Most studies concern the presentation of information on web pages [e.g., Hodemacher et al. 2005; Marcus 2003; Dormann 2005; Baumgartner 2003; Marcus and Gould 2000; Stengers et al. 2004; Sun 2001 and Callahan 2005a)].

Only since about 2006 have there been studies that examine stand-alone systems and applications that are not web applications (e.g., Kralisch 2006; Kamentz 2006; Lewandowitz et al. 2006; Braun et al. 2007).[1]

In the investigations, most researchers concentrate on the "visible" cultural variables (VIVs, cf. Chap. 5.4.1) such as colors (NASA color standard, Currie and Peacock 2002 or Ou et al. 2004), icons (application of pictorial or abstract icon Röse 2002, p. 135), date and time, telephone number and address formats, spelling, typography, reading and writing directions and sorting methods (Shneiderman et al. 2009, pp. 23–24), text length, word processing, number of characters (Rätzmann 2004, p. 77), and multimedia (Krömker 2000). Isa et al. (2009) compared cultural regulations and the perception of information architecture among users of a culture-determined website in a study of Muslim online users. Tateishi and Toma (2010) asked the question why social media can cross seas, but nationalist tendencies cannot, when comparing cross-cultural interfaces of use. Endrass et al. (2008) confirm the spread of the proverb "Speaking is silver, silence is gold" in some cultural contexts through a cross-cultural analysis of the use of speech breaks. Koda et al (2008) conducted a cross-cultural evaluation of the facial expressions of avatars designed by Western graphic artists. Lee (2007) explored culture and its impact on human interaction design between Korea and Japan with a focus on cross-cultural perspectives. Kankanhalli et al. (2004) focused on cross-cultural differences and the values of information system developers.

There is also some research in the field of intercultural HMI design concerning the design of intercultural web pages and research on international product design [cf. international workshops on the internationalization of products and systems (IWIPS)] as well as guidelines concerning the visible areas of graphical user interfaces for the internationalization and localization of software.

Thus, in the field of intercultural HMI design, much research is being done into cross-cultural design for websites and international product design (see International Workshop for the Internationalization of Products and Systems (IWIPS) and the manifold guidelines for international and local software adaptation of the visible areas of graphical user interfaces (GUI)).

Cultural influences on the values of the directly visible cultural variables (VIVs) of the HMI (cf. Chap. 5.4.1) are thus already empirically proven in the secondary

---

[1]Cf. https://www.usabilityblog.de/nutzen-sie-kulturdimensionen-zur-erfolgreichen-internationalisierung-und-lokalisation/, last access 9th of February 2019.

literature on internationalization (cf. Nielsen 1990; Evers and Day 1997) and largely realized in products at the user interface level (with regard to information display, language, and general hardware design) and at the functional localization level (with regard to machine functions, maintenance, and technical documentation) (e.g., in operating systems such as Windows or iOS).

▸ The TLCC model by Sturm (2002) shows the internationalization and localization steps in HMI design, represented by four levels: technical affairs, language, culture, and cognition (see Chap. 7.4.3). Cultural aspects of technology and language are taken into account in industry. Aspects relating to more specific cultural characteristics and cognition are still predominantly research-based (cf. Fig. 6.2).

The current status of industrial products comprises the inclusion of cultural aspects in design up to about the first half of the model (green area in Fig. 6.2). The other half of the model has so far been mainly researched (red area in Fig. 6.2). Accordingly, this development can also be seen in today's industrial products.

At the lowest levels of technology (T), technical aspects (e.g., mains plug) are adapted and corresponding character sets (e.g., Unicode) are used (cf. e.g., B. the checklist of Esselink 1998) so that the products can be used in any country. The adaptation of the software to Unicode is an example of a prerequisite for being able to use Asian languages at the language (L) level. Adaptation at the cultural level (C) concerns country-specific aspects including format, currency, colors, modalities, menu structure, content of menus, help, number of messages, length of texts, number of references, degree of entertainment, or relationship of information to entertainment. At the highest level, cognition (C), cognitive styles must be taken into account, which encompasses different types of human thought such as problem-solving techniques or decision-making processes (cf. Nardi 1996; Norman and Draper 1986, see also Chap. 2).

However, the use of internationalization concepts beyond the technical and linguistic level is only being promoted slowly in industry. Kersten et al. (2002), Aykin (2005) or Law and Perez (2005) suggest, for example, how to implement cross-cultural information systems. In industry today, at least technical and linguistic aspects are taken into account when designing products for other cultures, while academic approaches also take cultural and cognitive aspects into account (Fig. 6.2). Previous industrial process models for the development of intercultural user interfaces do not yet take intercultural aspects, which go beyond language, writing, and data formats, sufficiently into account. Also, evaluation techniques for those cultural circles in which Western methods fail are often still lacking.[2]

---

[2]Adaptive systems or agent systems offer a promising approach for the successful globalization of user interfaces through the integration of cultural imprinting in the user model used (cf. Heimgärtner 2012 and Dagstuhl Workshop 2014).

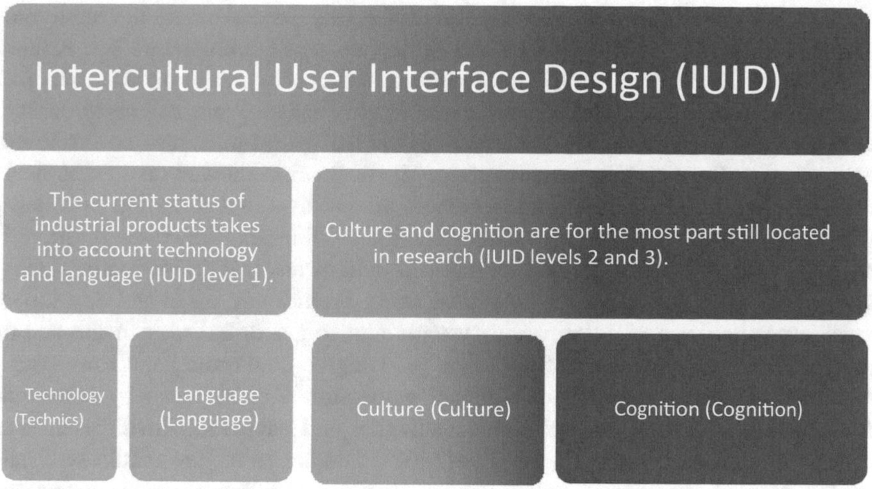

Fig. 6.2 Relationship between the "TLCC" model (after Storm 2002) and IUID (Heimgärtner 2014) (green: productive in industry, red: still researching in science)

► There is still a significant need for mediation between science and industry with regard to cultural and cognitive aspects in the development of intercultural user interfaces (IUID).[3]

► The detailed analysis of current research in the field of intercultural user interface design showed that especially hidden cultural variables (NVIVs) (under the iceberg's water surface) have not yet been thoroughly investigated.

The secondary literature in IUID research so far hardly covers anything essential on hidden intercultural variables at the level of interaction. The cultural influence on human–machine interaction related to navigation, system structure and mental models as well as flexible functionality has not yet been investigated in detail with the intention to develop optimal products for specific cultures. Furthermore, there is little literature on the connection between cultural aspects and the hidden intercultural variables (NVIVs) for HMI design. The literature study does not reveal much about the research on directly hidden cultural variables at the localization level of interaction for intercultural HMI design: Some of these interesting studies and their contents are addressed below.

---

[3]This book is intended to make an initial contribution by presenting the most important principles of IUID. As an author, I am happy to answer your questions and provide feedback on the book as well as on the IUID topic in general. Further information can also be found at https://www.iuic.de.

Komlodi (2005) investigated cultural differences in information search processes. Guidelines are accessible when setting up an IT architecture (cf. Koning et al. 2002); Evers et al (1999) noted cultural differences in the understanding of metaphors in user interfaces. Since the real-world changes from culture to culture, the metaphors used in the HMI that refer to the real world must also be taken into account when localizing the user interface. The evaluation showed that test subjects from different cultures understand metaphors differently and that their expectations, which they associate with the metaphors, are also different. However, these variables are also predominantly seen as an open field of research in intercultural HMI design. Lee (2002) wrote an intercultural study on the way users and developers experience their use of information systems and found differences in the use of mobile Internet between users from Japan (e.g., high e-mail traffic) and Korea (e.g., many downloads) depending on different value structures imposed by culture in Japan and Korea. Consequently, personalization and adaptation of different user needs are necessary. According to Lee (2002), Internet strategies should be localized or adapted to unique cultures, since people expect different values even from the same services in different cultures. Mobile Internet services must be personalized for individual users because value structures and usage patterns are influenced by numerous factors in different countries. In order to develop personalized services, mobile Internet providers must divide their user groups into cultural, demographic, or socioeconomic populations and monitor them, which can give them the ability to efficiently track the rapidly changing needs or values of users. Nisbett (2003) postulated that the thought patterns of East Asians and Westerners differ greatly (holistic vs. analytical). Holistically thinking people tend to perceive a scene globally; they are more field-dependent. Analytically thinking people are more field-independent because they tend to perceive an object detached from the scene and assign such objects to categories. Dong & Lee studied the relationship between cognitive styles and webpage perception. They explained the culturally different behavior of the eye movement (Dong and Lee 2008). The different viewing patterns of Chinese, Koreans, and Americans indicate that web page designers should not ignore the cognitive differences that exist among holistic and analytical people, and that web pages should be designed to match the cognitive styles of users in order to increase usability. Holistic people (e.g., Chinese) do not fly over the entire webpage in a straight line. Consequently, content design should reflect the overall context of the website, as well as the harmony between foreground and background, and the relationships between content areas. In contrast, webpage design for analytical people (e.g., Germans) should be kept as simple and clear as possible. These tend to apply a sequential reading behavior and read from the center of the page to the periphery. Consequently, the structure of all content areas must be carefully considered. Categories and navigation elements should be named as clearly as possible, as analytical people pay more attention to such elements and thus get an overall impression of the website.

In further studies (Dong and Lee 2008), the relationship between cognitive styles and webpage layout design will be defined. Lee et al (2008) have examined the user's life on the basis of a cross-country and cross-product analysis of the cultural characteristics of the user by means of cultural dimensions. Lee (2002) conducted a cross-cultural study on the experience of users and developers in using information systems. In addition, an exploratory study (Rızvanoğlu and Öztürk 2009) with French and Turkish users of an e-learning website improved the cross-cultural understanding of the dual structure of metaphorical icons.

▸ The number of studies that underline the importance of taking cultural aspects into account in the development of user interfaces is constantly growing (see Evers 2003; Smith et al. 2004). There are also activities to investigate trends in intercultural HMI (see Jetter 2004; Clemmensen and Roese 2010; Heimgärtner 2014).

This is also the case, for example, with driver navigation systems in the automotive sector (Rößger and Hofmeister 2003). However, there is hardly any secondary literature on the subject and there are only a few guidelines for intercultural dialogues or design guidelines for intercultural interaction design (Kamentz 2006; Kralisch 2006) and even fewer for special areas such as "embedded systems".

▸ In the field of intercultural user interface design, the exploration of difficult, receptive methodological intercultural factors such as different usages of the system, different expectations with regard to navigation within hyperspace, or different mental models is only now slowly taking off in order to achieve practice-relevant results.

Even though the first pragmatic guidelines exist, e.g., for intercultural web design (cf. Marcus and Gould 2000) or intercultural HMI design (cf. Röse 2001), there are none that could be applied very easily and effectively by HMI designers, because these guidelines are strongly dependent on the specific context of use. This is also supported in the overview by Sturm und Mueller (2003) as well as by Fitzgerald (2004) and the overview by Thiessen on intercultural information design (cf. Thissen 2008), which present many activities and models for intercultural website design. Röse (2002) and Zühlke and Röse (2000) explicitly mention intercultural HMI design and the design of global products for the Chinese market. Only recently have there been newer findings regarding interactive design (e.g., Heimgärtner 2012).

▸ Figure 6.3 summarizes the current state of research on intercultural HMI design using the iceberg metaphor.

The colors in Fig. 6.3 are related to the localization levels (interface, interaction, functionality (program and operating system)). In contrast to visible cultural variables, which influence the interface of the user interface (i.e., the visible elements of the user interface), invisible cultural variables affect the level of interaction. For example, "UC, coding" in the blue triangle in Fig. 6.3 denotes "Unicode coding". It is marked blue, similar to the system, because the system architecture has to be changed. In any case, the effect is visible on the surface (e.g., the representation of Chinese symbols instead of German characters). Therefore, Unicode (UC) can be found on the surface level of the localization (i.e., above the "Water surface"). The different colors (dark blue, blue, light blue, turquoise) show that there are different

Status of IUID research 2001

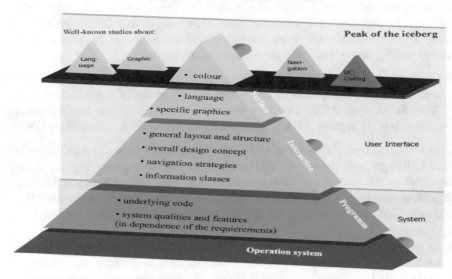

Status of IUID research 2016

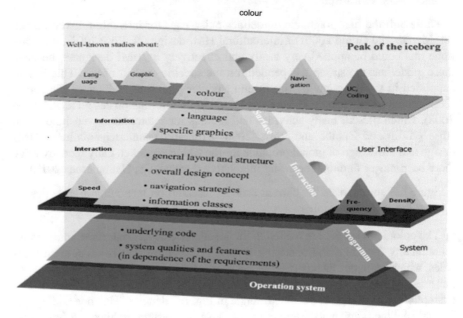

Fig. 6.3 Lack of well-elaborated theoretical work based on empirical results in the field of intercultural interaction and dialogue design with regard to non-visible cultural variables (*Source* Röse 2001, p. 161) (the light red level indicates the current state of intercultural HMI design; the dark red level indicates scientific progress up to 2016 on the interaction level) [Following the iceberg metaphor of Hoft (1995), re-published in Galdo and Nancy (1996), edited by Röse (2001) and updated by the author 2016]

relationships in the entire system that must be taken into account in the intercultural HMI design. Consequently, it is crucial for intercultural user interface design to close the gap between cultural aspects and those for user interface design, e.g., the current lack of research on culturally shaped interaction and dialogue design. The progress of IUID research to date is illustrated by the shift of the dark red marking.

6.2 Methods for Obtaining an Explanatory Model for Culture-Dependent HMI

Usability is a product quality of interactive systems. Knowing the cultural differences in HMI helps to improve the intercultural usability of technical systems. Empirical studies show that there are correlations between user interaction with the computer and user cultural imprinting. The values of cultural variables from the studies can be used for intercultural HMI design guidelines and for intercultural usability engineering. In an explanatory model for culturally influenced HMI, the relations between culture and HMI can be described using cultural interaction indicators, thus establishing and demonstrating the connection between culture and HMI.

> Due to the necessity of collecting current requirements and user wishes for the respective context and the respective target culture, a constant exchange between theory and practice is necessary: on the one hand, the newly collected results must be incorporated into further theoretical research, on the other hand, new theoretical findings affect the method of collecting and interpreting the results. Therefore, close interlocking of theory and practice is indispensable for intercultural HMI research. The link between theory and practice is of utmost importance, especially in an intercultural context.

▶ There is nothing more practical than a good theory to move from theoretical considerations to practical application in intercultural user interface design.

The so-called "Grounded Theory" (cf. Kelle 2003) is particularly suitable for areas that have yet to be researched in depth. "Grounded theory" encompasses a method that is applied in research areas that have not yet been explored in detail—such as the development of intercultural user interfaces (IUID). The "Grounded Theory" was not specifically conceived as a qualitative method, but rather as an alternative approach to general theory formation in social research. Since the hypothetical deductive model of the hypothesis test is not sufficient to capture the essence of the research interest, both quantitatively and qualitatively, there is still a great demand today for a concept of empirically proven theory formation in social research methodology (Kelle 2003, p. 1). Due to the lack of empirical data and the large research gaps remaining in the field of intercultural HMI, it makes sense to use the basic multistage research process of Grounded Theory to develop new theories. Through the analytical reflection of already known theories, models, and intuitive ideas, hypotheses for a new integration theory can be formed. Then, empirical data must establish a basic foundation (introductory position) to test and verify the hypotheses in order to obtain a new theory. Based on this theory, new hypotheses and predictions can then be developed in order to test them empirically (cf. Vollhardt et al. 2008).

▸ The "Grounded Theory" represents an iterative scientific process which resembles the iterative software development cycles (cf. Balzert 2005). The theoretically based processes are predominantly based on the "Grounded Theory" and the established and proven processes in practice are based on software engineering.

> The creation of an explanatory model for culture-dependent HMI does not, therefore, lie in the collection of loose recommendations for the design of obvious system components within the framework of "internationalisation". Nor should an attempt be made to draw up a list of simple static rules assigned to cultural standards according to which generalist systems are designed. Rather, a basic procedure for the scientific creation of a sustainable explanatory model of culturally influenced HMI should be proposed and empirical results used as a basis. Both qualitative and quantitative empirical studies must then show whether culturally influenced user behavior correlates with cultural models. If this is the case, the statements of the explanatory model can be used as guidelines for intercultural HMI design and for intercultural usability engineering.

An improvement in usability in the cultural context and in the methods of intercultural usability engineering can be derived purely analytically from basic scientific knowledge. The possible so-called "potential cultural interaction indicators (PCII)" are formed from the reflection of the connection between cultural dimensions, which serve for the comparative description of the behavior of people of different cultures, and HMI dimensions, which represent the interaction style of the user with the system. These represent HMI variables whose values are potentially culture-dependent (such as the mouse movement speed or the number of information units per drawing area).

▸ In an explanatory model for culturally influenced HMI, the relations between culture and HMI are described using cultural interaction indicators, thus illustrating the relationship between culture and HMI. These relations can be determined in particular in the following ways: data-driven or hypothesis-driven.

▸ The data-driven approach first collects data. The resulting patterns provide information about the connection between culture and HMI.

In the hypothesis-driven approach, hypotheses are derived from existing cultural theories and empirically verified. Finally, in the hybrid approach, the approaches are brought together and if necessary, extended by additional methods.

6.2.1   Data-Driven Approach

▸ Data-driven approach: Hypotheses are formed from data already collected.

In order to find out where the way in which users from different cultural groups interact with an interactive system is different and to derive possible correlations between cultural dimensions and HMI dimensions, the interaction behavior of users with the computer is observed and analyzed. Using automated analytical tools, dynamic aspects of the HMI can be measured by seamless chronological recording of user behavior (cf. e.g., Nelius 2003).

▸ In order to encourage the culturally different user to interact with the computer, and then to record and analyze this interaction, task scenarios were developed which were implemented in a specially developed PC tool (IIA-Tool, Heimgärtner 2008).

This tool allows the measurement of the values of cultural interaction indicators, as well as, the expressions of relevant cultural dimensions for the HMI design during the user's interaction with the system by processing test items and applying the VSM94 questionnaire of Hofstede (1994) within the IIA-Tool.

For example, the Map Display test case was generated to measure the amount of information on the map display (e.g., restaurants, roads, POIs, etc.) that represents an aspect of information density (Fig. 6.4).

The user can set the amount of information in the map display by scrolling (number of POIs, number of maneuvres, etc.). The test tool records the values set by the users. Based on this principle, the test tool can also be used to examine the values of other cultural variables, such as device position, menu, layout and dialogue structuring, information flow speed, etc. The number, size, distance, and uniformity of the arrangement of the information units can be set. In addition, parameters such as test duration, the abruptness and speed of mouse movements,

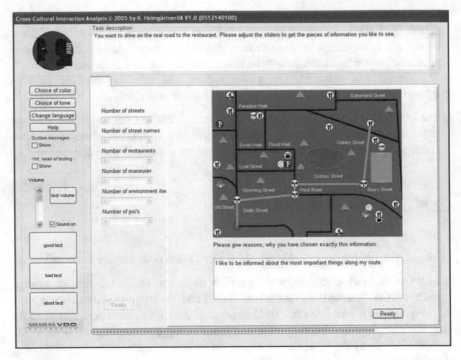

Fig. 6.4 Screenshot of the "Map Display Test Task" during the test session with the IIA-Tool

the sequence and speed of controller changes (e.g., scrollbars) and the entire sequence of interactions can be recorded, and average values or maxima and minima can be determined. In addition, measured variables of common usability metrics such as task time, number of errors, or number of functions used are recorded (cf. Dix et al. 2001).

This data shows which correlations occur between the user's interactive behavior and his culture or cultural dimensions and which implications can be derived from this for intercultural HMI design.

In 2006 and 2007, two empirical remote online studies with a total of 14500 Chinese-(C), German-(G), and English (E)-speaking employees of Siemens VDO worldwide collected interaction data and determined which cultural differences in human–computer interaction (MCI) can be quantitatively determined (Heimgärtner 2007). Subsequently, the results were examined for possible implications for intercultural usability engineering.

During the completion of test tasks by the test persons on their respective work computers (Windows PC system), their interaction behavior was recorded. Almost 1000 complete and valid data sets could be evaluated (Heimgärtner 2007).[4] Culturally induced differences in the HMI could be made visible by statistical means using the quantitative data collected (e.g. Explorative Factor Analysis, Discriminant Analysis, ANOVA, Kruskal–Wallis Test, Post Hoc tests, etc.). On this basis, usability metrics (cf. Nielsen 2001) of high empirical value for measuring relevant quantitative variables for the culturally influenced HMI can be derived.

▸ The evaluation of the data collected in the studies showed that there are correlations between the interaction of users with the computer and the cultural character of users (Heimgärtner 2007).

▸ The cultural differences in HMI between Chinese and German users concern layout (complex vs. simple), information density (high vs. low), personalization (strong vs. low), language (icons vs. characters), interaction speed (higher vs. lower), and interaction frequency (higher vs. lower).

▸ Cultural interaction indicators are HMI parameters that correlate with variables representing the user's culture. The cultural interaction indicators found in Table 6.1 mainly concern the localization level of the interaction.

▸ It has been empirically shown that user interaction with the system is influenced not only by culturally related variables such as nationality, mother tongue, country of birth, etc., but also by parameters such as experience and age (Heimgärtner 2007).

It is difficult to separate cultural influences from experience, because experience is also culturally shaped. However, the use of different statistical methods has shown that there are corroborative aspects which suggest that the statistical results of the two studies are sufficiently reliable and valid: there is a high discrimination rate of over 80% for classifying users in (C) and (G) by cultural interaction indicators.

Significant correlations between culture and HMI could be derived from the cultural interaction indicators obtained from the empirical studies and the cultural interaction patterns (represented by the conglomerate of all constructed cultural interaction indicators).

---

[4]Experimental setup, data evaluation, and results are described in detail in Heimgärtner (2007).

Table 6.1 Cultural differences in the HMI between Chinese-(C) and German (G)-speaking users

Cultural interaction indicator (CII)	Relationship between Chinese-(C) and German (G)-speaking users
Number of error clicks (clicks without functional effect)	2:1
Number of open applications	2:1
Speed of mouse movements	1,6:1
Number of mouse movements	1,3:1
Number of mouse clicks (left mouse button)	1,2:1
Interaction pauses with the mouse > 10 s	1:1,22

▶ Information density, information, and interaction frequency, as well as information and interaction parallelism, are lower for (G) than for (C) according to the relationship orientation, the density of information networks and the time orientation of the users.

This fact also seems to be the reason for the significant differences in the use of anthropomorphic agents, relational dialogues and message content as well as chat programs between (G) and (C).

▶ The way in which the system interacts with the user within the HMI must be adaptable through an adequate modification of the system parameters according to the development of the cultural interaction indicators and the HMI dimensions.

This enables the system to cope with the user's requirements regarding the HMI, which mainly depend on the cultural imprint, age, and experience of the user as well as on the situational context.

Similar cultural differences in the HMI (not only related to China and Germany) can also be found in studies by Röse (2002) or Kralisch (2006) (see also Clemmensen and Roese 2010).

▶ The significant cultural interaction indicators (CIIs) identified in Table 6.1 concern the different interaction behaviors in the HMI between Chinese-(C) and German (G)-speaking user groups.

This data-driven approach deals with the correlation of HMI data and demographic variables such as citizenship, mother tongue, country of birth, etc. This is a predominantly descriptive approach in which cultural standards or cultural dimensions are still largely ignored and demographic variables such as nationality or country of birth are used instead. As soon as explanations for the behavior of the user with the system are required from a cultural point of view—as is the case in the hypothesis-driven explanative approach explained in the next section—cultural models must be included in the considerations.

The high discrimination rate of over 80% for the classification of users in (C) and (G) by the CIIs proves the validity of the statistical results. The statistical

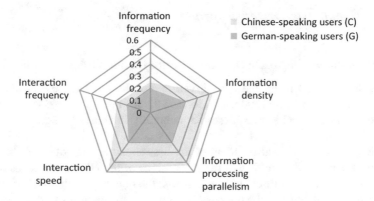

Fig. 6.5 Characteristics of the HMI dimensions representing the culture-dependent differences in the user's interaction with a computer system

evaluation of the empirical studies showed significant correlations between the culture of corresponding user groups ((C) and (G)) (here defined by demographic variables such as nationality, country of birth and mother tongue—(C) Chinese used as test language, (G) German used as test language) and the HMI.

According to the empirically determined values of the cultural interaction indicators, the characteristics of the HMI dimensions information frequency, information processing parallelism, information density, interaction speed, and interaction frequency are significantly higher for Chinese than for Germans. The numbers in Fig. 6.5 represent ratio values. For example, the interaction speed at (C) was about twice as high as at (G): (0.57–0.30).

From this, preliminary design recommendations regarding the system architecture can be derived:

▸ The way in which the computer interacts with the user must be adaptable in such a way that the system can cope with the user requirements, which depend as much on the cultural imprint and experience of the user as on the current situation. The necessary variables must be taken into account in the design of the system architecture.

For driver navigation systems, this design recommendation is reflected, for example, in the implementation of additional variables for the number of points of integration or for the number of color styles in the map display.

These results also serve as a basis for the optimization of the methods and processes of intercultural usability engineering because they describe the interaction behavior of users during communication with technical systems depending on the culture of the user.

6.2.2   Hypothesis-Driven Approach

▸ Hypothesis-driven approach: Data are collected for the verification of hypotheses.

The results obtained using the data-driven approach (see Sect. 6.2.1) led to the conviction that it is justified and useful to use CIIs for intercultural HMI research in order to obtain reasonable hypotheses for culturally influenced HMI.

▸ The hypotheses are based on some of the best classifications of the CIIs, which support the basic hypothesis that the expressions of the HMI dimensions depend on the cultural imprint of the user as follows: the higher the relational orientation (collectivism), the higher the information density, information speed, information frequency, interaction frequency, and interaction speed (and vice versa).

Heimgärtner (2007) examined some of these hypotheses and confirmed the trend that such relationships exist (see also Heimgärtner 2012). Although these findings cannot yet be really viable prognostic aids within the framework of a hypothesis-driven approach (because causal relations do not yet exist), it is necessary for further research to integrate the tendentious correlations found so far into an initial relationship model in order to be able to use them as a starting point for explanations of the connections between the cultural imprint of the user and his interaction with the system, and thus to establish an initial provisional model of culture-dependent HMI.

Table 6.2 shows possible connections between HMI dimensions, cultural interaction indicators, and cultural dimensions or variables of cultural models. For example, based on the Hall (1959) action chain hypothesis (see Chap. 2), it is assumed that the answers to questions from German users are linear (i.e., question after question) and is processed nonlinearly by Chinese users (which can be determined by analyzing the mouse movements and the sequence of fields when filling out the questionnaire).

Furthermore, the number of dialogue steps until completion of the task could be lower for German users than for Chinese users due to their higher task orientation. For German users, it is assumed that the number of interactions during the completion of the task, such as the number of optional functions (e.g., online help or color setup), is higher for German users due to the desire to work very accurately. On the other hand, the number of mouse movements or clicks of German users should be lower than for Chinese users due to the high uncertainty avoidance and strong task orientation. For these reasons, an interaction step during the completion of the task (and thus the entire test duration) might take longer for Germans than for Chinese users. Chinese users may not use the help button as often as German users to face-saving (see Victor 1998). The speed of mouse movements could be lower for German users due to high uncertainty avoidance and low communication speed or low context and relationship orientation.

Table 6.2 Cultural interaction indicators represent possible correlations between HMI dimensions and variables or dimensions of cultural models

HMI dimension	Cultural interaction indicator	Examples/characteristics of cultural interaction indicators	Cultural dimension/ variables of cultural models
Information frequency	Number of information units per time unit	Number of words, sentences, dialogues, Propositions, etc., per minute, reference distance	Unsteady avoidance, action chains, network density
Information density	Distance of information units from each other, number of simultaneously presented information units	Picture–text ratio, number of places of interest	Uncertainty avoidance, network density
Information or interactional parallelism	Sequential or parallel Presentation or reception of information units, information arrangement	Number of parallel tasks, discarded System messages, time until deactivation of virtual agents, layout	Mono-chrone versus. poly-chrone Time orientation,
Interaction speed	Duration of an interaction process	Mouse usage, mouse motion pauses less than 1 ms, mouse track length per second, Inputs	Mono-chrone versus poly-chrone time orientation
Interaction frequency	Number of interaction processes per time unit	Number of mouse clicks, mouse movements, function or help initiatives per session	Monochronic versus polychronic time orientation

Some of the postulated connections between culture and HMI known from the literature were examined with the help of a specially developed tool for intercultural interaction analysis [IIA-Tool, (Heimgärtner 2008)].

A user test with this tool included several successive parts. First, the demographic data of the subject were collected. Then the task presentation takes place: The subject was to perform a series of different tasks, each of which served to examine other cultural aspects of HMI according to the hypotheses. In order to determine the cultural value of the test person, a questionnaire had to be completed (cf. Hofstede 1994). The final debriefing clarified the purpose of the test and asked questions about the usability of the test system, the difficulty of the tests and whether the hypotheses had already been guessed during the test (and thus the test validity was lost) or not.

The hypotheses were tested, for example, by presenting the same task to subjects from different cultures. For example, the hypothesis "there is a high correlation of high information density to relation-oriented cultures such as Chinese" could be confirmed by the recruitment of more POIs by German users compared to Chinese users.

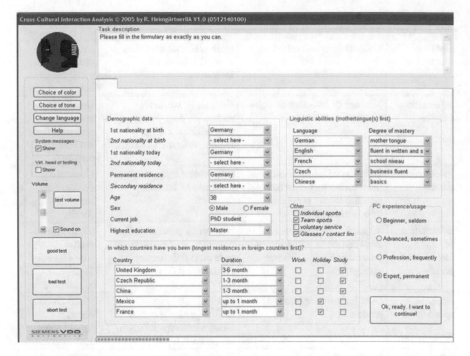

Fig. 6.6 "Special" demographic questionnaire that also records the user's interaction with the system as he completes the questionnaire (*Source* Heimgärtner 2012)

In addition, the demographic "questionnaire" provides common knowledge of demographic research that concerns the cultural background of the user, such as mother tongue, other languages, nationality, stays abroad, educational level, job title, age, and PC experience. By filling in the demographic questionnaire, parameters relating to the user's interaction with the system (in addition to the contents of the question fields) are also determined (Fig. 6.6).

Figure 6.7 shows the results of the investigation on the basis of the differences in the effective values of the measurement variables in contrast to the values of the parameters assumed in the hypotheses. For example, it was assumed that the number of interactions with the system per time unit (INH) of Chinese users is about four times higher than that of German users (0.8: 0.2 = 4). However, the ratio is in reality only 1.4 with respect to the number of average mouse movements in a test session (10566:7529). This ratio can be seen as an indicator of the strength of the postulated hypothesis.

▶ The confirmation strengths of six out of eight hypotheses were estimated a priori approximately correctly, and all postulated eight hypotheses were confirmed a posteriori using the online studies using the IIA-Tool. This shows that the analytical preparatory work and the methods and tools used in the studies were correct and that the results can be considered plausible and correct.

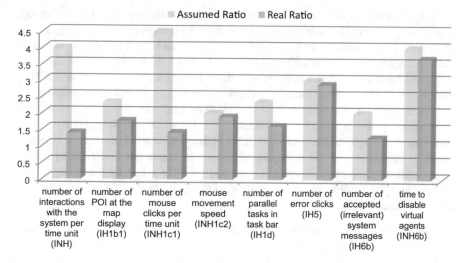

Fig. 6.7 Assumed and actual relationship of values of cultural interaction indicators with respect to Chinese- and German-speaking users (*Source* Heimgärtner 2012)

6.2.3   Hybrid Approach

Cultural dimensions and cultural standards serve to describe and compare cultural systems (cf. e.g., Hall 1959; Thomas 1996; Victor 1998; Hofstede and Hofstede 2005a). The characteristics of cultural dimensions influence the user experience and provide orientation for the usability engineering process (see Chap. 5.2). Differences between cultures can be found by analyzing critical interaction situations between people (Thomas 1996); Honold (2000c) made this method available for cultural differences in HMI. Critical interaction situations that arise due to problematic user interfaces are based on the given system functionality are analyzed. The mental model of the user about the system depends on the culture of the user, his expectations about the characteristics of the system and his experience of interaction with the system. Vöhringer-Kuhnt (2002) found that, e.g., Hofstede's individualism index is related to user satisfaction and usability of the product and has a significant influence on intercultural usability. Röse (2002) proposed the "Method for Culture-Oriented Design", which integrates the factors of new concepts of culture-oriented HMI design and the knowledge of cultural differences into existing concepts of HMI design. Relevant cultural variables for intercultural HMI design must be determined analytically on the basis of literature research and requirement studies. Their values represent culture-dependent variations that occur at all levels of HMI localization (interface, functionality, and interaction) and can be used for intercultural user interface design (IUID). A similar focus (Shen et al. 2006) was on culture-oriented design. Further methods are the user interface characteristics of Marcus (2006) or the cultural markers of Badre and Barber

(1998). More recent approaches are based on semiotic theory (e.g., Castro Salgado et al. 2013). One of the most promising methods to preserve cultural differences in HMI is the observation and analysis of user interaction with the system (see Heimgärtner 2008). The results of these observations in the form of cultural variables and their manifestations serve as a basis for guidelines in intercultural HMI design and for intercultural usability engineering [e.g., cultural interaction indicators, cf. Abdelnour-Nocera et al. (2011)]. Based on feedback from previous tutorials and workshops on IUID (M&C, Interact, IHCI, SouthCHI, ICCHP, HCII) and the summary of the state of research on IUID in Heimgärtner 2013, the author reviewed all IUID methods and the synopsis of the most important IUID methods was compiled into a corresponding IUID method mix (or IUID toolbox). Figure 6.8 shows exemplary results from the application of the IUID method mix and Fig. 6.9 IUID variable values.

▶ A hybrid approach integrates several IUID methods into an IUID method mix (Heimgärtner 2014). Based on the method of the culture-oriented HMI design (MCD, see Röse 2002), cultural differences are identified on the basis of cultural

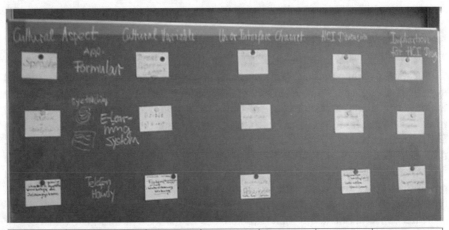

Applicatio n/ Use Case	Cultural aspect / cultural dimension	Cultur al variab	UI character	HMI dimension	Cultural interactio n	IUID Implication
form	Language	Direct (word length),	Presentat ion, Layout			
e-learnin		Visible	Presentati on,			
Phone	Communicati on speed, density of the information network	Indirect (operatin g manual)	Presentat ion, button size	Interacti on speed and interactio n style	Interacti on pauses	Other input method necessary (IME), other sorting algorithm

Fig. 6.8 Application of the IUID method mix (extract from an IUID workshop of the author)

Fig. 6.9 Examples of characteristics of decisive variables for the development of intercultural user interfaces (extract from an IUID workshop of the author)

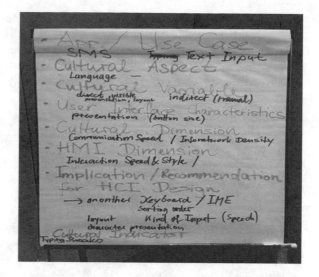

dimensions and cultural variables are derived for the project. With this knowledge of cultural differences and affected aspects of the HMI system, further effects on the HMI design are determined and supported by hypothesis-driven data transmission using user interface characteristics (see Marcus 2006) and HMI dimensions (see Heimgärtner 2012).

6.3   Path to an Explanatory Model of Culture-Dependent HMI

Some culturally influence factors on the HMI postulated in the literature were confirmed by quantitative empirical studies (Heimgärtner 2012). Cultural models and cultural interaction indicators, which have been generated by the analysis of user interaction, can be used to describe the needs of the user in terms of the HMI depending on his culture as well as to develop an explanatory model for culturally influenced HMI and to improve the methods of intercultural usability engineering. With the help of an explanatory model of culture-dependent HMI, examples of different culturally conditioned behavior of users can be explained with interactive systems.

For this purpose, the explanatory models must be determined on the basis of analytical considerations and verified using empirical data and statistical methods. Due to the lack of existing modeling and available cultural HMI theories, an iterative, i.e., alternately analytical and empirical approach is necessary (i.e., alternately data-and hypothesis-driven), so that an "evolutionary explanatory model" gradually emerges.

▸ Successful explanatory models can be applied to new examples or application cases and thus verified, which in turn allows predictive design recommendations to be generated. Finally, complete metrics for representing the usability of interactive systems (usability measurement systems, cf. Nielsen 2001) can be derived from high empirical values for the culturally influenced HMI.

In addition, the analysis of cultural models (cultural dimensions, cultural standards, etc.) can be intensified within the framework of explanatory models with regard to the usability engineering process and can be carried out using well-known methods of process and quality management (e.g., PDCA, FMEA, Six Sigma—cf.Lunau and Roenpage (2007) in order to prove and optimize the efficiency of the intercultural usability engineering process and to reduce its costs. As a result, these "new" methods of intercultural usability engineering and intercultural user interface design for the industry also lose their obviously still "foreign" character, namely when they can be embedded in the well-known method portfolio of companies.

One of the first steps toward a theory of culturally influenced HMI was the identification of significantly classifying cultural interaction indicators (CII) (cf. Heimgärtner 2007).

▸ Cultural interaction indicators (CIIs) represent cultural differences in the user's interaction behavior by expressing the relationship between the values of cultural dimensions and the values of HMI dimensions.

Cultural dimensions represent the cultural imprint of a user and HMI dimensions represent user interaction behavior (such as information speed, information density, interaction speed, and interaction frequency).

▸ HMI dimensions represent the characteristics of the respective HMI by describing the user's HMI style through the type of information processing in the respective HMI as well as its interaction characteristics.

In information processing, frequency, density, sequence, and structure are particularly affected; in interaction, their frequency and speed are particularly affected. The quality of information processing and interaction is represented by its effectiveness and efficiency. In order to measure the parameters, the characteristics of the HMI dimensions must be very precise and concrete. Therefore, the HMI dimensions are operationalized in many quantitative variables in order to obtain a basic measurement instrument and link it to cultural dimensions, thus generating empirical hypotheses.

▸ In order to analyze the interaction of the user with the system, dynamic aspects of the HMI must be measured by means of automated analysis tools by seamless chronological recording of the user behavior. [The Intercultural Interaction Analysis Tool (IIA-Tool) (Heimgärtner 2008) was used for this purpose (see Chap. 7.4.5)].

6.3.1 Presumed Connections Between Cultural Dimensions and HMI Dimensions

▸ The cultural influence on the HMI design can be represented by the relationships between the expressions of cultural dimensions and the expressions of the variables relevant for the HMI design.

With the help of cultural dimensions, it is possible to derive hypotheses that are relevant for intercultural HMI design. Heimgärtner 2012 derived several basic assumptions regarding the connection between cultural dimensions and HMI dimensions, mainly from the work of (Hall 1959).

▸ The empirical hypotheses concern Hall's cultural dimensions as basic behavioral patterns relevant to user behavior: Time orientation, density of information networks, communication speed as well as action chains.

In this respect, it is reasonable to assume that variables associated with HMI design such as information speed (distribution speed and frequency of information occurrence), information density (number and distance of information units), or information structure (order and arrangement of information units) are related to these culturally different behavioral patterns. If this is the case, the cultural differences found by Hall (1959) also imply differences in information speed ("duration of information representation"), information density ("number of information units represented in parallel") and information frequency ("number of information representations per time unit") as well as interaction frequency and interaction style. Table 6.3 shows some of the hypotheses generated, which were empirically tested.

6.3.2 Approaches to an Explanatory Model of Culturally Influenced HMI

▸ The results found in the studies led to the conviction that it is justified and useful to use cultural interaction indicators for intercultural HMI research in order to obtain a reasonable explanatory model for culturally influenced HMI.

Table 6.3 Hypotheses for possible relationships between HMI dimensions and variables or dimensions of cultural models (Table 6.3 to be continued on next page)

Cultural dimension	Germany	China	HMI dimension	HMI variable/operationalization (metrics)	Germany (German)	China
Context orientation	Low	High	Information redundancy	Number of redundant information units	Low	High
Monochronous versus polychronic time orientation	Mono	Poly	Information frequency	Time between the output of two information units by the system.	Low	High
Monochronous versus polychronic time orientation	Mono	Poly	Interaction sequence	Number of (quasi) parallel interactions/number, length and speed of mouse click sequences or mouse movements	Low	High
Density of the communication network	Low	High	Information density (spatial)	Number of information units displayed in parallel (e.g., POIs on the map display)	Low	High
Density of the communication network	Low	High	Information density (temporal) (corresponds to information frequency)	Number of information units issued per time unit	Low	High
Density of the communication network	Low	High	Interaction density (temporal)	Number of parallel tasks in the "Taskbar"/Task interrupt tolerance	Low	High
Communication speed	Low	High	Information frequency	Number of intentional interactions with the system per time unit	Low	High
Communication speed	Low	High	Interaction frequency	Number of interactions with the system per time unit (e.g., mouse clicks)	Low	High
Monochronous versus polychronic time orientation	Mono	Poly	Information Sequentiality	Number of parallel tasks in the "Taskbar"	Low	High
Monochronous versus polychronic time orientation	Mono	Poly	Interaction sequence	Number of (quasi) parallel interactions/number, length and speed of mouse click sequences or mouse movements	Mono/linear	Poly/nonlinear
Density of the communication network	Low	High	Information frequency	Number of information units displayed per time unit (NIT),	Low	High

(continued)

Table 6.3 (continued)

Cultural dimension	Germany	China	HMI dimension	HMI variable/operationalization (metrics)	Germany (German)	China
				Time between sequential display of two information units (TPI), error clicks		
Density of the communication network	Low	High	Interaction frequency	Number of interactions with the system per time unit	Low	High
Uncertainty avoidance	High	Low	Information Sequentiality	Number of parallel tasks in the "Taskbar"	Low	High
Uncertainty avoidance	High	Low	Information Sequentiality	Number of parallel tasks in the "Taskbar"	Low	High
Uncertainty avoidance	High	Low	Interaction sequence	Number of parallel tasks in the "Taskbar"	Low	High
Uncertainty avoidance	High	Low	Information tolerance	Number of accepted irrelevant system messages	low	high
Monochronous versus polychronic time orientation	Mono	Poly	Information Sequentiality	Number of parallel tasks in the "Taskbar"	Low	High
Monochronous versus polychronic time orientation	Mono	Poly	Interaction sequence	Number of (quasi) parallel interactions/number, length and speed of mouse click sequences or mouse movements	Mono/linear	Poly/nonlinear
Density of the communication network	Low	High	Information frequency	Number of information units displayed per time unit (NIT), Time between sequential display of two information units (TPI), error clicks	Low	High
Monochronous versus polychronic time orientation	Mono	Poly	Information Sequentiality	Number of parallel tasks in the "Taskbar"	Low	High
Monochronous versus polychronic time orientation	Mono	Poly	Interaction sequence	Number of (quasi) parallel interactions/number, length and speed of mouse click sequences or mouse movements	Mono/linear	Poly/nonlinear
Density of the communication network	Low	High	Information frequency	Number of information units displayed per time unit (NIT), Time between sequential display of two information units (TPI), error clicks	Low	High

(continued)

Table 6.3 (continued)

Cultural dimension	Germany	China	HMI dimension	HMI variable/operationalization (metrics)	Germany (German)	China
Density of the communication network	Low	High	Interaction frequency	Number of interactions with the system per time unit	Low	High
Uncertainty avoidance	High	Low	Information Sequentiality	Number of parallel tasks in the "Taskbar	Low	High
Uncertainty avoidance	High	Low	Information Sequentiality	Number of parallel tasks in the "Taskbar	Low	High
Uncertainty avoidance	High	Low	Interaction sequence	Number of parallel tasks in the "Taskbar	Low	High
Uncertainty avoidance	High	Low	Information tolerance	Number of accepted irrelevant system messages	low	high
Uncertainty avoidance/ relationship versus task orientation	High	Low	Interaction/interruption tolerance	Time until the virtual agent is switched off by the user.	Low	High
Relationship versus task orientation	Low	High	Information frequency/speed	Number of information units displayed in parallel (e.g., POIs on the map display)	Low	High
Relationship versus task orientation	Low	High	Interaction frequency/speed	Number of interactions with the system per time unit (e.g., mouse clicks)	Low	High
Relationship versus task orientation	Low	High	Interaction style	Number of interaction pauses	High	Low
Monochronous versus polychronic time orientation	Low	High	Interaction style	Length of interaction pauses	High	Low
Face-saving dimension	Low	High	Interaction equipment/frequency	Mouse, touch screen, language control button, functional initiations, number of dialogue steps	Low/ mouse button	High/ touch screen
Face-saving dimension	Low	High	Interaction frequency/style	Number of help calls per time unit	High/ direct	Low/ indirect
Relationship versus task orientation	Low	High	Information speed	Duration of the information presentation ("information presentation time")	Long	Brief

For this reason, initial considerations were made which reflect the relationships between the HMI dimensions and cultural aspects.

▸ Table 6.4 gives an overview of possible correlations between HMI dimensions and cultural dimensions based on the cultural interaction indicators determined.

▸ The aim is to find out the actual connection between the interaction indicators and their (postulated cultural) causes. Structural equation models[5] can be used to identify these relationships between cultural dimensions and HMI dimensions and their expressions.

The relationships between latent variables (cf. Byrne 2001 or Bortz und Döring 2006) that elude direct observation are identified, and the correctness of the postulated relationships between the values of cultural definitions and the values of the HMI dimensions is examined. For this purpose, cultural variables or expressions of cultural dimensions on the one hand and expressions of HMI dimensions, on the other hand, can be represented in the structural equation models and linked with the assumed connections both among themselves and with the corresponding measurement variables. Confirmational factor analysis or regression analysis can support this process. The main objective is to determine the causal relations between culture and HMI through cultural interaction indicators. A theory based on the modeled variables has the best explanatory quality when the left and right sides correspond to the best. The modeling of the structural equation is done by adding or removing variables or relations for the purpose of improving the explanatory quality.

▸ An attempt has been made to generate a structural equation model for the relationship between HMI dimensions and cultural dimensions. The connections between cultural, information-related, and interaction-related dimensions were modeled using intercultural interaction indicators. The explanatory model of culture-dependent HMI is all the better the more variances in the empirical data can be statistically explained by the modeled structural equations.

---

[5]Structural equation models (SEM) are among the statistical methods of conformative factor analysis. An SEM consists of a set of equations. On the left side of the equations are the effect variables and on the right side are the effect variables that probably influence these effect variables —the causation variable (endogenous variable) multiplied by a causal factor. Variables without effect are exogenous variables. If there are no feedback loops, one speaks of a hierarchical SEM (Kenny 1979, p. 32 ff.). SEMs have two basic elements: variables and parameters. Unlike variables, parameters do not vary across individuals or groups, but describe the entire population (e.g., average or variance). In SEMs, parameters are multiplied by variables. The sum of such parameter–variable combinations corresponds to the effect variable. The resulting equation is called the structural equation. AMOS is a software application to graphically model such equations. AMOS is the abbreviation for "analysis of moment structures". Details on AMOS can be found in Arbuckle (2005) or Byrne (2001).

Table 6.4 Possible relationships between HMI dimensions and cultural dimensions

HMI dimension	Ratio of (C):(G)	Cultural interaction indicator (CII)	Examples	Cultural dimension
Information frequency	1,25	Distance between notes, number of information units per time unit	Number of words, sentences, dialogues, propositions etc. per minute	Uncertainty avoidance, action chains, network density
Information density	1,77	Number of places of interest	Picture–text ratio, distance of information units from each other, number of simultaneously presented information units	Uncertainty avoidance, network density
Information and interaction parallelism	1,61	Number of parallel tasks, rejected system messages, time to deactivate the virtual agent ("life-like character", e.g., "Merlin" in Word)	Sequential or parallel presentation or reception of information units and information arrangement (e.g., layout)	All time-relevant cultural dimensions (such as uncertainty avoidance, action chains or time orientation)
Interaction speed	1,89	Mouse motion pauses less than 1 ms	Mouse usage, keyboard entries, length of mouse track per time unit	All time-relevant cultural dimensions
Interaction frequency	1,41	Mouse clicks with left mouse button, number of mouse movement events	Total number of mouse clicks/mouse movements or number of function or help initiatives per session	All time-relevant cultural dimensions

Figure 6.10 shows a partial model of one side of a complete structural equation model (modeled in AMOS), which has emerged from literature studies, postulated hypotheses in Heimgärtner (2007) and empirical results from Heimgärtner (2012). It shows the relations between partial expressions of HMI dimensions (e.g., display parameters as part of information density and information frequency or interaction errors as part of interaction accuracy). Other combinations of cultural interaction indicators (CIIs) are also possible for allocation to HMI dimensions. However, further modeling still must show which of the possibilities are the most useful. In addition, the other side of the structural equation model must also be explored more closely, on which the cultural dimensions must be introduced and linked.

▸ The explanatory model is based on some of the best-classifying cultural inter-action indicators, which have emerged from the hypothesis that the expressions of the HMI dimensions depend on the cultural imprint of the users, which can be

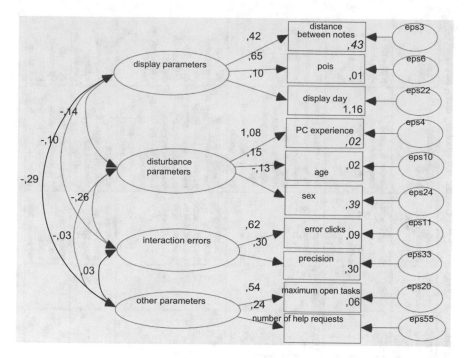

Fig. 6.10 Partial model to explain the relation between preliminary stages of the HMI dimensions and cultural interaction indicators (CIIs)

described by the expressions of cultural dimensions: the higher the relationship orientation (collectivism), the higher the information density, information speed, information frequency, interaction frequency, and interaction speed (and vice versa).

The entire model for culturally influenced HMI consists of more than 300 mainly quantitative potential parameters that are relevant for intercultural HMI design and depending on the culture, have been analytically determined from the literature study (see Heimgärtner 2012). 118 quantitative parameters were implemented in the IIA-Tool and empirically tested.

Table 6.5 shows an excerpt of the most proven results to date (relations between HMI and culture) from the explanatory model to a culture-dependent HMI.

The model in Table 6.5 was also partially modeled in an SEM. On the left side of the structural equation model, the cultural variables or expressions of cultural dimensions (Fig. 6.11 left) and on the right side of the structural equation model, the expressions of the HMI dimensions (Fig. 6.11 middle) were modeled and linked to the assumed connections (parameter–variable combinations). This approach shows the relations between partial expressions of HMI dimensions (such as information density and information speed based on display parameters or interaction errors based on interaction parameters) and the user culture, as well as, to

Table 6.5 Model for intercultural HMI design (contains both assumed and actual values for Chinese- (C) and German (D)-speaking users, respectively)

HMI dimension	Presumed situation (C):(G)	Effective holding (C):(G)	Assumed standardized value (G)	Effective standardized value (G)	Presumed standardized value (C)	Effective standardized value (C)	Effective value (G), utter	Effective value (C), utter	Cultural Interaction Indicator (CII)	UMTM Measurement class (es)	Cultural dimension
Information frequency (IF)	4	1,25	0,2	0,8	0,2	0,25	0,007	0,008	Message Distance (MG), Number of information units per time unit (NIT)	Number of words/dialogues/sentences/propositions per minute	BCD + UV + action chains + communication network density [yes]
Information density (ID)	2,333	1,77	0,3	0,7	0,3	0,53	19,91	35,26	Number of places of interest (POI)	Number of images per page, number of words/sentences/propositions per dialogue, image/text ratio, or Distribution, distance of information units from each other, number of simultaneously displayed information units	BCD + UV + communication network density [yes]
Parallel Information Processing (IP)	2,333	1,61	0,3	0,7	0,3	0,53	2,87	4,63	Maximum open tasks (PT), Rejected system requests, time to shutdown virtual agents (TDA)	Sequential or parallel presentation or reception of information units, layout/information arrangement (e.g., widget positions, image/text arrangement/information sequence (e.g., regularity), order, arrangement, priority of information units)	BCD + all time-stressed culture dimensions (such as UV, action chains), time orientation) [no]
Interaction speed (INS)	2	1,89	0,3	0,6	0,3	0,57	3,27	6,19	Micro-interaction pauses of 1 ms (~IN, MMS)	mouse click speed, character input speed, mouse track length per second	BCD + all time-stressed culture dimensions [no]
Interaction frequency (INF)	4,5	1,41	0,2	0,9	0,2	0,28	85,74	121,23	Mouse clicks (MC), Mouse movements (MM)	Total number of mouse clicks/mouse movements/function or help initiations per session	BCD + all time-stressed culture dimensions [no]

disturbances such as age, gender, or PC experience. In this model, information density, information speed, and interaction errors are latent variables (Fig. 6.11 middle). These are not directly measurable but can only be captured via the cultural interaction indicator variables (number of tasks, number of help messages, number of POIs, reference spacing, display duration, functionless mouse clicks, and mouse click accuracy) (Fig. 6.11 right).

In this model approach, the cultural imprinting of the user is determined by the variable "Nationality" is linked to the HMI dimensions. The effect of nationality on the variables "interaction errors" and "information density" is considerable—even if there is a general influence of user age. In contrast, however, gender and PC experience have far less impact on the information density in the HMI than nationality. This structural equation model shows that nationality has a much higher influence on information speed, information density, and interaction errors than age, PC experience, or gender—even if age is a significant disturbance (but not on interaction errors). In addition, interaction errors (which are directly related to the interaction with the interaction medium "mouse") are much less influenced by disturbance variables than information density and information speed.[6] According to Hofstede, there is a correlation between nationality and collectivism (see Hofstede and Hofstede 2005b). Thus, the variable "nationality" in this structural equation model represents to a certain extent the variable "collectivism versus individualism" (or Power Distance Index of Hofstede). The empirical findings from the study presented in Sect. 6.2.1 and the hypotheses derived from them in Sect. 6.2.2 (the higher the relationship orientation, the higher the information density, information speed, etc.) are reflected by corresponding trends in the parameter values of the structural equation model. This supports the assumption that further connections between cultural dimensions and HMI dimensions and cultural interaction indicators can be modeled and explained using structural equation models.

6.3.3   Methodological and Empirical Problems of Modeling

The correctness of the explanatory model varies greatly with the number of cultural interaction indicators (CIIs) used for each HMI dimension. The explanatory power of the model is still very weak because so far, the individual HMI dimensions have only been supported by a few CIIs and, in addition, only some of the CIIs exhibit a high degree of selectivity. Nevertheless, it makes sense to continue along this path in order to

---

[6]Further details on these structural equation models and detailed explanations on parameter estimation can be found in Heimgärtner (2012).

understand the connections between HMI and culture in one day. However, enough questions remain unanswered until then.

The danger is that one actually finds differences in interaction behavior which, however, are not culture-dependent, but have, e.g., demographic causes (different interaction behavior due to age differences) are based on experience in dealing with PCs. In order to avoid this problem, appropriate measures have to be taken (e.g., select sensible random checks, clean up data records, keep disturbance variables constant).

Moreover, it is difficult to derive generally valid guidelines from the results of the methodological problems in intercultural HMI design that have just been discussed. The results of the qualitative studies on interaction analysis have a very subjective character, since very dynamic phenomena (such as interaction speed or information frequency) are not observed and objectively interpreted by humans without the support of special tools (e.g., IIA-Tool, see Sect. 7.4.5). Therefore, the qualitative studies conducted in Heimgärtner 2012 did not show any concrete design recommendations. Furthermore, considerable subjective interpretation is necessary (also in quantitative studies) in order to conclude any implications from the results.

In the choice of methods, both qualitative and quantitative survey methods have their advantages and disadvantages. The qualitative survey can provide very many different, diverse, or multifaceted and nuanced opinions as well as a determination of variance to assess the "average opinion". However, only consciously chosen statements can be used from the collected data, which does not imply a reliable "average opinion". The problem is that only explicit, not implicit, knowledge can be collected, but the latter would be the much more effective category of knowledge for culture.

This means that the appropriate use of the variable "culture" is a challenge because it can be represented differently (e.g., by nationality, country of birth and primary residence, etc., or by the values of cultural dimensions). The obvious cultural imprint on the "cultural side" of the structural equation model (Fig. 6.11 left) should, therefore, be explored in more detail. Not only explicit demographic variables such as "country of birth" (which does not necessarily correspond to "nationality") or the expressions of cultural dimensions such as "high versus low uncertainty avoidance" must be considered. It is also necessary to take into account the implicit influence of the cultural imprint on all other variables (both on the interaction indicators and on the disturbance variables) in the model.

In addition, when testing systems with causal hypotheses—as is the case in structural equation models—fundamental feasibility problems exist which make it difficult to verify the hypotheses (cf. Kenny 1979). This applies in particular to the underlying data. These may have been lost or not collected or may be out of date (i.e., out of date or changing) or inadequate (e.g., due to inappropriate distribution, lack of validity or category errors).

Moreover, due to their nature, models are subject to a decisive disadvantage, making it impossible in principle to bring cultural models into complete agreement with dimensions of human–machine interaction (HMIDs): 1. due to cultural complexity, all possible disturbing variables can possibly never be taken into account and 2. models cannot, in principle, completely describe reality. This means that the explanatory model as well as the results obtained by the explanatory model always differ from reality: A systematic combination of all explanations into an overall explanatory model is only possible to a limited and gradual extent due to the diversity of external influences (since the model is an incomplete system) and mutual influence of system-internal components.

▶ It is problematic to bring cultural models fully in line with HMI dimensions, as not all possible interfering variables can be considered due to cultural complexity and models cannot fully describe reality because of their nature. The results obtained by the explanatory model therefore also differ from reality.

For example, different uses of chat systems in India and Germany may be due to cultural differences in the expressions of the HMI dimensions "information density", "interaction speed", and "interaction errors" (represented by the cultural interaction indicators in Fig. 6.11)—but there may also be other cultural interaction indicators and combinations of them which can be assigned to the HMI dimensions (in Fig. 6.11 or others) and could nevertheless result in equally plausible explanations. Further modeling must, therefore, show which cultural interaction

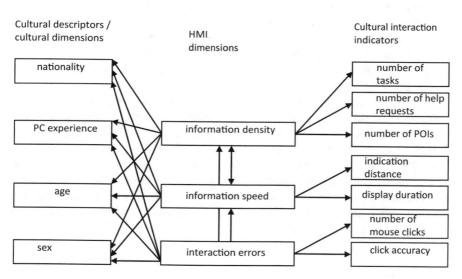

Fig. 6.11 Approach for a model to explain the relations between HMI dimensions and cultural interaction indicators as well as between HMI dimensions and nationality

indicators and which of their combinations will provide the highest quality of explanation. More detailed studies are therefore needed in order to further verify, refine, and optimize such an initial explanatory model.[7]

▶ Nevertheless, the results so far (postulated and confirmed hypotheses) serve to reveal a basis and some proven facts that are useful to obtain recommendations for intercultural HMI design with tendency character in general and for culturally adaptive systems in particular (see Heimgärtner 2012). In addition, it is very reasonable for further development and research to consider some rules of thumb, even if they have to be considered provisional and should therefore still be treated with the greatest possible care.

Although research on methods for intercultural usability engineering has increased in recent years (Clemmensen and Roese 2010), there are still gaps that cannot be ignored, especially in the area of usability testing and usability evaluation with regard to the reliability and interpretation of results (Hahn et al. 2009).

▶ The test methodology of intercultural usability engineering still leaves questions unanswered and is sometimes a costly factor for companies wishing to adapt their products to international markets. As the most reliable and profitable human-centered evaluation method, however, it is still the method of choice for the development of intercultural user interfaces (cf. Sect. 7.4).

It is true that guidelines for the design of internationally applicable software and isolated country-specific design recommendations can provide clues for the cultural adaptation of an HMI system. However, the former are quite general and therefore have limited action-relevant value, while the latter are specifically tailored to certain sales markets and interface types and are therefore not fully applicable. This creates a gap which can be closed by means of product and market-oriented usability testing, especially by user-related testing.

However, it is precisely this area that is used in industry due to the high costs involved—e.g., due to qualitative on-site investigations—and is therefore often not available to industry as action-relevant knowledge. In industry, cultural adaptations to HMI systems concentrate primarily on the technical and linguistic level (cf. Sturm 2002; Heimgärtner 2007; Best 2009_ENREF_5) and are based primarily on techno-centric cultural comparisons. Anthropocentric testing, which reveals profound cultural differences (cf. Honold 2000c; Röse 2002), often fails because of the means, the time required and the lack of knowledge about cultural impassability in the test (cf. Heimgärtner 2006).

---

[7]This requires, in particular, the clarification and delimitation of the blurriness of the concept of culture, which can be achieved by a suitable working definition of culture (cf. Chap. 2.1), in order to obtain a clear and concise explanatory model. Future research must also show to what extent cultural interaction indicators can ultimately be derived systematically from cultural models or linked in a very concrete and detailed way to cultural dimensions.

▶ Chapter 7.4 shows how culture-independent methods can lead to reliable results and at the same time save resources.

6.4 Challenges of IUID Research

6.4.1 Complexity of Cultural Systems

▶ According to Hall (1976), the methodological problems in the study of culture are that transmission in simple systems is simpler than the integration of complex systems that require human creativity.

This refers superficially to cultural issues that encompass and integrate the whole context of a member of a culture. This problem also arises in the design of inter-cultural user interfaces, which makes an examination of the connection or combination of culture with HMI design unavoidable. Besides the usual concerns and challenges in HMI, in HMI design (see Chen 2001 and Reiterer 2008) and in the life of the usability engineering process (Andreas Holzinger, Karl-Heinz Weidmann (ed.) 2005—Empowering Software Quality 2005), problems arise because every-thing has to function in a specific cultural context (see Honold 2000a; Heimgärtner et al. 2011; Clemmensen 2012 or Hertzum und Clemmensen 2012). Rehm et al (2007) have investigated the problems of adapting the HMI to the cultural back-ground of a user. Many aspects must be considered simultaneously in order to gain possible cultural explanations for their influence on the HMI. In other words, the impact of culture on HMI cannot be explained by a single aspect due to the complexity of culture. Another problem in cultural research stems from the impossibility of predicting how individual pieces of the cultural puzzle fit together (see Hall (1976, p.130). This unpredictability has consequences for the use of methods of intercultural HMI design and intercultural usability engineering (see Nielsen 2006).

6.4.2 Different Approaches

▶ The determination of intercultural variables and their values is still too unsys-tematic and too selective due to various research approaches and complex cultural contexts.

Intercultural factors for HMI design can be derived from cultural dimensions. The results obtained in this way enjoy discursive and deductive validity, but often lack empirical confirmation (Marcus and Gould 2000). Cyr and Trevor-Smith (2004) found in 2004 that the link between cultural dimensiveness and HMI design was not investigated in enough depth. Either detailed empirical studies of the derived results will follow, or these results will only serve as examples, but not as a statistic basis for further research. The counterpart to the deductive approach is the inductive approach: cultural characteristics have been determined in empirical studies (e.g., Badre and Barber 1998; Dormann 2006; Sun 2001), which refer to a specific culture and are preferably used in this culture. Badre and Barber (1998) show the direct influence of cultural characteristics on the performance of users interacting with the system, thus demonstrating the link between culture and usability (confirmed by the studies of, for example, Sun 2001 and Vöhringer-Kuhnt 2002).

6.4.3   High Research Expenditure

▸ Hidden (hidden) cultural variables are difficult to identify because they only become recognizable over time.

The reason for the lack of results on direct hidden intercultural variables at the interaction level often lies in the difficulties in recording and assessing them, which can generate high research expenditures. In order to overcome these methodological and logical obstacles to the observation of hidden variables, it makes sense to some extent to strictly separate interaction design and dialogue design. First, the cultural differences in the user's interaction with the system have to be elucidated and then how the interaction influences the flow of information between user and system can be examined. Then, the dialogue design for culturally different users can be examined, which can finally lead to initial design recommendations for the development of intercultural user interfaces.

6.4.4   Lack of Empirical Confirmation

▸ Not all recommendations regarding the five areas of user interface characteristics (presentation, navigation, metaphor, mental mental delta, interaction) have been empirically confirmed so far—although there is already some research in this area.

Röse et al (2001) confirmed some of the aspects highlighted by Marcus and Gould (2000) in qualitative studies from China with regard to different page layouts in the layout for Chinese and German users (cf. Chap. 7). In addition, due to the high "power distance" values in China, hierarchical taxonomies and classification models are more likely to be used as metaphors than in Germany (cf. Chap. 2).

Most of the recommendations presented have yet to be tested and empirically confirmed in detail in additional investigations before they can be proposed as model solutions (design patents) or even guidelines (or even standards). In addition, empirical studies on intercultural user interface characteristics are necessary. Strictly speaking, some different systems from different cultures have to be compared and usability tests have to be carried out in order to determine the usability of the different systems (benchmark tests on intercultural usability).

▸ The results must therefore not yet be generalized to the extent that they apply to an entire country or a particular cultural group, as the sampling is too small and too selective, thus ruining high-quality statistical results. This is also one of the reasons why so few qualitative empirical studies and even fewer quantitative research reports exist (cf. Smith et al. 2004; Maier et al. 2005; Heimgärtner 2012).

6.4.5   Use of Cultural Dimensions

▸ There is disagreement among scientists about the effect of using cultural dimensions in the development of intercultural user interfaces.

On the one hand, critics of Hofstede claim that the evidence from the original 1957–72 worldwide IBM employee survey study is not representative. It would not provide data on national cultural differences between countries but would represent differences within IBM's corporate culture. Hofstede's approach also ignores differences within a nation. The model treats a people as a homogeneous collection of individuals sharing the same value structure. This is not true in most cases (see House and Aditya 1997 and House 2004). Some studies, e.g., by Komischke et al. (2003), show inconsistencies with Hofstede's values: Power Distance Index (PDI) values for Japan, China, and the USA differ from those calculated by Hofstede. Furthermore Komischke et al. (2003) points out that although much has been said about what should be considered culturally, little empirical research is actually done on this topic. Different behavior does not necessarily mean a different cultural (e.g., propositional) attitude, e.g., a different cognitive status in the network of believed content (propositions within the web of belief). According to Rathje (2003), limited assessment and mediation of the cultural dimension and its models can lead to ineffective and even restrictive strategies of action. In this case, little cultural understanding proves to be just as disadvantageous—or worse—than no cultural understanding at all. For this reason, Rathje (2003) pleads for cultural models that are not dependent on a cultural dimension, because they enable the derivation of concrete patterns of behavior, the explanation of which derives directly from the concrete phenomena of the culture described.[8]

On the other hand, the supporters of Hofstede's theory reject the distancing of cultural dimensions because numerous independent replication studies have verified Hofstede's results. Hofstede's results also referred to different subgroups of the respective populations and nevertheless showed similarities in national differences —which is consistent with Hofstede's dimensional values. Hofstede also draws particular attention to the different cultural levels, while distancing himself from accompanying question lists (VSM). After Hofstede (2006) this distancing was necessary because one consequence of his further research and results—and a justified starting point for criticism—was the "unreflected" adoption and application of his cultural model.

▸ Hofstedes Kulturmodell can be seen as a useful research tool (see Bryan et al. 1994) and a useful starting point for researching user interfaces in the cultural context, especially when a well-founded theory is the intended goal of the research.

6.4.6   Future Research Directions

▸ The trend in research on culture and HMI is toward verifying preliminary models and theories through extensive empirical research in different cultural contexts and the empirical collection of the connections between user and system (HMI) in concrete cultural context of use in order to derive practical and concrete recommendations for the development of intercultural user interfaces.

The close relationship between culture and HMI design will have to be further elaborated in detail. The focus of the investigation of cultural differences will shift from the national level to the regional or individual level in order to cover all cultural contexts. By considering empirical studies, methods, models, and theories will be modified and improved in the near future in order to derive and then optimize the processes for intercultural HMI design and intercultural usability techniques. In this way, international standards can be established, and instruments

---

[8]This has a particular impact on culturally adaptive HMI systems. For example, the combination of cultural interaction indicators (CIIs) with NLP principles means a "cultural" adaptation on the individual level—as suggested by Heimgärtner (2012). Criticism of the validity of Hofstede's cultural dimensions and indices weakens confidence in them. This in turn implies that it would be better or at least advisable to build a culturally real-adaptive HMI system not on cultural dimensions, but on parameters that reflect the user's direct behavior with the system. A proposed solution can be found in Heimgärtner (2012).

can be developed which supplement international research standards and thus in future include and cover cultural contexts in the HMI (hopefully in part completely automatically or involuntarily) in the development of user interfaces.[9]

In recent years, research and literature involving cultural contexts in HMI design have grown rapidly (Shen et al. 2006; Plocher et al. 2012). Until recently, culture in the HMI was considered exclusively a question of internationalization or localization (see Clemmensen 2009). However, as formulated by Clemmensen (2009), these traditional approaches to culture and HMI turned out to be seriously flawed as the computer continued to spread around the world. According to Honold (2000b) and Röse (2002), successful intercultural design goes far beyond the usual design processes, since different mentalities, thought patterns and problem-solving strategies are anchored in the respective culture. Depending on the culture, application patterns differ with regard to different power structures (see Hofstede et al. 2010, flat versus hierarchical). Problem-solving strategies can be more linear or nonlinear (see Röse et al. 2001; Honold 2000b). Therefore, the design expert must know exactly what the user needs or wants (i.e., why and in what context, see Holzinger 2005). In addition, on-site design engineers must adapt general HMI methods to their needs (see Clemmensen et al. 2009; Röbig et al. 2010; Bidwell et al. 2011b).

▸ Intercultural HMI design must in future be adapted in such a way that cultural aspects are taken into account both at the local level (indigenous, local cultural context) and at the national level (cf. Abdelnour-Nocera et al. 2011).

Within culturally diverse groups, dependence on context, situation, and experience must be taken into account (cf. Bidwell et al. 2011b). Such knowledge can be recorded most precisely with survey approaches or methods based on communication, such as interviews, focus groups, or questionnaires (cf. Hampe-Neteler 1994). Furthermore, it will be the task of future IUID research to illuminate all elements of user experience design in an intercultural context and to make them available for the development of intercultural user interfaces. The focus of these overlapping areas is on user interface design and usability engineering (upper two levels of the IUID pyramid, cf. Fig. 5.4 in Chap. 5).[10]

---

[9]Through the author's collaboration with DIN, corresponding findings on intercultural HMI design are incorporated into German and (via the ISO mirror committees at DIN) international standards of the 9241 series of standards.

[10]Initial approaches in this direction were undertaken in 2010 at the IAD in Darmstadt with corresponding workshops (cf. Röbig et al. 2010).

6.5   Summary, Conclusion, Outlook

From the analysis of publications in the field of intercultural HMI, it is possible to identify some IUID "hypes". The first hype occurred in the early 1990 s. The next was around 2000 and since about 2010, research in the field of intercultural HMI or the IUID has increased by leaps and bounds.

However, there are only a few qualitative studies or tests on intercultural user experience that would provide meaningful answers to these questions (cf. Jameson 2007). The number of studies underlining the importance of cultural aspects in the development of user interfaces is constantly growing (see Evers 2003; Smith et al. 2004). There are also activities to investigate trends in intercultural HMI (see Jetter 2004; Clemmensen and Roese 2010; Heimgärtner 2014). Even though there is now relevant literature on usability engineering (e.g., Nielsen 1993; Holzinger 2005 etc.), reliable and above all generalizing literature on intercultural usability engineering [e.g., on evaluation in an intercultural context (cf. Clemmensen and Clemmensen 2012)] and above all on intercultural usability engineering (cf. Heimgärtner 2014) is increasing only very moderately. Most studies concern the presentation of information on web pages (e.g., Hodemacher et al. 2005; Marcus 2003; Dormann 2005; Baumgartner 2003; Marcus and Gould 2000; Stengers et al. 2004; Sun 2001 and Callahan 2005a). The detailed analysis of current research in the field of intercultural user interface design also shows that in particular hidden cultural variables (NVIVs) (under the water surface of the iceberg model, cf. Sect. 6.1.3 and Fig. 6.3) have not yet been investigated thoroughly enough.

The TLCC model of (Sturm 2002) shows the internationalization and localization steps in HMI design, represented by four levels: technical affairs, language, culture, and cognition (cf. Fig. 6.2). There is still a significant need for mediation between academia and industry with regard to cultural and cognitive aspects in the development of intercultural user interfaces (IUID).[11]

There is nothing more practical than a good theory to move from theoretical considerations to practical application in intercultural user interface design. The process of "grounded theory" is an iterative scientific process that resembles iterative software development cycles (cf. Balzert 2005). Theoretically based processes are predominantly based on "Grounded Theory" and established and proven processes are based on software engineering. In an explanatory model for culturally influenced HMI, the relations between culture and HMI are described using cultural interaction indicators, thus showing the relationship between culture and HMI.

---

[11]This book is intended to make an initial contribution to this by presenting the most important principles of IUID. As an author, I am happy to answer your questions and provide feedback on the book as well as on the IUID topic in general. Further information can also be found at https://www.iuic.de.

These relations can be determined in particular in the following ways: data-driven or hypothesis-driven. In the data-driven approach, data is first collected. The resulting patterns provide information about the connection between culture and HMI. In the hypothesis-driven approach, hypotheses are derived from existing cultural theories and are empirically verified. Finally, in the hybrid approach, the first two approaches are combined with other methods.

Data-driven approach: Hypotheses are formed from data already collected. In order to encourage the culturally different user to interact with the computer and then to record and analyze this, task scenarios were developed which were implemented in a specially developed PC tool (IIA-Tool, Heimgärtner 2008). The author conducted two online studies with approximately 15000 Chinese-(C), German-(G), and English (E)-speaking test subjects. The evaluation of the collected data of the studies showed that there are correlations between the interaction of the users with the computer and the cultural character of the users (Heimgärtner 2007). The cultural differences in HMI between the tested Chinese and German users concern layout (complex vs. simple), information density (high vs. low), personalization (strong vs. low), language (icons vs. characters), interaction speed (higher vs. lower), and interaction frequency (higher vs. lower). It has been empirically shown that the user's interaction with the system is influenced not only by culturally related variables such as nationality, mother tongue, country of birth, etc., but also by parameters such as experience or age (Heimgärtner 2007). Information density, information, and interaction frequency, as well as information and interaction parallelism, are lower for (G) than for (C) according to the relationship orientation, the density of information networks and the time orientation of the users. The way in which the system interacts with the user within the HMI shall be adaptable by adequately modifying the system parameters according to the nature of the cultural interaction indicators and the HMI dimensions. The significant cultural interaction indicators (CIIs) identified in Table 6.1 concern the different interaction behavior in the HMI between Chinese-(C) and German (G)-speaking user groups. It has been empirically confirmed that the interaction of the user with the system is influenced not only by variables describing the cultural affiliation of the user, such as nationality, mother tongue, country of birth, etc., but also by parameters such as experience or age (Heimgärtner 2007). The way in which the computer interacts with the user must be adaptable so that the system can cope with the user requirements, which depend as much on the cultural imprint and experience of the user as on the current situation. The necessary variations must be taken into account in the design of the system architecture. Cultural interaction indicators (CIIs) are, for example, such HMI variables that correlate with variables that represent the culture of the user. They represent cultural differences in the interactive behavior of the user by expressing the relationship between the values of cultural dimensions and the values of HMI dimensions. HMI dimensions represent the characteristics of the respective HMI by describing the HMI style of the user by means of the type of information processing in the respective HMI as well as its interaction characteristics.

Hypothesis-driven approach: Data are collected for the verification of hypotheses. The empirical hypotheses concern basic user behavior: Time management, density of information networks, communication speed as well as action chains. The hypotheses are based on some of the best classifications of the CIIs, which support the basic hypothesis that the expressions of the HMI dimensions depend on the cultural imprint of the user as follows: the higher the relationship orientation (collectivism), the higher the information density, information speed, information frequency, interaction frequency, and interaction speed and vice versa. The confirmation strengths of six out of eight hypotheses were estimated a priori approximately correctly, and all postulated eight hypotheses were confirmed a posteriori in the online studies. This shows that the analytical preparatory work and the methods used were correct and that the results can be considered plausible and correct. In order to analyze user interaction with the system, dynamic aspects of HMI must be measured using automated analyzing tools by gapless chronological recording of user behavior. For this purpose, the intercultural interaction analysis tool (IIA-Tool) (Heimgärtner 2008) was used (see Chap. 7.4.5).

A hybrid approach integrates several IUID methods into an IUID method mix (Heimgärtner 2014). Based on the method of culture-oriented HMI design (MCD, see Röse 2002), cultural differences are identified on the basis of cultural dimensions and cultural variables are derived for the project. With this knowledge of cultural differences and affected aspects of the HMI system, User Interface Characteristics (see Marcus 2006) and HMI dimensions (see Heimgärtner 2012) are used to determine and support further hypothesis-driven effects on HMI design.

The cultural influence on the HMI design can be represented by the relationships between the expressions of cultural dimensions and the expressions of the variables relevant for the HMI design. The results found in the studies led to the conviction that it is justified and useful to use cultural interaction indicators for intercultural HMI research in order to obtain a reasonable explanatory model for culturally influenced HMI. Successful explanatory models can be applied to new examples or use cases and thus verified, which in turn allows predictive design recommendations to be generated. Finally, complete metrics for representing the usability of interactive systems [usability measurement systems, cf. (Nielsen 2001)] can be derived from a high empirical value for the culturally influenced HMI. The aim is to find out the actual connection between the interaction indicators and their (postulated cultural) causes.

Structural equation models can be used to identify these relationships between cultural dimensions and HMI dimensions and their manifestations. An attempt has been made to generate a structural equation model for the relationship between HMI dimensions and cultural dimensions. The connections between cultural, information-related and interaction-related dimensions were modeled using intercultural interaction indicators. The explanatory model of culture-dependent HMI is all the better the more variances in the empirical data can be statistically explained by the modeled structural equations. The resulting explanatory model is based on some of the best-classifying cultural interaction indicators, which were created by the hypothesis that the expressions of the HMI dimensions depend on the cultural imprint of the users, which can be described by the expressions of cultural dimensions: the higher the relationship orientation (collectivism), the higher the information density, information speed, information frequency, interaction frequency, and interaction speed (and vice versa).

In the field of intercultural user interface design, the difficult investigation of methodological intercultural factors is still in its infancy: Data and results for phenomena such as different system integration habits, different expectations with regard to navigation in hyperspace or different mental models still have to be collected. In the field of intercultural user interface design, the gap between cultural aspects and specific technical aspects remains to be bridged.

According to Hall (1976), the methodological problems in the study of culture are that transmission in simple systems is simpler than the integration of complex systems that require human creativity. The determination of intercultural variables and their values is still too unsystematic and selective due to different approaches and complex cultural contexts. It is problematic to bring cultural models fully into line with HMI dimensions, as not all possible interfering variables are taken into account due to cultural complexity and models cannot fully describe reality: the results obtained by the explanatory model differ from reality. Nevertheless, the results obtained so far (postulated and confirmed hypotheses) serve to reveal a basis and some proven facts that are useful to obtain recommendations for intercultural HMI design with tendentious character in general and for cultural-adaptive systems in particular (see Heimgärtner 2012). Moreover, it is very reasonable that development and research should take into account some rules of thumb, even if they must be considered preliminary and should be treated with the utmost care. The results must therefore not yet be generalized to the extent that they apply to an entire country or a particular cultural group, as the sampling is too small and too selective, thus ruining high-quality statistical results. This is also one of the reasons why so few qualitative empirical studies and even fewer quantitative research reports exist. cf. Smith et al. (2004) and Maier et al. (2005 and Heimgärtner 2012). In addition, hidden (hidden) cultural variables are difficult to identify because they only become apparent over time. By no means all recommendations regarding the five areas of user interface characteristics (presentation, navigation, metaphor, mental model, interaction) have been empirically confirmed so far, although there is some research in this area. The test methodology of intercultural usability engineering still leaves questions unanswered and is sometimes a cost-intensive factor for companies wishing to adapt their products to international markets. There is disagreement among scientists about the effect of using cultural dimensions in the development of intercultural user interfaces.

The empirical results of the described study partly confirm the relationships between HMI dimensions and cultural dimensions postulated in literature. There is a measurement system consisting of cultural interaction indicators (CIIs) to measure culturally influenced HMI. The characteristics of the CIIs open interesting tendencies in the user interaction behavior related to the cultural imprint of the user. This first fundamental research, based on the analysis of cultural models, has produced the ten most relevant cultural dimensions and the culture-dependent HMI styles that can be calculated from them, which should be taken into account in the development of intercultural user interfaces and in the intercultural HMI design process (Heimgärtner 2012). This also revealed hidden cultural variables of human–machine interaction, namely information speed and information frequency as well as interaction speed and interaction frequency. The explanatory model of culturally dependent HMI variables gained so far can be optimized and further developed with the help of statistical methods (such as factor analysis or structural equation models) by revising the relationships between user interaction and user culture. However, there is still a lot of work to be done here (e.g., concerning the selectivity of the CIIs or the explanatory power of the model). Despite everything, these variables remain an open field of research in human–machine interface design because there is still too little empirical evidence.

The investigation and consideration of hidden cultural variables for intercultural HMI design are still ongoing. This is particularly the case in relation to the current lack of research, which relates to culturally shaped interaction and dialogue design and is based on empirical research. Even if research on culture-centric HMI design has grown enormously, it remains extremely important that the results of empirical studies on cultural contexts are integrated into HMI design, thereby providing both the basis of input data for the model and theory approaches and the basis of the measured scale with which they can be verified. Nevertheless, there is a sensible approach toward an explanatory model for culturally influenced HMI, where areas such as intercultural usability engineering and intercultural user interface design (IUID) can benefit to the extent that the model is further developed and validated.

The trend in research on culture and HMI is toward verifying preliminary models and theories through extensive empirical research in different cultural contexts and the empirical investigation of the relationships between users and systems (HMI) in concrete cultural context of use in order to derive practical and concrete recommendations for the development of intercultural user interfaces. Intercultural HMI design must be changed in the future so that cultural aspects are taken into account both at the local level (cultural context/indigenous) and at the national level (cf. Abdelnour-Nocera et al. 2011).

Norms	√
9241-171	☐
9241-210	☐
9241-220	☐

Checklist	√
Insight into the state of IUID research has been gained	☐
Data-driven approach is known and is applied	☐
Hypothesis-driven approach is known and is applied	☐
Hybrid approach (IUID method mix) is known and is applied	☐
· Cultural models	☐
· Intercultural variable	☐
· User interface characteristics	☐
· HMI dimensions	☐
· Method of Culture Oriented Design (MCD)	☐
Possible connections between HMI dimensions and cultural dimensions are known	☐
Concepts "culture-dependent explanatory model" and "structural equation model" are well-known	☐
Methodological challenges of the IUID are known	☐
· Cultural complexity	☐
· Different approaches	☐
· Increased research expenditure	☐
· Low empirical confirmation	☐
· Use of cultural dimensions controversial	☐
Insight into future IUID research gained	☐

References

Abdelnour-Nocera J, Kurosu M, Clemmensen T, Bidwell N, Vatrapu R, Winschiers-Theophilus H, Yeo A et al. (2011) Re-framing HCI through local and indigenous perspectives. Paper presented at the Lecture Notes in Computer Science. Berlin/New York

Apel K-O (2002) Language analysis, semiotics, hermeneutics (vol 164, 1st ed, [6th ed]). Suhrkamp, Frankfurt a.M

Arbuckle J L (2005) AMOS 6.0 user's guide. SPSS, Chicago

Austin JL, von Savigny E (1962) Zur Theorie der Sprechakte, Bd 9396/9398. Reclam, Stuttgart

Aykin N (2005) Usability and internationalization of information technology. NJErlbaum, Mahwah

Aykin N (Hrsg) (2004) Usability and internationalization of information technology. Lawrence Erlbaum Associates

Badre A, Barber W (1998) Culturabilty: The merging of culture and usabilty proceedings of the 4th conference on human factors and the web. AT and T Labs, Basking Ridge

Balzert H (2005) Textbook Grundlagen der Informatik: Konzepte und Notationen in UML 2, Java 5, C++ und C, Algorithmik und Software-Technik, Anwendungen; with CD-ROM and e-learning- Online-Kurs (2nd edition). Elsevier Spektrum Akad. Verl, Munich

Baumgartner V-J (2003) A practical set of cultural dimensions for global user-interface analysis and design. Fachhochschule Joanneum, Graz

Best R (2009) Software internationalization. VDMA Publishing House, Frankfurt a. M

Beynon M, Nehaniv CL, Dautenhahn K (2001) Cognitive technology: instruments of mind. In Proceedings of the international cognitive technology conference. Springer-Verlag, Warwick

Bidwell NJ, Winschiers-Theophilus H, Koch Kapuire G, Rehm M (2011b) Pushing person- hood into place: situating media in the transfer of rural knowledge in Africa. Int J Hum Comput Stud. (Hrsg), Cheverst K, Willis K, Special Issue on Locative Media 69(10):618–631

Black M (2008) Introduction to cognitive linguistics (3rd, fully revised and extended edition, vol. 1636). Francke, Tübingen

Bortz J, Döring N (2006) Research methods and evaluation: for human and social scientists. 4th, revised edn http://dx.doi.org/10.1007/978-3-540-33306-7resp. http://link.springer.com/book/10.1007%2F978-3-540-33306-7. Access 29 Feb 2019

Braun B-M, Röse K, Rößger P (2007) Localizing for the Korean Market: „Actually being there with a multi-method approach". In Evers V, Sturm C, Alberto M, Rocha M, Cambranes Martinez E, Mandl T (Eds) Designing for global markets 8, IWIPS 2007, Actually being there, June 28–30 2007, Merida, Mexico, proceedings of the eighth international workshop on internationalisation of products and systems. Product & Systems Internationalisation, S 55–62

Brekle HE (1972) Semantics: an introduction to the linguistic theory of meaning (vol 102). Fink, Munich

Bryan NB, McLean ER, Smits SJ, Burn J (1994) The structure of work perceptions among Hong Kong and United States IS professionals: a multidimensional scaling test of the Hofstede cultural paradigm proceedings of the 1994 computer personnel research conference on Reinventing IS: Managing information technology in changing organizations: managing information technology in changing organizations. ACM, Alexandria, S 219–230

Byrne BM (2001) Structural equation modeling with AMOS: basic concepts, applications, and programming. Lawrence Erlbaum, Mahwah

Cagiltay K (1999) Culture and its effects on human-computer-interaction. In Collis B, Oliver R, (Hrsg) Proceedings of world conference on educational multimedia, hypermedia and telecommunications 1999. AACE, Chesapeake, S 1626–1626

Callahan E (2005a) Cultural similarities and differences in the design of university web sites. J Comput Med Commun 11(1):239–273

Callahan E (2005b) Interface design and culture. Ann Rev Inf Sci Technol 39(1):255–310

Castro Salgado LC, Leitão CF, Souza C (2013) Semiotic engineering and culture a journey through cultures. Springer, London, pp 19–42

Chen Q (2001) Human computer interaction issues and challenges. http://search.ebscohost.com/login.aspx?direct=true&scope=site&db=nlebk&db=nlabk&AN=60706

Clemmensen T (2009) A framework for thinking about the maturity of cultural usability./z-wcorg/database

Clemmensen T (2012) Usability problem identification in culturally diverse settings. Inf Syst J 22 (2):151–175. https://doi.org/10.1111/j.1365-2575.2011.00381.x

Clemmensen T, Goyal S (2004) Studying cross cultural think-aloud usability testing–some suggestions for an experimental paradigm. Paper presented at the proceedings of the fourth danish human-computer interaction research symposium 16th November 2004, Aalborg University, Denmark

Clemmensen T, Roese K (2010) An overview of a decade of journal publications about culture and Human-Computer Interaction (HCI). In Katre D, Ørngreen R, Yammiyavar P, Clemmensen T (Hrsg), Human work interaction design: usability in social, cultural and organizational contexts. IFIP Advances in Information and Communication Technology, Bd 316. Springer, Heidelberg, S 98–112

Clemmensen T, Hertzum M, Hornbæk KAS, Shi Q, Yammiyavar P, Clemmensen T, Yammiyavar P et al (2009) Cultural cognition in usability evaluation. Interact Comput 21 (3):212–220. https://doi.org/10.1016/j.intcom.2009.05.003

Currie NJ, Peacock B (2002, September). International space station robotic systems operations-a human factors perspective. In Proceedings of the human factors and ergonomics society annual meeting (Vol 46, No 1). SAGE Publications, S 26–30

Cyr D, Trevor-Smith H (2004) Localization of web design: An empirical comparison of German, Japanese, and United States web site characteristics. J Am Soc Inf Sci Technol 55(13):1199–1208

Davidson D (1993) The Myth of the Subjective: philosophical essays, vol 8845. Reclam, Stuttgart

Day DL (1991) The cross-cultural study of human-computer interaction: a review of research methodology, technology transfer, and the diffusion of innovation

Dennett DC (1998) The intentional stance (7. printing. Hrsg), MIT Press, Cambridge

Dix A, Finaly J, Abowd G, Beale R (2001) Human-computer interaction. (2. Aufl 11. Pr. Aufl Prentice Hall Europe, London

Dong Y, Lee K (2008) A cross-cultural comparative study of users' perceptions of a webpage: with a focus on the cognitive styles of Chinese, Koreans and Americans. Int J Des 2:2 [Online]

Dormann C (2006) Cultural representations in web design: differences in emotions and values. In McEwan T, Benyon D, Gulliksen J (Hrsg), People and computers XIX—the bigger picture. London, S 285–299

Dormann C (2005, September 5–9 2005). Cultural Representations in web design. Paper presented at the People and Computers XIX–The Bigger Picture: Proceedings of HCI 2005, Edinburgh

Dörner D (2001) Building plan for a soul, vol 61193. Rowohlt Paperback-Verl, Reinbek near Hamburg

Empowering Software Quality (2005) How can Usability Engineering reach these goals? 1st Usability symposium, HCI&UE workgroup, Vienna, 8 Nov 2005, Bd 198. Austrian Computer Society

Endrass B, Rehm M, André E, Nakano Y (2008) Talk is silver, silence is golden: a cross cultural study on the usage of pauses in speech. Paper presented at the proceedings of the IUI workshop on Enculturating conversational interfaces (2008)

Esselink B (1998) A practical guide to software localization: for translators, engineers and project managers, vol 3. Benjamins, Amsterdam

Evers V (2003) Cross-cultural aspects of user understanding and behaviour: Evaluation of a virtual campus website by user from North America, England, the Netherlands and Japan. In Evers V, Röse K, Honold P, Coronado J, Day D (Hrsg) Proceedings of the fifth international workshop on internationalisation of products and systems. IWIPS 2003, Berlin, 17–19 July 2003. Kaiserslautern: University of Kaiserslautern, S 189–210

Evers V, Day D (1997) The role of culture in interface acceptance. In Proceedings of the IFIP TC13 international conference on human-computer interaction. Chapman & Hall, S 260–267.

Evers V, Kukulska-Hulme A, Jones A (1999) Cross-cultural understanding of interface design: a cross-cultural analysis of icon recognition. Paper presented at the Proceedings of the International Workshop on Internationalisation of Products and Systems. IWIPS 1999, Rochester, NY

Fitzgerald W (2004) Models for cross-cultural communications for cross-cultural website design. http://nparc.cisti-icist.nrc-cnrc.gc.ca/eng/view/fulltext/?id=c34a8e11-1943-4cd3-9d5e-0dfcca40f8a8. Access 29 Feb 2019

Gadamer H-G (1975) Truth and method: basic features of philosophical hermeneutics (4th ed, unchanged. 3rd ed, extended ed.). Mohr, Tübingen

Galdo D, Elisa M, Nielsen J (1996) International user interfaces. Wiley, New York

Grewendorf G (1979) Speech act theory and semantics (vol. 276, 1st ed). Suhrkamp, Frankfurt a. M

Grice P (1993) Studies in the way of words. Harvard University Press, Cambridge

Gudykunst WB, Mody B (2002) Handbook of international and intercultural communication (2nd upl). Sage, Thousand Oaks

Habermas J (2006) On the critique of functionalist reason (Vol. 2, [Nachdr.]). Suhrkamp, Frankfurt a. M

Hahn S, Didier M, Brother R (2009) Usability, usability, utilitsabilité, usability … a single meaning or national specificity? The human being at the centre of technical systems. Proceedings of the 8th Berlin Workshop Man-Machine-Systems 7–9 October

Hall ET (1959) The silent language. Doubleday, New York

Hall ET (1976) Beyond culture. Anchor Books, New York

Hampe-Neteler W (1994) Software-ergonomic evaluation between work design and software development (vol 2). Lang, Frankfurt a. M

Heimgärtner R (2006) On the necessity of intercultural usability engineering in the design of driver information systems. i-com 5(2):66-67. https://doi.org/10.1524/icom.2006.5.2.66

Heimgärtner R (2007) Cultural differences in human computer interaction: Results from two on-line surveys. Paper presented at the Open innovation, Konstanz

Heimgärtner R (2008) A tool for getting cultural differences in HCI. In: Asai K (ed) Human computer interaction: new developments. InTech, Rijeka, pp 343–368

Heimgärtner R (2012) Cultural differences in human-computer interaction: towards culturally adaptive human-machine interaction. Oldenbourg, Munich

Heimgärtner R (2014) Intercultural user interface design. In Blashki K, Isaias P (Hrsg) Emerging research and trends in interactivity and the human-computer interface (S 1–33). Information Science Reference (an imprint of IGI Global), Hershey

Heimgärtner R, Tiede L-W, Windl H (2011) Empathy as key factor for successful intercultural HCI design. Paper presented at the proceedings of 14th International Conference on Human-Computer Interaction, Orlando

Heindrichs W (1979) Dialogues: contributions to interaction and discourse analysis. Gerstenberg, Hildesheim

Hermeking M (2001) Cultures and technology. Waxman, Munich

Hertzum M, Clemmensen T (2012) How do usability professionals construe usability? Int J Hum Comput Stud 70(1):26–42. https://doi.org/10.1016/j.ijhcs.2011.08.001

Hodemacher D, JarmanF, Mandl T (2005) Culture and web design: an empirical comparison between Great Britain and Germany. Paper presented at the Mensch & Computer 2005: Art and Science—Crossing the boundaries of interactive ART, Vienna

Hofstede GH (1991) Cultures and organizations: software of the mind. McGraw-Hill, London

Hofstede G (1994) VSM94: values survey module 1994 manual. IRIC, Tilberg

Hofstede G (2006) What did GLOBE really measure? Researchers' minds versus respondents' minds. J Int Bus Stud 37(6):882

Hofstede G, Hofstede JG (2005a). Cultures and organizations: software of the mind (2. Aufl.). McGraw-Hill, New York

Hofstede G, Hofstede GJ (2005) Cultures and organizations: software of the mind; [intercultural cooperation and its importance for survival] (Rev. and expanded 2nd. Aufl.). McGraw-Hill, New York

Hofstede GH, Hofstede GJ, Minkov M (2010) Cultures and organizations: software of the mind, 3rd edn. McGraw-Hill, Maidenhead

Hoft NL (1995) International technical communication: how to export information about high technology. Wiley, New York

Hoft NL (1996) Developing a cultural model. In Del Galdo EM, ielsen J (Hrsg), International users interface. Wiley, S 41–73

Holzinger A (2005) Usability engineering methods for software developers. Commun ACM 48 (1):71–74. https://doi.org/10.1145/1039539.1039541

Honold P (2000a) Intercultural usability engineering: barriers and challenges from a German point of view. In Day D, del Galdo E, Prabhu GV (Hrsg), Designing for global markets 2. Second international workshop on internationalisation of products and systems. S 137–147

Honold P (2000b) Culture and context: an empirical study for the development of a framework for the elicitation of cultural influence in product usage. Int J Hum Comput Interact 12(3/4):327–345

Honold P (2000c) Intercultural usability engineering: an investigation into cultural influences on the design and use of technical products (vol 647, Als Ms. gedr.). VDI Verl, Düsseldorf

House RJ (2004) Culture, leadership, and organizations: the globe study of 62 societies. Sage

House RJ, Aditya RN (1997) The social scientific study of leadership: Quo vadis? J Manag 23 (3):409

Isa, WAWM, Noor, NLMd., Mehad S (2009) Cultural prescription vs. User perception of information architecture for culture centred website: A case study on Muslim online user. Paper presented at the proceedings of the 3d international conference on online communities and social computing: Held as Part of HCI International 2009, San Diego

Jameson A (2007) Adaptive interfaces and agents. In Jacko JA (Hrsg), Human-computer interaction. Interaction design and usability, 12th international conference, HCI international 2007, Beijing, 22–27 July 2007, Proceedings, Part I, Bd 4550. Springer, S 305–330

Jetter H-C (2004) Intercultural UI Design and UI Evaluation. Term paper. University of Constance

Kamentz E (2006) Adaptivity of hypermedial learning systems: a procedure model for the conception of a user modelling component under consideration of culture-related user characteristics. PhD Univ., Hildesheim. http://d-nb.info/986457256/34. Accessed 30 Sep 2016

Kamp H, Reyle U (1993) From discourse to logic: introduction to model theoretic semantics of natural language, formal logic and discourse representation theory (Student Aufl., Bd 42). Kluwer, Dordrecht

Kankanhalli A, Tan BCY, Wei K-K, Holmes MC (2004) Cross-cultural differences and information systems developer values. Decis Support Syst 38(2):183–195. https://doi.org/10.1016/S0167-9236(03)00101-5

Kaplan RB (1966) Cultural thought patterns in inter-cultural education. Lang Learn 16(1–2):1–20

Kersten GE, Kersten MA, Rakowski WM (2002) Software and culture: beyond the internationalization of the interface. J Global Inf Manag 10(4):86–101

Khaslavsky J (1998) Integrating culture into interface design. student posters: design: applications and approaches (Summary). Paper presented at the proceedings of ACM CHI 98: conference on human factors in computing systems, Los Angeles

Koda T, Rehm M, Andre E (2008) Cross-cultural evaluations of avatar facial expressions designed by western designers. Lecture Notes Comput Sci 5208:245–252

Komischke T, McGee A, Wang N, Wissmann K (2003) Mobile phone usability and cultural dimensions: China, Germany & USA. In Mühlbach L (Hrsg), Human factors in telecommunication. Proceedings of the 19th international symposium on human factors in telecommunication (HFT 03). Berlin

Komlodi A (2005) Cross-cultural study of information seeking. Paper presented at the proceedings of the international conference on human-computer interaction (HCII 2005). First international conference on usability and internationalization, Las Vegas

Koning H, Dormann C, van Vliet H (2002) Practical guidelines for the readability of IT-architecture diagrams

Kralisch A (2006) The impact of culture and language on the use of the internet empirical analyses of behaviour and attitudes. Dissertation, Berlin

Krömker H (2000) Introduction. Int J Hum Comput Interact 12(3&4):281–284

Ladle U (2003) "Grounded Theory" as a contribution to the general methodology of social research. In Behrens J (Ed), Hallesche Beiträge zu den Gesundheits- und Pfl gewissenschaften (Vol 12, p. 1–24). Kenny DA (1979). Correlation and causality. Wiley, New York

Law WK, Perez K (2005) Cross-cultural implementation of information system. J Cases Inf Technol 7(2):121–130

Lee K-P (2002) Development of tool for on-line usability testing of information appliances. Japanese J Ergon 38:80–83

Lee K-P (2007) Culture and its effects on human interaction with design: with the emphasis on cross-cultural perspectives between Korea and Japan

Lee I, Choi GW, Kim J, Kim S, Lee K, Kim D, An Y et al (2008) Cultural dimensions for user experience: cross-country and cross-product analysis of users' cultural characteristics. People Comput 1(22):3–12

Leidner DE, Kayworth T (2006) Review: A review of culture in information systems research: toward a theory of information technology culture conflict. MIS Q 30(2):357–399

Lewandowitz L, Rößger P, Vöhringer-Kuhnt T (2006) Asian vs. European HMI solutions of driver information systems Useware 2006, Vol 1946. VDI, Düsseldorf, S 279–287

Lunau S, Roenpage O (2007) Six Sigma+ Lean Toolset: Successful implementation of improvement projects. Springer, Berlin

Lyre H (2002) Information theory: a philosophical-scientific introduction (vol 2289). Fink, Munich

Maier E, Mandl T, Röse K, Womser-Hacker C, Yetim F (2005) Internationalization of information systems: cultural aspects of human-machine interaction. In Auinger A (ed), Workshops-Proceedings of the 5th interdisciplinary conference Mensch und Computer 2005 (pp 57–58). Vienna

Marcus A (2003) Global and intercultural user-interface design. In Julie AJ, Andrew S (Eds), The human-computer interaction handbook. L. Erlbaum Associates Inc, S 441–463

Marcus A (2006) Cross-cultural user-experience design. In Barker-Plummer D, Cox R, Swoboda, N (Hrsg), Diagrammatic representation and inference, Bd 4045. Springer, Berlin/Heidelberg, S 16–24

Marcus A, Gould EW (2000) Cultural dimensions and global web user-interface design: What? So what? Now what? http://bamanda.com/cms/uploads/media/AMA_CulturalDimensionsGlobalWebDesign.pdf. Accessed 29 Feb 2019

Moeschler J (1989) Dialogue modeling: representation of the Argumentative Inference. Hermès, Paris

Nardi BA (1996) Context and consciousness: activity theory and human-computer interaction. MIT Press, Cambridge

Nelius M(2003) Mousemap-based recognition of user problem areas when operating software. Dipl. Master Thesis, University of Rostock, Rostock

Nielsen J (1990).Designing user interfaces for international use, Bd 13. Elsevier, Amsterdam

Nielsen J (1993) Usability engineering. Academic Press, Boston

Nielsen J (2001) Usability metrics. nngroup. https://www.nngroup.com/articles/usability-metrics/. Accessed 19 Feb 2016

Nielsen J (2006) Usability engineering ([Nachdr.]). Merchant, Amsterdam

Nisbett RE (2003) The geography of thought: How Asians and Westerners think differently … why. Free Press, New York

Norman DA, Draper S (Hrsg) (1986) User centered system design: New perspectives on human-computer interaction. Lawrence Erlbaum Associates

Oldenburg H (1992) Applied text linguistics, vol 17. Fool, Tübingen

Ou LC, Luo MR, Woodcock A, Wright A (2004) A study of colour emotion and colour preference. Part I: colour emotions for single colours. Color Res Appl 29(3)

Plocher T, Patrick Rau P-L, Choong Y-Y (2012) Cross-cultural design handbook of human factors and ergonomics. Wiley, S 162–191

Preece J, Rogers Y et al (1994) Human-computer interaction, Reprinted edn. Addison-Wesley, Wokingham

Rathje S (2003) Is little cultural understanding better than none at all?—The problem of using dimensional models to describe culture. Interculture-Online. www.inter-culture-online.info

Rätzmann M (2004) Software-testing & internationalisierung (2. Aufl.). Galileo Press, Bonn

Rau P-LP, Plocher TA et al (2012) Cross-cultural design for IT products and services. Taylor & Francis, Boca Raton

Rehm M, Bee N, Endrass B, Wissner M, André E (2007) Too close for comfort?: adapting to the user's cultural background. Paper presented at the Proceedings of the international work- shop on Human-centered multimedia, Augsburg, Bavaria, Germany

Reinecke K, Reif G, Bernstein A (2007) Cultural user modeling with CUMO: an approach to overcome the personalization bootstrapping problem. In First international workshop on cultural heritage on the Semantic web at the 6th international semantic web conference (ISWC 2007), Busan

Reischer J (2002) Language: a phenomenon and its exploration. de Gruyter, Berlin

Reischer J (2006) Signs, information, communication. Analysis and synthesis of the sign and Information concept. http://www.opus-bayern.de/uni-regensburg/volltexte/2006/740

Reiterer H (2008) Seminar reader: Future challenges and trends in HCI [Seminar Reader]. Human-Computer Interaction Group. University of Konstanz

Rickheit G, Strohner H (1993) Basics of cognitive language processing: models, methods, results, vol 1735. Francke, Tübingen

Rızvanoğlu K, Öztürk Ö (2009) Cross-cultural understanding of the dual structure of metaphorical icons: an explorative study with French and Turkish users on an E-learning site. Paper presented at the proceedings of the 3rd International Conference on Internationalization, Design and Global Development: Held as Part of HCI International 2009, San Diego

Röbig S, Didier M, Brother R (2010) International understanding of usability and application of methods in the field of usability. Paper presented at the Grundlagen—Methoden— Technologien, 5th VDI symposium USEWARE 2010, Baden-Baden. http://tubiblio.ulb.tu-darmstadt.de/46312/. Access 29 Feb 2019

Röse K (2001) Culture as a variable of UI design. Paper presented at the Mensch & Computer 2001, Stuttgart

Röse K (2002) Methodology for the design of intercultural man-machine systems in production engineering, vol 5. Univ, Kaiserslautern

Röse K, Zühlke D (2001) Culture-oriented design: developers' knowledge gaps in this area. Paper presented at the 8th IFAC/IFIPS/IFORS/IEA symposium on analysis, design, and evaluation of human-machine systems, 18–20 Sept 2001, Kassel

Röse K, Zühlke D, Liu L (2001) Similarities and dissimilarities of German and Chinese users. In Johannsen G (Hrsg), Preprints of 8th IFAC/IFIP/IFORS/IEA symposium on analysis, design, and evaluation of human-machine systems. Kassel, S 24–29

Rößger P (2003) An international comparison of the usability of driver-information-Systems: tools, results and implications. http://dx.doi.org/10.4271/2003-01-2273

Saffer D (2008) Designing gestural interfaces: Touchscreens and interactive devices. Reilly Media, Canada, S 247

Searle JR, Kiefer CF, Lang MB (1980) Speech act theory and pragmatics. Reidel, Dordrecht

Shannon CE (1948) A mathematical theory of communication. Bell Syst Techn J 27(379–423):623–656

Shen S-T, Woolley M, Prior S (2006) Towards culture-centred design. Interact Comput 18(4):820–852. https://doi.org/10.1016/j.intcom.2005.11.014

Shneiderman B (1998) Designing the user interface: strategies for effective human-computer interaction (3. Aufl.). Addison-Wesley, Reading

Shneiderman B, Plaisant C, Cohen M, Jacobs S (2009) Designing the user interface: Strategies for effective human-computer interaction (5. Aufl., Bd Hardcover). Addison Wesley

Smith A, Dunckley L, French T, Minocha S, Chang Y (2004) A process model for developing usable crosscultural websites. Interact Comput 16(1):63–91

Stengers H, Troyer O, Baetens M, Boers F, Mushtaha A (2004) Localization of web sites: is there still a need for it? Paper presented at the International Workshop on Web Engineering (HyperText 2004 Conference), Santa Cruz

Sturm C (2002) TLCC-Towards a framework for systematic and successful product internationalization. Paper presented at the international workshop on internationalisation of products and systems, Austin/Texas

Sturm C, Mueller CH (2003) Putting theory into practice: how to apply cross-cultural differences to user interface design? In Rauterberg M, Menozzi M, Wesson J (Hrsg), Human-computer interaction: INTERACT '03; IFIP TC13 international conference on human-computer interaction, 1st 5th Sept 2003. International Federation for Information Processing, S 1051–1052

Sun H (2001) Building a culturally competent corporate web site: an exploratory study of cultural markers in multilingual web design. Paper presented at the proceedings of SIGDOC, New York. Sun H (2001b). Building a culturally-competent corporate web site: An exploratory study of cultural markers in multilingual web design. In Proceedings of the 19th annual international conference on Computer documentation. ACM, Sante Fe, S 95–102

Sun H (2012) Cross-cultural technology design: creating culture-sensitive technology for local users. Oxford University Press, Oxford/New York

Sundermeier T (1996) Understand the stranger: a practical hermeneutics. Vandenhoeck & Ruprecht, Göttingen

Tateishi M, Toma T (2010) A cross-cultural comparative study of user interface in social media: Why social media can cross seas but not nationalisms. http://koara.lib.keio.ac.jp/xoo-nips/modules/xoonips/detail.php?koara_id=KO40002001-00002010-0037. Access 29 Feb 2019

Thissen F (2008). Intercultural information design. In Weber W (ed), Compendium informations-design (p 387–424). Berlin/Heidelberg

Thomas A (1996) Psychology of intercultural action. Hogrefe, Göttingen/Seattle

Vatrapu R, Suthers D (2007) Culture and computers: A review of the concept of culture and implications for intercultural collaborative online learning. Lecture Notes Comput Sci 4568:260

Victor DA (1998) International business communication (7. Aufl.). Harper Collins, New York

Vöhringer-Kuhnt T (2002). The influence of culture on usability. M.A. master thesis, Freie Universität Berlin

Vollhardt JK, Migacheva K, Tropp LR (2008) Social cohesion and tolerance for group differences handbook on building cultures of peace. Springer, New York, pp 139–152

Wilss W (1988) Cognition and translation: to the theory and practice of human and machine translation, vol 41. Niemeyer, Tübingen

Wimmer FM (2004) Intercultural philosophy: an introduction (Vol. 2470). WUV, Vienna

Wittgenstein L, Schulte J (2000) Tractatus logico-philosophicus. Diaries 1914–1916. Philosophical studies (vol. 501, 1st ed, [repr.]). Frankfurt a. M.: Suhrkamp

Wonderful D (1975). Linguistic pragmatics (vol 12, 2nd ed, verb. repr.). Wiesbaden: Athenaion

Wonderful D (1978) Studies on speech act theory (Vol. 172, 2nd ed, 6th–8th thousand). Suhrkamp, Frankfurt a. M

Zühlke D, Röse K (2000) Design of global user-interfaces: Living with the challenge proceedings of the IEA 2000/HFES 2000 congress, July 29th trough August 4th 2000, Bd 6. San Diego, S 154–157

Chapter 7
IUID in Practice—Industrial Development

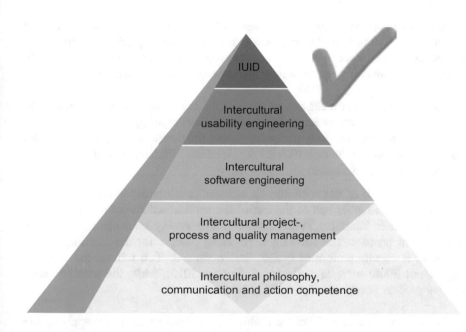

First, aspects of the procedural approach of IUID in practice are presented. Subsequently, the essential phases (requirements analysis and concept development, design elements and implementation, evaluation and test) of the process for the development of intercultural user interfaces (IUID) with regard to cultural differences to the established development process models (V-model and agile methods as well as U-CD and U-CD) are examined in more detail. Highlights are the U-CD approach extended by a cultural model, the use of a model for culture-dependent HMI design to derive design recommendations and their description, the use of an automated tool for intercultural interaction analysis and finally the signature and representation of culture-dependent and culture-independent evaluation methods.

© Springer Nature Switzerland AG 2019

R. Heimgärtner, *Intercultural User Interface Design*, Human–Computer Interaction Series, https://doi.org/10.1007/978-3-030-17427-9_7

7.1   Process

The development of physical products often follows the "Stagegate process" (Cooper et al. 2007), in which a number of decision points (gates) from research are often fed into the development process.

▸ In the development of digital products and services, development processes often follow the V model—a sequential iterative process model—or use agile software development methods such as Scrum or combinations of such approaches.
▸ Advanced software development processes also have corresponding gates (e.g., with regard to quality: quality gates/hurdles).
▸ The quality of these processes is often checked using maturity models (e.g., CHMI, SPICE).

With the competition in mind in the search for flexibility and a comprehensive reduction of effort in HMI design projects, in the past, it was particularly difficult to get all the required documents for the entire project approved by the customer right at the start of development. However, this procedure is not possible if:

• The product requirements are not clear at the beginning—which is very probable for preliminary projects of intercultural development,
• The requirements are only generated during the development phase and often change—which is the case with the development of intercultural user interfaces due to iterative evaluation (cf. Chap. 4).

Approximately half of all the efforts of a software development project relate to the user interface, the other half to the rest of the application. In the development of intercultural user interfaces, cultural influences inevitably influence the necessary development process. The software engineering process for the creation of user interfaces is usually performed systematically, since it often follows the V-model (cf. Balzert 2008) or agile methods (cf. Ferreira 2012), while the usability engineering process is often unsystematic in practice.

▸ The goal must be to perform the usability engineering process by applying the human-centered design principles (cf. ISO 9241-210) as systematically as the software engineering process.

To this end, the need for human-centered design for the respective intercultural context must be identified. The standard V-model process, which is based on a waterfall model, is less suitable for intercultural HMI design projects because the product requirements are still too unclear at the beginning (especially in the case of new product developments) and the requirements are developed iteratively during the development phases and thus often undergo changes. In addition, the feedback of the users must be permanently included in the human-centered design up to the last phase of the development of the user interface.

These challenges can be met well with agile methods. However, they require a lasting change in the cultural way of thinking, which can be achieved (in the long term) with appropriate training of the teams.[1] In practical use and with the appropriate development of some agile principles and methods, the focus is often more on the constant iterative (repeated, step-by-step) achievement of correct results (product quality) than on the correct achievement of results (process quality) (see also Chap. 3). Nevertheless, while maintaining the compatibility of SPICE's process capability model,[2] the following principles of agile manifesto can also be adhered to[3]:

- Individual interactions over processes and tools,
- Functioning software over extensive documentation,
- Customer participation over contract negotiation.

For many process areas it is possible to achieve "SPICE capability level 3 of 5", if the agile development processes are supported with corresponding auxiliary processes:

- Supplier processes related to product release and acceptance are performed by the product owner.
- Technological processes, especially regarding software (but also on system level), such as requirements analysis, design, implementation, integration, and testing, are the core of agile methods. They are carried out by the cross-functional core team and managed at system level by the product owner.
- Resource management, training, and project infrastructure are essential requirements of agile methods and are administered by product owners, scrum masters and other stakeholders.
- Process improvement is a constant focus in agile development, which requires constant monitoring of the learning curve and efficiency ("retrospectives").
- Product evaluation and modification management (including problem-solving management) are optimized through team coordination discussions regarding requirements and troubleshooting when defining a "sprint" plan.

---

[1]It is faster and more successful if management roles in the projects (e.g., Product Owner and Scrum Master) are filled with interculturally experienced team members right from the start.

[2]SPICE's "process capability model" includes 6 "process maturity levels": 0—incomplete, 1—performed, 2—managed, 3—established, 4—measurable, 5—optimized. A short and action-relevant introduction to SPICE can be found in Heimgärtner 2016. SPICE is explained in detail in ISO 15504. The successor and general standard for process assessments are ISO 330XX. When SPICE is mapped to SCRUM, some of the generic practices of the process attributes 3.1 and 3.2 can be largely or fully achieved.

[3]Different interpretations of the "agile manifesto", which is very abbreviated here because it is short and concise, are often represented by different methods (such as SCRUM, XP, Lean Driven, Kanban).

- Process-related documentation and configuration management is driven until the desired maturity of the product or skill level of the team is available.

To be able to fulfil all process attributes up to SPICE level 3 in all process areas, additional documentation and an intelligent extension of existing SCRUM templates are indispensable (even to achieve bidirectional traceability at SPICE level 1).

▸ In addition, the early recognition and consideration of cultural differences in product development play a decisive role in the development of intercultural user interfaces.

This is done by means of a planned process (engineering), which optimizes the interaction between users and product and increases the usability of the product under consideration of regional and cultural influence factors (intercultural) (see Chap. 4). This process comprises the determination of the necessary user requirements engineering, system and function design (concept development, e.g., information architecture, interaction concept), the comprehensible design of the functions with regard to the user interface design and the evaluation of functionality and user interface evaluation (ISO 9241-210, Honold 2000, see also Sect. 4.6: Intercultural Usability Engineering).

Project and development process always have the characteristics of the HMI concept development and the prototypes or product development. Figure 7.1 illustrates the connection between usability engineering and software engineering.

Initially, the HMI concept development (consisting of requirements analysis and creation of the concept for possible design solutions) will be started. Once this has been specified, it can be implemented in a prototype. Both HMI concept specifications and prototypes are iteratively optimized according to permanent evaluation loops.

If in a project only little is known about the influence of culture on the engineering processes, then the results from the process (work products) will be distorted, unexpected or insufficient. A corresponding cultural sensitivity of the process participants in all phases of intercultural usability engineering is, therefore, indispensable for a high-quality of the research and development results as well as their validity.

Fig. 7.1 Relationship between usability engineering and software engineering

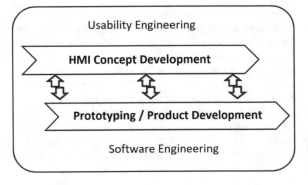

In the following, we will, therefore, explain where culture influences the individual phases of software engineering and how, which problems can arise, and which solutions exist to master these challenges in order to maintain adequate intercultural user interfaces.

In principle, the phases of intercultural software engineering (see Chap. 3) also correspond to the phases of software engineering as described by Balzert (2008) in the V-Modell. In addition, the close connection to the usability engineering process (see Chap. 4) is indispensable (shown in bold):

- Analysis phase (requirements analysis, specifications, **context of use description, user requirements specification, user research (cf. Urbas et al.** 2006)),
- Design phase (system architecture, software design, **information architecture, interaction design, UI design/style guide**),
- Implementation phase (creation of a prototype or the product),
- Test phase (software test, **heuristic evaluation, usability test**).

Before you start developing intercultural user interfaces, you should think about the overall process and plan the individual steps within the development project. In the following, the essential aspects (requirements analysis and concept development; design elements and implementation; evaluation and test) of the process for the development of intercultural user interfaces are examined.

▸ The introduction of agile methods can accelerate the process of unraveling diverse and changing stakeholder interests from different cultures.

7.2   Requirements Analysis and Concept Development

▸ The requirements analysis for the development of user interfaces essentially consists of understanding and describing the context of use and deriving and specifying user requirements as the basis for creating design solutions for interactive systems.

The user of an interactive system must perform certain tasks. Within the task domain, tasks have a certain structure (for example, sending electronic mail or preparing documents). The HMI should then have the same structure. Therefore, the discovery of the structure of the task domain is seen as part of the user interface design. This discovery process and its translation into user interfaces require special expertise (see Chap. 4).

▸ In the requirements analysis, the business processes must be included in accordance with the HMI action level model (cf. Chap. 4) in order to achieve the analysis of the requirements of the interactive system in the context of the entire

	Task appropriatenes	completenes s	Activity room	creative work	Exploratory learnin
Pragmatic level	✓ Is there a general relation to the task? ✓ Is the software with compatible/networkable with other organizational units? ✓ Is the software is functional	✓ Can overriding goals be independently subdivided into subgoals and mapped in the software? ✓ Can functions become de-fragmented	✓ Can the software be adapted to individual characteristics (e.g. font, text, etc.)? size, language)? ✓ Do several radio chains lead to the	✓ Are software modules clearly assignable? ✓ Can individual modules of the software be combined? Do multiple moduleand function chains	✓ Can the user's order and memory criteria be generated within the software? ✓ Voices software in accordance with mental models?
Semantic level	✓ Does the execution of functions serve to achieve objectives?	✓ Is the effect of a function reported back to the user? ✓ Can a software action match with the manual targets? ✓ Does the software offer communication possibilities?	✓ Can I choose between different functions? ✓ Can you distinguish and choose between different dialogues? ✓ Are exit and exit break possibilities available?	✓ Are the functional effects completely recognizable? ✓ Are the necessary thought processes also of a non- algorithmic nature? ✓ Can or must prior experience and action knowledge	✓ Are different learning strategies supported? ✓ Are the functions analogous to previous (non-computerized) activities? ✓ Can faulty executions of a
Syntactic level	✓ Do the misnomers correspond to the task vocabulary? ✓ Does the networking structure of the software reflect the organizational structure? ✓ Functions are named identically throughout the	✓ Are the terms and functional descriptions used familiar to the user from his working environment? ✓ Are these terms recognizable at the age of the user?	✓ Can I choose between control and command-line input?	✓ Will the same para- meters remain the same? ✓ Can designations be shared across modules?	✓ Is it possible to revive what has already been learned? ✓ Do the command designations represent the respective functions (meaningful activation of
Physical level	✓ Are the type and form of input and output adapted to the task?	✓ Do the type and form of input/output change? ✓ Are monotonous activities (e.g. data release)	✓ Can I choose between keyboard and mouse input? ✓ Are key assignments (Shortcuts) modifiable?	✓ Are the menu structure and key assignment consistent? ✓ Can the output individualized?	✓ Are learning and task contents clearly separated from each other? ✓ Can the incorrect input of data (typing error) be corrected easily?

Fig. 7.2 Requirements from the action level model of Herczeg (2005) to be examined for the cultural context of use. (*Source* Herczeg 2005)

work organization (Fig. 7.2). All these questions should be answered in the development of intercultural user interfaces for the respective cultural target contexts.

The requirements analysis collects facts about the users with their individual needs, tasks, and goals as well as the typical usage environment. The subsequent formulation of usage scenarios then forms the basis for the definition of requirements. Surveys and observations are methodically available, which can be carried out personally, online, by telephone or as a group discussion (focus groups). A large number of variables must be defined which, when combined, lead to useful results, e.g. considerations on the composition of the sample or on the quantitative or qualitative approach. The observation of users takes place when working with comparable products or when performing comparable tasks on site, in a usability test studio or remotely. A trained Usability Professional (e.g., User Requirement Engineer or Usability Engineer, see Sect. 4.4.4) observes and analyzes tasks, action sequences including stumbling blocks and the user environment. The user(s) are either observed in their typical work or the usability professional designs concrete usage scenarios, tailored to the questions of the user research study. Normally, interviews and observations are combined. There are different approaches for the collection of user requirements from which the user requirements can be derived, e.g.:

- Task analysis (Hackos and Redish 1998),
- Context analysis (Beyer and Holtzblatt 2007),
- Activity theories (Kaptelinin and Nardi 2012).

At the moment it is still questionable whether models for task analysis such as CTT, GOMS, TaskModL and Design Rationale such as problem-based information systems (IBIS) or Questions, Options, Criteria (QOC) as well as patterns also function without complications in an intercultural context.

▸ Even though there are already some studies on the analysis of suitable methods for the cultural context, the following techniques of user participation for early development phases, which are suitable for the cultural context, are still predominantly used: Focus groups (Honold 2000), interviews (Winschiers-Theophilus et al. 2010) and field observations (Röse 2002; Honold 2000).

The main focus of intercultural usability engineering and thus of intercultural UI design is the implementation of empirical intercultural studies (user studies or user research studies). Intercultural user research means the systematic investigation of the users of a product, their respective usage situations and their demands on the product in an intercultural context (cf. also Sect. 5.1).

In order to save resources in the process of data collection, procedures are required which guarantee an analysis of the user without having to carry out on-site testing, e.g., through online studies or remote testing (see Heimgärtner 2008). However, this is not without problems for various reasons. For example, the insight into the working environment and the view of the test leader (e.g., of a usability tester, see Sect. 4.4) on the cultural differences on site are missing.

Since in most cases employees (e.g., sales engineers, furnishing engineers, etc.) already work in the target environment before a planned localisation of the product (see Chap. 3), it is, therefore, advisable to conduct interviews with these employees in the corresponding branches about the local conditions.

The often experienced "culture shock" and the experiences of these people involved in it also contribute to giving the system developer a more real picture of the user of the system.

▸ In addition to statistical data on the country average (see, for example, the CIA's World Fact Book), information can be collected in this way which originates from the production environment and which already uncovers initial points of intersection or problems regarding user requirements and demographic data.

This knowledge is an essential yardstick for the development and design work of the interactive system meeting the requirements or the intercultural user interface— because the requirement is that the product has to adapt to people and not the other way round (cf. Chap. 4).

Intercultural user research makes sense before and during development in an iterative process. Before, respectively at the beginning of a development there is the collection of requirements and expectations of the users. As soon as initial operating concepts have been developed, they must be made tangible (prototyping) in order to evaluate the fit of the concepts to the previously collected requirements and expectations of the users. Through iterative optimization based on the knowledge from user research activities (see Chap. 4), a product with optimal usability is created.

▶ The ultimate goal is a structured process for intercultural HMI design. To date, there are generally only a few complete and consistent systemized methods in the HMI design process that support the designer in the creation of user interfaces (UIs)—especially for the consideration of cultural aspects.

In order to meet this difficult task, it makes sense to choose a model-based systematic approach. A model-oriented approach that combines many of these approaches within a structured way of working is the usage-centered design approach (see Constantine and Lockwood 2003). Due to a consistently structured working method, cultural aspects can also be systematically included in the product development process with this model-based approach (Windl and Heimgärtner 2013). Use case modeling (UML) can also be used as business process and workflow modeling according to BPMN with corresponding activity diagrams. The task of all those involved in the process is to analyze at which points in the process cultural influences come into play in order to counteract possible obstacles in intercultural projects (Hoffmann et al. 2004).

▶ The inclusion of cultural aspects in HMI design plays a decisive role, especially in the analysis of user and system requirements, as a lack of cultural aspects can have a negative impact on the entire further UI development process in the form of higher error rates and project costs. This is made possible by a systematic intercultural design process.

In addition, such a procedure helps developers of user interfaces to:

- Successfully start the development process (i.e., determine what needs to be done and in what order),
- To have guidance from requirements to specification,
- To develop better systems.

7.2.1 Excursion: Usage-Centered Design Approach to Systematic Modeling

A hybrid model approach integrates activity theory into the proven and successful usage-centered design approach for systematic model-based requirements analysis and extends it by cultural models to take cultural aspects into account in the design of HMI systems and to cover cultural contexts (Windl and Heimgärtner 2013). This ensures clear and clean guidance through the entire design process to an intercultural user interface, providing an alternative to trial-and-error approaches, which attempt to find and fix flaws and problems of bad design through iterative testing and repair. In contrast to user-centered design, which first places the user in the foreground and then moves on to system design via the tasks, usage-centered design begins with the tasks and then moves on from the user to the system concept.

▶ Intercultural Usage-Centered Design (IU-CD) serves as a systematic and model-based method for determining the user requirements for the design of intercultural user interfaces (cf. Windl und Heimgärtner 2013).

This approach helps developers of intercultural user interfaces to get started directly with their work and to maintain an overview and insight into reusable models during the entire construction process by means of structured orientation aids and thus to achieve better intercultural systems. Usage-Centered Design (Constantine and Lockwood 1999) is a systematic process with abstract models to design user interfaces for software systems that support all tasks and thus reach the user completely. The user interfaces are derived directly and systematically from a series of interconnected core models. At the heart of the process is the robust, fine-grained Task Model, which includes a user view of the functionality of the system and is essentially expressed in use cases. Usage-Centered Design (UCD) has a clear focus on user performance. This approach creates systems that allow users to perform their tasks more accurately, reliably and in less time (cf. Constantine 2004). Developed for the first time in the early 1990s, UCD is a proven, industry-strength approach that has been used to develop everything from industrial automation systems (cf. Windl 2002) and consumer electronics to banking and infotainment applications (cf. Constantine and Windl 2009). This is possible because the Usage-Centered Design (UCD) approach activates a lean process driven by simple models that are well scalable. This approach has been used for projects ranging from a few months in duration to major projects (Constantine and Lockwood 1999; Ferr et al. 2001).

▶ The Usage-Centered Design procedure (UCD) is divided into an analysis and a discard phase (Fig. 7.3). Role and task models are the results of user and task analysis. The content model together with the implementation model are the results of the design phase.

The Usage-Centered Design is grouped around three simple core models that represent the relationships between user and system (role model), the user tasks (task model), and the content and structure of the user interface (content model). The content model is derived directly from the task model, which in turn is derived from the role model. All models consist of two parts, a description and an additional model that models the relationship between the descriptions.

Looking at the cultural aspects, we find a variety of different aspects. Intercultural variables (Röse and Zühlke 2001), properties of the user interface (Marcus 2001) and HMI dimensions (Heimgärtner 2012) can be combined with cultural aspects and thus represent more or less overlapping specific cultural HMI design rules and guidelines that influence the visual design and interaction design of a system (cf. Chap. 5). Since these are static (i.e., independent of the purpose of the

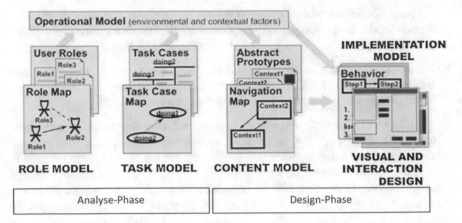

Fig. 7.3 Main components of the Usage-Centered Design (UC-D) process. (*Source* Windl and Heimgärtner 2013)

system), they apply to almost all systems and are not specific to a particular system. System specific cultural aspects are specifically designed for a particular system. The aspects are usually the result of user requirement and task analysis and are influenced by user roles and task structures. For example, a user role has different distinctive backgrounds in different countries and therefore requires different task structures in different countries.

Another example would be that one and the same task has a radically different course in different countries. An example of this is entering addresses in a GPS navigation system in the USA and China. In China, the usual strategy for finding a position is not to use the postal address, but either to find a crossroads or a point of interest (POI, see Chap. 6) near the desired location. Which method is used also depends on where you are in China at the moment, i.e., at which location the navigation system is currently used. In addition to the different types of cultural aspects, it is important to consider methods of localization and internationalization within an intercultural UI design to reduce future development times of the software.

▸ In order to integrate the cultural aspects and the internationalization requirements into UCD, it is necessary to expand it and make adjustments to the existing procedure in various places. The common aspects of intercultural UI design are taken up in a cultural model similar to the existing "operation model" (Fig. 7.4).

Since the content of the cultural model influences the visual design and inter-action design, this new model influences the transitions from the task model to the content model and from the content model to the implementation model. The cultural model captures the common rules for those cultures for which the system is to be designed.

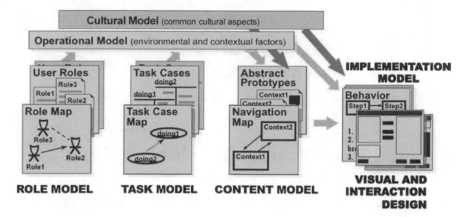

Fig. 7.4 Extended usage-centered design process through a cultural model. (*Source* Windl and Heimgärtner 2013)

▸ Each culture has its own cultural model (Fig. 7.5).
  The content of the cultural model is primarily related to the characteristics of the user interface (cf. Marcus 2007) and the HMI dimensions (cf. Heimgärtner 2012) and describes a user interface on an abstract level, which is filled with the special values for the desired culture.

In internationalized systems, which are used in different cultures, it is necessary to implement different cultures at the level of role and task models, as there may be culture-dependent versions of the same user roles and task structures. The role and task models for different cultures are extended with a cultural identifier that corresponds to the ISO country code with a rhombus at country level (Fig. 7.6).

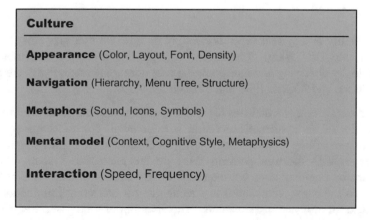

Fig. 7.5 Qualitative content of the cultural model. (*Source* Windl and Heimgärtner 2013)

Fig. 7.6 Notation for a cultural identifier expressing validity for all cultures except China

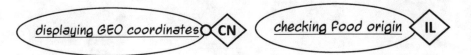

Fig. 7.7 Task cases with different cultural identifiers. *Source* Windl und Heimgärtner (2013)

► In order to be able to cover cultural aspects that do not fit into this country scheme (such as religious denominations, locations, or any other cultural target groups), it is possible to use project-specific cultural identifiers.

 The task case map contains all task cases as well as the relationships between the task cases. The task cases are provided with their names including one or more cultural identifiers (Fig. 7.7).

► The approach of intercultural usage-centered design (IU-CD) helps developers of intercultural user interfaces to systematically collect and model system and user requirement and to create suitable interactive systems of high usability and UX on the basis of exact models.

7.2.2   Context of Use and User Requirements

► The usability of a system depends strongly on how the user gets along with the system (see DIN 2006). The degree of compliance can be determined, for example, by observing and questioning a user during interaction with the system (cf. Nielsen and Molich 1990 and Nielsen 1990).

 In this case, the user articulates his wishes and thus also his needs with regard to the usability of the system. Observation is a technique for collecting contextual information regarding requirements. During an observation, the User Requirements Engineer watches the user perform tasks on the interactive system. The User Requirements Engineer does not intervene unless there is a need for a clarifying answer. An interview (contextual) is a technique for collecting information about the context of use and requirements. The interviewer (the User Requirements Engineer) asks the user questions about current processes in the light of the planned interactive system. The interview takes place where the user's interaction with the interactive system usually takes place, e.g., at the user's workplace.[4] A written interview checklist with appropriate questions and hints, which is used during an interview, ensures that all relevant topics are considered.

If these methods are not used within the HMI design, both the user requirement engineer, and the developer lack the knowledge about the user requirements. If then not all necessary requirements and user requirements can be derived or if they are wrong, a product with inferior design is obtained.

The consequences are obvious: The user shows no interest in the product because it does not cover his needs, or he cannot use the product properly because essential components of the user interface are missing and therefore a specific task processing takes too long, or tasks cannot be solved at all.

▸ The individual cultural context of use must be specified for relevant usage situations in order to develop a deeper understanding of the individual culture-specific needs of the user. In addition to qualitative techniques of market research, quantitative methods must also be used. International requirements must also be taken into account.

For example, in the case of navigation systems, it could be the case that managing directors worldwide have similar requirements for implemented functions, such as e-mail reception and regularly updated messages, while taxi drivers, in contrast, require a precise prediction of traffic obstacles. Detailed observations of the user "in situ", i.e., in typical behavior scenarios, are useful here.[5] On this basis, the HMI dimensions, the UI characteristics, the intercultural variables, and the cultural dimensions within the context of use can then be described.

▸ The determination of all different requirements from all stakeholder groups requires that all requirements of the preceding process steps are identified and that these requirement specifications are collected and consolidated (i.e., clarified and purified) regardless of their origin.

All needs, interests, expectations and behavior patterns of the different user groups must be recorded. In an international context, it is important to note that there is not a single homogeneous user group, but that there are thousands or even millions of individual users worldwide, as in the case of a consumer product such as the mobile phone. In order to get a better grip on the complexity of this survey, these users are condensed into imagined user groups. A conceived, specific and concrete representation of the target user

---

[4]The contextual interview therefore always has a contextual reference and is therefore often referred to as "contextual inquiry".

[5]Principles of "design thinking", for example, can be used here. In this example it could be determined, for example, when, where, how and for how long a user enters data into the navigation system.

('persona') helps the product teams to understand the user better and therefore to improve their products (cf. Cooper 1999 and Cooper et al. 2007). The IUID process requires more than one persona; different personas represent culturally different user groups.

An investigation of the human-centered design process (cf. ISO 9241-210) showed (see Chap. 4) that the current process does not fully meet these requirements (cf. Heimgärtner 2014). If the user requirements are not fully understood at the very beginning of the development process, there is a risk that a uniform general basic structure cannot be developed which can then be adapted to the local culture-specific requirements (according to the principles of localization and internationalization, see Chap. 3).

In addition, requirements must be compared with the strategic objectives of the manufacturer of the product and those requirements that do not correspond to the corporate strategy must be removed. Furthermore, all conflicts of interest must be resolved during the requirements analysis (e.g., small screen versus large screen, touch screen versus keyboard).

▸ The consolidated requirements define the production objectives of the project. Compliance with these objectives, which are separate from their solutions, can ultimately be achieved by meeting the requirements according to the SMART principle: specific, measurable, attainable, realistic and timely.

7.3 Components of a Localization Project

This section presents the components, the people involved and the localization processes in a conventional software localization project and thus the embedding of directly usable action-relevant knowledge in the processes of internationalization and localization of software. The basic requirement for a localization project is that a software product becomes localized. Although each localization project is unique, factors such as software type, customer requirements, budget, and schedule can identify some components that are critical to a localization project (Fig. 7.8).

▸ Normally, software products contain two main components: software and documentation.[6]

Documentation includes (Esselink 2000) printed documentation, online documentation, web pages, online manuals, and online help. Software products usually

---

[6]This distinction increasingly disappears with the use of integrated localization tools (see Sect. 7.4.4).

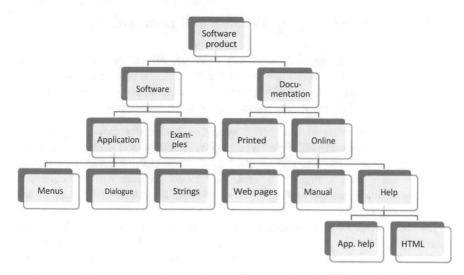

Fig. 7.8 Typical components of a localization project. (*Source* eColore website of the University of Saarbrücken, http://fr46.uni-saarland.de/index.php?id=662. Accessed 26.10.2016)

include one or two printed manuals: for ordinary ones, an installation guide (which explains to the user how to install the software), and

A guide to the first steps (it provides a brief introduction to the application). Other printed documents that can be delivered with a software product are reference cards, marketing material, registration cards, product packaging, etc. Software vendors often prefer online documentation because it reduces printing costs and makes it easier to distribute updates or revise via the Internet. Online documentation includes Web pages, online manuals, and online help. Websites enable software companies to publish texts and other information about their software applications dynamically and interactively on the Internet. Online manuals are usually published in an electronic exchange format (e.g., Portable Document Format (PDF)). They can either be opened and read or printed with an appropriate program. Online help is directly accessible from the software application on the screen. It allows users to search for specific topics and jump back and forth between different topics.

▸ Localization projects usually begin with software translation, which involves translating the components of an application's graphical user interface, such as menus, dialogue boxes, and strings (error messages, questions, etc.), and any sample files that may be provided with the software for demonstration purposes. The translation of the documentation should be iterative and parallel to the maturity of the software.

7.3.1   Core Elements of Translation and Localisation

▸ When internationalizing and localizing software, all parties involved should always be aware of the core elements of localization and take them into account accordingly, otherwise they could be potential sources of problems that can cause excessive user effort and inacceptance during the development process.

Localization elements include terminology, symbols, diagrams, graphics and photos, colors, character sets, fonts/typography, language and style, formats and other aspects such as space requirements, layout, menu customization, icon design, metaphor usage, and navigation design. A detailed presentation of localization elements and guidelines can be found, for example, in Fernandes (1995) and Tuthill and Smallberg (1997).

The localization of a software product contains the localization of all its components (application, documentation, other materials). A software application consists of a program code and an HMI specification or HMI elements. The program code contains the commands to monitor the performance and functions of the program.

HMI elements form the basis for "communication" between the user and the program. Both program code and HMI elements must be localized. In the program code, for example, date, time, number, currency, and paper format, hotkey or shortcut combinations and character sets must be adapted and in the HMI elements button labels, tooltips, menus, submenus, dialogue boxes and their internal elements (options, lists, etc.), system messages (error or status messages), etc. must be adapted.

The adaptation of the documentation includes the software documentation and localizable text in the application. The outsourcing of these documents and the HMI elements for translation takes place with so-called exchange formats (e.g., inx format (InDesign Interchange Format) or XML) (cf. eColore WebSite University of Saarbrücken), which is increasingly diminishing due to the distinction between software and document localization (Schildhauer 2000, Passolo, Linguatec).

▸ In times of globalization it is very important for companies, institutions or products to be present on the Internet. This presence in the form of a web site should also be tailored to the local target markets.

A multilingual website is often not planned at the beginning and therefore the localization will be done later as the market grows. Web pages consist of several elements that can contain text to be translated or that must be adapted to the target market, such as text blocks, graphics, audio or video recordings, buttons, animations, hyperlinks and navigation elements. These elements are closely linked and form a complex text. Web pages can be static or dynamic, depending on the type of text they display. Static web pages consist of static text in HTML files. Dynamic web pages contain texts that have been created from databases and are regularly updated. Therefore, when preparing a localization project for a website, it is necessary to analyze the language and design, file formats and strategies for using the file formats (HTML, XML, ASP, JSP, etc.) and content (text, graphics, animation, audio, video, etc.) to determine, for example, which translatable text or culture-specific content is contained that needs to be adapted.

▸ Since the content of websites changes very often, it is advisable to develop and systematize a localization workflow.

Content management systems (CMS) can be used for this purpose (e.g., Typo3, Joomla, etc.). With these platforms, it is possible to develop and organize content so that new or modified text can be extracted and forwarded to translators. CMS also allows version control, i.e., only the most current versions of the website are displayed, for example, (cf. Zerfaß 2005).

After localizing a website, the following aspects must be considered to ensure the quality of the final product (i.e. the localized website):

- Check that the navigation of the localized website works correctly.
- Check all links.
- Show all localized graphics and icons to see if they are displayed correctly.
- Check dynamic sites, e.g. whether user queries that depend on database functions work correctly.
- Try different browsers to verify that the localized website is displayed correctly.
- Update.

7.3.2 Localization Kits (LocKits)/L10 N-KIT

▸ A "locale" is the culture-dependent component of the software and is rich in units that are specific to particular target culture.

These elements combine things like dialogue and error messages and menu names, which are translated and stored in a separate folder. There is a folder for each culture, which allows an adaptation of the page orientation (from left to right in Danish or English and from right to left in Arabic) and the vocabulary ("color" in American English and "color" in British English). If an interface in a new language is required, the localization takes place in the culture-dependent components—only the folders are localized; there is no modification of the culture-independent component of the software.

▸ A localization kit (LocKit) should contain all the information the translator needs
  for localization. Zerfaß (2005) gives step-by-step tips on how to create a LocKit
  (see also the I18 N-L10 N checklist in Appendix B of this book).

LocKits are target-oriented and contain—besides the files to be localized—a
description of the workflow, the resources (glossaries, style guidelines for user
interfaces, etc.) and partly also tools for localization (L10 N tools, translation
memories, editors, etc.)—often as free translation tools which only allow the
translator to edit the corresponding project and which do not allow the creation of
new own projects (Müller 2005). Of course, software localization projects require
many organizational details that the project manager takes care of.

▸ One way to avoid communication problems within a localization team is to give
  everyone involved in the project an overview of all project phases using an L10 N
  plan.

The localization plan provides an overview of all project phases. It contains the
product description (product name, usage, website, previous versions, and word
count), previous versions (in which languages are previous versions available, who
was responsible for the localization?), the team (name and area of responsibility of
the team members; organization table) as well as the objective of a project and the
schedule. An overview of files to be translated and file structure allows each team
member to know who is responsible for creating, modifying and translating each
file, if changes need to be made or terminology questions arise, etc.

7.4 Design Elements and Their Implementation

7.4.1 Cultural Influence on Information Architecture and Interaction Design

Cultural dimensions represent an aspect of a culture that is measurable in
dependence on other cultures (see Chap. 2). Cultural dimensions are good
indicators of possible differences between cultures (cf. Hofstede 1991). In
addition, recommendations are available regarding which cultural dimensions
are most interesting for intercultural HMI design (see Sect. 5.2.2). The
knowledge of the values of cultural dimensions gives an impression of the
possible cultures to which a user might belong. For example,
relationship-oriented cultures allow high information speeds in contrast to
task-oriented cultures, which like to concentrate on their tasks instead of
wasting time talking to other people when communication is not related to the
task (see Halpin and Winer 1957; Hall 1959). Task-oriented users prefer to
perform tasks within working hours instead of maintaining relationships. The
knowledge as to whether the user is more relationship-oriented or

task-oriented can be seen from the interaction behavior of the user. For example, pressing buttons very precisely and navigating very directly without disturbances or interruptions increases the likelihood that the user is task oriented and takes the task very seriously.

▸ Trends in cultural differences can be used both for the development and design of intercultural user interfaces and for further reflection and research.

Thus Marcus (2001) developed characteristic factors for user interfaces with the aim of making cultural dimensions accessible for user interface design. It provides examples of effects on the design of user interfaces (see Sect. 5.4.3). The five following characteristics are linked to the five cultural dimensions of Hofstede: 'metaphor', 'mental model', 'navigation', 'interaction' and 'presentation'. Marcus pursued a purely deductive approach in order to establish these connections. Marcus and Gould (2000) have therefore derived possible recommendations for web design mainly on the basis of Hofstedes cultural dimensions—without empirical foundation of the connections. This model therefore still requires empirical validation. Röse confirmed this for example by qualitative studies in China, e.g. different layout for Chinese and German users (see Röse 2001). Chinese users are traditionally strong (Marcus 2001; Röse et al. 2001) because of the hierarchical social structures are more relationship- and family-oriented. In stark contrast, German users are described as event-oriented or task-oriented in terms of actions, tools, work, employment and competition. Table 7.1 shows a summary of implicit general recommendations for intercultural user interface design based on Röse (2002).

However, there are also some recommendations that are not very intuitive and clear, as they partly contradict each other and in the literature. For example, German users cope better with fuzzy logic and ambiguities than Chinese users. This view can also be found in the literature on cognitive styles (cf. Beynon et al. 2001; Houghton 2005), which contradicts the attributes from Tables 2 and 3 in Röse (2002, p. 138).

In addition, metaphors, taxonomy as hierarchical and classifying instruments are applied more in China than in Germany due to the high-power distance values. Nevertheless, the recommendations presented must be empirically tested in detail before they are available for practices or even helpful guidelines.

▸ In addition to reading literature, empirical studies on intercultural user interface characteristics are necessary to determine the intercultural usability of the systems (e.g., by comparing several systems of different cultures and performing usability tests).

Table 7.1 Recommendations for intercultural HMI design according to the user interface characteristics of China and Germany (summarized by the author based on "Table 6-3" in Röse (2002, p. 138) and Röse (2002, pp. 305–317)

User interface	China	Germany
Metaphor	Using clear hierarchies and concrete representation instead of abstraction	Flat hierarchy and abstraction can be used
Mental model	Use many references without relevant arrangement in simple mental models; clear formulations, limited interaction options, and binary logic	Few references from a relevant order; "fuzzy" logic
Navigation	Using restricted, predefined options in navigation	Use open access, arbitrary selection, and individual destination information when navigating
Interaction	Use personalized, but team-based systems that deliver direct error messages, guided assistance and face-to-face interaction	Use distant but helpful error messages that allow open and flexible interaction with the system
Presentation	Use formal language style with strong contextual, relational information and "feminine" colors	Use informal language style with little contextual, but strongly goal-oriented information and "masku line" colors

For example, in the design of information stimuli interculturality is shown in the evaluation of the stimuli themselves, but also in the effectiveness of these stimuli for subsequent action tendencies. Overdrawn security features such as strong snap-lock symbols or even threateningly designed "security guards", which are intended to prevent the user from triggering a particular action option, are rated significantly more negatively by German users under acceptance aspects than by Indian persons of a comparable population (Brau 2009). There are clear indications of how the characteristics of an individualistic culture have an effect on system perception in comparison to those of a hierarchically autocratic culture. Direct deductions from the effectiveness of such incentives cannot, however, be made. For example, it can be seen that users in Germany and the Benelux countries feel less disturbed than Indian users by real restrictions (e.g., on usage rights) and try less often to ignore restrictions (Brau 2009).

▸ When developing intercultural user interfaces, all aspects concerning the characteristics of the user interface must be considered in the cultural context:

- Wireframes: schematic structure, layout, and navigation structure,
- Seven dimensions of visual design: shape, size, saturation, texture, color, orientation, position,
- Layout,
- Navigation,
- Paper-based mockups,

- Coding forms, information views, text representation, colors, (in context),
- Gestalt laws,
- Icons.

▸ However, the methods for obtaining and evaluating intercultural user interfaces also require cultural inspection:

- User participation and methods used such as think aloud, etc.,
- Heuristics,
- Card sorting tests,
- Interaction techniques.

Initial approaches in this direction were described in Chap. 6 (see Sect. 6.4.6, cf. also Röbig et al. 2010).

7.4.2   Model for Culture-Dependent HMI Design

Culturally   influenced basic variables in HMI design are frequency, density, arrangement and structure. They are particularly involved in information processing and interaction activity.

▸ HMI dimensions may be considered as main factors in HMI design because they designate the basic classes of variables relevant to HMI design and must, therefore, be considered and used in the development of intercultural user interfaces.

▸ The view of space, time and mental perspectives is strongly dependent on culture (cf. Hall 1959). HMI is also culturally dependent because HMI dialogues, interaction and information representation are strongly linked to time (interaction, communication) and space (layout, structure) as well as mental aspects (relationships, thoughts) (cf. Preim und Dachselt 2010; Honold 2000; Röse 2002). At least one potential indicator must exist as a measurement variable in order to realize the expression of an HMI dimension. Table 7.2 presents some examples of indicators for some HMI dimensions.

For example, the indicator "number of information units per room unit" belongs to the HMI dimension "information density" and can be expressed by the number of words displayed on the screen. The HMI Dimension "Interaction frequency" contains the variable "Number of interactions per time unit", which can be expressed by the number of mouse clicks per second.

Table 7.2 Excerpt from the model for intercultural HMI design—characteristics of the HMI divisions are represented by certain indicators. (*Source* Heimgärtner 2012)

HMI dimension	Manifestations	Indicator(s)
Interaction frequency	Number of interactions per time unit	Mouse clicks and mouse movements per second or per session
Information density	Number of information units per room unit	Number of words per message or on the screen
Information/ interaction parallelism/ arrangement	Appearance sequence of the information units	Number and sequence of dialogue steps (for example, the number of message windows that are displayed to display a single system error message)

7.4.3   Design Elements

Mandel (1997) lists a number of aspects that have to be considered with regard to cultural influences when designing graphic interfaces of internationally distributed systems:

- Upper case,
- Table labels,
- Date formats,
- Fonts,
- Time formats,
- Descriptive texts,
- Suitable keyboard shortcuts,
- Person and speech,
- Navigation over the first letter of commands,
- Currency formats,
- Design of icons,
- Numeric Formats,
- Use of colors,
- Use of symbols,
- Formats for paper sizes,
- Prompts,
- Formats for telephone numbers,
- Formats for separators,
- Suitable function key assignment,
- Keyboard combinations,
- Acronyms,
- Text length,
- Abbreviations,

- Information sorting,
- Humor,
- Bidirectional language,
- Dimensions,
- Formats,
- Selection of memory aids.

In addition to these partially obvious design aspects, which often result from language differences or country-specific units of measurement, usability effects can be observed in practice which are barely superficially discernible and therefore partially or completely elude the foresighted design of persons who are outside the target culture (cf. iceberg metaphor in Chap. 2 and hidden direct intercultural variables (NVIVs) in Chap. 5).

▸ Both obvious and at first sight invisible aspects of design must be taken into account.

The manifestations of interculturality are far less clear than might initially be assumed, which is why no generally applicable guidelines for the design of interculturally "correct" systems can be derived. Nevertheless, the effects of cultural contexts on controls (Table 7.3) are clear.

Areas of a software product that—in addition to a functional translation of the text—require localization are primarily elements of the formal language level as well as visible components of the layout design. These include character systems, writing and reading directions, punctuation rules, calendar types, sorting rules, national formats for dates and times, measures and weights, numbers, currency units, but also more complex information such as the spelling of titles and addresses. The area of layout design includes special elements such as the use of colors or the design of icons and symbols.

Fernandes (1995, p. 2) assigns the elements to the first group to "national localization", while he includes aspects of layout design in the area of "cultural localization" (cf. TLCC model in Chap. 4). When designing intercultural user interfaces, all components of a localization project must be considered with regard to their cultural aspects (cf. Sect. 7.4.3).

In the following, some differences to be considered in these areas are shown by means of examples.

7.4.3.1 Terminology

▸ Since the users of a certain target market should (and want to) be addressed in their native language, terminology in the target language is an important aspect of software localization.

Table 7.3 Impact of cultural differences on control elements (from Dr. International 2003)

Control	Impact of cultural contexts on the control element
Button	Right-aligned lettering, reading direction RTL (right to left)
Checkbox	The box is on the right instead of the left side of the text
Combination field (combo box)	Text right-justified, reading direction RTL, pop-up arrow on left side
Menu	Menus are displayed right-justified, as are the entries in the menus, reading direction RTL
Tab views	Right-justified display, reading direction RTL
Lists and data tables (list viewsand Data Grids)	Texts arranged right-justified, scrollbars on the left side, tables and lists are mirrored
Progress bar	Runs from right to left (RTL)

When localizing software, terminology often does not exist in the target language. Therefore, the terminology of the source language must be structured, and possible target language equivalents defined before the start of the project. This is the only way to ensure consistent use of terminology from the start of the project through to the final phase—a basic requirement in software localization.

Another reason for determining the terminology to be used in the early stages of projects is that software localization projects are often complex and have to be completed within very tight deadlines. At the same time, several actors are involved in the project (cf. Schmitz und Wahle 2000; Schmitz 2005, pp. 9–10).

▸ Context information and the available reference materials are very important for terminology work.

Translators should know the context of text elements, which can also appear as individual elements on the user interface, for example. They should also be familiar with the software context, i.e., the environment to which the software belongs, as this may require the use of special, predefined terminology—e.g., Windows terminology. The following materials, for example, can be used as context or reference (cf. Ottmann 2002, 2005, p. 149):

- Glossaries of operating systems,
- Help files, online help,
- Reference manuals with descriptions of individual elements,
- Operating system in the target language,
- Current version of the application in the target language,
- Earlier version of the application in the target language.

▸ Generally used terminology data categories (e.g., ISO12620 1999) are not suitable for terminology work in software localization because within the software a single term can refer to different terms depending on its immediate context (e.g., in a menu, a dialogue box or an error message).

Software documentation can be described as a "normal" technical text containing terms that can be treated as terminological entries. However, considering certain terminology used in user interfaces, such as "Save As", "Insert Table", "Set Index Entry", etc., and other types of system messages, it is not easy to define the terminology (according to the rules of terminology theory) of such "terms".

▸ There are differences between the terminology used in the software documentation (online help and web pages) and that used in the user interface.

> This problem can partly be solved by managing such user interface terminology (e.g. system messages) using translation memory tools (TM tools) rather than terminology management systems. However, TM tools do not provide the ability to accurately describe localization units based on data categories. Another possibility is to use special data categories for localization units. Table 7.4 shows the proposal of Reineke and Schmitz (2005) for the introduction of localisation-specific data categories. They are located at all levels of the terminological entry and enable a terminological description of elements in user interfaces (cf. Schmitz 2005; Zerfaß 2005, pp. 42–44).
>
> Esselink (2000, p. 28) recommends the following for terminology work in software localization:
>
> • Create a glossary or (even better) a terminology database with product, company or industry specific terms for each localization project.
> • Use simple and concise sentences. So, you should determine from the beginning which words you want to use for the description of commands.
> • Use terminology consistently across all software components (user interface) and documentation (online help, printed documentation, and product-related Web pages).

7.4.3.2   Icons and Symbols

Cultural differences in the meaning of icons and symbols present a challenge to the developers of graphical user interfaces (GUIs) for international target groups—especially if they want to do without the use of internationally understandable pictograms and plan the design of specific icons and symbols whose meaning is to be understood in several cultures. The difference between icons and symbols is the degree of abstraction. While icons are pictorial signs representing familiar objects or persons, symbols move on a more abstract level. Their specific meaning must first be learned in the course of the respective culture-specific socialization (cf. Marcus 1996, p. 257). If, for example, the call of the mail function is to be marked

Table 7.4 Data categories for software localization according to Reineke (to be specified for each term/localization unit). *Source* Schmitz (2005, p. 44)

Localization type	Type of localization unit (main resource type) (menu, dialogue box, system message, etc.)
Menu type	Type of menu item (menu bar, menu option, etc.)
Dialogue box type	Control type of the dialogue box element (checkbox, button, static element, etc.)
Message type	Type of system message (string type) (message, status bar, etc.)
Environmental component inventory	Specifies the validity within a particular environment (environment subset) (e.g., Windows)
Partial product stock	Specifies the validity for a particular program (product subset) (for example, Notepad)
Localization number	Unique number of the localization unit (resource ID) (actually the entry level, important for data exchange)
Origin of localization	Locale of the original software (localization source) (e.g., en-US)
Localization target	Locale of the localized software (localization target) (e.g., de-DE)

Germany (German)   Denmark   Italy   USA

Fig. 7.9 Different mailbox icons. (*Source* VDMA 2009, p. 37)

with an icon, it is more convenient to choose the representation of an envelope, since this object is associated worldwide with mail. The illustration of a letterbox is problematic, however. As the following examples in Fig. 7.9 show, the appearance of letterboxes differs considerably between countries so that the meaning of an icon representing a specific country-specific letterbox type is either not recognized or even confused with another object by users of the software from other cultures.

This example belongs to the visible or relatively easy to work out elements of a culture-specific system of values and norms. However, Hoft (1995) points to the need to adapt to elements which are less or even completely invisible to outsiders, but which at the same time are self-evident to members of a certain culture, of which they are often hardly aware.

The fact that text has to be translated means that the graphics have to be edited, which can be a very time-consuming task. Very often the text to be translated is embedded in the program code, so that when updating the application all strings must be edited again and there is a risk that translators accidentally change or delete encodings. It is also more difficult for translators to identify the text to be translated

Fig. 7.10 Examples of failed internationalization. *Source* Zerfaß 2005, p. 44 and Heimgärtner et al. (2011)

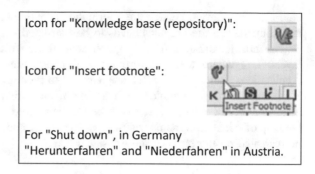

if this is mixed with the programming code. To verify that code and text are separate, developers and copywriters can use evaluation tools (e.g., developer tools, internationalization tools, localization tools) (see Sect. 7.4.4).

When using variables in messages, developers and copywriters should be aware that the grammar of the target language may require parameter reordering. The use of symbols from general areas of life for the representation of abstract ideas with concrete examples and as substitutes for linguistic elements to be localized is common practice in the area of software development and internationalization.

▸ Particularly problematic in software localization is the use of allusions and puns (referring to other terms using homonyms) and the inclusion of symbols in the user interface, since editing and customizing these symbols can be a complicated and time-consuming process.

The illustrations in Fig. 7.10 show examples of successful and unsuccessful internationalization (cf. Zerfaß 2005, p. 44; Heimgärtner et al. 2011).

7.4.3.3 Diagrams, (Animated) Graphics, Photos

Like symbols, diagrams, graphics and photos can refer to culture-specific situations (e.g., religion, appearance, clothing) and must be adapted or replaced in the software or its components during localization. A typical mistake in internationalization is the use of linguistic elements in diagrams, graphics or photos. This should be avoided to avoid time-consuming creation of new graphic files.

Similarly, diagrams, graphics, and photos can refer to specific products that look different in different target markets, for example, a car may have the steering wheel on the left or right side depending on the country. In addition, the customs for the presentation of diagrams, graphics and photos may also vary depending on the target market, e.g., in the order of presentation and layout (cf. Schmitz 2005, pp. 11–12).

When localizing graphics, it is important to know whether the graphic is culturally acceptable and understandable or whether it needs to be adapted, whether colors and background match the information contained in the text, and whether the text contained in the graphics needs to be translated.

The most localization-friendly graphics are those which are composed of several layers, i.e., where text, background, and image are stored in different layers. Applications such as Paint.NET are required to process these types of files. When localizing animated graphics such as Flash, the individual graphics have to be adapted and any existing text has to be translated into its own text files (also with the help of translation memory systems). Normally, audio and video files must also be recreated on the basis of the translated text.

7.4.3.4 Sign Systems

In order to make a software product accessible to the international market right from the start, English is often the language of development in Germany. However, this procedure entails two disadvantages which have a negative influence on the quality of the product. For one thing, software developers are not authors and cannot be expected to use terminology consistently or to have knowledge of standard formulations and writing styles. On the other hand, nonnative-speaking software developers often only have technical English skills, which sometimes lead to rather amusing results for the customers of a product.

The quality of a translation depends heavily on the quality of the source language texts. It is not uncommon, however, for translators only to discover how poor the quality of the source language is at the beginning of the localization process. Frequently, the companies then make do with a preliminary translation from "developer English" into "correct English", which then also forms the basis for the translation of other languages.

▶ If you want to ensure the quality and consistency of the source language right from the start, you should have it developed in your native language and can also provide the development team with a technical author (e.g., from the documentation department). This can guarantee a high-quality translation of the textual elements of the user interface already during the development.

There is a general distinction between phonetic and ideographic sign systems. While in phonetic sign systems, such as the Latin, Cyrillic, Greek, Hebrew or Arabic alphabet, a sign or a group of signs stands for a sound, the ideographic sign systems contain symbols (ideograms) that represent individual morphemes (e.g., Hanzi in China, Kanji in Japan, and Hanja in Korea).

▶ For the development of intercultural user interfaces from a German/Western European perspective, at least six writing systems can be formed worldwide (Fig. 7.11). As the font system number increases, internationalization and localization efforts increase (Table 7.5).

SG I: Westeuropäisches Schriftsystem
SG II: Osteuropäisches Schriftsystem
SG III: Kyrillische/ Griechische/ Südostasiatisches Schriftsystem
SG IV: Asiatisches Schriftsystem
SG V: Arabisches Schriftsystem
SG VI: Indisches Schriftsystem

Fig. 7.11 Distribution of writing systems. *Source* DCC GmbH in VDMA (2009, p. 18)

The writing system I (Western Europe) is characterized by 256 characters, the character set comprises 128 ASCII characters plus 128 for the Western European extension. The character input takes place directly via keyboard. A uniform code page is used for character encoding. If fonts from Central/Eastern Europe or Turkey are to be displayed (font system II), a different code page is required. For the implementation, this means switching the code page. The characters are still legible for Western Europeans. A code page switch is also required for the Cyrillic/Greek/ Southeast Asian writing system III. Furthermore, these letters are no longer legible for most Western Europeans. For the writing system IV (Asian fonts) more than 256 characters are necessary. This requires a multibyte encoding for character management and an input editor for character input. Also, the sign matrix of Asian signs is larger than that of European signs. In the writing system V, (Arabic languages), the writing direction is from right to left. In addition, the characters are spelled differently depending on the context of the surrounding characters. For Indian languages (writing system VI) a concept-dependent spelling of the characters with rearranging of the sequence is necessary (which also requires a layout engine).

Further information on character encoding (e.g., Unicode) can be found in the checklists in Appendix B of this book.

This results in the following order of effort for the internationalization of the writing system of intercultural user interfaces (from the highest to the lowest effort):

1. Hebrew languages,
2. Arabic languages,
3. Indian languages,
4. Eastern European languages,
5. Western European languages.

Table 7.5 Effort for localization of different language areas (*Source* DCC GmbH in VDMA 2009, p. 18) Writing

Writing systems

	I Western Europe	II Eastern Europe	III Cyrillic languages/Greek	IV Asian languages	V Arabic languages/Hebrew	VI Indian languages
Languages	German, French, English, Spanish, Portuguese, Dutch, Italian, …	Polish, Hungarian, Czech, Slovenian, Slovak, Estonian, Latvian, Lithuanian, Turkish, …	Cyrillic scripts (Russian, Bulgarian, Serbian, Northen Macadonian, Tajik, Mongolian) and Greek	Chinese, Japanese and Korean	Arabic and Persian languages, Hebrew	North and South Indian languages such as Hindi and Bengali
Effort (points)	1	2	3	4	3	3
Technical adaptations	Date/number formats	Date/number formats Character set Character encoding	Date/number formats Character set Character encoding	Date/number formats Character management for more than 256 characters Character matrix larger than in Europe Character encoding: Input Method Editor (IME)	Date/number formats Change the writing direction and layout to right-to-left character output by layout engines	Date/number formats Character output through layout engines (ligatures)
Effort (points)	1	3	3	5	4	3
Surface layout	Adaptation of the surface due to different running length of the texts	Adaptation of the surface due to different running length of the texts	Adaptation of the surface due to different running lengths of the texts	Adaptation of the surface due to different running lengths of the texts; cultural differences in colors and icons	Surface adjustment due to writing direction of right-to-left icons with moving direction have to be adjusted	cultural differences in colors and icons

(continued)

Table 7.5 (continued)

Writing systems

	I Western Europe	II Eastern Europe	III Cyrillic languages/ Greek	IV Asian languages	V Arabic languages/ Hebrew	VI Indian languages
Effort (points)	1	1	1	2	5	2
Character set size	Latin I (ISO 8859-1)	Latin-2, Latin-5 (ISO 8859-2, ISO 8859-9) Code page switching and character set required Characters based on Latin characters supplemented by diacritical characters	ISO8859-5 (Cyrillic), ISO 8859-7 (Greek) Code page and character set switching required Greek and Cyrillic characters not legible for Western Europeans	GB12345, Shift-JIS, BIG5, KSC One language- and culture-adapted character set per country Character encoding; Unicode character set range from 8,000 to 80,000 to be used Characters not legible for Europeans	ISO 8859-6 Character set must match layout engine Character not readable by Europeans	Character set must match the layout engine Character not readable by Europeans
Effort (points)	0	0	0	3	3	1
Total effort (points)	3	6	7	14	15	9

7.4.3.5 Formats

▸ Formats for displaying information such as date, time, numbers, currency or units
  of measurement are subject to country-specific conventions.

Paper formats must also be adapted. Measurement units (such as distances, weights,
and filling quantities) can also play a role in application programs. Their adaptation
or conversion into an equivalent measure for the target language depends on the
function of the respective information (cf. Schmitz 2005, p. 16, Fig. 7.12). In some
localization projects, the customization of sample files and templates that accom-
pany the application program makes up a large part of the project scope. For
example, in a project to localize a word processing program for the translator, the
localization of templates for standard letters may also be required. When it comes to
software for creating business cards, the templates for business cards, typical
example names, places, addresses, etc. must be localized (cf. Schmitz 2005, p. 17).
      With regard to the number format, for example, differences can be observed in
the coding of the decimal separator and the symbol for number grouping
(Table 7.6). Date formats differ in terms of the coding of the date separator and the
order in which they are displayed (Table 7.7).

EN: Allow at least 6 inches of clearance on all sides and 12 inches above the printer.
       (6 inches = 15.24 cm)

DE: A minimum distance of 15 cm must be maintained on all sides of the printer and
       30 cm above it.

Fig. 7.12 Example for length adjustment

Table 7.6 Different number formats in selected countries (from Fernandes 1995, p. 54)

Number format	Country
1 234, 56	France, Luxembourg, Portugal, Sweden
1.234,56	Argentina, Belgium, Denmark, Greece, Netherlands, Germany, Ireland, Italy, Spain, Germany
1.234 56	Russia
1'234.56	Switzerland
1,234.56	USA, Canada, Great Britain, China

Table 7.7 Different date formats in selected countries (from Fernandes 1995, p. 61)

Date format	Country
31.1.95	Austria, Germany, Belgium, Canada, Ireland, Italy, Norway, Portugal, United Kingdom
31.01.95	France, Germany, Norway, Portugal
31.1.'95	Iceland
95/1/31	Arab countries
95-1-31	Sweden
1/31/95	USA

7.4.3.6 Colors

▸ Since colors also have different meanings in different cultures, they should also be adapted to the target culture, otherwise they will be misinterpreted.

Table 7.8 shows the differences between individual countries with regard to the meaning of colors, although this compilation does not claim to be exhaustive. For example, the importance of green as the color of Islam should also be emphasized.

Certain colors have several culturally specific meanings, which in certain contexts even make them undesirable, as they can evoke negative associations. The different aesthetic sensitivities from country to country make country-specific adjustments necessary. It is also common practice, for example, to use the national colors when creating web pages—for example, the colors of the national flag of a particular country.

7.4.3.7 Character Sets and Fonts

▸ The appropriate representation and processing of the target languages using appropriate character sets or character coding and matching fonts is a basic prerequisite for the localization of the linguistic elements of a product.

Character coding can be defined as the representation of a character set using another character set, e.g., the representation of natural speech characters (such as an alphabet) by a set of other values such as digits or electrical impulses. Since machines cannot work directly with characters from different human writing systems, each character is assigned a binary value. This is made possible by the character encoding. Therefore, every character available in human writing must be encrypted in order to be recognized by a machine.

The characters are therefore encoded differently within different operating systems, e.g., Microsoft Windows and Apple iOS. A connection between a character

Table 7.8 Culture-specific meanings of colors (from Hoft 1995, p. 26; Russo and Boor 1993, cited by Tuthill and Smallberg 1997, p. 30 ff., see also Schmitz 2005, p. 13 and VDMA 2009)

Color	Country	Significance
Red	Egypt	Death
	China	Prosperity, wealth, happiness, cheerfulness
	France	masculinity, aristocracy
	Great Britain	The first place, masculinity
	India	Life, creativity
	Japan	Anger, danger
	USA	Power, STOP, danger
Green	Egypt	Fertility, strength
	China	Ming dynasty, religion
	France	Crime, cosmetics
	Republic of Ireland	Patriotism
	USA	Progress, capitalism, envy, security
	Many Western countries	Hope, environmentally friendly
White	Egypt	Joy
	China	Death, purity
	Christian countries	Purity, faith, innocence
	France (France)	Neutrality
	Japan and many Asian countries	Death and grief
		Purity
	Muslims and Hindus	Purity and peace
Blue	Egypt	Truth, virtue, faith
	China	Heaven, immortality
	France	Freedom, peace
	Ghana	Joy
	India	Divine enlightenment
	Japan	Abomination
	USA	First place, masculinity, stability
	Many European countries	Rest, sleep
Yellow	Egypt	Happiness, possessions
	China	Joy, prosperity, authority, birth, strength, health
	Europe, Canada, Australia, New	Happiness and other positive connotations
	France	Transience
	India	Achievement
	Japan	Nobleness, mercy
	USA	Caution, warning of physical danger, cowardice

and its encryption is established by assigning a numerical value, a so-called code point, to each character. The number of available code points depends on the number of available bits. An 8-bit encoded character set can encrypt 256 characters.

A second problem area is fonts that are used to display and print characters. Although an application may be able to interpret a particular character encoding, it may not be able to display a particular character because it cannot find a suitable font. Even a text that is predominantly or wholly in a language such as English, in which the Latin alphabet is used without diacritical characters, is not necessarily free of problems with character coding. An English text from the field of mathematics may contain Greek letters. In addition, the British pound sign (£), for example, is not available in all co-operating systems.

UNICODE is a uniform and unique basis for the handling of (almost) all languages of the world. Therefore, the use of UNICODE standards is common in the development of software products. Before UNICODE and after the introduction of operating systems and their localized versions for the Asian markets, various so-called code pages (character coding tables) were created in order to make different character sets available for the Asian languages. This solution was not entirely successful and became particularly problematic when Western and Asian character sets were used together in one text (cf. Schmitz 2005, p. 11). The following graphic illustrates the problem of using several character sets within the same document if not all character sets are supported. If the western code page (for Latin-based languages) is used, German characters are displayed correctly in the dialogue box. However, Japanese and Greek character sets are not supported by the western code page. Therefore, they cannot be interpreted correctly and displayed as question marks, as can be seen in Fig. 7.13 (cf. Sachse 2005, p. 151). Figure 7.14 shows that UNICODE contains the missing information for decoding the Japanese and Greek character set.

▸ When selecting fonts, it is important that the fonts and character sets used to match. If a font does not support a certain character set, the information cannot be displayed correctly (Fig. 7.15).

The Japanese and Greek character set is not supported by the font used. Therefore, another symbol is displayed to represent the missing characters (the vertical bar). Only if character set and font match, i.e., the UNICODE application uses a font that can display the required character sets, then the information is displayed correctly.

7.4.3.8   Language and Style

▸ Each culture has different customs and therefore culture-specific linguistic conventions with regard to syntax and style, which must be taken into account and adapted during software localization.

Fig. 7.13 Characters in unsupported character sets are displayed as question marks in Windows, depending on the code page

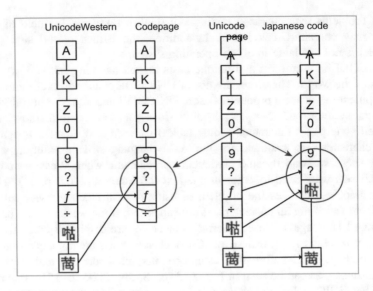

Fig. 7.14 UNICODE representation

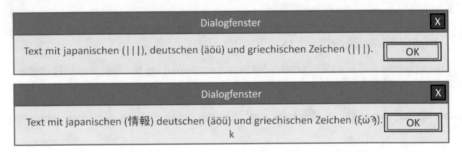

Fig. 7.15 Top: Missing fonts are displayed as bars in Windows depending on the code page; Bottom: Correctly displayed information

Table 7.9 shows some examples of general principles for translations in the English/German language pair.

Headings, composites and highlighting as linguistic elements must also be adapted to cultural conventions or customer wishes. In IT texts, highlighting takes place in elements of the user interface or in continuous text. Software manufacturers often have their own style guidelines ("style guides", cf. Schmitz 2005, p. 15–16).

7.4.3.9 Layout

Especially with user interfaces, developers must be aware that the length of a translated text usually differs from the original (Fig. 7.16). It is common to use

Table 7.9 Principles for syntax and style for translations in English/German language pairs (from Schmitz 2005, pp. 14–15)

English	German
The reader is addressed personally	Reader is not addressed personally, passive constructions
Use of simple verbs	Use of application-specific verbs
Repetition of text parts	Avoidance of repetitions
Random use of terms	Avoidance of synonyms

abbreviations for space reasons, but this becomes a problem if developers do not use them uniformly. Therefore, it should be possible to customize elements (e.g., buttons and dialogue boxes should accept longer texts and in (especially embedded) systems additional memory should be reserved for longer error messages.

▸ Due to the different number of characters in the translation of words into different languages, it is necessary to adjust the size of widgets to display corresponding text lengths (so-called "resizing", see Fig. 7.16).
▸ In addition, the widget positions must also be adjusted according to the preferences of the cultural user group (Fig. 7.17).

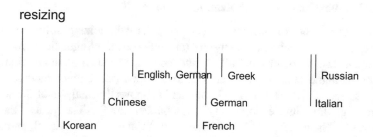

Fig. 7.16 Automatic adjustment of widget size for complete display of texts in different languages

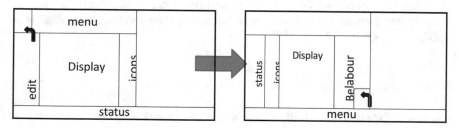

Fig. 7.17 Adaptation of widget positions according to the preferences of the cultural user group (left: Germany, right: China; from Röse 2002)

7.4.4   Tool Support

▸ Tools for internationalization support the development of hard-coded texts from the source code of the software.

Furthermore, API functions such as date display in your source code, which should then be checked by the developers.

▸ Localization tools usually offer functions for pseudo translation (see also VDMA 2007). This allows the test of internationalization to be carried out. For example, hard-coded texts, texts that are not to be translated and internal text buffers that are too short are discovered.

Pseudo-translation can lengthen texts, insert characters specific to the target language and enlarge dialogues, and supports developers in creating executable software that can be tested on the target system. This makes it possible to check whether the software translated in this way works at all and whether the corresponding lines of the target language are displayed correctly.

▸ Tools offer partly automatic support for the management of the project, the translation and adaptation of the terminology as well as the software to the cultural context and for the evaluation of the results.

There are more tools for localizing than for internationalizing software. This is obviously due to the fact that mostly the translation of the linguistic elements of a software and less so other culturally influenced aspects such as navigation, interaction or dialogue behavior are taken into account (for known methodological reasons), s. Sect. 5.4.1). The tool "Globalizer" supports the analysis of the software structure regarding its "exportability" (Globalizer 2009). The tools "Passolo", "Multilizer", "Sisulizer", "RC-Win-Trans" or "Catalyst", "Reviser" and others support the adaptation of the software to the target country.

In addition, translation tools greatly simplify translation work (see VDMA "Translation Guide", VDMA 2007). In addition to machine translation tools, there are translation memories, for example. These translation memories contain already translated fragments which can be reused in other subsequent translations. Furthermore, formats for the exchange of translations and localization settings were defined (e.g., OLIF, TBX or TMX).

7.4.4.1   User Interface Toolkits

▸ User interface toolkits, which usually have a basic window system and a window manager as integral components, support the deepest level of dialogue design, the lexical design (cf. action level model in Sect. 4.1.2). Rapid prototyping tools also cover the mental level of the action level model.

They map primitive hardware properties to meaningful elements of the dialogue language (such as command, location or name). This is done using dialogue objects such as forms, text fields or control knobs.

User Interface Toolkits thus represent a first step towards supporting the development of high-quality user interfaces. They can be understood as libraries of interaction techniques that provide the application programmer with functions for creating and manipulating dialogue elements.

The various toolkits usually offer a set of very similar dialogue objects. A distinction can be made between objects for implementing basic dialogue functions, such as:

- Single and multiple selections (menus, radio buttons, radio buttons, palettes, toolboxes),
- Trigger actions (pushbutton, menus),
- Text display and entry (text label, single and multi-line editable text fields, tables),
- Setting of analog values (scrollbars, sliders).

In addition, the toolkits offer a number of elements which serve in various ways to organize and arrange basic dialogue objects, such as forms, lists, grouping objects, and bulletin boards.

Since not all application requirements can be solved by the basic dialogue mechanisms mentioned above, the toolkits usually still offer objects whose graphical characteristics and semantics the application can freely dispose of (windows, sub-windows, drawing areas, etc.) and/or they offer mechanisms for extending the existing basic set of dialogue options.

In any case, the toolkit ensures a correct, consistent basic behavior (e.g., opening a menu cascade and selecting a menu item), which means that the application only needs to add the problem-specific semantics of the objects.

7.4.4.2 Benefits and Limitations of Toolkits

The benefit of using User Interface Toolkits for the development of interactive graphical applications is quite considerable compared to a pure use of the basic window system. The use of toolkits brings advantages in terms of software ergonomics, in addition to the more technical development advantages, such as savings in development effort, lower susceptibility to errors, better modularization and thus increased maintainability:

- The toolkit ensures a correct, uniform and consistent basic behavior of the used dialogue objects.
- The dialogue elements and dialogue mechanisms offered by the Toolkit are usually verified and have proven themselves.

- The toolkits are used for a wide range of application developments. This automatically achieves a kind of standardization of the dialogue mechanisms supported by the toolkit.

The standardization effect can be further increased if the toolkit offers additional height dialogue objects that have already been extended by a higher semantics for solving recurring use cases (design pattern). Examples include forms for opening, saving application files with a convenient option for navigating in the file system, or for selecting and displaying help texts. The dialogue elements of this level are usually composed of the basic objects of the toolkit and can be created by the toolkit user with one call.

▸ The use of UI toolkits drastically reduces the development effort for intercultural user interfaces.

Further developments of these L10N/I18 N toolkits can, therefore, be seen as the first stage in the realization of tools for rapid prototyping of intercultural user interfaces.

If new findings arise about the course of certain dialogue mechanisms, these can ideally be integrated into the toolkit and are thus available to all applications implemented with the toolkit without costly intervention in the applications.

▸ However, the software ergonomic advantages of using toolkits only come into their own if the toolkit is flexible enough to offer solutions for a wide range of application requirements while remaining consistent and manageable in its range of dialogue objects and mechanisms.

UI tools are usually focused on the concrete design of user interfaces and less on the analysis and implementation of intercultural design requirements. In the following an initial approach of a tool on the way to rapid prototyping for the development of intercultural user interfaces with the so called "IIA-Tool" (see Heimgärtner 2007) is presented.

7.4.5 Excursion: Tool Support via IIA Tool

Literature surveys by Heimgärtner (2005) showed that there are no adequate tools for determining cross-cultural differences in cultural aspects of HMI, although there are some treatises on recording interactions (cf. Spannagel 2003). Some tools for user interaction measurement are (no claim to completeness of the enumeration):

- ObSys (recording and visualization of window messages) (see Gellner and Forbrig 2003),
- Interact (coding and visualization of user behavior (cf. Mangold 2005)),
- Reviser (automatic criterion-oriented usability evaluation of interactive systems, see Hamacher 2006),

- Tool set for log file analysis (see Köppen and Wandke 2002),
- UserZoom (recording, analysis and visualization of online studies).

There are other instrumental tools such as Noldus, SnagIt, Morae, A-Prompt or Leo- Trace. All these tools offer a certain functionality for (partly remote) usability tests and for measuring the interaction behavior of users with an interactive system.

▶ In 2006, no commercially available interaction analysis tool had current cultural usability metrics (cf. UMTM, Table 6.5 in Sect. 6.3.2) or possibilities for implementing special use cases to measure the interaction behavior of an HMI system in a cultural context.

In addition, the required knowledge about culture-dependent variables could not be subsequently implemented into the existing tools (and manufacturers had no way to implement cultural usability metrics such as UMTM when programming their tools, because these cultural usability metrics did not yet exist).

▶ Heimgärtner (2007) developed a new tool for measuring the intercultural inter-action behavior of the user.

In order to motivate the user to interact with the computer and to verify intercultural hypotheses (cf. Chap. 6), adequate task scenarios were developed and implemented in this new test tool. The resulting intercultural interaction analysis tool (IIA Tool) provides a data collection, data analysis, and data evaluation module for data collection, analysis, and evaluation with the following features:

- Recording, analysis, and visualization of user interaction behavior and user preferences,
- Intercultural usability testing using localized use cases for different cultures,
- Usability evaluation and report for all interactions,
- Qualitative assessments of quantitative data to improve the correctness and validity of tests.

▶ The Intercultural Interaction Analysis Tool (IIA Tool) allows the interaction of culturally different users to be observed who perform the same task under the same controlled environment and test conditions (same hardware and software, language and test tasks). This makes the tests and their results comprehensible at any time, mutually comparable and transferable to similar applications.

The collection and preparation of the data is mainly carried out automatically by the IIA data collection module. This saves a lot of time, costs and effort. The collected data can be quantitative (related to all test subjects, e.g., the significance of a Likert scale, cf. Lienert and Raatz 1998) as well as qualitative (related to a single test subject, e.g., answering open questions (cf. La Cruz et al. 2005)).

In addition, the collected data volumes can be saved in standard format (e.g., CSV), allowing additional statistical analyses to be carried out with any standard statistical tool (e.g., SPSS).

▸ Studies and their results using the IIA tool are reproducible.

Collected data is stored by the IIA Data Acquisition Module in databases in a format that is read immediately by the IIA Data Analysis Module and is read using a data conversion and preparation process into usable data for evaluation by the IIA data evaluation module. In addition to the evaluation of the data with regard to intercultural interaction indicators on the basis of a classification using neural networks, this also enables the comprehensive validation of results from other data analyses.

The IIA Tool can be installed online via the Internet or offline via CD. In order to avoid download and interaction delays, the IIA tool has been integrated as an executable program file on a server from which it can be downloaded to the local hard disk by worldwide users. The reason for this is that the tool must measure the interaction behavior of the user during the online test correctly and comparably in real time. This is only possible if the program is running on the target system in order to avoid delays in the program execution due to high network traffic.

▸ The IDE of the tool allows a very fast implementation of new HMI concepts into good looking prototypes, which can be tested very quickly within the iterative development process. For example, some hypotheses from the culture-dependent explanatory model (cf. Chap. 6 or Heimgärtner 2012) were implemented within one month as use cases in the IIA Tool and quantitatively verified by a representative number of users after data collection and analysis.

The use of the IIA Tool means a fast application case design including data collection and evaluation, i.e., the creation of rapid prototypes with user interfaces for different cultures as well as the collection of a large amount of valid data, which can be quickly and easily collected and evaluated worldwide online in real time.[7]

7.5 Evaluation and Testing

Evaluation and testing of intercultural user interfaces refer in particular to the areas of usability engineering (evaluation) and to the areas of software engineering (SW test). The evaluation checks whether the system meets the user requirement. This also includes usability tests. SW tests are used to check whether the software meets the requirements—especially those resulting from I18 N and L10 N (see Chap. 3).

---

[7]Further information on the IIA Tool can be found in Heimgärtner (2007) and can also be obtained directly from the author and at URL=https://www.iuic.de.

7.5.1 Software Technical Quality Assurance

Typically, localization or test engineers are responsible for completing the tasks that arise in the test phase, such as:

- Preparation of the project: checking the source material for completeness, bug fixing after compiling the software, checking the translations.
- Developing and testing localized software: This involves activities such as customizing the translated software user interface (buttons, dialogue boxes, etc.), checking and testing hotkeys (underlined letter or number in a menu command or dialogue box in combination with the Alt key), compiling the localized resource files into an executable application (in the case of software or online help), as well as testing the functionality of the software (ensuring that the translated version of the software works), and taking screenshots of the localized version (see Sect. 7.4.3—all aspects addressed there must also be evaluated).
- Testing internationalization: Check whether the software architecture, text and software source codes are separated and whether the character sets and local standards of the target languages or countries are supported.
- Help for localization projects: Software developers should help project managers, translators, and all localization stakeholders at all times during the localization process if technical problems arise.

7.5.2 Software Ergonomic Quality Assurance

The object of consideration of software ergonomics is the individual user with very different intellectual, social, psychomotor and professional backgrounds—embedded in his cultural context (cf. Chap. 4). Therefore, software ergonomic quality assurance must not be limited to individual objects, e.g., to the input and output area of a software's user interface but must also focus on the entire complex of dialogue guidance.

▸ As soon as initial concepts and ideas of the user interface can be made tangible, e.g., in the form of prototypes, they must be evaluated with users in an intercultural context.

The strengths and weaknesses of the concepts and ideas up to supposedly mature products are recognized by user research studies and can flow into further development. As with requirements collection and analysis, interviews and observations are considered, with a clear focus on observation.

In an observation, representative users use the product or prototype in realistic usage scenarios. A usability engineer recognizes whether the product meets the requirements of the users, whether it supports typical tasks and procedures and whether it can be operated effectively and efficiently.

A variety of methods and possibilities are also available for evaluation, ranging from simple usability tests in the usability test studio (Fig. 7.18) to on-site studies and international user experience studies aimed at understanding the entire product life cycle. These range from initial commissioning to disposal and from operating instructions to the training concept and service hotline.

Evaluation is needed whenever decisions have to be made about the design process. This will be the case both in the analysis and in the specification. Evaluating analysis decisions mainly refers to the phase in which the future tasks are presented. During the detail specification development process, many decisions have to be made that relate the technical details to usability aspects.

▸ Evaluation doesn't solve problems but shows them. A valid diagnosis often requires several complementary techniques and experience. Therefore, it always makes sense and is often necessary to involve usability professionals (see Chap. 4) in the evaluation process.

A distinction is made between formative evaluation during the iterative development cycle and summative evaluation at the end of the development cycle.

7.5.3   Culture-Dependent Evaluation Methods

▸ The cultural framework conditions that cause cultural differences in service must be determined by detailed analyses of the country and user profile for the respective target culture.

Without evaluation methods and "getting to know" the user and his culture, the user requirements cannot be developed. It is, therefore, necessary to develop a user profile that is as detailed as possible (see Chap. 5).

The necessary tests and resulting changes should always be carried out by the developer and tester in the culture of the user in order to meet the cultural requirements of the user (Honold 2000).

However, such culturally influenced data collection methods are less suitable for intercultural usability testing. Due to cultural differences, distortions can be expected in the following methods:

- Structured or expert interviews,
- Card sorting,
- Questionnaires,
- Thinking aloud.

▸ Due to the subjective character of personal survey methods, the results are strongly influenced by the cultural background of the persons involved. Because of this "intercultural subjectivity" a comparison between country-specific results becomes meaningless. Only through objective, intercultural evaluation methods can the results be compared.

First of all, there is "intercultural subjectivity". Comparative studies of two cultures can be used to determine a corresponding "compensation factor", which could be included in the method box for comparative cultural studies and thus guarantee "intercultural objectivity". The subjectivity of a comparison without considering the cultural mentality has a negative influence on the analysis (Zühlke 2004). For example, culture-dependent answer tendencies in a question box could be investigated. By using an empirically collected "conversion factor", the results of a question could be made interculturally comparable.

▸ But also the possibilities of applying the methods and their practical application differ from culture to culture (see Shi and Copenhagen Business School 2010, p. 208).

In a test setting in China, it may well happen that test persons within a defined test setting are spontaneously supported in their choice of answer by colleagues who have not been invited, thus influencing the results (cf. Zühlke 2004, p. 154).

During usability tests, Chinese respondents may rate calls from friends higher than the current test and interrupt it, accordingly, thereby falsifying test times (cf. Heimgärtner 2012).

7.5.4   Culture-Independent Evaluation Methods

The process of interpreting is culturally shaped. The less interpretation in tests, the less cultural distortion of the results is present. If not interpreted, there is no cultural distortion of the results. If differences are nevertheless found within the results, there are cultural differences in the use. Therefore, quantitative measurement methods are more reliable than qualitative ones because they are less subject to cultural interference. However, due to the lack of levels of interpretation, only efficiency and effectiveness can be measured with purely quantitative measuring methods, but user satisfaction or "joy of use" cannot be measured. The strength of quantitative methods lies rather descriptively in the description of facts, and not explanatively in the explanation and model generation as with qualitative methods.

▸ Numbers do not have to be assigned additional meaning by interpretation since they represent mathematically *worldwide* (i.e., culture-independent) identically defined order values.

In comparison to qualitative culture-dependent methods, which require considerable personal (subjective and thus culturally strongly influenced) additional interpretation services, there are quantitative methods which are almost independent of

Fig. 7.18 Minimalistic usability test station

the respective culture. Due to their objectivity, they are largely insensitive to cultural influences and can, therefore, be used across cultures.

▶ For culture-independent data collection and evaluation, theory and task-oriented tests with an objective character must be used[8]:

- Log file analyses,
- Evaluation of stress tests on hardware (humidity, temperature, contamination, etc.),
- Evaluation of repair and maintenance statistics,
- User observations (video recording),
- Concealed screen recording,
- Concealed eye tracking,
- Event recording (mouse, keyboard, touchscreen, function calls, etc.),
- Video analysis,
- Biometric data of the user (heart rate (HR), heart rate variability (HRV), galvanic skin response (GSR) etc.).

Most of these methods are tool-based and, for example, integrated in the "Tool for Intercultural Interaction Analysis" ("IIA Tool", cf. Sect. 7.4.5) (cf. Heimgärtner 2008). By the setting of tasks in tests, the user is brought into cognitive situations

---

[8]This means as independent as possible of a subjective (and thus culturally influenced, i.e., culturally dependent) interpretation by a person. In this way, the usability engineer is able to make statements about culture-dependent findings on the basis of the evaluation of culture-independent methods.

which demand or distract him in such a way that he does not think of the underlying experimental hypotheses. Therefore, cases are conceivable in which the test setting cannot be identified as such. With log file analyses or hidden tests, the data is collected from the natural (working) environment.

▸ The use of quantitative methods, which are less susceptible to failure or culturally sensitive due to a lack of interpretation performance in data collection, is particularly beneficial to remote studies, which contribute significantly to cost savings in intercultural usability engineering (no travel costs, no test setting, laboratory conditions do not have to be created, no test leader, no training necessary, high time savings, etc.).

With log file recording it is possible to objectively determine interaction differences between users with different cultural backgrounds by analyzing interaction data such as mouse events, system errors, user preferences regarding system usage (number of applications) or problem-related parameter settings in applications.

▸ A purely quantitative survey method is log file recording.

In the environment of tool systems (e.g., in plant operation), data from real production environments are more reliable than under laboratory conditions due to the pressure of employees to succeed. Chinese and German machine users, for example, are confronted with the same problem and asked to solve it. Here, the procedure for system operation is analyzed for the same problem. This is expressed as follows when troubleshooting a labeling machine: Glue escapes and contaminates the sensor. The question arises how the machine should continue to operate. Correct the fault or allow the machine to continue running under poorer performance or start an emergency program or change the parameters (e.g., deactivate the sensor)? By means of a simple quantitative recording, i.e., the counting and recording of problem-solving strategies planned and not planned by the developer, a methodically culture-independent evaluation of culturally different approaches can be carried out. Therefore, the evaluation of real log file data, e.g., from a labeling machine is more reliable than the evaluation of log files, which were determined by simulation tests.

▸ Log files from the field cannot contain data falsified by an artificial test environment (as is the case in the laboratory), since the real tasks have no test character.

In this way, quantitative comparisons are also possible with regard to compliance with country-specific (quantitative) standards (e.g., tolerance measures or productivity values, etc.).

7.6   Summary, Conclusion, Outlook

In the development of digital products and services, development processes often follow the V-model—a sequential iterative development model—or use agile software development methods such as Scrum or combinations of such approaches. Advanced software development processes have corresponding gates (e.g., with regard to quality: quality gates/hurdles). The quality of these processes is often checked using maturity models (e.g., CHMI, SPICE).

The aim must be to enliven the usability engineering process just as systematically as the software engineering process by applying human-centered design principles (cf. ISO 9241-210). In addition, the early recognition and consideration of cultural differences in product development play a decisive role in the development of intercultural user interfaces. The usability of a system depends strongly on how the user gets along with the system (cf. DIN 2006). The degree of usability of an interactive system can be determined, for example, by observing and questioning a user during interaction with the system (cf. Nielsen and Molich 1990; Nielsen 1990). The individual cultural context of use must be specified for relevant usage situations in order to develop a deeper understanding of the individual culture-specific needs of the user. In addition to qualitative techniques of market research, quantitative methods should therefore also be used. Trends in cultural differences can be used for the development and design of intercultural user interfaces and further reflection and research. In addition to reading literature, empirical research on intercultural user interface characteristics is needed to find out how well the systems can be used (e.g., by comparing several systems of different cultures and performing usability tests). In the development of intercultural user interfaces, all those aspects in the cultural context which are the properties of the user interface. But also, the methods for obtaining intercultural user interfaces and their evaluation require cultural inspection.

The requirements analysis during the development of user interfaces essentially consists of understanding and describing the context of use and deriving and specifying user requirements. In the requirements analysis, the business processes must be included in accordance with the HMI action level model (cf. Chap. 4) in order to achieve the analysis of the requirements of the interactive system in the context of the entire work organization (Fig. 7.2). All these aspects should be considered when developing intercultural user interfaces for the respective cultural target contexts. The determination of all different requirements of all stakeholder groups requires that all requirements of the preceding process steps are identified, collected depending on their origin and consolidated (clarified and adjusted) accordingly. The consolidated requirements define the production objectives of the project. These objectives, which are not linked to their solutions, must be specific (specific, measurable, attainable, realistic and timely) according to the SMART principle.

Intercultural Usage-Centered Design (IU-CD) serves as a systematic and model-based method for determining user requirements for the design of intercultural user interfaces (cf. Windl und Heimgärtner 2013). The Usage-Centered Design process (U-CD) is divided into the analysis and design phases (Fig. 7.3). The role and task model are the result of the user and task analysis. The content model together with the implementation model represent the results of the design phase. In order to integrate the cultural aspects and the internationalization requirements into U-CD, it is necessary to expand it and make adjustments to the existing procedure in various places. The common aspects for intercultural UI design are included in a cultural model similar to the existing "operation model" (Fig. 7.4). A separate cultural model is used for each culture (Fig. 7.5). The content of the cultural model is primarily related to the characteristics of the user interface (cf. Marcus 2007) and the HMI dimensions (cf. Heimgärtner 2012) and describes a user interface on an abstract level, which is filled with the special values for the desired culture. In order to also cover cultural aspects that do not fit into this country scheme (such as religious denominations, locations, or any other cultural target groups), it is possible to use project-specific cultural identifiers. The approach of intercultural usage-centered design (IU-CD) helps developers of intercultural user interfaces to systematically collect and model system and user requirements and to create suitable interactive systems on the basis of exact models.

HMI dimensions are major factors in HMI design because they denote the basic classes of variables relevant to HMI design. They are to be considered and used in the development of intercultural user interfaces. Both obvious and at first glance invisible design aspects must be taken into account. Since the users of a certain target market are (and want to be) addressed in their native language, terminology in the target language is an important aspect of software localization. Context information and the available reference materials are very important for terminology work. Generally used terminology data categories (e.g., ISO12620 1999) are not sufficient for terminology work in software localization because within the software a single term can refer to different terms depending on its immediate context (e.g., in a menu, in a dialogue box or in an error message). There are differences between the terminology used in the software documentation (online help and web pages) and that used in the user interface. Particularly problematic in software localization is the use of allusions and wordplay (reference to other terms via homonyms) and the inclusion of symbols in the user interface, since editing and adapting these symbols can be a complex and time-consuming process. For the development of intercultural user interfaces from a German/Western European perspective, at least six writing systems can be distinguished worldwide (Fig. 7.11). As the font number increases, internationalization and localization efforts increase (Table 7.5). Notations for the representation of formats such as date, time, numbers, currency units or units of measurement are subject to country-specific Conventions. The appropriate representation and processing of the target languages using appropriate character sets, character coding and fonts is a basic prerequisite for the localization of linguistic elements of a product. When selecting fonts, it is important that the fonts and character sets used to match each other. If a font does not support a certain character set, the information cannot be displayed correctly (Fig. 7.15). Each culture has its own set of cultural conventions in terms of syntax and style, which must be taken into account and adapted during software localization. Depending on the different number of characters in the translation of words into different languages, it is necessary to adjust the size of widgets to display the corresponding text lengths (so-called "widgets", cf. also "Resizing", see Fig. 7.16). In addition, the widget positions must also be adapted according to the preferences of the cultural user group (Fig. 7.17). Since colors also have different meanings in different cultures, they should also be adapted to the target culture, otherwise, they will be misinterpreted (Fig. 7.9).

Localization tools usually offer functions for pseudo translation (see also VDMA 2007). This will allow the test of internationalization to be carried out. For example, hard-coded texts, texts that are not to be translated and internal text buffers that are too short are discovered. Tools offer partly automatic support for the management of the project, the translation, and adaptation of terminology and software to the cultural context as well as for the evaluation of the results. User Interface Toolkits, which usually have a basic window system and a window manager as integral components, support the deepest level of dialogue design, the lexical design, as a tool. By using UI toolkits, the development effort is drastically reduced. However, the software ergonomic advantages of using toolkits only come to bear if, on the one hand, the toolkit is flexible enough to offer solutions for the most diverse application requirements and, on the other hand, its range of dialogue objects and mechanisms remains consistent and manageable. In 2006, no commercially available interaction analysis tool had current cultural usability metrics (cf. UMTM, Table 6.5 in Sect. 6.3.2) or possibilities for implementing special use cases to measure interaction behavior in a cultural context. Therefore, the author developed a tool in 2006 to measure the intercultural interaction behavior of the user (cf. Heimgärtner 2007). With this tool, the interaction of culturally different users can be observed who perform the same task under the same controlled environment and test conditions (same hardware and software, same language and test tasks). This makes the tests and their results comprehensible, mutually comparable and transferable to similar applications. Studies using the IIA tool are fully reproducible. The IDE of the tool allows a very fast conversion of new HMI concepts into good looking prototypes, which can be tested very quickly within the iterative development process.

Software testing includes technical aspects of software localization that must be addressed at the beginning and end of a localization project. As soon as initial concepts and ideas of the user interface can be experienced, e.g., in the form of prototypes, these must be evaluated with users. Evaluation does not solve problems, but it does reveal them. A valid diagnosis in the evaluation phase often requires several complementary techniques and experience. Therefore, it makes sense and is often necessary to involve usability professionals (see Chap. 4) in the evaluation process. User testing and user-centric development (U-CD) are an important means to measure and ensure user satisfaction with a technical system. In intercultural usability testing/engineering, indirect user participation is to be preferred (Zühlke 2004). The possibilities of applying methods and their practical application also differ from culture to culture (see Shi and Copenhagen Business School 2010,

p. 208). The cultural framework conditions, which cause cultural differences of use, must be determined by detailed analyses of the country and user profile for the respective target culture. Due to the subjective character of person-related survey methods, the results are strongly influenced by the cultural background of the persons involved. On the basis of this "intercultural subjectivity", therefore, a comparison between country-specific results become meaningless. Only through objective, intercultural evaluation methods can the results be compared. Distortions of the developer's impression of the user's image (Honold 2000) by cultural influence factors must, therefore, be circumvented by culturally objective, task-oriented survey methods. The more independent their use of cultural influences and the more sensitive their sensitivity to cultural aspects is, the higher the reliability of methods that are supposed to measure cultural differences. This describes a paradox that arises from different levels of explanation and can be resolved by them: methodical insensitivity to cultural influences while at the same time metrical sensitivity to quantitatively ascertainable differences in the culturally influenced interaction of the user with the system. This is the only way to make cultural comparisons of user behavior possible. Then, the causes of previously identified errors can be determined through comparative studies, found violations of guidelines and statistically proven cultural differences. As a result, the problems of culturally determined "culturally subjective" test results and resource-intensive on-site testing can be avoided. Culture-dependent methods can thus save costs and deliver reliable results with regard to cultural differences and thus cultural knowledge on a physical-objective measurement basis in the form of numbers. Numbers do not have to be assigned additional meaning by interpretation, since they represent mathematically *worldwide* (i.e., culturally independent) identically defined order values. In addition, for culture-independent data collection and evaluation, theory and task-oriented tests with an objective character must be generated. The use of quantitative methods, which are less susceptible to failure or less culturally sensitive due to a lack of interpretation performance in data collection, is particularly beneficial for remote studies, which contribute significantly to cost savings in intercultural usability engineering (no travel costs, no test setting, no laboratory conditions need not be created, no trainer, no training necessary, high time savings, etc.). Log file recording is a purely quantitative survey method. Log files from the field cannot contain falsified data from an artificial test environment (as is the case in the laboratory), as the tasks do not have a "laboratory character". However, these numbers and the process from which they originate must eventually be interpreted semantically. Unfortunately, all interpretation (which is not influenced by universal conventions such as norms) is culturally influenced and there is still considerable need for research into culturally dependent—i.e., culturally influenced—methods (such as interpretation methods based on culturally dependent thought patterns and cognitive styles). The test methodology of intercultural usability engineering, therefore, remains an exciting field of research.

Norms   √

ISO 15504   ☐
ISO 9241-210   ☐
ISO 12620   ☐
ISO 8859   ☐
Unicode   ☐
GB12345   ☐
Shift JIS   ☐
BIG5   ☐
KSC   ☐
                                                                                             ☐

Checklist   √

Activities in the global product development process are well known   ☐

The meaning and contents of the process phases (requirements analysis, design and   ☐
    evaluation) are well known and are embodied

Usage Centered Design approach is known   ☐

Team knows the relationship between software engineering and usability engineering and   ☐
    embodies the interfaces between the processes

Tools for I18N and L10N are well known and are used   ☐

Intercultural interaction analysis is well known and is performed using a tool
    (e.g. IIA Tool); results are considered in information architecture and   ☐
    interaction design

Description of context of use and specification of user requirements are available   ☐

Model for culture-dependent HMI design is known and used   ☐

Recommendations for intercultural HMI design are considered   ☐

Intercultural software quality assurance measures   ☐
    (e.g. the L10N/I18N) are known and are performed

Intercultural software ergonomic quality assurance measures   ☐
    (e.g. intercultural usability tests) are known and are performed

Culture-dependent and culture-independent evaluation methods are known   ☐
    and used correctly

Problems with the evaluation of intercultural user interfaces are known and   ☐
recommendations are considered

References

Balzert H (2008) Textbook of Software Technology. [2], software management. Heidelberg: Specter, Akad. Verl

Beyer H, Holtzblatt K (2007) Contextual design: defining customer-centered systems ([Reprint] Aufl.). Morgan Kaufmann, San Francisco

Beynon M, Nehaniv CL, Dautenhahn K (2001) Cognitive technology: Instruments of mind. In: Proceedings of the international cognitive technology conference. Springer, Warwick

Brau H (2009) Unpublished internal project report. Daimler AG, Stuttgart

Constantine L (2004) Beyond user-centered design and user experience: designing for user performance. Cutter IT J 17(2):16–25

Constantine LL, Lockwood LAD (1999) Software for use: a practical guide to the models and methods of usage-centered design. Addison Wesley, Reading

Constantine LL, Lockwood LAD (2003) Usage-centered software engineering: An agile approach to integrating users, user interfaces, and usability into software engineering practice. Paper presented at the proceedings of the 25th international conference on software engineering, Portland

Constantine L, Windl H (2009) Safety, speed, and style: Interaction design of an in-vehicle user interface. Paper presented at the CHI '09 extended abstracts on human factors in Computing Systems, Boston

Cooper A (1999) The inmates are running the asylum. Macmillan, Indianapolis

Cooper A, Reimann R, Cronin D, Cooper A (2007) About face 3: the essentials of interaction design. Wiley, Indianapolis

DIN (2006) DIN EN ISO 9241-110 Ergonomics of humans-system interaction Part 110: dialogue principles. Beuth

Dr. International (2003) Developing International Software

Esselink B (2000) A practical guide to localization. J. Benjamins, 4. Aufl Amsterdam/Philadelphia

Fernandes T (1995) Global interface design: a guide to designing international user interfaces. AP Professional, Boston/Chestnut Hill

Ferr X, Juristo N, Windl H, Constantine L (2001) Usability basics for software developers. IEEE Softw 18(1):22–29. https://doi.org/10.1109/52.903160

Ferreira J (2012) Agile development and UX design: towards understanding work cultures to support integration. In: Bajec M, Eder J (eds) Advanced information systems engineering workshops, vol 112. Springer, Berlin/Heidelberg, pp 608–615

Gellner M, Forbrig P (2003) ObSys—a tool for visualizing usability evaluation patterns with mousemaps. In Human computer interaction: theory and practice. Ellis Horwood, New York

Globalizer. (2009). Infralution globalizer .NET. http://www.infralution.com/products/globalizer. html. Accessed 29 Feb 2019

Hackos JAT, Redish JC (1998) User and task analysis for interface design. Wiley, New York

Hall ET (1959) The silent language. Doubleday, New York

Halpin AW, Winer BJ (1957) A factorial study of the leader behavior descriptions. In: Stogdill RM, Coons AE (eds) Leader behavior: Its description and measurement. Bureau of Business Research, Ohio State University, Columbus, pp 39–51

Heimgärtner, R. (2005). Measuring cultural differences in human-computer interaction. In: Auinger A (ed) Workshop-Proceedings Mensch und Computer, pp 89–92. OCG, Vienna

Hamacher NA (2006) Automatic criteria-oriented assessment of the usability of interactive systems, 1st edn. Dr. Hut, Munich

Heimgärtner R (2007) A tool for cross-cultural human computer interaction analysis. In: Aykin NM (ed) Usability and internationalization. HCI and culture, second international conference on usability and internationalization, UI-HCII 2007, held as part of HCI international 2007, Beijing, China, July 22–27, 2007, Proceedings, Part I, vol 4559, pp 89–98. Springer, Heidelberg

Heimgärtner R (2008) A tool for getting cultural differences in HCI. In: Asai K (ed) Human computer interaction: new developments. InTech, Rijeka, pp 343–368

Heimgärtner R (2012) Cultural differences in human-computer interaction: towards culturally adaptive human-machine interaction. Oldenbourg, Munich

Heimgärtner R (2014) ISO 9241-210 and Culture?—The impact of culture on the standard usability engineering process. In: Marcus A (ed) Third international conference on design, user experience, and usability. User experience design practice, DUXU 2014, held as part of HCI international 2014, Heraklion, Crete, Greece, June 22–27, 2014, Proceedings, Part IV, pp 39–48. Springer, Cham

Heimgärtner R, Windl H, Solanki A (2011) The necessity of personal freedom to increase HCI design quality. In: Marcus A (ed) Design, user experience, and usability. Theory, methods, tools and practice, vol 6769, pp 62–68. Springer, Berlin/Heidelberg

Herczeg M (2005) Software ergonomics: basics of human-computer communication (2nd, fully revised edition). Oldenbourg, Munich

Hoffmann H-E, Schoper Y-G, Fitzsimons C-J (2004) International project management: intercultural cooperation in practice (original edition vol. 50883: Beck-Wirtschaftsberater; 50883). Munich: German Paperback-Verl

Hofstede GH (1991) Cultures and organizations: software of the mind. McGraw-Hill, London

Hoft NL (1995) International technical communication: how to export information about high technology. Wiley, New York

Honold P (2000) Intercultural usability engineering: a study on cultural influences on the design and use of technical products (published as Ms. gedr. vol 647). Düsseldorf village: VDI Verl

Houghton G (2005) Connectionist models in cognitive psychology. Psychology Press, Hove

ISO12620 (1999) Computer applications in terminology: data categories = computer aids in terminology: data categories. ISO, Geneva

Kaptelinin V, Nardi B (2012) Activity theory in HCI: fundamentals and reflections. Synth Lect Hum-Cent Inf 5(1): 1–105. https://doi.org/10.2200/s00413ed1v01y201203h-CI013

Köppen N, Wandke H (2002) Development of a toolset to support logfile studies Useware 2002. Deutscher Ingenieur-Verlag, Düsseldorf, pp 27–32

La Cruz T, Mandl T, Womser-Hacker C (2005) Cultural dependency of quality perception and web page evaluation guidelines: results from a survey. In: Day D, del Galdo E, Evers V (eds) Designing for global markets 7: proceedings of the seventh international workshop on internationalization of products and systems (IWIPS 2005), pp 15–27, Amsterdam

Lienert GA, Raatz U (1998) Test construction and test analysis, 6th edn. Beltz Psychologie-Verl.-Union, Weinheim

Mandel T (1997) The elements of user interface design: [foundations of user interface design; graphical and object-oriented user interfaces; the user interface design process; Internet interfaces, agents, and social interfaces]. Wiley, New York

Mangold P (2005) Proceeding studies on behavior—not only a challenge for professional tools. In: Andreas H, Karl-Heinz, W (eds) Empowering software quality: how can usability engineering reach these goals? 1st usability symposium, HCI&UE workgroup, pp 127–140, Vienna, 8 Nov 2005

Marcus A (1996) Icon and symbol design issues for graphical user interfaces International users interface. Wiley, New York, pp 257–270

Marcus A (2001) Cross-cultural user-interface design. In Smith MJSG (ed) Proceedings conference on human-computer interface internat (HCII), New Orleans, vol 2, pp 502–505. Lawrence Erlbaum Associates, Mahwah

Marcus A (2007) Global/intercultural user-interface design. In: Jacko J, Spears A (eds) The human-computer interaction handbook. Lawrence Erlbaum Associates, Mahwah

Marcus A, Gould EW (2000) Crosscurrents: cultural dimensions and global web user-interface design. Interactions 7(4):32–46

Nielsen J (1990) Designing user interfaces for international use, vol 13. Elsevier, Amsterdam

Nielsen J, Molich R (1990) Heuristic evaluation of user interfaces. Paper presented at the proceedings of the SIGCHI conference on human factors in computing systems, Seattle

Ottmann A (2002) Software localization. In: Hennig J, Tjarks-Sobhani M (ed) Publications on Technical Communication Tekom. Volume 6 Localization of Technical Documentation, pp 146–163

Ottmann A (2005) Localization of software interfaces. In: Reineke D, Schmitz K-D (ed) Introduction to Software Localization, pp 101–115. Gunter Narr Publishers, Tübingen

Preim B, Dachselt R (2010) Interactive systems—volume i: basics, graphical user interfaces, information visualization. Springer, Heidelberg

Reineke D, Schmitz K-D (2005) Introduction to software localization. Gnv Narr, Tübingen

Röbig S, Didier M, Brother R (2010) International understanding of usability as well as metrology application in the field of usability. Paper presented at the Grundlagen—Methoden—Technologien, 5th VDI Symposium USEWARE 2010, Baden-Baden. http://tubiblio.ulb.tu-darmstadt.de/46312/. Accessed 29 Feb 2019

Röse K (2001) Culture as a variable of UI design. Paper presented at the Mensch & Computer 2001, Stuttgart

Röse K (2002) Methodology for the design of intercultural man-machine systems in production technology, vol 5. Univ, Kaiserslautern

Röse K, Zühlke D (2001) Culture-oriented design: developers' knowledge gaps in this area. Paper presented at the 8th IFAC/IFIPS/IFORS/IEA symposium on analysis, design, and evaluation of human-machine systems, 18–20 September 2001, Kassel

Röse K, Zühlke D, Liu L (2001) Similarities and dissimilarities of German and Chinese users. In: Johannsen G (ed) Preprints of 8th IFAC/IFIP/IFORS/IEA symposium on analysis, design, and evaluation of human-machine systems, pp 24–29, Kassel

Russo PBS (1993) How fluent is your interface? Designing for international users. Paper presented at the human factors and computer systems, Boston

Sachse F (2005) Localization formats. http://translation-tools.de/pdf/fs_LocFormate_old.pdf. Accessed 29 Feb 2019

Schildhauer E (2000) Localization of documentation and online help. In: Schmitz KD, Wahle K (eds) Software localization. Stauffenburg, Tübingen, pp 117–125

Schmitz K-D (2005) Internationalization and localization of software. In: Reineke D, Schmitz K-D (ed) Introduction to Software Localization, pp 11–26. Gunter Narr Publishers, Tübingen

Schmitz K-D, Wahle K (2000) Software localization. Stauffenburg-Verl, Tübingen

Shi Q, Copenhagen Business School, CBS (2010) An empirical study of thinking aloud usability testing from a cultural perspective. Frederiksberg: Copenhagen Business School (CBS)/Institut for Informatik (INF)/Department of Informatics, INF

Spannagel C (2003) Qualitative und quantitative Analyse von Interaktionsaufzeichnungen (Dipl.), Technical University of Darmstadt, Darmstadt

Tuthill B, Smallberg D (1997) Creating worldwide software: solaris international developer's guide. Prentice Hall, Upper Saddle River

Urbas L, Steffens C, Beu A, Jakob F (2006) The user is the focus—usability in the industry. In: Jahrbuch Elektrotechnik 2007—Data, Facts, Trends, vol 26. VDE-Verlag GmbH

VDMA (2007) Translation management. VDMA Publishing House, Frankfurt

VDMA (2009) Software Internationalization Guide. VDMA Software Association, Frankfurt a. M.

Windl H (2002) Designing a winner. Paper presented at the for USE 2002 1st international conference on usage-centered design

Windl H, Heimgärtner R (2013) Intercultural design for use—extending usage-centered design by cultural aspects. In: Marcus A (ed) Design, user experience, and usability. Health, learning, playing, cultural, and cross-cultural user experience, vol 8013, pp 139–148). Springer, Heidelberg

Winschiers-Theophilus H, Chivuno-Kuria S, Kapuire GK, Bidwell NJ, Blake E (2010) Being participated: a community approach. Paper presented at the proceedings of the 11th Biennial participatory design conference, Sydney

Zerfaß A (2005) Localization of internet presences. In: Reineke D, Schmitz K-D (ed) Introduction to software localization, pp 127–143. Gunter Narr Publishers, Tübingen

Zühlke D (2004) Useware systems for international markets useware engineering for technical systems. Springer, Heidelberg, pp 142–164

Chapter 8
Summary, Conclusion and Outlook

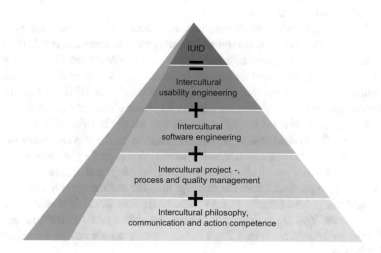

The need to develop intercultural user interfaces is more urgent than ever due to global competition. By using appropriate IUID methods, processes and tools, cultural differences in user interface design for other cultures can and must be considered. IUID research has developed rapidly in recent years, but this is also necessary in order to close research gaps and provide the developer of intercultural user interfaces with action-relevant but scientifically sound design recommendations. Explanation models for culture-dependent HMI design are the basis for this. In the following, relevant results and statements on the IUID are summarized and presented. Subsequently, the most important conclusions are drawn and relevant recommendations and calls for action are given. The chapter concludes with an outlook on the future development of intercultural user interfaces.

© Springer Nature Switzerland AG 2019
R. Heimgärtner, *Intercultural User Interface Design*, Human–Computer Interaction Series, https://doi.org/10.1007/978-3-030-17427-9_8

8.1 Summary

8.1.1 Introduction

Increasing globalization requires a new perspective on user interface design. Due to the intercultural overlap between product definition and product use and in order to meet the expectations of the user, his cultural preferences must be taken into account during product development. Already the awareness that products for the international market must be adapted accordingly, represents the first large step in the development of international IT products. Many designers and project managers have no idea to what extent people in other countries are different and therefore—especially with regard to the development of user interfaces—require special attention. International usability has a great influence on market success. Actually, meeting the requirements of international users is a serious design problem that requires serious work and effort.

The development of intercultural user interfaces encompasses all necessary process steps for the adequate design of human–machine interaction (HMI), taking cultural influences into account. Intercultural Human–Machine Design becomes beneficial and profitable when designers or developers know and apply the principles and recommendations for the design of intercultural HMI in each product development phase (as suggested in this book). Intercultural user interfaces allow users from different cultural backgrounds to use products from different cultural manufacturers. The consideration of cultural aspects in the development of intercultural user interfaces is just as necessary as the corresponding sensitization of the product manufacturers and through education, training and consultation of the stakeholders of the product (from the concept initiator and designer to the developer to the evaluator, product manager and salesman). This book is meant to make a contribution here. You are welcome to contact the author or IUIC for questions and further services (https://www.iuic.de). Further contact details can be found on page 344 of this book.

8.1.2 Thinking and Acting

There are many cultural terms which make it difficult to define culture unambiguously. For the development of intercultural user interfaces, culture is understood as an image of common values, ways of thinking and acting of a group of individuals that contributes to the formation of this community (Röse 2002). Cultural models describe these images and allow them to be compared with each other. Cultural differences extend across all areas of human life and have an impact on the development of intercultural products ranging from project, process and quality management to software engineering to usability engineering and thus the development of intercultural user interfaces.

Culture represents an orientation system and influences the interaction with other individuals as well as the interaction with technical devices and thus has a considerable influence on human–machine interaction and thus on the operation of user interfaces. Culture influences learning behavior, expectations and cognitive processing. Interaction and dialogue design, in particular, must, therefore, be treated very carefully in the intercultural development process, which represents a corresponding challenge for all participants due to the cultural differences. This can only be countered by appropriate knowledge of the desired target cultures. Ethnocentrism and relying only on one's own culture should be avoided.

Cultural models help to look "beneath the surface of the cultural iceberg", i.e., to explore the initially not directly visible areas of cultures, in order to overcome previous methodological gaps. Cultural models describe the cultural distance, i.e., the differences between cultures, and enable mutual comparison. Cultural standards express the normal, typical, and valid attributes for the majority of the members of a particular culture by considering modes of perception, thought, judgment, and action. Cultural dimensions represent a cultural aspect that can be measured in relation to other cultures. They can be used to classify behaviors within and between cultures. Due to the affinities between cultural dimensions and personality dimensions, both concepts should be applied in the design of intercultural user interfaces.

Patterns of thought are determined by the philosophies (worldviews) of mankind, which are very different worldwide for cultural reasons. In intercultural philosophy research, two main directions are distinguished: Eastern and Western philosophy. Cognitive styles describe the way in which information is processed and how it is dealt with, which is typical for an individual. Cognitive styles tend to be different in different cultures, resulting in different patterns of thought. In the respective cultures, this, in turn, has an effect on the world view and thus on the approaches to reality. These differences in thinking also have implications for the development and operation of intercultural user interfaces. These are described in detail in Chap. 5.

Culture is mainly a communication system (cf. Hall 1959). Successful communication depends very much on the ability of the people involved to empathize. Above all, intercultural user experience designers must be able to put themselves in the position of the user in order to know and understand his or her intentions or needs, to experience them ideally and then take them into account in the product. At least the following aspects of the user must be analyzed in detail before the product can be developed:

- User's worldview (metaphysical approach),
- General knowledge (procedural and factual knowledge) of the user,
- The context in which the product will be used by the user,
- The tasks that the user wishes to perform by using the product.

Overall, management must be adapted to the globalization process. Project, process, and quality management are the basis for successful intercultural product development. The biggest problem area in international project work is the work culture based on cultural differences. Misunderstandings in project work arise mainly because–without training the complexity of the rules and norms of other cultures as well as one's own remain unconscious and therefore an adequate reaction in critical interaction situations in project work is impossible. There is a direct connection between the characteristics of cultural dimensities and the understanding of project planning. In an international project, the definition of objectives is a top priority and should be done together with the international team. Empathic skills are therefore required in order to put oneself in the position of a user as a developer and to be able to master it. There are also different cultural views about fulfilling the requirements of the project and the processes. Agreements on understanding quality should therefore be made with all stakeholders. Different cultural backgrounds require a different understanding of quality.

8.1.3 Software Engineering

The challenges facing global software development all have something to do with distance: time, geography and sociocultural distance. Intercultural software engineering considers cultural influences during software development based on the results of software ergonomics research and usability engineering. The ultimate goal of incorporating software ergonomics into software engineering is to produce software that is easy to understand and use, with which the user is satisfied (=software with high usability). Ethnocomputing refers to everything that is encompassed by computer science and culture. Not only ethnic groups are meant, but also nations, and individual regions down to the smallest user groups with their very own cultural context.

A product can only be successful on the international market if it arouses familiar associations and positive connotations in the customer. The disregard of this aspect can lead to a complete rejection of the product. Intercultural product development spans the entire product development cycle and consists of software internationalization and software localization. Internationalization and localization are interwoven processes. In their application, it is essential to take into account the different cultural backgrounds of the users in order to generate user models and thus adapt the system and its parameters to the cultural needs of the user.

Internationalization of a product means that the product is equipped with a basic structure on the basis of which a cultural adaptation for use in the desired target countries can later be carried out (cf. International 2003), which saves costs. The TLCC model (cf. Sturm 2002) shows the historical growth of the steps of internationalization and localization in HMI design and comprises four levels which categorize the activities into the classes: technology, language, culture, and cognition. At the beginning of the internationalization process, a decision must be made as to which components should be localized. On the basis of this definition, appropriate measures can then be taken to internationalize the software. When internationalizing and localizing software, all parties involved should always be aware of the core elements of localization and take them into account accordingly, as otherwise, they could represent potential sources of problems which can cause excessive user effort and inacceptance in the development process.

Localization means the adaptation of a system to certain cultural requirements of a local market, e.g., the adaptation of the look and feel of the user interface or the internal data structures to the cultural requirements of the user (cf. VDMA 2009). Hoft (1995) illustrates visible (language, colors, icons, symbols) and hidden localization elements (context, behavioral norms, thinking, communication, behavior, time aspect) using the iceberg model. In localization projects, the project objectives (e.g., scope and type of software localization, such as definition of exchange formats and checking the localization database) must be defined first. After that, a time schedule for the project and a calculation of the costs is created, followed by the implementation of the plan according to the specifications defined in the planning process. The preparation and delivery of a localization kit or package with all the resources required by the translators for the translation must then be prepared and delivered. After translation, at least one linguistic test must be carried out to ensure the quality of the translated product. After translation/ localization, some software components (such as user interfaces and help files) may require recompilation. One of the best strategies for using language and designing a localized product is to know the purpose of the translation and localize it directly in the target country with local translators and specialists. It is advisable to bring localization experts on board.

The study of the human-centered design process in the current ISO 9241-210 with regard to aspects of intercultural management, in particular, intercultural project management, shows that precisely these aspects are still missing in this process, especially in the important early project phase. Interculturally induced problems require an interculturally experienced, professional project manager to resolve them in a professional manner and avoid potential obstacles. In intercultural projects, the monitoring and control of projects, i.e., the checking and recording of project progress and costs as well as the correction of deviations from the project management plan, is of central importance. The communication between designer and user plays a decisive role in the requirements analysis. Successful intercultural communication depends on the personal ability to understand each other's web of faith by using empathic abilities (cf. Heimgärtner et al. 2011). Knowledge about users and their needs can be obtained most precisely by using methods based on communication, such as user surveys or interviews.

Difficulties in understanding the requirements analysis must be analyzed and solved in order to improve the cooperation between designers, managers, users, and customers. Intercultural communication can help to solve problems arising from cultural differences, as these are strongly influenced by the philosophy of the cultures concerned. In the design process step, the culturally diverse UI design team must generate new innovative solutions. In the international context, it is important to evaluate the design status from the perspective of different user groups defined to ensure that the design meets the different and often contradictory requirements of all stakeholders. The introduction of agile methods can accelerate this process of disentangling diverse and changing stakeholder interests from different cultures.

Normally, software products contain two main components: software and documentation. Localization projects usually begin with software translation, which involves translating the components of an application's graphical user interface such as menus, dialogue boxes, and strings (error messages, questions, etc.) and any sample files that may be provided with the software for demonstration purposes. In times of globalization it is very important for companies, institutions or products to be present on the Internet. This presence in the form of a website should also be tailored to the local target markets. Since the content of websites changes very often, it is advisable to develop and systematize a localization workflow. A "locale" is the culture-dependent component of the software and is rich in units that are specific to a particular target culture. A localization kit (LocKit) should contain all the information the translator needs for localization. Zerfaß (2005) gives step-by-step tips for creating a LocKit. One way to avoid communication problems within a localization team is to give everyone involved in the project an overview of all project phases using an L10N plan.

8.1.4 Usability Engineering

Ergonomics deals with the relationship between human characteristics and artifacts. Software ergonomic criteria or guidelines are used to design, evaluate and compare user interfaces and their dialogues. The supreme principle of software ergonomics is that the software must be adapted to people and not the other way around.

The interaction in which information is exchanged between user and system via User Interface (UI) is referred to as "human–machine interaction" (HMI) or "human–computer interaction (MCI)" (cf. Jacko and Sears 2003). The interface between the user and the technical system is the "user interface" according to ISO standard 9241 (often referred to as user interface, user interface, user interface). The action level model according to (Herczeg 2005) describes the steps of man-machine communication. Metaphors represent a known real situation or object, facilitate learning for the user and give a certain direction to his expectations.

Mental models are a means of depicting the shared knowledge of communication partners (cf. Johnson-Laird 1983). The product developer is not forced to prognosticate the mental models of the users, but they can empirically collect them systematically with the help of the methods of intercultural usability engineering. Therefore, intercultural usability engineering is also indispensable for intercultural product development.

Interactive systems must be designed in such a way that all user requirements are met. The more different the cultural imprint between designer and user is, the higher the transformation effort of the user is to bridge the distances in the interaction on all levels of the action level model. Genetic recommendations (such as guidelines, norms, standards, dialogue principles, etc.) must be broken down by experts (such as usability professionals) into the concrete design situation and filled with the corresponding knowledge. A usability professional (cf. Sect. 4.4.4) is a person who is qualified and methodically derives, implements or verifies the usability of interactive systems (hardware and software).

A dialogue is an interaction between a user and an interactive system in the form of a sequence of actions by the user (inputs) and responses by the interactive system (outputs) to achieve a goal. Principles of dialogue are general objectives for the design of dialogues. Dialogue principles are abstract guidelines derived from experience for dialogue design at the highest level. Dialogue principles often cannot be strictly separated when it comes to their application. The seven principles of dialogue design DIN EN ISO 9241-10 (DIN 1996) (task adequacy, error tolerance, self-explanatory ability, learning facilitation, expectation conformity, controllability, and individualizability) are not *laws*, but lead to interculturally variable interpretations. Therefore, they need to be thoroughly analyzed in order to derive recommendations on how to correctly apply these principles of dialogue in international contexts. For example, a dialogue regarding the dialogue principle of task adequacy should provide the user with the information related to the successful completion of the task. But both the presentation of the information, the requirement to fulfil the task and the task itself can be culture-specific (see Windl and Heimgärtner 2013). If the requirements of the task are culture-specific, the required quality, quantity, and type of information to be presented are also culture-specific. The analysis of the application of the dialogue principle "task adequacy" in the intercultural context with cultural dimensions at the national level shows that the existing dialogue principles defined in ISO 9241-110 should be applied with caution in order to successfully grasp intercultural contexts. If only one of the dialogue principles in ISO 9241-110 cannot be applied internationally because of an intercultural conflict at the national level, optimizations or modifications of the dialogue principles must take place so that they function at least in international contexts at the national level.

Usability is the extent to which a product can be used by specific users in a specific context of use in order to achieve specific objectives effectively, efficiently and satisfactorily. (DIN EN ISO 9241-11 1999, S. 94). Users evaluate the quality of a software system based on the degree to which it helps them perform their tasks and the pleasure they experience when using it. The context of use includes the user himself, his work tasks, the work tools available to him, and the physical and social environment (Fig. 4.3). A usability problem occurs when aspects of a system make it unpleasant, inefficient, cumbersome or impossible for users with sufficient prior knowledge to achieve the goals for which the system was designed in a typical context of use (Sarodnick and Brau 2011).

User Experience (UX) comprises all effects that an interactive product has on the user both before (anticipated use) and during or after use (identification with the product or dissociation) (Fig. 4.5).

Usability engineering is the methodical way to generate the property of usability and UX. It is a sub-process of the development and design of technical systems and supplements classical engineering—for example software engineering—with ergonomic perspectives. The human-centered design process (usability engineering process) follows six principles, which must also be considered in an intercultural context. In order to establish a stable intercultural engineering process, cultural aspects must be considered in the phases of the software engineering process as well as in the usability engineering process (human-centered design process) (cf. Chaps. 3, 4 and 7). Empathy is an essential prerequisite for successful intercultural communication, which requires successful intercultural HMI design and intercultural usability engineering and, as a consequence, a positive user experience. It should, therefore, be ensured and disseminated that usability professionals receive, know and apply empathy.

The analysis of the human-centered design process (cf. ISO 9241-210) with regard to intercultural management showed (cf. Heimgärtner 2014b) that aspects in this process are missing with regard to the cultural context of use. In drawing up this standard, no particular emphasis was placed on a thorough analysis of the cultural aspects and their effects within the process, because the necessary concepts such as HMI dimensions, UI characteristics, intercultural variables, and cultural dimensions had not yet been sufficiently received. Even if the analytical ideas propagated here are preliminary and unsolicited or have to be described in detail in order to be universally valid, they can still provide a reasonable basis for future research. In addition, the examples presented, which bridge the gap between the principle of dialogue and culture, should be sufficient to give an impression of how principles of dialogue can be affected in intercultural contexts.

"Intercultural" Usability Engineering is a method for designing good usability products for users from different cultures (Honold 2000). Through the use of specific *intercultural* usability engineering, differences in approaches and preferences of different cultures can be addressed in order to be globally successful (Holzinger 2005; Honold 2000).

The application of this engineering method requires knowledge of cultural differences in HMI as well as the corresponding methodological competence and its consideration in the design and implementation of the product. In an intercultural context, knowledge about the target culture and about which methods can be used for intercultural usability engineering is required, thus allowing the development of intercultural user interfaces (cf. Chap. 5).

The development of intercultural HMI begins before the context of use and requirements analysis and long before the actual design of the HMI is started. Differences between cultures can be found by analyzing critical interaction situations (Thomas 1996). Due to the intercultural overlap between product definition and product use and in order to meet the expectations of the user, his cultural preferences must be taken into account in product development. The product must, therefore, be internationalized and localized. This process refers both to the functionality of the device and to the user interface design. The use of methods of intercultural usability engineering ensures the usability of the products. Therefore, intercultural user interface design should be included in the curriculum of HMI design.

Culture influences all phases and all participants in the development of intercultural user interfaces. The knowledge about these influences and the use of appropriate measures does not represent insurmountable problems for a project in theory or in the practical application of methods but motivates to include cultural aspects in research and development. Ultimately, users of any cultural imprint and in any cultural context should be able to use the product—through Intercultural Usability Engineering. Bad or missing intercultural usability engineering within the development process of the product increases the development and maintenance costs considerably due to frequent change requests. Comparative cultural studies of human–machine interaction are a necessary prerequisite for improving the intercultural usability of software, which in turn is a necessary prerequisite for global sales opportunities. It is necessary to examine the cultural context of use and the user culture on site. An international software product, which can be used effectively and efficiently by users of different cultures due to the use of intercultural usability engineering, increases both customer satisfaction with the product and its functional security. A satisfied user will not change the manufacturer of the product in the future, because he appreciates his efforts for usable products and optimized user interfaces. Intercultural usability engineering is, therefore, a must for every product development in the global market.

Even if the propagated analytical ideas regarding the examination of dialogue principles in an intercultural context have a preliminary character and still have to be examined and described in detail in order to attain general validity, they can nevertheless provide a reasonable basis for future research. In addition, the examples presented, which bridge the gap between the principle of dialogue and culture, should be sufficient to give an impression of how principles of dialogue can be affected in intercultural contexts.

It remains open, for example, to empirically prove the postulated hypothesis that dialogue principles are "culturally sensitive" in this respect, that their core characteristics change in intercultural contexts because they contain terms whose meaning, or reference variables also change in intercultural contexts. Until then, a more profound discussion on the relationship between dialogue principles and culture has yet to take place. In this sense, a thorough discussion is still pending. Nevertheless, some of the ideas suggest that the HMI development process currently defined in ISO 9241-210 could be expanded with roles and activities in order to be successful in all cultural contexts worldwide and to meet its international claim. In addition, the methods for developing user interfaces should be systematically complemented by cultural aspects to ensure that new systems can be designed from the outset for one or more cultures and that developers can adapt to the various global user requirements and thus react faster to changes using agile methods and modules of usage-centered design. In any case, it is reasonable for experts in international HMI standardization committees to have intercultural experience and knowledge in the development of intercultural user interfaces and intercultural usability engineering.

8.1.5 User Interface Design

Culture-related user differences must be taken into account when designing modern user interfaces and integrated sensibly into product development. The design of intercultural HMI has a lot to do with intercultural communication and requires appropriate know-how and procedures. Intercultural overlapping situations (cf. Honold 2000, p. 42 ff.) arise when a product is defined and formed within a culture and this product is then transferred into another culture and then also used there. A developer from culture X has to make the operation of the product understandable for a user from culture Y (see Röse 2002, p. 68 ff.). A cultural user group is a group of people who consciously (self-assessment) or unconsciously (by feature/context/role, assigned from outside) share values, rules, and behavioral patterns and thus represent a culture. The assignment to a cultural user group is made by belonging to a culture and the characteristics implicitly assumed with it. The cultural focus is not on single individuals, but on user groups. This means that the user is considered an individual or representative of a group/role. Multiple user groups require different user interface styles for the same application, and sometimes a single user will require different user interface styles to run the same application.

The cultural conditions in which a person grows up determine what is remembered and stored. This also has an influence on structuring and memory. The resulting actions—as a result of the information processing process—are also directly dependent on it. There are cultural differences in performance in the area of short-term and long-term memory. Culture thus also shapes people's learning and performance capacity. Language is an obvious characteristic for the differentiation of cultures. Asian cultures have a "top/bottom" typeface and Western cultures have a "left/right" typeface. The same arrangement principle also applies to the horizontal or vertical menu arrangement (see Röse 2002 and Heimgärtner 2012). The consideration of cultural aspects should not only refer to visual design and elementary UI components, but also to basic design concepts, metaphors, and workflows. There is still a significant need for mediation between academia and industry with regard to cultural and cognitive aspects in the development of intercultural user interfaces (IUID).[1]

The multidimensional cultural imprinting of users can be described using cultural models. The most interesting cultural models for the design of intercultural HMI are those that are directly linked to communication, information, interaction, and dialogue design, i.e., those cultural dimensions that concern the culturally different concepts of space, time and communication (Heimgärtner 2005, 2007, 2012):

---

[1]This book is intended to contribute to this. As the author of this book, I am happy to help you with questions and feedback about the book and the IUID. Further information can be found at http://www.iuic.de.

- Individualism (task) versus collectivism (relationship) (containing related cultural dimensions such as face-saving or power distance),
- Nonverbal communication,
- Perception of space (e.g., distance between user and system, network density, context),
- Time perception (containing all related cultural dimensions such as uncertainty avoidance or communication speed).

All the cultural dimensions analyzed provide space- and time-specific aspects. It, therefore, makes sense to assume that cultural dimensions based on time deal with interaction and information processing in HMI (e.g., use of dialogue). Cultural dimensions, which instead are based on space, concern the presentation of information as well as the structure and layout of user interfaces. Culture influences the HMI at all levels of the interaction model (cf. action level model after Herczeg 2005 and Heinecke 2004, as well as Norman and Draper 1986). Cultural dimensions can be reduced to a basic cultural dimension (BCD) in which the very similar dimensions "individualism versus collectivism", "task versus person orientation" and "role versus relationship orientation" are combined.

Intercultural HMI design describes the user- and culture-oriented design of interactive systems and products, including the cultural context of the user in relation to tasks and product use (Röse 2002, p. 87; Honold 2000, pp. 42–43) and thus the "process of HMI design in the cultural context". "Process of HMI Design" generally refers to the process of human-centered design according to ISO 9241-210 and in particular to the development of user interfaces. The perception and consideration of the customs and requirements of other cultures by the developers of intercultural user interfaces is one of the main tasks of intercultural HMI design. Intercultural User Interface Design (IUID) refers to the process of adequately designing human–machine interaction, taking into account the cultural requirements of the user. The development of intercultural user interfaces (IUID) focuses on a specific product or service and its use in a specific cultural context. The system checks whether the user interface is suitable for the user in the respective cultural context or whether it can be adapted by the user accordingly. Intercultural user interface design is a necessary prerequisite for improving the intercultural usability of software, which in turn is a necessary prerequisite for global sales opportunities. Using methods of intercultural usability engineering, further design guidelines can be iteratively derived from the results of the tests and the dialogues with potential users from all over the world for intercultural user interface design. Intercultural interface design is divided into three levels according to Thissen (2008). On the first level (signs) the cultural coding of signs takes place, i.e., the way in which information is presented (=semiotic systems of a culture—Cassirer 1994)—signs as expressions of cultural values ("cultural markers"). The second stage (social behavior) deals with forms of cultural perception described on the basis of cultural models. At the third level of intercultural user interface design, culture is captured and understood in its entirety and complexity (understanding of otherness).

Cultural dimensions are too rough for intercultural user interface design. For this reason, additional cultural variables are necessary which—in relation to user interface design—break down the cultural aspects into smaller units (cf. Röse 2002). These cultural aspects can be empirically determined using qualitative and quantitative methods. Although cultures are constantly changing, for a product life cycle of a few years at least trends can be determined, and for special applications even selective parameters can be determined which serve the intercultural user interface design. There are correlations between the interaction behavior of the user and his culture or between the cultural dimensions and information science variables such as information density or interaction frequency at the interaction level (cf. middle level of the "iceberg" in Fig. 6.3 in Chap. 6).

Intercultural variables describe the differences in HMI design with respect to the preferences of users from different cultures (Table 5.3). Direct intercultural variables are most important because they have a direct and significant influence on the HMI design. "Visible" intercultural variables (VIVs) are immediately perceptible at a given time (font, color, window size, navigation bar, etc.). In contrast to this, "invisible" (or "hidden") intercultural variables (NVIVs) are only recognizable over a certain period of time (speed of interaction, duration of information presentation, frequency of dialogue presentation, use of the navigation bar, etc.).

The localization of hidden intercultural variables is very difficult to realize because the contextual relation to the cultural background as well as to the product is very high for interaction and dialogue design. However, it is precisely this high context and consequently the cultural dependency that makes these patterns and invisible intercultural variables so important for the design of interaction and for the resulting dialogues (Röse 2002, p. 98, 108) uses intercultural variables within her "Method of Culture-Oriented Design" (MCD), which she developed for the development of intercultural human–computer systems (Fig. 5.6).

The user interface characteristics "Metaphor", "Mental Model", "Navigation", "Interaction" and "Presentation" are linked to five of Hofstede's cultural dimensions (see Chap. 2). User interface characteristics can be used in conjunction with empirical surveys of their characteristics for the corresponding cultural target context to derive recommendations for the development of intercultural user interfaces.

Information science quantities such as information speed (speed of dissemination and frequency of occurrence of information), information density (number and distance of information units) or information order (sequence of occurrence and arrangement of information) correlate with culturally different basic patterns of behavior. HMI dimensions (HMID) describe the behavior of a user (HMI style) with an interactive information processing system (Heimgärtner 2007). HMI dimensions represent classes of HMI variables (expressions of HMI dimensions) useful for HMI design, which are operationalized using (interaction) indicators in HMI metrics (Table 5.8). At least one potential indicator must exist as a measurement variable in order to be able to represent the expression of an HMI dimension. For real use, however, several empirically proven indicators should be used. If HMI dimensions are consistently represented by cultural variables, one could speak of "(inter-)cultural HMI dimensions", which express a culturally influenced HMI style. The HMI style coefficient describes the cultural HMI style of a user by representing the average amount of information density, information frequency, interaction frequency and interaction speed expected by members of the intended cultural group.

It is important that there is agreement between the developer and the users in different cultures about the meaning and interpretation of information; otherwise, misunderstandings or no understanding at all arise (see Chap. 2). In order to be competitive as a product manufacturer in the world market, it is important that users accept the product. Therefore, cultural influences during the development of products for other markets must be taken into account. The communication level forms the basic level, followed by the levels of project management, software and usability engineering on the way to the successful development of intercultural user interfaces (Fig. 5.4).

In order to be able to design user interfaces for the global market that meet the cultural needs of users, the first step is to find out the differences in the cultural needs of users and thus the cultural differences in HMI at all levels of HMI localization (interface, functionality and interaction) (Röse and Zühlke 2001). Areas such as information presentation and language or dialogue design as well as interaction design are affected (Lewandowitz et al. 2006) (cf. Chap. 7).

Bevan (2001) described the international standards for HMI design and usability engineering. The human-centered HMI design process is defined in ISO 9241-210 and the resulting extension ISO 9241-220. Relevant parts of the ISO 9241 series for usability professionals and user interface designers are practically summarized in a two-volume edition of DIN-VDE paperback 354 by Beuth-Verlag.

In addition to descriptive models, there are several other approaches to a theory culturally influenced HMI. However, there is still no definitive theory that explains all the relevant factors that would be necessary to derive general design recommendations for culture-centric HMI design. This remains a challenge for the future. In the field of intercultural user interface design, the difficult investigation of methodological intercultural factors is still in its infancy: data and results for phenomena such as different system interaction habits, different expectations with regard to navigation in hyperspace or different mental models still have to be collected. In the field of intercultural user interface design, the gap between cultural aspects and specific technical aspects remains to be bridged. This is particularly the case in relation to the current lack of research that relates to culturally shaped interaction and dialogue design and is based on empirical research on hidden cultural variables. Even if research on culture-centric HMI design has grown enormously, it remains extremely important that the results of empirical studies on cultural contexts are integrated into HMI design, thereby providing both the basis of input data for the model and theory approaches and the basis of the measured scale with which they can be verified.

8.1.6 IUID in Theory—Scientific Research

From the analysis of publications in the field of intercultural HMI, some IUID "hypes" can be identified. The first hype occurred in the early 1990s. The next one was around 2000 and since about 2010 research in the field of intercultural HMI and IUID has increased by leaps and bounds. To date, however, there are only a few qualitative studies or tests on intercultural user experience that would provide reasonable answers to these questions (cf. Jameson 2007). The number of studies underlining the importance of cultural aspects in the development of user interfaces is constantly growing (see Evers 2003; Smith et al. 2004). There are also activities related to the study of trends in the intercultural HMI (cf. Jetter 2004; Clemmensen and Roese 2010; Heimgärtner 2014a). Even though there is now relevant literature on usability engineering (e.g., Nielsen 1993; Holzinger 2005 etc.), reliable and above all general literature on intercultural usability engineering [e.g., on evaluation in an intercultural context (cf. Clemmensen 2012)] and above all on intercultural usability engineering (cf. Heimgärtner 2014a) is increasing only very cautiously. Most studies concern the presentation of information on web pages (e.g., Hodemacher et al. 2005; Marcus 2003; Dormann 2005; Baumgartner 2003; Marcus and Gould 2000; Stengers et al. 2004; Sun 2001 and Callahan 2005). The detailed analysis of the current research in the field of intercultural user interface design also showed that in particular hidden cultural variables (NVIVs) (under the water surface of the iceberg model, cf. Sect. 6.1.3 and Fig. 6.3) have not yet been investigated thoroughly enough.

The TLCC model of (Sturm 2002) shows the internationalization and localization steps in HMI design, represented by four levels: technical characteristics, language, culture, and cognition (cf. Fig. 6.2). There is still a significant need for mediation between academia and industry with regard to cultural and cognitive aspects in the development of intercultural user interfaces (IUID).[2]

There is nothing more practical than a good theory to move from theoretical considerations to practical application in intercultural user interface design. The process of "Grounded Theory" is an iterative scientific process that resembles iterative software development cycles (cf. Balzert 2005). Theoretically based processes are predominantly based on "Grounded Theory" and established and proven processes are based on software engineering. In an explanatory model for culturally influenced HMI, the relations between culture and HMI are described using cultural interaction indicators, thus showing the relationship between culture and HMI. These relations can be determined in particular in the following ways: *data-driven* or *hypothesis-driven*. In the *data-driven approach*, data is first collected. The resulting patterns provide information about the connection between culture and HMI. In the *hypothesis-driven approach*, hypotheses are derived from existing

---

[2]This book is also intended to make a contribution here. As the author of this book, again it would be an honor to answer your questions and feedback about the book and the IUID. Further information can be found at https://www.iuic.de.

cultural theories and empirically verified. Finally, in the *hybrid approach,* the first two approaches are combined with other methods.

Data-driven approach: Hypotheses are formed from data already collected. In order to encourage the culturally different user to interact with the computer and then to record and analyze this interaction, task scenarios were developed which were implemented in a specially developed PC tool (IIA Tool, Heimgärtner 2008). The author conducted two online studies with approximately 15000 Chinese (C), German (G) and English (E) speakers.

The evaluation of the data collected in the studies showed that there are correlations between the interaction of users with the computer and the cultural imprint of users (Heimgärtner 2007). The cultural differences in HMI between the tested Chinese and German users concern layout (complex vs. simple), information density (high vs. low), personalization (strong vs. low), language (icons vs. characters), interaction speed (higher vs. lower) and interaction frequency (higher vs. lower). It has been empirically shown that the user's interaction with the system is influenced not only by culturally related variables such as nationality, mother tongue, country of birth, etc., but also by parameters such as experience or age (Heimgärtner 2007). Information density, information, and interaction frequency as well as information and interaction parallelism are lower for (G) than for (C) according to the relationship orientation, the density of information networks and the time orientation of the users. The type of interaction of the system with the user within the HMI must be adaptable by an adequate change of the system parameters according to the characteristics of the cultural interaction indicators and the HMI dimensions. The significant cultural interaction indicators (CIIs) identified in Table 6.1 concern the different interaction behavior in the HMI between Chinese (C) and German (G) speaking user groups. It has been empirically confirmed that the interaction of the user with the system is influenced not only by variables describing the cultural belonging of the user such as nationality, mother tongue, country of birth, etc., but also by parameters such as experience or age (Heimgärtner 2007). The way in which the computer interacts with the user must be adaptable so that the system can cope with the user requirements, which depend on the cultural imprint and experience of the user as well as on the current situation. The necessary variables must be taken into account in the design of the system architecture. Cultural interaction indicators (CIIs), for example, are such variables in the HMI that correlate with variables that represent the culture of the user. They represent cultural differences in user interaction behavior by expressing the relationship between the values of cultural dimensions and the values of HMI dimensions. HMI dimensions represent the characteristics of the respective HMI by describing the HMI style of the user by means of the type of information processing in the respective HMI as well as its interaction characteristics.

Hypothesis-driven approach: Data are collected for the verification of hypotheses. The empirical hypotheses concern basic user behavior: Time orientation, density of information networks, communication speed as well as action chains. The hypotheses are based on some of the best classifications of the CIIs, which support the basic hypothesis that the expressions of the HMI dimensions depend on the cultural imprint of the user as follows: the higher the relationship orientation (collectivism), the higher the information density, information speed, information frequency, interaction frequency and interaction speed, and the higher the information density, the higher the information speed, the higher the interaction frequency and interaction speed and vice versa. The confirmation strengths of six out of eight hypotheses were estimated a priori approximately correctly, and all postulated eight hypotheses were confirmed a posteriori in the online studies. This shows that the analytical preparatory work and the methods used were correct and that the results can be regarded as plausible and correct. In order to analyze the interaction of the user with the system, dynamic aspects of the HMI must be measured by means of automated analyzing tools by gapless chronological recording of the user behavior. For this purpose, the intercultural interaction analysis tool (IIA Tool) (Heimgärtner 2008) was used (see Sect. 7.4.5).

A hybrid approach integrates several IUID methods into an IUID method mix (Heimgärtner 2014a). Based on the method of culture-oriented HMI design (MCD, see Röse 2002), cultural differences are identified on the basis of cultural dimensions and cultural variables are derived for the project. With this knowledge of cultural differences and affected aspects of the HMI system, further effects on the HMI design are determined and supported by hypothesis-driven and data-driven user interface characteristics (see Marcus 2006) and HMI dimensions (see Heimgärtner 2012).

The cultural influence on the HMI design can be represented by the relationships between the expressions of cultural dimensions and the expressions of the variables relevant to the HMI design. The results found in the studies led to the conviction that it is justified and useful to use cultural interaction indicators for intercultural HMI research in order to obtain a reasonable explanatory model for culturally influenced HMI. Successful explanatory models can be applied to new examples or use cases and thus verified, which in turn allows predictive design recommendations to be generated. Finally, complete metrics for representing the usability of interactive systems (usability measurement systems, cf. Nielsen 2001) can be derived from high-empirical value for the culturally influenced HMI. The aim is to discover the actual connection between the interaction indicators and their (postulated cultural) causes. Structural equation models can be used to identify these relationships between cultural dimensions and HMI dimensions and their manifestations. An attempt was made to generate a structural model for the relationship between HMI dimensions and cultural dimensions. The connections between cultural, information-related and interaction-related dimensions were modeled using intercultural interaction indicators. The explanatory model of culture-dependent HMI is all the better the more variations in the empirical data can be statistically explained by the modeled structural equations. The resulting explanatory model is based on some of the best-class-scoring cultural interaction indicators that emerged from the hypothesis that the expressions of the HMI dimensions depend on the cultural imprint of the users, which can be described by the expressions of cultural dimensions: the higher the relationship orientation (collectivism), the higher the information density, information speed, information frequency, interaction frequency and interaction speed and vice versa.

In the field of intercultural user interface design, the difficult investigation of methodological intercultural factors is still in its infancy: data and results for phenomena such as different system interaction habits, different expectations with regard to navigation in hyperspace or different mental models still have to be collected. In the field of intercultural user interface design, the gap between cultural aspects and specific technical aspects still needs to be bridged.

According to Hall (1976), the methodological problems in the study of culture lie in the fact that transmission is simpler in simple systems than the integration of more complex systems that require human creativity. The determination of intercultural variables and their values is still too unsystematic and selective due to different approaches and complex cultural contexts. It is problematic to bring cultural models fully in line with HMI dimensions, as not all possible interfering variables are taken into account due to cultural complexity and models cannot fully describe reality: the results obtained by the explanatory model differ from reality. Nevertheless, the results obtained so far (postulated and confirmed hypotheses) serve to reveal a basis and some proven facts that are useful for obtaining recommendations for intercultural HMI design with tendency character in general and for cultural real-adaptive systems in particular (see Heimgärtner 2012). In addition, it is very reasonable that development and research should consider some rules of thumb, even if they must be considered provisional and should be treated with the utmost care. The results from these approaches must not be generalized to the extent that they apply to an entire country or a particular cultural group, as the number of experiments is too small, and the limited justifiability of the subjects thwarts high-quality statistical results. This is also one of the reasons why so few qualitative empirical studies and even fewer quantitative research reports exist (cf. Smith et al. 2004) and (Maier et al. 2005 and Heimgärtner 2012). In addition, hidden (hidden) cultural variables are difficult to identify because they only become recognizable over time. Not all recommendations regarding the five areas of user interface characteristics (presentation, navigation, metaphor, mental model, interaction) have been empirically confirmed so far, although there is some research in this area. The test methodology of intercultural usability engineering still leaves questions unanswered and is sometimes a cost-intensive factor for companies wishing to adapt their products to international markets. There is disagreement among scientists about the effect of using cultural dimensions in the development of intercultural user interfaces.

The empirical results of the described study partly confirm the relationships between HMI dimensions and cultural dimensions postulated in literature. There is a measurement system consisting of cultural interaction indicators (CIIs) to measure culturally influenced HMI. The characteristics of the CIIs open interesting tendencies in the user interaction behavior related to the cultural imprint of the user. This first fundamental research has been carried out on the basis of the analysis of cultural models, the ten most relevant cultural dimensions and the culturally dependent HMI styles that can be calculated from them were produced, which should be taken into account in the development of intercultural user interfaces and in the intercultural HMI design process (Heimgärtner 2012). This also revealed hidden cultural variables of human–machine interaction, namely information speed and information frequency as well as interaction speed and interaction frequency. The explanatory model of culturally dependent HMI variables gained so far can be optimized and further developed with the help of statistical methods (such as factor analysis or structural equation models) by revising the relationships between user interaction and user culture. However, there is still a lot of work to be done here (such as improving the selectivity of the CIIs or the explanatory power of the model). Despite everything, these variables remain an open field of research in human–machine interface design because there is still too little empirical evidence.

The investigation and consideration of hidden cultural variables for intercultural HMI design is still ongoing. This is particularly the case in relation to the current lack of research, which relates to culturally shaped interaction and dialogue design and is based on empirical research. Even if research on culture-centric HMI design has grown enormously, it remains extremely important that the results of empirical studies on cultural contexts are integrated into HMI design, thereby providing both the basis of input data for the model and theory approaches and the basis of the measured scale with which they can be verified. Nevertheless, there is a sensible approach towards an explanatory model for culturally influenced HMI, where areas such as intercultural usability engineering and intercultural user interface design (IUID) can benefit to the extent that the model is further developed and validated.

The trend in research on culture and HMI is towards verifying preliminary models and theories through extensive empirical investigations in different cultural contexts and the empirical collection of the connections between user and system (HMI) in concrete cultural context of use, in order to be able to derive practical and concrete recommendations for the development of intercultural user interfaces. Intercultural HMI design must be changed in the future so that cultural aspects are taken into account both at the local level (cultural context/indigenous) and at the national level (cf. Abdelnour-Nocera et al. 2011).

8.1.7 IUID in Practice—Industrial Development

In the development of digital products and services, development processes often follow the V-model—a sequential iterative development model—or use agile software development methods such as Scrum or combinations of such approaches. Advanced software development processes also have corresponding gates (e.g., with regard to quality: quality gates/hurdles). The quality of these processes is often checked using maturity models (e.g., CHMI, SPICE).

The aim must be to embody the usability engineering process just as systematically as the software engineering process by applying human-centered design principles (cf. ISO 9241-210). In addition, the early recognition and consideration of cultural differences in product development plays a decisive role in the development of intercultural user interfaces. The usability of a system strongly depends on how the user gets along with the system (see DIN 2006). The degree of success can be determined, for example, by observing and questioning a user during interaction with the system (cf. Nielsen and Molich 1990 and Nielsen 1990). The individual cultural context of use must be specified for relevant usage situations in order to develop a deeper understanding of the individual culture-specific needs of the user. In addition to qualitative techniques of market research, quantitative methods must also be used in order to gain a deeper understanding of user needs. Trends in cultural differences can be used for the development and design of intercultural user interfaces and further reflection and research. In addition to reading literature, empirical studies on intercultural user interface characteristics are necessary to find out how well the systems can be used (e.g., by comparing several systems of different cultures and performing usability tests). When developing intercultural user interfaces, all those aspects in the cultural context that affect the properties of the user interface must be considered. But also, the methods for obtaining intercultural user interfaces and their evaluation require cultural inspection.

The requirements analysis during the development of user interfaces essentially consists of understanding and describing the context of use and deriving and specifying user requirements. In the requirements analysis, the business processes must be included in accordance with the HMI action level model (cf. Sect. 4.1.2) in order to achieve the analysis of the requirements of the interactive system in the context of the entire work organization (Fig. 7.2). All these questions should be answered when developing intercultural user interfaces for the respective cultural target contexts. International requirements must be taken into account. The determination of all different requirements from all stakeholder groups requires that all requirements of the preceding process steps are identified and that these requirement specifications are collected and consolidated (clarified and cleansed) accordingly, regardless of their origin. The consolidated requirements define the production objectives of the project as the objectives of the project and compliance with these objectives, which are separate from their solutions, is verified according to the SMART principle: Goals must be specific, measurable, attainable, realistic and timely bound.

Intercultural Usage-Centered Design (IU-CD) serves as a systematic and model-based method for determining user requirements for the design of intercultural user interfaces (cf. Windl and Heimgärtner 2013). The Usage-Centered Design process (U-CD) is divided into the analysis and design phases (Fig. 7.3). The role and task model are the results of the user and task analysis. The content model together with the implementation model are the results of the design phase. In order to integrate the cultural aspects and the internationalization requirements into U-CD, it is necessary to expand it and make adjustments to the existing procedure in various places. The common aspects for intercultural UI design are included in a cultural model similar to the existing "operation model" (Fig. 7.4). A separate cultural model is used for each culture (Fig. 7.5). The content of the cultural model is primarily related to the characteristics of the user interface (cf. Marcus 2007) and the HMI dimensions (cf. Heimgärtner 2012) and describes a user interface on an abstract level, which is filled with the special values for the desired culture. In order to also cover cultural aspects that do not fit into this country scheme (such as religious denominations, natives, or any other cultural target groups), it is possible to use project-specific cultural identifiers. The approach of intercultural usage-centered design (IU-CD) helps developers of intercultural user interfaces to systematically collect and model system and user requirements and to create suitable interactive systems on the basis of exact models.

HMI dimensions may be considered as the main factors in HMI design because they define the basic classes of variables relevant to HMI design and are therefore to be considered and used in the development of intercultural user interfaces. Both obvious and at first glance invisible design aspects must be taken into account. Since the users of a specific target market should (and want to) be addressed in their native language, terminology in the target language is an important aspect of software localization. Context information and the available reference materials are very important for terminology work. Generally used terminology data categories (e.g., ISO12620 1999) are not sufficient for terminology work in software localization, because within the software a single term can refer to different terms depending on its immediate context (e.g., in a menu, a dialogue window or an error message). There are differences between the terminology used in the software documentation (online help and web pages) and that used in the user interface. Particularly problematic in software localization is the use of allusions and puns (referring to other terms via homonyms) and the inclusion of symbols in the user interface, since editing and adapting these symbols can be a complicated and time-consuming process.

For the development of intercultural user interfaces from a German/Western European perspective, at least six writing systems can be formed worldwide (Fig. 7.11). As the font system number increases, internationalization and localization efforts increase (Table 7.5). Formats for displaying formats such as date, time, numbers, currency units or units of measurement are subject to country-specific conventions. The appropriate representation and processing of the target languages using appropriate character sets, character encoding and fonts is a basic prerequisite for the localization of linguistic elements of a product. When selecting fonts, it is important that the fonts and character sets used match. If a font does not support a certain character set, the information cannot be displayed correctly (Fig. 7.14). Each culture has different customs and therefore culture-specific linguistic conventions with regard to syntax and style, which must be taken into account and adapted during software localization. Depending on the different number of characters in the translation of words into different languages, it is necessary to adjust the size of widgets to display the corresponding text lengths (so-called "resizing", see Fig. 7.17). In addition, the widget positions must also be adjusted according to the preferences of the cultural user group (Fig. 7.18). Since colors have different meanings in different cultures, they should also be adapted to the target culture, otherwise, they will be misinterpreted.

Localization tools usually offer functions for pseudo translation (see also VDMA 2007). This allows the test of internationalization to be carried out. For example, hard-coded texts, texts that are not to be translated and internal text buffers that are too short are discovered. Tools offer partially automatic support for project management, translation and adaptation of terminology and software to the cultural context as well as for evaluation of results. User Interface Toolkits, which usually have a basic window system and a window manager as integral components, support the deepest level of dialogue design, the lexical design, as a tool. The use of UI toolkits drastically reduces the development effort. However, the software ergonomic advantages of using toolkits only come to bear if, on the one hand, the toolkit is flexible enough to offer solutions for a wide range of application requirements and, on the other hand, its range of dialogue objects and mechanisms remains consistent and manageable. In 2006, no commercially available interaction analysis tool had up-to-date cultural usability metrics (cf. UMTM, Table 6.5 in Sect. 6.3.2) or possibilities for implementing special use cases to measure interaction behavior in a cultural context. Therefore, a new tool was developed by the author in 2006 to measure the intercultural interaction behavior of the user (see Heimgärtner 2008). With this tool, the interaction of culturally different users can be observed who perform the same task under the same controlled environment and test conditions (same hardware and software, same language and test tasks). This makes the tests and their results traceable, comparable and transferable to similar applications at any time. Studies using the IIA tool are fully reproducible. The IDE of the tool allows a very fast conversion of new HMI concepts into good looking prototypes, which can be tested very quickly within the iterative development process. For example, some of the hypotheses were implemented within a month as use cases in the IIA tool and quantitatively confirmed by many users after data collection and analysis.

The processes of software engineering and software testing include technical aspects of software localization that need to be addressed at the beginning and end of a localization project. As soon as initial concepts and ideas of the user interface can be made tangible, e.g., in the form of prototypes, these must be evaluated with users. Evaluation doesn't solve problems, it shows them much more. A valid diagnosis often requires several complementary techniques as well as experience. Therefore, it always makes sense and is often necessary to involve usability professionals (see Chap. 4) in the evaluation process. User testing and user-generated development (U-CD) are an important means to measure and ensure user satisfaction with a technical system. In intercultural usability testing/engineering, indirect user participation is to be preferred (Zühlke 2004). But also, the possibilities of applying the methods and their practical application differ from culture to culture (see Shi and Copenhagen Business School 2010, S. 208). The cultural framework conditions, which cause cultural differences of use, must be determined by detailed analyses of the country and user profile for the respective target culture.

Due to the subjective character of person-related survey methods, the results are strongly influenced by the person's cultural background. Because of this "intercultural subjectivity" a comparison between country-specific results becomes meaningless. Only through objective, intercultural evaluation methods can the results be compared. Distortions of the developer's impression of the user image (Honold 2000) by cultural influencing factors and must, therefore, be circumvented by culturally objective, task-oriented survey methods. The more independent their use of cultural influences and the more sensitive their sensitivity to cultural aspects is, the higher the reliability of methods that are supposed to measure cultural differences. This describes a paradox that arises from different levels of explanation and can be resolved by them: methodical insensitivity to cultural influences while at the same time metrical sensitivity to quantitatively ascertainable differences in the culturally influenced interaction of the user with the system. Cultural comparisons of user behavior only become possible through (as far as possible) culturally independent measurement methods, i.e., precisely when no cultural interpretation of quantitative data is required. Then, the causes of previously identified errors can be determined through comparative studies, found violations of guidelines and statistically proven cultural differences. As a result, the problems of cultural-subjective test results and resource-intensive on-site testing can be avoided. Culture-independent methods can thus save costs and provide reliable results regarding cultural differences and thus cultural knowledge on a physical-objective measurement basis in the form of numbers. Numbers do not have to be assigned additional meaning by interpretation, since they represent mathematically *worldwide* (i.e., culture-*in*dependent) identically defined order values. For a culture-independent data collection and evaluation, theory and task-oriented tests with an objective character must be used. The use of quantitative methods, which are less susceptible to disruptions or culture-sensitive due to a lack of interpretation performance in data collection, is particularly beneficial for remote studies, which contribute significantly to cost savings in intercultural usability engineering (no travel costs, no test setting, laboratory conditions do not have to be created, no test leader, no training necessary, high time savings, etc.). Log file recording is a purely quantitative survey method. Log files from the field cannot contain data falsified by an artificial test environment (as is the case in the laboratory), since the real tasks have no test character. However, these numbers and the process from which they originate must eventually be interpreted semantically. Unfortunately, any interpretation is culturally influenced and there is still considerable need for research on culturally dependent—i.e., culturally influenced—methods (such as interpretative methods based on culturally dependent thought patterns and cognitive styles). The test methodology of intercultural usability engineering, therefore, remains an exciting field of research.

8.2 Conclusion

▸ To know the cultural differences of human–machine interaction (HMI) helps to improve the intercultural usability of machines. Accordingly, it is important to sensitize and advise both product manufacturers and product stakeholders (from concept developers and designers to developers, evaluators, product managers, and salesmen) as well as their education and training.

Differences between cultures can be found by analyzing critical interaction situations between people (Thomas 1996; Honold 2000) made this method available for cultural differences in the HMI.

▸ Intercultural usability engineering serves as a means to develop products of good usability for users of different cultures (Honold 2000).

Critical interaction situations that arise due to problematic user interfaces or are based on the given system functionality are analyzed. In addition, systems can also be regarded as (artificial) agents with their own culturally influenced behavior caused by the culture of the developer. The internal model of the user about the system is shaped by the culture of the user, his expectations about the characteristics of the system and his experience of interaction with the system. Some culturally influencing factors on the HMI postulated in the literature have been confirmed by quantitative empirical studies.

▸ Badre & Barber (1998) empirically demonstrated the direct influence of cultural markers on the performance of user interaction with the system and thus on the connection between culture and usability.

Cultural dimensions and cultural standards represent cultural orientation systems (Hofstede and Hofstede 2005; Thomas 1996). These cultural models can be used to obtain explanatory models for intercultural HMI design as well as to improve the methods of intercultural usability engineering.

▸ Vöhringer-Kuhnt (2002) found that e.g., Hofstede's individualism index is related to user satisfaction and usability of the product and has a significant influence on intercultural usability.

However, the most culturally influenced aspects (such as cognition or ethics) are not directly visible on the surface. Rather, these aspects are reflected in the behavior of the user. Therefore, the analysis of user behavior, in particular, provides information on the cultural imprinting of the user (Röse 2002). One of the most promising methods to preserve cultural differences in HMI is, therefore, the observation and analysis of user interaction with the system.

▸ Relevant cultural variables for intercultural HMI design must be determined analytically on the basis of literature research and requirement studies.

Their values represent culture-dependent variations that occur at all levels of HMI localization (surface, functionality, and interaction) (Röse 2002) and can be used for intercultural user interface design (IUID) (Heimgärtner 2007). In 2002 Röse proposed the "Method for Culture-Oriented Design", which integrates the factors of new concepts of culture-oriented HMI design and the knowledge of cultural differences into existing concepts of HMI design.

▸ Empirical qualitative and quantitative studies have shown that culturally influenced user behavior correlates with cultural models.

The cultural interaction indicators determined by the analysis of user interaction can be used for intercultural HMI design guidelines and for intercultural usability engineering to describe the user's needs for HMI depending on his culture as well as to develop an explanatory model for culturally influenced HMI. From the findings of the explanatory model of culturally influenced HMI, implications can be drawn for the derive culturally appropriate product design, which ultimately leads to better usability and higher sales of those products that are equipped with a corresponding HMI for global markets.

▸ There is a measurement system consisting of cultural interaction indicators (CIIs) to measure culturally influenced HMI ("Cultural HMI Style Coefficient"). The characteristics of the CIIs open up interesting tendencies in user interaction behavior in relation to the cultural imprint of the user and serve as guidelines for the development of intercultural user interfaces.

The explanatory model of culturally dependent HMI variables gained so far can be optimized and further developed with the help of statistical methods (such as factor analysis or structural equation models) by revising the relationships between user interaction and user culture. However, there is still a lot of work to be done here (what z. B. the selectivity of the CIIs or the explanatory power of the model). Nevertheless, the ideas presented in this paper represent a reasonable measure towards an explanatory model for culturally influenced HMI, from which areas such as intercultural usability engineering and intercultural user interface design (IUID) can benefit to the extent that the model is developed and validated.

8.3 Outlook

In recent years, research and literature looking at the cultural contexts in human–computer interaction design have grown rapidly (Shen et al. 2006; Plocher et al. 2012). According to Honold (2000) and Röse (2002), successful intercultural HMI design goes far beyond the normal design process by taking into account different

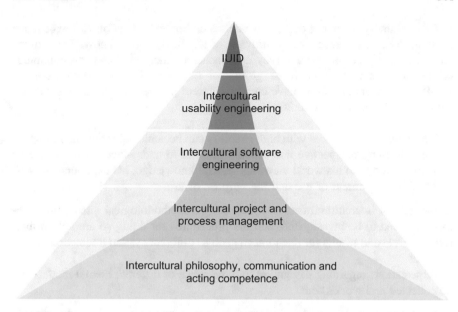

Fig. 8.1 Current status of research in the necessary areas for the development of intercultural user interfaces

mentalities, thought patterns and problem-solving strategies anchored in culture. However, not all relevant areas are adequately covered here yet (Fig. 8.1).

Use patterns differ from culture to culture according to different power structures (cf. Hofstede et al. 2010), e.g., "flat" versus "hierarchical" or according to problem-solving strategies such as "linear" versus "nonlinear" (cf. Röse et al. 2001; Honold 2000). A designer must, therefore, know exactly what a user needs or wants (i.e., why and in what context, cf. Holzinger 2005). To this end, local designers must adapt general HMI methods to their needs (see Clemmensen et al. 2009; Röbig et al. 2010; Bidwell et al. 2011). Sustainable recommendations and guidelines for the capture, design, and evaluation of the issues involved in implementing standard HMI perspectives in local contexts, as practiced by German developers of products for Chinese, can be found in (Heimgärtner and Tiede 2008). Related studies on culture and HMI have been combined by Clemmensen and Roese (2010), Marcus and Baumgartner (2004), Röbig et al. (2010) and (Heimgärtner 2012).

It has now become apparent that traditional approaches, which view culture in HMI only as a question of internationalization or localization, have proved to be seriously inadequate (Clemmensen 2009) because the use of computers has spread and changed worldwide.

▸ "Changing the HMI" means that, beyond the national level, cultural aspects at the local level—the cultural context of the locals—must be taken into account.

Within culturally diverse groups, dependence on context, situation and experience must be taken into account (cf. Bidwell et al. 2011). Such knowledge can be recorded most precisely with survey approaches or methods based on communication, such as interviews, focus groups or questionnaires (cf. Hampe-Neteler 1994). Developers and users have clearly different perspectives in an intercultural context (cf. Eigenbrode et al. 2007).

▶ Only good user interfaces with high usability can be achieved if the HMI designer takes the user's perspective into account in order to understand his requirements in connection with his world view, his general knowledge, his experience as well as within the context of use and the purpose of use.

In the field of intercultural user interface design, methodological intercultural factors still need to be investigated, and the procedures for doing so are still in their infancy. Data and results for phenomena such as different system interaction habits, different
    Expectations regarding navigation in hyperspace or different mental models can be collected and worked out.

▶ It remains crucial to bridge the gap between cultural aspects and the specific aspects of the user interface.

This is due to a lack of empirical research on hidden cultural variables, especially with regard to culturally shaped interaction and intercultural dialogue design.

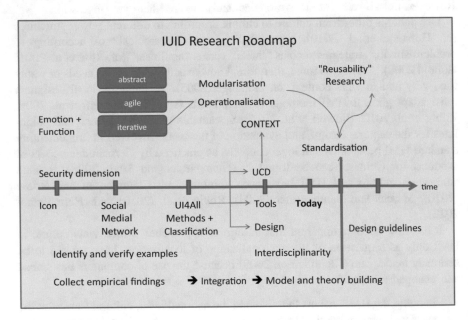

Fig. 8.2 Research roadmap (Excerpt from the results of the IUID workshop "On research in the field of "development of intercultural user interfaces" at the conference "Mensch & Computer 2013")

▸ Precisely because research on culture-oriented HMI design is growing rapidly, it remains extremely important to integrate the results of empirical research into cultural contexts in HMI design and thereby provide the basis for the data, which can serve as input for models and the formulation of theories as well as an evaluation yardstick for their verification.

The research trend towards the development of intercultural user interfaces is in the direction of verifying first preliminary models and theories through exhaustive empirical studies in different cultural (including indigenous) contexts [Fig. 8.2, cf. also "Designing for the Wild" (cf. Rogers 2011)].

Furthermore, the relationship between culture and HMI design must be discussed in detail. The focus of the study of cultural differences will shift from a national to a regional level to any sublevel in order to cover all cultural contexts. Methods, models, and theories will be adapted in the near future and improved by the results of a variety of empirical studies. This will result in new insights into the necessary processes for intercultural HMI design and intercultural usability engineering, which will affect international research and development standards as well as corresponding development tools and thus drive the development of high-quality intercultural user interfaces in practice.

Norms	√
ISO 9241	☐
ISO 9241-10	☐
ISO 9241-11	☐
ISO 9241-110	☐
ISO 9241-210	☐
ISO 9241-220	☐
ISO 9241-12620	☐
ISO9241 -15504	☐
Checklist	√
Consolidate the summary by reading the corresponding chapters where necessary	☐
Take book content to heart in the development of intercultural user interfaces	☐

References

Abdelnour-Nocera J, Kurosu M, Clemmensen T, Bidwell N, Vatrapu R, Winschiers-Theophilus H, Yeo A et al (2011) Re-framing HCI through local and indigenous perspectives. Paper presented at the lecture notes in computer science. Berlin

Balzert H (2005) Grundlagen der Informatik: Konzepte und Notationen in UML 2, Java 5, C+ + und C, Algorithmik und Software-Technik, Anwendungen; with CD-ROM and e-learning-Online-Kurs, 2nd edn. Elsevier Spektrum Akad. Verl., Munich

Baumgartner V-J (2003) A practical set of cultural dimensions for global user-interface analysis and design. Fachhochschule Joanneum, Graz

Bevan N (2001) International standards for HCI and usability. Int J Hum-Comput Stud 55(4):533–552

Bidwell NJ, Winschiers-Theophilus H, Koch Kapuire G, Rehm M (2011) Pushing person-hood into place: situating media in the transfer of rural knowledge in Africa. Int J Hum-Comput Stud 69(10):618–631. (Hrsg Cheverst K, Willis K Special Issue on Locative Media)

Callahan E (2005) Cultural similarities and differences in the design of university web sites. J Comput-Mediat Commun 11(1):239–273

Cassirer E (1994) Nature and effect of the concept of symbol. Scientific Book Society, Darmstadt

Clemmensen T (2009) Towards a theory of cultural usability: a comparison of ADA and CMU theory. In: Publications about culture and human-computer interaction (HCI). In Human work interaction design: usability in social, cultural and organization contexts. IFIP advances in information and communication technology 316/2010. HCD 2009, Held as Part of HCI international 2009, San Diego. July 19–24, S 98–112

Clemmensen T (2012) Usability problem identification in culturally diverse settings. Inf Syst J 22 (2):151–175. https://doi.org/10.1111/j.1365-2575.2011.00381.x

Clemmensen T, Roese K (2010) An overview of a decade of journal publications about culture and human-computer interaction (HCI). In: Katre D, Ørngreen R, Yammiyavar P, Clemmensen T (Hrsg) Human work interaction design: usability in social, cultural and organizational contexts. IFIP advances in information and communication technology, Bd 316. Springer, Berlin, S 98–112

Clemmensen T, Hertzum M, Hornbæk K, Shi Q, Yammiyavar P (2009) Cultural cognition in usability evaluation. Interact Comput 21(3):212–220. https://doi.org/10.1016/j.intcom.2009.05.003

DIN (1996) DIN EN ISO 9241-10 (1996): ergonomics requirements for office work with display screen equipment–Part 10: principles of dialogue design. Berlin/Vienna/Zurich: Beuth-Verlag

DIN (2006) DIN EN ISO 9241-110 Ergonomics of humans-system interaction Part 110: Dialogue principles. Beuth, Berlin

Dormann C (2005) Cultural representations in web design. Paper presented at the people and computers XIX–The bigger picture: proceedings of HCI 2005 (September 5–9, 2005), Edinburgh

Eigenbrode SD, O'Rourke M, Wulfhorst JD, Althoff DM, Goldberg CS, Merrill K, Bosque-PÉRez NA (2007) Employing philosophical dialogue in collaborative science. Bioscience 57(1):55–64. https://doi.org/10.1641/b570109

Evers V (2003) Cross-cultural aspects of user understanding and behaviour: evaluation of a virtual campus website by user from North America, England, the Netherlands and Japan. In: Evers V, Röse K, Honold P, Coronado J, Day D (Hrsg) Proceedings of the fifth international workshop on internationalisation of products and systems, IWIPS 2003, Berlin, 17–19 July 2003. University of Kaiserslautern, Kaiserslautern, S 189–210

Hall ET (1959) The silent language. Doubleday, New York

Hall ET (1976) Beyond culture. Anchor Books, New York

Hampe-Neteler W (1994) Software-ergonomic evaluation between work design and software development, vol 2. Frankfurt a. M.: Lang

Heimgärtner R (2005) Measuring cultural differences in human-computer interaction. In: Auinger A (ed) Workshop-proceedings mensch und computer 2005. OCG Vienna, Vienna, pp 89–92

Heimgärtner R (2007) Cultural differences in human computer interaction: results from two on-line surveys. In: Oßwald A (ed) Open innovation, vol 46. UVK, Konstanz, pp 145–158

Heimgärtner R (2008) A tool for getting cultural differences in HCI. In: Asai K (Hrsg) Human computer interaction: new developments. InTech, Rijeka, S 343–368

Heimgärtner R (2012) Cultural differences in human-computer interaction: towards culturally adaptive human-machine interaction. Oldenbourg, Munich

Heimgärtner R (2014a) Intercultural user interface design. In: Blashki K, Isaias P (Hrsg) Emerging research and trends in interactivity and the human-computer interface. Information Science Reference (an imprint of IGI Global), Hershey, S 1–33

Heimgärtner R (2014b) ISO 9241–210 and culture?–The impact of culture on the standard usability engineering process. In: Aaron M (Hrsg) Design, user experience and usability. User experience design practice: third international conference, DUXU 2014, held as part of HCI international 2014. Heraklion, Crete, Greece, June 22–27, 2014. Proceedings, Part IV. Springer International Publishing, Cham, S 39–48

Heimgärtner R, Tiede LW (2008) Technology and culture: intercultural experience in product development for China. In: Rösch O (ed) Interkulturelle Kommunikation (Technik und Kultur), vol 6. Publisher News & Media, Berlin, pp 149–162

Heimgärtner R, Tiede L-W, Windl H (2011) Empathy as key factor for successful intercultural HCI design. Paper presented at the proceedings of 14th international conference on human-computer interaction, Orlando

Heinecke AM (2004) Human-computer interaction. Reference book edition Leipzig in the Carl Hanser Verl, Munich

Herczeg M (2005) Software ergonomics: basics of human-computer communication, 2nd, fully revised edn. Oldenbourg, Munich

Hodemacher D, Jarman F, Mandl T (2005) Culture and web design: an empirical comparison between Great Britain and Germany. Paper presented at the Mensch & Computer 2005: art and science–crossing the boundaries of interactive ART, Vienna

Hofstede GH, Hofstede GJ, Minkov M (2010) Cultures and organizations: software of the mind, 3 Aufl. McGraw-Hill, Maidenhead

Hoft NL (1995) International technical communication: how to export information about high technology. Wiley, New York

Holzinger A (2005) Usability engineering methods for software developers. Commun ACM 48 (1):71–74. https://doi.org/10.1145/1039539.1039541

Honold P (2000) Intercultural usability engineering: a study on cultural influences on the design and use of technical products, vol 647. VDI Verl, Düsseldorf. (Als Ms. gedr. Hrsg)

International Dr (2003) Developing international software, 2 Aufl. Microsoft Press, Redmond

ISO12620 (1999) Computer applications in terminology: data categories = Computer aids in terminolgy: data categories. ISO, Geneva

Jacko JA, Sears A (2003) The human-computer interaction handbook: fundamentals, evolving technologies and emerging applications. Erlbaum, Mahwah

Jameson A (2007) Adaptive interfaces and agents. In: Jacko JA (Hrsg) 12th international conference on human-computer interaction. Interaction design and usability, HCI international 2007, Beijing, China, July 22–27, 2007. Proceedings, Part I, Bd 4550. Springer, S 305–330

Jetter H-C (2004) Intercultural UI design and UI evaluation. University of Constance, Term paper

Johnson-Laird PN (1983) Mental models: towards a cognitive science of language, inference and consciousness, Bd 6. Harvard University Press, Cambridge

Lewandowitz L, Rößger P, Vöhringer-Kuhnt T (2006) Asian vs. European HMI solutions of driver information systems Useware 2006, vol 1946. VDI, Düsseldorf, S 279–287

Maier E, Mandl T, Röse K, Womser-Hacker C, Yetim F (2005) Internationalization of information systems: cultural aspects of human-machine interaction. In: Auinger A (ed) Workshops-proceedings of the 5th interdisciplinary conference man and computer. OCG, Vienna, pp 57–58

Marcus A (2003) Global and intercultural user interface design. In: The human-computer interaction handbook: fundamentals, evolving technologies and emerging applications. Lawrence Erlbaum Associates, Mahwah

Marcus A (2006) Cross-cultural user-experience design. In: Barker-Plummer D, Cox R, Swoboda N (Hrsg) Diagrammatic representation and inference, Bd 4045. Springer, Berlin, S 16–24

Marcus A (2007) Global/intercultural user-interface design. In: Jacko J, Spears A (Hrsg) The human-computer interaction handbook. Lawrence Erlbaum Associates, Mahwah

Marcus A, Baumgartner V-J (2004) A practical set of culture dimensions for global user-interface development. In: Masood M, Jones S, Bill R (Hrsg) 6th Asia pacific conference on computer human interaction, APCHI 2004. Rotorua, New Zealand, June 29–July 2 2004, Proceedings, S 252–261

Marcus A, Gould EW (2000) Cultural dimensions and global web user-interface design: what? So what? Now what? http://www.amanda.com

Nielsen J (1990) Designing user interfaces for international use, Bd 13. Elsevier, Amsterdam

Nielsen J (1993) Usability engineering. Academic, Boston

Nielsen J (2001) Usability metrics. nngroup. https://www.nngroup.com/articles/usability-metrics/. Accessed 29 Feb 2019

Nielsen J, Molich R (1990) Heuristic evaluation of user interfaces. In: Proceedings of the SI-GCHI conference on human factors in computing systems. ACM, Seattle, S 249–256. https://doi.org/10.1145/97243.97281

Norman DA, Draper S (Hrsg) (1986) User centered system design: new perspectives on human-computer interaction. Lawrence Erlbaum Associates, Hillsdale

Plocher T, Patrick Rau P-L, Choong Y-Y (2012) Cross-cultural design handbook of human factors and ergonomics. Wiley, Hoboken, S 162–191

Rogers Y (2011) Interaction design gone wild: striving for wild theory. Interactions 18(4):58–62. https://doi.org/10.1145/1978822.1978834. Zugegriffen am 26 Sept 2016

Röbig S, Didier M, Brother R (2010) International understanding of usability as well as metrology application in the field of usability. Paper presented at the Grundlagen–Methoden–Technologien, 5th VDI symposium USEWARE 2010, Baden-Baden. http://tubiblio.ulb.tu-darmstadt.en/46312/. Accessed 29 Feb 2019

Röse K (2002) Methodology for the design of intercultural man-machine systems in production engineering, vol 5. Univ, Kaiserslautern

Röse K, Zühlke D (2001) Culture-oriented design: developers' knowledge gaps in this area. Paper presented at the 8th IFAC/IFIPS/IFORS/IEA symposium on analysis, design, and evaluation of human-machine systems, September 18–20, 2001, Kassel

Röse K, Zühlke D, Liu L (2001) Similarities and dissimilarities of German and Chinese users. In: Johannsen G (Hrsg) Preprints of 8th IFAC/IFIP/IFORS/IEA symposium on analysis, design, and evaluation of human-machine systems. Kassel, S 24–29

Sarodnick FF, Brau H (2011) Methods of usability evaluation. Scientific basics and practical application, 2nd, revised and updated edn. Huber, Bern

Shen S-T, Woolley M, Prior S (2006) Towards culture-centred design. Interact Comput 18(4):820–852. https://doi.org/10.1016/j.intcom.2005.11.014

Shi Q, Copenhagen Business School CBS (2010. An empirical study of thinking aloud usability testing from a cultural perspective. Copenhagen Business School (CBS)/ Institut for Informatik (INF)/Department of Informatics. INF, Frederiksberg

Smith A, Dunckley L, French T, Minocha S, Chang Y (2004) A process model for developing usable cross-cultural websites. Interact Comput 16(1):63–91

Stengers H, Troyer O, Baetens M, Boers F, Mushtaha A (2004) Localization of web sites: is there still a need for it? Paper presented at the international workshop on web engineering (HyperText 2004 Conference), Santa Cruz

Sturm C (2002) TLCC-towards a framework for systematic and successful product internationalization. Paper presented at the international workshop on internationalisation of products and systems, Austin/Texas

Sun H (2001) Building a culturally-competent corporate web site: an exploratory study of cultural markers in multilingual web design. In: Proceedings of the 19th annual international conference on computer documentation. ACM, Sante Fe, S 95–102

Thissen F (2008) Intercultural information design. In: Weber W (ed) Compendium Informationsdesign. Springer, Berlin, pp 387–424

Thomas A (1996) Psychology of intercultural action. Hogrefe, Göttingen/Seattle

VDMA (2007) Translation management. VDMA Publishing House, Frankfurt

VDMA (2009) Software Internationalization Guide. VDMA Software Association, Frankfurt a. M.

Vöhringer-Kuhnt T (2002) The influence of culture on usability. MA master thesis, Freie Universität Berlin

Windl H, Heimgärtner R (2013) Intercultural design for use–Extending usage-centered design by cultural aspects. Paper presented at the HCII 2013, Las Vegas

Zerfaß A (2005) Assembling a localization kit. The guide from multilingual computing & technology. Beiheft 75:8–11

Zühlke D (2004) Useware systems for international markets. Useware engineering for technical systems. Springer, Berlin, pp 142–164

Chapter 9
Annex A: Norms and Standards

This annex lists the norms and standards relevant for the development of intercultural user interfaces (IUID) and provides comments. In addition to the UCD standard, further types of standards for HMI and usability are described with regard to terminology and their contextual applicability. Finally, the usability maturity level of organizations and models for determining the maturity level of processes is discussed.

9.1 Norms and Standards Used in Chaps. 1–8

ISO 3166	☐
ISO 8859	☐
ISO 9241	☐
ISO 9241-1	☐
ISO 9241-8	☐
ISO 9241-10	☐
ISO 9241-11	☐
ISO 9241-20	☐
ISO 9241-110 (Dialogue principles)	☐
ISO 9241-171	☐
ISO 9241-210 (Process)	☐
ISO 9241-220	☐
ISO 12620	☐
ISO 15504	☐
DIN 66234	☐
DIN EN 29241-2	☐
DIN EN 62366	☐

(continued)

© Springer Nature Switzerland AG 2019
R. Heimgärtner, *Intercultural User Interface Design*, Human–Computer
Interaction Series, https://doi.org/10.1007/978-3-030-17427-9_9

(continued)

ISO 3166	☐
DIN EN ISO 14915-1 DIN SPEC 33441-100	☐
ISO/TR 16982	☐
ISO/TS 18152	☐
ISO/IEC TR 25060	☐
ISO/IEC 25062	☐
Unicode	☐
GB12345	☐
Shift-JIS	☐
BIG5	☐
KSC	☐

9.2 User-Centered Design Standards

The most important standards for human-centered design can be found in the ISO 9241 standard family. The most relevant parts for professional usability engineering and user interface design are listed in the brochure of the German UPA (cf. references in the occupational field brochure of the German UPA, 2010). Figure 9.1 gives an overview of the first 17 parts, some of which are now available in highly revised form as new parts from 100 upwards (e.g., Part 110 as a successor to Part 11). Based on Nigel Bevan's overview of HMI standards, the main topics for intercultural user interface design are listed and briefly explained.

9.3 Standard Types for HMI and Usability

Standards regarding usability can be categorized as primarily concerned with

1. The use of the product (effectiveness, efficiency, and satisfaction in a particular context of use),
2. The user interface and user interaction,
3. The process used to develop the product,
4. The ability of an organization to apply human-centered design.

Standards for HMI and usability are developed under the auspices of the International Organization for Standardization (ISO) and the International Electrotechnical Commission (IEC). The status of an ISO and IEC document is indicated by the title of the standard. The ISO 9241 standard family refers to hardware and software ergonomics.

9.4   Usability Definitions

ISO 9241-11: Usability control (1998)

This standard (which is part of the ISO 9241 series) provides a definition of usability that is used in the following related ergonomic standards: Usability is the extent to which a product can be used by specific users to achieve specific goals of effectiveness, efficiency, and satisfaction in a specific context of use.

ISO 9241-11 explains how the necessary information can be identified when specifying or evaluating usability in terms of user performance and satisfaction measures. A guideline is given on how to explicitly describe the context of use of the product and the usability measures. This part of the standard includes an explanation of how the usability of a product can be specified and evaluated as part of a quality system that conforms to ISO 9001.

ISO/IEC 9126: Software product evaluation—Quality characteristics and guidelines for their use (1991)

In the software engineering community, the term usability was closely associated with user interface design. ISO/IEC 9126, developed as a software engineering standard, defines usability as a relatively independent contribution to software quality associated with the design and evaluation of the user interface and user interaction.

ISO/IEC FDIS 9126-1: Software engineering—Product quality—Part 1: Quality model (2000)

ISO/IEC 9126 (1991) was replaced by a four-part standard that balances the two approaches to usability. ISO/IEC 9126-1 describes the same six categories of software quality that are relevant during product development: Functionality, reliability, usability, efficiency, maintainability, and portability.

The definition of usability is similar: Usability is the ability of the software product to be understood, learned and applied under certain conditions and to be attractive to the user.

The term "use under certain conditions" (equivalent to the "context of use" in ISO 9241-11) has been added to clarify that a product has no intrinsic usability, but only the ability to be used in a particular context.

The standard now recognizes that usability plays two roles (Bevan 1999): A detailed software design activity (presupposed by the definition of usability) and the general goal that software meets user needs (similar to the concept of usability in ISO 9241-11). ISO/IEC 9126-1 uses the term "quality of use" for this broad objective.

Quality in use is the combined effect of the six categories of software quality in product use. The general goal is to achieve quality in use, both for the end user and the supporting user. Functionality, reliability, efficiency, and usability determine the quality of use for an end user in a particular context. The support user is concerned with the quality of use with regard to maintainability and portability tasks. Other parts of ISO/IEC 9126 define metrics for usability and quality of dialogues.

The term "serviceability metrics" refers to the use of a product, i.e., usability metrics and quality metrics.

9.5   Application in Context

ISO/IEC DTR 9126-4: Software engineering—Product quality—Part 4: Quality in application metrics (2001)

This technical report contains sample metrics for effectiveness, productivity, safety, and satisfaction. Specifying usability requirements and verifying that they have been achieved in a usability test is an important component of user-centric design (ISO 13407). ISO/IEC 9126-4 recommends metrics for effectiveness, productivity, satisfaction, and security that can be used for this purpose. The results can be documented using the common industry format for usability test reports, which is contained in the form of an example template in the appendix of ISO/IEC 9126-4.

ISOWS 20282: Usability of everyday products (2001)

A multi-part standard to specify the information on usability that should be given for a consumer product so that a consumer can assess the usability of the product (Bevan and Schoeffel 2001).

9.6   Software Interface and Interaction

Standards can be used to support user interface development as follows:

1. ISO 14915 and IEC 61997 contain recommendations for multimedia interfaces. From this, details on the appearance and behavior of the user interface can be derived. More specific guidance can be found for icons in ISO/IEC 11581, for PDAs in ISO/IEC 18021, and for cursor control in ISO/IEC 10741.
2. They provide detailed guidance for the design of user interfaces (ISO 9241 Parts 12–17).
3. They contain criteria for the evaluation of user interfaces (ISO/IEC 9126 Parts 2 and 3).

ISO 9241: Ergonomic requirements for office work with visual display terminals

ISO 9241 provides requirements and recommendations regarding the attributes of the hardware, software, and environment that can contribute to usability. Parts 10 and 12–17 deal specifically with the attributes of the software. Parts 14–17 should be used by both designers and evaluators of user interfaces. But the focus is mainly on the designer.

The standards provide an authoritative source of references, but designers without usability experience have great difficulty applying these types of guidelines (de Souza and Bevan 1990). To apply directives successfully, designers must understand the design objectives and benefits of each directive, the conditions under which the directive should be applied, the precise nature of the proposed solution and any procedures that must be followed to apply the directive.

Several checklists have been prepared to measure the conformity of the software with the main principles of ISO 9241 (Gediga 1999; Oppermann and Reiterer 1997; Prümper 1999).

Part 10: Principles of dialogue (1996)

This part deals with the general ergonomic principles applicable to the design of dialogues between people and information systems: Task measurement, learning facilitation, individualization, expectation conformity, self-descriptiveness, controllability, and fault tolerance.

Part 12: Information presentation (1998)

This section contains recommendations for presenting and representing information on visual displays. It contains a guide to ways in which complex information can be represented using alphanumeric and graphic/symbolic codes, screen layout and design, and the use of windows.

Part 13: User manual (1998)

This part contains recommendations for the design and evaluation of attributes of the user manual of software user interfaces, including operator notes, feedback, status, online support, and error management.

Part 14: Menu dialogues (1997)

This section provides recommendations for designing menus used in user–computer dialogues. The recommendations cover the menu structure, navigation, option selection and execution, as well as menu presentation (through numerous techniques including windowing, panels, buttons, fields, etc.).

Part 15: Command dialogues (1997)

This section provides recommendations for the design of command languages applied in user–computer dialogues. The recommendations cover command language structure and -syntax, command representation, input and output considerations, feedback, and help.

Part 16: Dialogues of direct manipulation (1999)

This part provides recommendations for the ergonomic design of direct manipulation dialogues and includes the manipulation of objects and the design of metaphors, objects, and attributes. It covers those aspects of graphical user interfaces that are directly manipulated and not covered by other parts of ISO 9241.

Part 17: Dialogues in Forms (1998)

This section provides recommendations for the ergonomic design of formulating dialogues. The recommendations cover the form structure and output views, input views, and form navigation.

ISO/IEC 9126: Software Engineering—Product Quality

ISO/IEC 9126-1 defines usability in terms of comprehensibility, learnability, practicability, and attractiveness. Parts 2 and 3 contain examples of metrics for these characteristics. These can be used to specify and evaluate detailed usability criteria.

Part 2: External metrics (DTR: 2001)

This technical report describes metrics that can be used to evaluate the performance of the software when it is used by the user. For instance: How long does it take to learn to use a function? Can users undo functions? Can users react appropriately to error messages?

Part 3: Internal metrics (DTR: 2001)

This technical report describes metrics that can be used to create requirements that describe static peculiarities of the interface that can be evaluated by acceptance without operating the software. For instance: What ratio of functions is documented? How many functions can be undone? How many error messages are self-explanatory?

ISO/IEC 11581 Icon symbols and functions

Part 1: Icons—General (2000)

This part contains a framework for the development and design of icons, including general requirements and recommendations, applicable to all icons.

Part 2: Object icons (2000)

This part contains requirements and recommendations for icons that represent functions by association with an object, and that can be moved and opened. It also contains specifications for the function and appearance of 20 icons.

Part 3: Note Icons (2000)

This part contains requirements and recommendations for eight common hint icons that represent a hint associated with a physical input device.

Part 4: Control icons (CD: 1999)

This part contains requirements and recommendations for 14 common control icons that allow the user to operate in windows, lists, and other graphical elements.

Part 5: Tool icons (FCD: 2000)

This part contains requirements and recommendations for 20 common tool icons and specifies the relationships between the tool and hint icons.

Part 6: Action icons (1999)

This part contains requirements and recommendations for 23 common icons, which are typically used for toolbars that represent actions in conjunction with objects that help the user retrieve the desired actions.

ISO/IEC 10741-1: Dialogue Interaction—Cursor Control for Text Editing (1995)

This standard specifies how the cursor should move on the screen according to the use of the cursor control keys.

ISO/IEC FCD 18021: Information Technology—User Interface for Mobile Tools (2001)

This standard contains user interface specifications for PDAs with data exchange capability with corresponding servers.

ISO 14915: Software ergonomics for multimedia user interfaces

Part 1: Design principles and framework (DIS: 2000)
   This part provides a complete introduction to the standard.
   Part 2: Multimedia control and navigation (CD: 2000)
   This section provides recommendations for navigation structures and aids, media controls, basic controls, media control policies for dynamic media, and controls and navigation involving multiple media.
   Part 3: Media selection and combination (DIS: 2000)
   This part provides general guidelines for media selection and combination, media selection for information types, media combination and integration, and directing user attention.
   Part 4: Domain-specific multimedia interfaces (AWI)
   This part covers computer-based training, computer-assisted collaborative work, kiosk systems, online help and testing, and evaluation.

IEC CDV TR 61997: Guidelines for user interfaces in multimedia equipment for universal use (2000)

This technical report provides general principles and detailed design guidance for media selection and mechanical, graphical, and auditory user interfaces.

Hardware Interface

These standards can be used in the design and evaluation of workstations, screens, keyboards, and other input devices. Unlike software standards, most of these standards contain explicit requirements. ISO 9241 and ISO 13406 contain requirements for visual display terminals in offices. These standards can be used to support compliance with European guidelines for the use of display screens (Bevan 1991). Gestures for pen-based systems are covered in ISO/IEC 14754. ISO 11064 contains ergonomic requirements for the design of control centers.

ISO 9241: Ergonomic requirements for office work with visual display terminals

Parts 3 through 9 contain hardware design requirements and instructions. Part 3: Visual Display—Requirements (1992)
   This part specifies the ergonomic requirements for display screens that ensure that these can be read comfortably, safely and efficiently to perform office tasks. Although this part specifically deals with displays used in offices, it is also useful for most applications that require the use of universal displays in office-like environments.

Part 4: Keyboard requirements (1998)

This part specifies the ergonomic design characteristics of an alphanumeric keyboard that can be used conveniently, securely, and efficiently to perform office tasks. Keyboard layouts are handled separately in many parts of ISO/IEC 9995: Information Processing—Keyboard Layouts for Text and Office Systems (1994).

Part 5: Workplace Layout and Posture Requirements (1998)

This part specifies the ergonomic requirements for a Visual Display Terminal workstation that allows the user to adopt a comfortable and efficient posture.

Part 6: Guidance on the working environment (1999)

This section provides a guide to setting up the Visual Display Terminal working environment (including lighting, noise, temperature, vibration, and electromagnetic fields) to provide the user with comfortable, safe, and productive working conditions.

Part 7: Requirements for displays with reflection (1998)

This part specifies measurement methods of glare effects and reflections from the surface of the display screen, including those with treated surfaces. It is aimed at display manufacturers who want to ensure that anti-reflection treatments do not degrade image quality.

Part 8: Requirements for the colors shown (1997)

This part specifies the requirements for multicolor displays, in addition to the monochrome requirements in Part 3.

Part 9: Requirements for input devices without a keyboard (2000)

This part specifies the ergonomic requirements for keyboardless input media that can be used in conjunction with a Visual Display Terminal. It covers devices like mouse, trackball, and other pointing instruments. It also includes a performance test. It does not refer to language input.

ISO 13406: Ergonomic requirements for working with visual displays based on flat panels

Part 1: Introduction (1999)

Part 2: Ergonomic requirements for flat panel displays (2001)

This standard establishes the ergonomic image quality requirements for the design and evaluation of flat panel displays and specifies methods for determining the image quality.

ISO AWI 18789: Ergonomic requirements and measurement techniques for electronic visual displays (1999)

This standard is intended to correct and replace ISO 9241 Parts 3, 7, and 8 and ISO 13406.

ISO/IEC 15754: Pen-based interfaces—Common gestures for text editing with pen-based systems (1999)

This standard defines a set of basic gesture commands and feedback for pen interfaces. The gestures include select, delete, insert space, split, move, copy, cut, paste, scroll, and undo rows.

ISO 11064: Ergonomic design of control centers

This eight-part standard contains ergonomic principles, recommendations, and guidelines.

Part 1: Principles for the design of control centers (2000)
Part 2: Principles for the construction of the control suite (2000)
Part 3: Control room layout (1999)
Part 4: Workplace layout and dimensions (CD:2000)
Part 5: Human–system interfaces (WD: 1999)
Part 6: Environmental requirements for control rooms (WD: 2000)
Part 7: Principles for the evaluation of control centers (WD: 2000)
Part 8: Ergonomics requirements for specific applications (WD: 2000)

Documentation

ISO/IEC 15910 provides a detailed process for the development of a user documentation (written and online help, often referred to (not quite aptly because the user is not documented) as "user documentation"), while ISO/IEC 18019 provides more guidance on how to produce the documentation that meets the user's needs.

ISO/IEC 15910: Software User Documentation Process (1999)

This standard specifies the minimum process for creating user documentation for software that has a user interface, including a printed presentation (e.g., user manuals (better "user manual") and quick reference cards), online documentation, help text, and online documentation systems.

ISO/IEC WD 18019: Guidelines for the Design and Preparation of Software User Documentation (2000)

This standard describes how to establish what information users need, how to determine the way in which this information should be presented to users, and how to prepare the information in order to make it accessible. It covers both online and printed documentation and was developed from two British standards:

   BS 7649: Guidelines for the design and preparation of documentation for users of application software (1993)
   BS 7830: Guidelines for Design and Preparation of Screen Documentation for Application Software Users (1996).

The Development Process

ISO 13407 explains the activities required for user-centric design and ISO 16982 discusses the types of methods that can be used. ISO/IEC 1458 provides a general framework for the evaluation of software products using the model in ISO/IEC 9126-1. ISO 13407 has been revised and optimized and newly published using ISO 9241-210.

ISO 13407: Human-centered design processes for interactive systems (1999) and ISO 9241-210, respectively

This standard provides a guide to human-centered design activities throughout the life cycle of interactive computer-based systems. It is a tool for those who control design processes and provides a guide of information sources and standards relevant to the human-centric approach. It describes human-centered design as a multidisciplinary activity that combines human factors and ergonomic knowledge and techniques with the aim of increasing effectiveness and efficiency, improving human working conditions and counteracting the possible negative effects of application on human health, safety and performance. The recommended process is shown below:

The EU-funded INUSE project has developed a more detailed procedure and set of criteria that can be used to assess how strictly a development process follows the principles of ISO 13407. The TRUMP project has proposed specific methods for user-centric design based on ISO 13407.

ISO DTR 16982: Usability Methods for the Support of Human-Centered Design (2001)

This technical report highlights the different types of usability methods that can be used to support user-centric design.

ISO/IEC 14598: Information Technology—Evaluation of Software Products (1998–2000)

This multi-standard specifies the process to be used to evaluate software products.

9.7 Capability of the Organization

The usability maturity model in ISO TR 18529 contains a structured set of processes derived from ISO 13407 and a recognized survey. It can be used to measure the extent to which an organization is capable of performing user-centric design. Each HCD process (such as "specifying user and organizational requirements") can be evaluated against the ISO 15504 software process evaluation scale: Incomplete, Performed, Controlled, Established, Predictable, Optimized (Earthy et al. 2001).

ISO TR 18529: Ergonomics of human–system interaction—Human-centered life cycle process descriptions (2000)

This technical report contains a structured and formalized list of human-centered processes:

HCD.1 Ensure HCD content in system strategy
HCD.2 Plan and control HCD process
HCD.3 Specify user and organizational requirements

HCD.4 Understand and specify context of use
HCD.5 Create design solutions
HCD.6 Balance designs against requirements
HCD.7 Introduce and use the system

The usability maturity model in ISO TR 18529 is based on the model developed by the INUSE project.

Other Related Standards

ISO 9241-1: Ergonomic requirements for office work with visual display terminals (VDTs)—Part 1: General introduction (1997)

This part introduces the ISO 9241 multipart standard for ergonomic requirements for the use of visual display terminals for office tasks and explains some of the basic principles. It provides guidance on how to use the standard and describes how compliance with parts of ISO 9241 should be reported.

ISO 9241-2: Part 2: Guidance on task requirements (1992)

This section covers the design of tasks and jobs that involve working with visual display terminals. It provides guidance on how to identify and specify task requirements within individual organizations, and how task requirements can be merged with the system design and implementation process.

ISO 10075-1: Ergonomic principles relating to mental workload—General terms and definitions (1994)

This part of ISO 10075 explains the terminology and provides definitions on the mental workload.

ISO DTS 16071: Guidance on accessibility for human–computer interfaces (2000)

This technical specification (derived from ANSI HFS 200) provides guidelines and recommendations for the design of systems and software that enable users with limitations to more easily access the computer system (with or without assistive technology). It includes users with impaired vision, hearing impaired users, deaf users, users with physical and cognitive impairments and older users.

How do you get international standards?

ISO standards must be acquired. They can be purchased directly from ISO, or from a national standard institute. NSSN: A national source of global standards also has an extensive list of standards, some of which can be acquired electronically (see Table 9.1). In principle, ISO standard drafts can also be acquired.

In Germany, Beuth Verlag distributes all DIN and ISO standards—often in handy, thematically organized editions.

Table 9.1 National standards	National Standards
	BSI: British Standards Institute
	ANSI: American National Standards Institute
	ANSI HCI standards (IMB list)

Support for Jurisprudence

The European Display Screen Equipment Directive (EEC 1990) specifies a minimum of ergonomic requirements for workplace equipment and environment. These can be fulfilled by adhering to ISO 9241 Parts 3–9. The directive also requires that the "principles of software ergonomics" be applied in the design of user interfaces. ISO 9241 Part 10 contains appropriate principles. The other requirements for the user-friendliness of software can be met by considering Parts 12–17.

The Machinery Directive (EC 1998) requires that suppliers offer machines that meet essential health and safety requirements, one of which is that interactive software must be "user-friendly". Countries of the European Union have a national jurisdiction that implements these directives.

9.8   CHMI and SPICE

ISO 15504 describes capability levels of process areas in degrees or levels from 1 to 5. The process areas comprise both performance, value-added and support processes. Appropriate tools support the HMI development process (e.g., Methodpark stages). Assessments and continuous process improvement are an everyday business (see van Loon 2007). Every member of the project team knows the current process and its optimization potential. With a seamless software development process, errors can be avoided. The quality of the products as the result of a better process increases continuously and sustainably (see Heimgärtner, Solanki, Windl: "Cultural User Experience in Cars—Towards a Standardized Systematic Intercultural Automotive UI-UX Design Process", published in 2017).

Reference

van Loon H (2007) Process assessment and ISO/IEC 15504. A reference book. Springer, New York

Chapter 10
Appendix B: Checklists

By combining the checklists of this book in this appendix, the state of knowledge on the IUID topic can be reviewed, deepened, and applied in practice. In addition, further II18N/L10N checklists are available for the localization process, translation, SW localization, documentation, and usability testing in an intercultural context. In addition, further tips and information on information processing in Asia (CJKV checklist, Unicode) as well as on the translation of user interfaces are given. Design and evaluation criteria for intercultural user interfaces complete the chapter.

© Springer Nature Switzerland AG 2019
R. Heimgärtner, *Intercultural User Interface Design*, Human–Computer
Interaction Series, https://doi.org/10.1007/978-3-030-17427-9_10

10.1   Checklists from Chaps. 1–8

10.1.1   Introduction

Norms	√
ISO 9241	☐
Checklist	√
Conceptual knowledge	☐
· Product	☐
· Process	☐
· User Interface (UI)	☐
· Internationalization (I18N)	☐
· Localization (L10N)	☐
· Intercultural User Interface Design (IUID)	☐
IUID includes or builds on the following areas:	☐
· Interculturalphilosophy, communication and action competence	☐
· Intercultural project, process and quality management	☐
· Intercultural software engineering	☐
· Intercultural usability engineering	☐
Do you want to develop user interfaces of products for target markets of other cultures or get to know the process of intercultural HMI design? Then read this book!	☐

10.1.2 Thinking and Acting

Norms	√
ISO 3166	☐

Checklist	√
Team (at least key roles) was trained in intercultural action competence	☐
Team members are familiar with their own culture	☐
There are no fears of contact with other cultures in the team Team has	☐
been trained in intercultural communication Project managers have	☐
relevant intercultural project experienceEthno-centred thinking and	☐
procedures are avoided	☐
Culture models are known and used to describe cultures	☐
Different cultural understanding of quality is taken into account	☐
Methods of intercultural projects, process and quality management are known and are applied	☐

10.1.3   *Software Engineering*

Norms	√
ISO 9241-210	☐

Checklist	√
Cooperation with other cultures is mindset of the team	☐
Team is trained in intercultural communication and action competence	☐
SW development team is trained in intercultural software engineering	☐
Team (at least owners of process roles with pronounced intercultural contact) are trained in intercultural project management (e.g. PM, QM, TM, RM)	☐
HMI developers are trained in intercultural usability engineering and UI design.	☐
Planning system adapted to target culture	☐
Requirements analysis is culturally appropriate (not ethnocentric, empathic, systematic, culture-oriented)	☐
Context of use (user, tasks, system and environment) were determined and described with adequate means for (inter-)cultural context determination	☐
User requirement were derived and specified with adequate means for the (inter-)cultural context.	☐
Methods of internationalization and localization are familiar to the team	☐
Team knows the possible cultural influences on the context of use (users, tasks, etc.), environment, technology) and on product design (information architecture and interaction design) and acts accordingly.	☐
Team knows potential recommendations for the development of intercultural user interfaces (e.g. intercultural design guidelines)	☐
team is familiar with the TLCC model and is guided by it.	☐
Team knows the core elements of localization	☐
Localization KIT available	☐
Localization tools are known and used	☐
Intercultural differences in quality are known and there is a corresponding understanding of quality.	☐
Relevant norms and standards are used and taken into account in the intercultural context (e.g. assessed and used on the basis of cultural dimensions).	☐
Problems with the evaluation of intercultural user interfaces are known and recommendations are taken into account.	☐

10.1.4   Usability Engineering

Norms	√
ISO 3166	☐
DIN 66234	☐
ISO 9241-8	☐
ISO 9241-10	☐
ISO 9241-11	☐
DIN EN ISO 9241-110 (Dialogue principles)	☐
ISO 9241-210 (process)	☐

Checklist	√
The principle of human-machine interaction is well known ☐	
Concepts and sense of ergonomics, usability and user experience are known and introduced ☐	
Users, tasks, context and technology are considered (PACT) ☐	
Dialogue principles or usability heuristics are used and applied ☐	
Usability and user experience of the system are given ☐	
Influence of culture on usability is known	☐
Influence of culture on usability engineering is well known	☐
· Process	☐
· methods	☐
· Use of the	☐
· interpretation	☐
· documentation	☐
The influence of culture on the dialogue principles and their application is well known.	☐
Basic methods and approaches of intercultural usability engineering are well known and organizationally installed.	☐

10.1.5 *User Interface Design*

Norms √
DIN EN 29241-2 ☐
DIN EN 62366 ☐
DIN EN ISO 9241-1 ☐
DIN EN ISO 9241-11 ☐
DIN EN ISO 9241-20 ☐
DIN EN ISO 9241-110 ☐
DIN EN ISO 9241-171 ☐
DIN EN ISO 9241-210 ☐
DIN EN ISO 9241-220 ☐
DIN EN ISO 14915-1 ☐
DIN SPEC 33441-100 ☐
ISO/TR 16982 ☐
ISO/TS 18152 ☐
ISO/IEC TR 25060 ☐

ISO/IEC 25062 ☐

Checklist √

The basics of the intercultural user interface design are known (Cultural

Influences on the context of use (PACT), Significant new findings from research are ☐
   available)

Level 1 of intercultural user interface design achieved (cultural differences in language and symbols ☐
   taken into account)

Level 2 of intercultural user interface design achieved (cultural behavior considered) ☐

Level 3 of intercultural user interface design achieved (cultural values considered) ☐
Level 1 of the TLCC model is implemented (Technology) ☐

Level 2 of the TLCC model is implemented (language) ☐

Level 3 of the TLCC model is implemented (culture) ☐

Level 4 of the TLCC model is implemented (cognition) ☐

Relevant cultural dimensions for HMI development are known ☐

User interface characteristics are known and applied ☐

HMI dimensions are known and applied ☐

The relationship between cultural dimensions and HMI dimensions is reflected and integrated in the ☐
   Design process included

Intercultural variables are known and used ☐

Method of culture-oriented design is applied systematically ☐

Challenges in the Application of Methods and Approaches of Intercultural Usability ☐
      Engineerings and corresponding solutions are well known (data-driven,
      hypothesis-driven and hybrid approaches)

Procedure for the creation of explanatory models for the connection between culture ☐
   and human-machine interaction is well known.

Empathy as a key factor in the development of intercultural user interfaces is ☐
   is known and applied

The possibility of using agile methods in the development of intercultural ☐
      User interfaces are known

10.1.6   IUID in Theory—Scientific Research

Norms	√
ISO 9241-171	☐
ISO 9241-210	☐
ISO 9241-220	☐

Checklist	**√**
Insight into the state of IUID research has been gained	☐
Data-driven approach is well known and is applied	☐
Hypothesis-driven approach is well known and is applied	☐
Hybrid approach (IUID method mix) is known and applied	☐
· Cultural Models	☐
· Intercultural variable	☐
· user interface features	☐
· HMI Dimensions	☐
Possible connections between HMI dimensions and cultural dimensions are known.	☐
Concepts "culture-dependent explanatory model" and "structural equation model" are well	☐
known Methodological challenges of the IUID are well known	☐
· Cultural complexity	☐
· Different approaches	☐
· Increased research expenditure	☐
· Low empirical confirmation	☐
· Use of cultural dimensions controversial	☐
Insight into future IUID research gained	☐

10.1.7   IUID in Practice—Industrial Development

Norms	√
ISO 15504	☐
ISO 9241-210	☐
ISO 12620	☐
ISO 8859	☐
Unicode	☐
GB12345	☐
Shift JIS	☐
BIG5	☐
KSC	☐

Checklist	√
Activities in the global product development process are well known	☐
The meaning and contents of the process phases (requirements analysis, design and evaluation) are well known and are embodied	☐
Usage Centered Design approach is known	☐
Team knows the relationship between software engineering and usability engineering and embodies the interfaces between the processes	☐
Tools for I18N and L10N are well known and are used	☐
Intercultural interaction analysis is well known and is performed using a tool (e.g. IIA Tool); results are considered in information architecture and interaction design	☐
Description of context of use and specification of user requirements are available	☐
Model for culture-dependent HMI design is known and used	☐
Recommendations for intercultural HMI design are considered	☐
Intercultural software quality assurance measures (e.g. the L10N/I18N) are known and are performed	☐
Intercultural software ergonomic quality assurance measures (e.g. intercultural usability tests) are known and are performed	☐
Culture-dependent and culture-independent evaluation methods are known and used correctly	☐
Problems with the evaluation of intercultural user interfaces are known and recommendations are considered	☐

10.1.8 *Summary, Conclusion, Outlook*

Norms	√
ISO 9241	☐
ISO 9241-10	☐
ISO 9241-11	☐
ISO 9241-110	☐
ISO 9241-210	☐
ISO 9241-220	☐
ISO 9241-12620	☐
ISO 9241-15504	☐
Checklist	**√**
Consolidate the summary by reading the corresponding chapters where necessary	☐
Take book content to heart in the development of intercultural user interfaces	☐

10.2 General I18N-L10N Checklist

The following are various checklists for the interculturalization of user interfaces with a rather general character. These include process, language, software, and documentation (see Irina Spitznagel 2001, Internationalization of Software as a Prerequisite for Localization).

Account must be taken of:

- Interaction elements (the BOF, the program, enclosed examples, installation routine, etc.),
- Documentation (online help, manual, tutorials, etc.),
- Packaging, CD labeling, warranty cards, etc.,
- Text, graphics and sounds, formats, determinations,
- Dialogue box, menu, status bar, toolbar, tooltip, error messages.

You have to create a localization kit, which includes the following:

- Software including documentation,

- Build environments of software and online help,
- Glossaries,
- Guidelines for language and style, etc.,
- Checklists,
- Project tracking documents,
- Localized previous versions.

Internationalization concerns:

- Character sets,
- Sorting,
- Hardware support,
- Audio files,
- Formats (date and time, numbers, currencies, units of measurement, paper formats, address formats),
- Pictures,
- Language.

I18N rules:

- No concatenation of texts,
- Separation of program code and data/texts,
- Allow resizing,
- Avoid text in images.

10.2.1   Localization Process

Make sure you go through all the steps of the entire localization process:

- Pre-sales phase,
- Kick-off meeting,
- Analysis of the purchasing material,
- Scheduling and budgeting,
- Terminology setup,
- Preparation of source materials,
- Software translation,
- Engineering and software testing,
- Screenshots,
- Help engineering and DTP of the documentation,
- Translation of online help and documentation,
- Process updates,
- Product quality assurance and delivery,
- Project closure.

10.2.2   *Language*

Terminology
Glossary, consistency.

Style
Clear, unambiguous, short active sentences, no culture-specific text, no time references, no acronyms and abbreviations, conversion of units of measurement.

Expansion
Enough space for text in vertical direction.

Country-Specific Elements
Completely write out data, different calendars and address formats, use of globally known, general examples.

10.2.3   *Software*

Character Set Support
Use international sorting standards, multi-byte support, cut/paste functionality between applications, open/save files with multi-byte characters and names; use international code sets for input and output.

Identification of the Entities to be Translated
Consider all resource files and include files (bitmaps, symbols) that require localization, avoid too many separate resource files, use variable names with "unreal" words, provide a context for translators in code using comments, remove all untranslatable text strings from resource files.

User Interface Design
Allow text extension by buffers of sufficient size, avoid \n for manual text encapsulation, avoid concatenation of strings at runtime, do not "hard" code keyboard commands, string variables must not have grammatical endings, key combinations must be accessible from any keyboard; third-party controls must be localizable, use generic images, pay attention to colors, no text in bitmaps and icons; insert additional spaces when using variables within a string.

Local Support
DBCS (Double-Byte Character Sets) for Asian languages to allow users to input, store, retrieve, distribute, display and print DBCS languages; use IME (Input Method Editor) for Asian languages, use the language support of each operating system, and the corresponding different calendar, date, time and number formats, different currencies, weights and measures, international paper and envelope sizes, and address formats.

10.2.4 Documentation

Creation
Use appropriate applications for document type, target languages, output formats, use design templates and standard or combined fonts, ensure consistency in text flow, links, and styles, use computer-aided translation (CAT) tools.

Use
No manual hard line breaks in running text, index marks outside the sentence, no manual hyphenation, import of graphics using references, no conditional text, single text flow, no product delivery without review and approval, keep documents (or chapters) shorter than 50 pages.

Graphics
Generic and internationally accepted graphics, graphics with text over a separate text layer, use standard color scheme and font settings; make sure screen captures are reproducible, link graphics instead of embedding them, no outline text in graphics.

10.2.5 Usability Test

- Application of checklists and guidelines to the product,
- Mäeutic development (method of Socrates to help people to get the desired solution by themselves) of an own product-related kit,
- Summary, lessons learned, and final discussion,
- Check all I18N/L10N guidelines and checklists,
- Think about what to do and how to do it (e.g., architectural change),
- Read further literature,
- Answer product-related questions,
- Discussion of interesting aspects or open points,
- Definition of topics for further promotional measures (usability course, etc.),
- Avoidance of inconsistencies, etc.,
- Survey of cultural preferences with the help of tools (especially IIA tool(s)),
- Choice of the right tools,
- Use of external know-how where necessary,
- Examine which methods and tools are right for determining user preferences for intercultural HMI design,
- Elucidation of cultural differences (methodology and content),
- Use of suitable aids (tools).

10.3 Tips for Translating User Interfaces

10.3.1 General Information

Since the text to be translated within the strings is usually enclosed in quotation marks (" "), you should avoid using them within the text or delete them in the original. The use of the character (&) should be avoided as this can confuse the compiler and cause hotkey malfunctions. If it must be used anyway, it should be set twice or replaced ("&&"). It is often advisable not to change the date, time, or number format in the source files, even if they are to be adapted to the target language at runtime. The reason is that these formats sometimes must remain unchanged in order to retain the correct formats from the operating system. File names or extensions are only transferred if the software provider expressly requests it (e.g., "Readme.txt"). When working with online help source files, hidden text must never be translated, changed or moved. Only the terms linked with hidden text or tags can be moved if the grammar requires it. Coding elements such as references to screen dumps, index placeholders, encodings, or formatting tags may not be translated, modified, or deleted. Do not sort the icons until the files have been converted back to their original format. Do not delete or insert line or page breaks or word separations and do not adjust lines manually. Use the Search and Replace function carefully, as a translation can overwrite a hidden part of the text, which can be difficult to correct. Document settings should not be changed. Examples of this are: Tab stops, margins, page size, line spacing, paragraph spacing, templates, etc.

10.3.2 Language and Style

When translating a function or option of software, the meaning must first be clarified before one becomes creative, not vice versa. It must be ensured that the translation of software strings within and between software products is consistent. For frequently used operating systems (e.g., Apple Mac OS, Microsoft Word, etc.), there is a standard terminology that should be adhered to. In news, the use of the first and second person is to be avoided. If terminology and style specifications are available, the translators should adhere to them. In addition, they should try to create their own terminology list with translations of common terms or phrases from the text. This list should be approved by the project manager or software vendor. Culture-specific information should be adapted to the target market. These are: Information hotlines, popular sports, holidays, etc. As far as style is concerned, active and imperative are suitable for technical texts; passive and sentences with many nouns are to be avoided. The style to be applied should be agreed upon by the translation/localization team before the start of the translation, e.g., acronyms, lists (numbered or enumerated), capitalization, spelling of numbers, style to be used for image captions, etc. In order to translate the software links within the text, the application itself should already be translated. If this is not the case, it is advisable to leave all software references untranslated and change them afterward.

10.3.3   Elements Not to Be Translated

Strings can contain parts with elements that should not be translated. Some of these elements are: Capitalized terms (e.g., EDIT), terms containing underscores (e.g., size_is) and combinations of terms (e.g., ConnCount). However, it must be noted that the distinction between string elements to be translated and string elements not to be translated is not always easy. In such cases, the help of a software developer may be useful.

10.3.4   Quality Assurance Tips

In order to make sure that the online help works correctly, you should proofread the online help, especially with regard to the following elements: Table of Contents: All translated points of the table of contents should correspond to the actual headings in the online help document and tree structures should correspond to the actual headings in the online help document. The sequence of the contents in the document must be the same.

Graphics: Since graphics are usually linked and not embedded, they do not become visible to translators until the source help files are compiled. The translators should check if all graphics are localized, if the text refers to the images, if the graphics contain callouts with image descriptions (in this case the references and the localized images must be consistent), etc.

Tables: Tables should be checked because translation memory tools often display them in a different format than the compiled help file (see Esselink 2000, pp. 65–172). The user interfaces should always be localized first and only then the associated documents (online help, websites and written documents) should be created in order to avoid inconsistencies in terminology.

10.4   CJKV

The following aspects must be considered when designing user interfaces for China, Japan, Korea, and Vietnam (CJKV) (more information can be found in Lunde (2009). CJKV information processing. O'Reilly Media, Inc., Sebastopol, CA.):

- Multiple writing systems,
- Writing systems,
- Latin characters and transliteration,
- Zhuyin,
- Kana,
- Hangul,
- Chinese characters,
- Non-Chinese Chinese characters,
- Character set standards,
- Non-coded character set standards,
- Coded character set standards,
- International character set standards,
- Character set standard oddities,
- Non-coded versus coded character sets,
- Information interchange versus professional publishing,
- Advice to developers,
- Encoding methods,
- Locale-independent encoding methods,
- Locale-specific encoding methods,
- Comparing CJKV encoding methods,
- International encoding methods,
- Charset designations,
- Code pages,
- Code conversion,
- Repairing unreadable CJKV text,
- Beware of Little- and Big-Endian issues,
- Input methods,
- Transliteration techniques,
- Input techniques,
- User interface concerns,
- Keyboard arrays,
- Other input hardware,
- Input method software,
- Font formats,
- Typeface design issues,
- Bitmapped fonts,
- Outline fonts,
- Ruby fonts,
- Host-based versus printer-resident fonts,
- Creating your own fonts,
- External character handling,
- Typography (→also the contents of the DTP document!),
- Typographic units and measurements,
- Horizontal and vertical layout,
- Line breaking and word wrapping,

- Character spanning,
- Alternative metrics,
- Kerning,
- Line length issues,
- Multilingual text,
- Glyph substitution,
- Annotations,
- Typographic software,
- Output methods,
- Font memory,
- Printer output,
- PostScript CJKV printers,
- Computer monitor output,
- Other printing methods,
- Printer drivers,
- Output management,
- Information processing techniques,
- Language, country, and script codes,
- Programming languages,
- Code conversion algorithms,
- Miscellaneous algorithms,
- Byte versus character handling,
- Character sorting,
- Natural language processing,
- Regular expressions,
- Search engines,
- Code processing tools,
- Basic concepts and terminology,
- Environment and tools,
- Viewing CJKV text on non-CJKV systems,
- Operating systems,
- Hybrid environments,
- Text editors,
- Word processors,
- Internet and WWW,
- Content versus presentation,
- Displaying Web documents,
- Authoring HTML, XML, PDF documents,
- Dictionaries and software,
- Chinese character dictionary indexes,
- Character dictionaries,
- Dictionary hardware,
- Dictionary software,
- Machine translation software,
- Machine translation services,

- Learning aids,
- Tables,
- Glossary,
- Literature.

10.5   User Interfaces

- Text length check,
- Word wrapping,
- "Resizing",
- Resource management,
- Locale technology,
- Character set problem,
- Icons/metaphors,
- Ink usage,
- Arrangement/layout,
- Navigation/interaction,
- Writing systems in China and Japan.

Necessary aspects to be considered for the Asian region (especially Japan and China):

- ISO-2022-JP,
- Shift JIS,
- EUC-JP,
- GB 2312-80: character set standard representing the most widely implemented character set for Chinese,
- GB18030-2000: name for the official character set of the People's Republic of China (PRC) superseeding GB2312-80,
- GB/T (guojia biaozhun tui),
- GBK (guojia biaozhun kuozhan),
- JIS (Japanese Industrial Standard),
- JISC (Japanese Industrial Standards Committee),
- JSA (Japanese Standards association).

CJK Processing:

- Multiple writing systems,
- Character set standards,
- Encoding methods,
- Input methods,
- Font formats,

- Typography,
- Output methods,
- Information processing techniques,
- Environment,
- Tools,
- Character sorting,
- Natural language processing,
- Regular expressions,
- Search engines,
- Code processing tools,
- Basic concepts and terminology.

10.6 Unicode

Unicode ['juːnɪkoʊd] is an international standard that defines a digital code for each meaningful character or text element of all known font cultures and character systems. The goal is to solve the problem of different, incompatible encodings in different countries or cultures. Further information and links can be found in Appendix C.

10.7 Design and Evaluation Criteria for Intercultural User Interfaces

- How big is the order of information?
- How closely is the information arranged (character spacing, line spacing, etc.)?
- How large are the information units displayed (image size, font size)?
- How many information units are represented simultaneously (images, sentences, letters, words, propositions, prompts, etc.)?
- What is the color distribution of the information presentation (in pictures, on the whole page, background, foreground)?
- What are the time intervals for the sequential presentation of two information units?
- What type of information presentation is available (direct, indirect, clear, overfilled, simple, complex, etc.)?
- Which style of information presentation is used (font, etc.)?
- Which selection types (interaction tools/types) are used (radio buttons, combo box, list box, menu, toolbar, toolbar, etc.)?
- Which interaction hierarchy exists (menu (hierarchical) versus toolbar (flat), etc.)?

- Which means of interaction are used (mouse, I-drive, touchscreen, softkeys, hardkeys)?
- How often are which means of interaction used?
- How long is the pause between interactions (between output and input, between input and output, between two outputs, between two inputs, etc.)?
- How long does it take to communicate an (inter)action (action analysis) (duration until output or input is complete)?
- How long does an interaction path for a function selection take (duration from the first click through the menu to the desired function point, duration of linguistic navigation)?
- How many steps does an interaction path contain?
- How many steps does a dialogue have?
- How long does a dialogue last?
- What dialogues are there (hint, explanation, justification, question dialogue, etc.)?
- How are the widgets arranged (vertical, horizontal, grouped, even, uneven, logical, illogical, etc.)?
- What widgets are there (panels, forms, toolbars, frames, etc.)?
- How many widgets are there?
- What are the steps of a dialogue? (Initial, Mid, End)?
- How many polite phrases does a dialogue contain?

References

Lunde K (2009) CJKV information processing. O'Reilly Media Inc., Sebastopol
Spitznagel I (2001) Internationalization of software as a prerequisite for localization. University, Saarbrücken. (specialization 4.6)

Chapter 11
Annex C: Further Information

This appendix contains further literature as well as valuable information and links on the subject of IUID (e.g., institutions, committees, conferences, tool manufacturers, IUID service providers).

11.1 Further Literature

Bevan, N. (1999) Quality in use: meeting user needs for quality In: Journal of Systems and Software, 49(1), 89–96.

Bevan, N., Claridge, N., Earthy, J., Kirakowski, J. (1998) Proposed Usability Engineering Assurance Scheme. INUSE Deliverable D5.2.3.

Bevan N., Schoeffel R. (2001) A proposed standard for consumer product usability. Proceedings of 1st International Conference on Universal Access in Human Computer Interaction (UAHCI), New Orleans, August 2001.

de Souza, F., and Bevan, N. (1990) The Use of Guidelines in Menu Interface Design: Evaluation of a Draft Standard. Proceedings of IFIP INTERACT'90: Human-Computer Interaction 1990 S. 435–440.

Earthy, J. (1999) Usability Maturity Model: Processes, version 2.2.

Gediga, G., Hamborg, K., Düntsch, I. (1999) The IsoMetrics usability inventory: An operationalisation of ISO 9241–10. Behavior and Information Technology

Heimgärtner, R. (2017) Using Converging Strategies to Reduce Divergence in Intercultural User Interface Design (Vol. 05).

Heimgärtner, R. (2018) Culturally-Aware HCI Systems. In C. Faucher (Ed.), Advances in Culturally-Aware Intelligent Systems and in Cross-Cultural Psychological Studies (pp. 11–37). Cham: Springer International Publishing.

Heimgärtner, R. (2019) Method-Mix for the Development of Intercultural User Interfaces - Exemplified. Paper presented at the International Human-Computer Interaction.

© Springer Nature Switzerland AG 2019
R. Heimgärtner, *Intercultural User Interface Design*, Human–Computer Interaction Series, https://doi.org/10.1007/978-3-030-17427-9_11

Heimgärtner, R. (2019) IUID Method-Mix: Towards a Systematic Approach for Intercultural User Interface Design. Journal of Computer and Communications.

Heimgärtner, R., Solanki, A., & Windl, H. (2017) Cultural User Experience in the Car—Toward a Standardized Systematic Intercultural Agile Automotive UI/UX Design Process (pp. 143–184).

Heimgärtner, R., Sturm, C., Womser-Hacker, C., Linxen, S., & Mandl, T. (2017) Interkulturelle Erforschung und Gestaltung von Benutzungsschnittstellen (UI) und Benutzererfahrung (UX). https://doi.org/10.18420/muc2017-ws03-0421

Oppermann, R., Reiterer, R. (1997) Software Evaluation Using the 9241 Evaluator Usability Evaluation Methods. Behavior and Information Technology v. 16 n. 4/5 S. 232–245.

Prümper, P. (1999) Test it: ISONORM 9241/10. In: Bullinger H-J and Ziegler J (Hrsg.), Proceedings of HCI International, Munich, 22–27 August 1999. Lawrence Erlbaum, Mahwah, NJ, USA.

Rüdiger, H. (2016). Intercultural User Interface Design. In A. Information Resources Management (Ed.), Web Design and Development: Concepts, Methodologies, Tools, and Applications (pp. 113–146). Hershey, PA, USA: IGI Global.

Usability Professionals' Association, UPA. (2009). www.uxpa.org. accessed 29.02.2019.

UsabilityNet. (2009). http://www.usabilitynet.org/home.htm. accessed 29.09. 2016.

11.2   Institutions

Unicode Consortium: www.unicode.org, last access February 29, 2019.

The Unicode consortium enables people around the globe to use computers in any language. It develops the Unicode Standard and Unicode Locales (CLDR). These specifications form the basis for software internationalization in all major operating systems, search engines, applications, and the internet.

"The aim of the W3C's internationalization activities is to propose and coordinate, within the consortium and together with other organizations, techniques, conventions, guidelines and activities that will enable and facilitate the worldwide use of W3C technology in different languages, scripts and cultures" from internationalisation activities of the W3C (WWW Consortium), last access 29 February, 2019.

LISA (Localization Industry Standards Association) developed a software localization standard as a committee from 2007 to 2011, which was published in ISO 30042. After its dissolution in 2011, LISA continues to work in a working group for software localization at the European Institute for Telecommunications Standards.

In addition, there are other professional associations, organizations, committees, and conferences that deal with intercultural user interfaces or the topic of IUID:

UXQB, DIN, VDMA, UPA, GUPA, HCII, IHCI, Man and Computer and IWIPS. The German UPA as professional association of usability professionals in Germany had the role descriptions of usability professionals created in its working group "Quality Standard" (see version 1.0, April 2012, http://docplayer.org/8048330-German-upa-qualitaetsstandard-fuer-usability-engineering.html. accessed February 29, 2019). The UXQB has emerged from this working group on an international level. Corresponding curricula are developed there in the context of the CPUX schema. IUID aspects are entered there by the author of this book as a personal UXQB member. In addition, the author of this book is currently initiating the establishment of a new GUPA working group on IUID.

OLIF (Open Lexicon Interchange Format).

OLIF is a standard for encoding lexicons and terminologies. It is primarily used by translators and software manufacturers to exchange software terminology. Standards related to usability, HMI and culture can be found at VDMA, Nigel Bevan, LUCID.

11.3 Tools

Software Localization Tools

	Catalyst Localization Environment
	Language Studio - ATIA Ltd., Sofia, Bulgaria
	Lingobit Localizer
	Multilizer - The Software Localization Solution
	PASSOLO Localization Software
	RC-WinTrans

(continued)

(continued)

	Sisulizer -Visual Software Localization Tool
	Visual Localize (AIT AG)
	PhraseApp

There are also open-source tools on the market: https://opensource.com/article/17/6/open-source-localization-tools, last access 29.2.2019.

Another overview on localization tools can be found at lingualizer.net: http://www.lingualizer.net/tools/files/category-localization-tools.html, last access 29.2.2019.

11.4   Links

Localization Associations and Organizations
Internationalization and Localization (WWW-Consortium)
Localisation Resources Centre
Silicon Valley Localization Forum (TGP Consulting)
Simultrans Globalization company in Silicon Valley

IUID Service Provider

There are specialized service providers for international user research. Only a few service providers have the possibility to work internationally with high quality. Industry knowledge and international experience are important criteria when selecting a service provider. The service provider directories of the Usability Professionals' Association UPA (Usability Professionals' Association 2009) or the EU project UsabilityNet (UsabilityNet 2009) are good sources. In the meantime, individual regional companies have joined together to form international networks, which have coordinated their methods with each other and enable interested parties to operate "from a single source" (International Usability Partners 2009). The author of this book is owner of a service company for training and consulting in the development of intercultural user interfaces:

Advantage through knowledge—quality instead of quantity

Dr. Rüdiger Heimgärtner

Owner and CEO

Lindenstraße 9

93152 Undorf Germany

Phone: +49 (0) 9404 96090

Fax: +49 (0) 9404 96091

Mobile phone: +49 (0) 0175 565 0 322

E-mail: ruediger.heimgaertner@iuic.de

URL: https://www.iuic.de

Index

Printed in the United States
By Bookmasters